Beginning SQL

Beginning SQL

Paul Wilton and John W. Colby

WILEY
Wiley Publishing, Inc.

Beginning SQL

Published by
Wiley Publishing, Inc.
10475 Crosspoint Boulevard
Indianapolis, IN 46256
www.wiley.com

Copyright © 2005 by Wiley Publishing, Inc., Indianapolis, Indiana

Published simultaneously in Canada

ISBN: 0-7645-7732-8

Manufactured in the United States of America

10 9 8 7 6 5 4 3 2 1

1MA/RW/QS/QV/IN

For general information on our other products and services or to obtain technical support, please contact our Customer Care Department within the U.S. at (800) 762-2974, outside the U.S. at (317) 572-3993, or fax (317) 572-4002.

Wiley also publishes its books in a variety of electronic formats. Some content that appears in print may not be available in electronic books.

Library of Congress Cataloging-in-Publication Data

Wilton, Paul, 1969-
 Beginning sql / Paul Wilton and John W. Colby.
     p. cm.
 Includes bibliographical references and index.
 ISBN 0-7645-7732-8 (paper/website : alk. paper)
 1. SQL (Computer program language) I. Colby, John W., 1954- II. Title.
QA76.73.S67W57 2005
005.75'65--dc22

                    2004031057

About the Authors

Paul Wilton

After an initial start as a Visual Basic applications programmer at the Ministry of Defense in the U.K., Paul found himself pulled into the Net. Having joined an Internet development company, he spent the last three years helping create Internet solutions and is currently working on an e-commerce Web site for a major British bank.

Paul's main skills are in developing Web front ends using DHTML, JavaScript, VBScript, and Visual Basic and back-end solutions with ASP, Visual Basic, and SQL Server. Currently, Paul is working on a new Web-based application that will hopefully make him millions. . . well, thousands at least!

Paul Wilton contributed Chapters 1–9 and Appendixes A, B and C to this book.

John W. Colby

John Colby is an independent consultant who has specialized in Access development since 1994. He has designed databases for companies in the U.S., Mexico, Canada, and Ireland. John is past president and current board member of Database Advisors, Inc. (www.databaseAdvisors.com), a not-for-profit organization dedicated to providing fellow developers with a place to discuss Access, SQL Server, Visual Basic, and other topics relative to modern database applications development. Database Advisors also allows developers to showcase their talents by sharing databases, wizards, and various code packages.

John lives in northwestern Connecticut with his wife and two small children. He enjoys music, travel, and all things computers, and he dreams of working from his laptop while enjoying travel with his family.

John W. Colby contributed Chapters 10–13 to this book.

Credits

Senior Acquisitions Editor
Jim Minatel

Development Editor
Brian Herrmann

Production Editor
Felicia Robinson

Technical Editor
Wiley-Dreamtech India Pvt Ltd

Copy Editor
Publication Services

Editorial Manager
Mary Beth Wakefield

Vice President & Executive Group Publisher
Richard Swadley

Vice President and Publisher
Joseph B. Wikert

Project Coordinator
April Farling

Graphics and Production Specialists
Lauren Goddard
Jennifer Heleine
Amanda Spagnuolo

Quality Control Technician
John Greenough
Leeann Harney
Jessica Kramer
Brian H. Walls

Proofreading and Indexing
TECHBOOKS Production Services

Paul Wilton: With lots of love to my darling Beci, who, now that the book's finished, will get to see me for more than ten minutes a week.

John W. Colby: Dedicated to my son Robbie and my daughter Allie, who give me so much inspiration, and to my wife Mary, a wonderful soul mate and mother.

Contents

Contents

Contents

Contents

Contents

Contents

Contents

Acknowledgments

Paul Wilton

Many thanks to Catherine who for many years supported me and ensured that my sanity chip remained plugged in. I'd also like to thank Brian Herrmann, who has been a great editor to work with and has done amazing work on the book and kept his professionalism and sense of humor even when faced with another of my "just a few more days and I'll get the chapter to you" emails! Thanks also to Jim Minatel for allowing me to subject the world to yet another of my books. Finally, pats and treats to my German shepherd Katie, who does an excellent job in warding off disturbances from door-to-door salespeople.

Introduction

Data, data, data! Data is where it's at as far as computers go, whether processing millions of calculations or keeping a record of your Aunt Maude's birthday. When it comes to storing data, the database is the king. In almost eight years of professional programming, every single project I've worked on has involved databases somewhere along the line—that's how essential they are to most business applications and projects. Admittedly, some areas, such as computer games, don't make the same use of databases. My guess is that "Mega Doom 99: The Final Bloody Massacre" isn't running an Oracle database in the background!

However, I have a confession! Around 10 years ago, when I first started learning about databases, I initially found them very confusing. I'd been programming in my spare time for a few years and was used to using text files to store information. I decided to leap right in and start creating databases and writing SQL, and I got very confused and odd results. Databases, their design, and their underlying concepts are very different from storing data in simple files, and the Structured Query Language (SQL) used to access and manipulate data in databases is very different from any procedural language. One of my first aims with this book is to soften the blow of new concepts and ways of doing things. To that end, I explain all the underlying concepts and theory you'll need to get started with databases and in programming with SQL. How to get the answers you want from a database and all the results you get will be fully explained, as SQL can throw up some surprises if you're not forewarned.

Another of my aims in writing this book is to get you quickly and effectively to the point where you're able to go off on your own and design your own databases and write your own SQL code in a practical environment. Personally, I dislike books that waffle on about every small detail and eventuality so that it takes months to be able to stand on your own feet and create your own work. I stick with the stuff that you'll find is used in most database applications, keeping the fine details and more advanced stuff for the later chapters. The first few chapters' aim is to get you up and running in SQL quickly, but they do not skimp on essential concepts, code, and techniques, which are all thoroughly discussed and backed up with lots of practical examples.

Finally, I'm a hands-on, practical person, and those are the sort of computer books I like to read, rather than books that contain lots of theory. This book reflects my "put it into action" nature and is full of examples and places where you can get hands-on experience. I do introduce and explain theory where it's necessary to build a foundation of understanding, but I do this only with the eventual aim of putting theory into practice. I use databases and SQL most days in my programming, and I hope to bring that real-world experience to this book.

Who This Book Is For

This book starts right from the basics with databases and SQL. Prior database or SQL knowledge is not necessary, as this book covers everything from database design to creating your first database and understanding how the SQL language is used with databases.

If you have some previous experience with databases and SQL, then you'll have a head start and you may want to just skim Chapter 1. You'll need to follow its instructions for creating the book's example database, as this is used for all the examples throughout the book.

What This Book Covers

This book will look at Structured Query Language, or SQL as it's usually abbreviated. SQL works with a database to create the database and to insert and extract data. Therefore, it's essential to understand the theory and concepts behind database systems. Hence, this book also covers database theory and database design, so that you're equipped to create an effective database.

The SQL code in this book reflects the modern SQL standards set by organizations such as the American National Standards Institute (ANSI) and the International Standards Organization (ISO). However, while standards are great, what's available for practical use is what really counts. This book, then, concentrates on the sort of SQL supported by most modern database systems. You should find that most of the code runs with little or no modification on most database systems released within the last six or seven years.

How This Book Is Structured

This book has been split into two main parts. The first part, which consists of Chapters 1–3, provides the foundations for understanding databases and SQL. The aim in this first part is to get you up to speed on all the essential details. These chapters take you through the following:

❑   The essentials of database theory

❑   Writing SQL code

❑   Good database design

❑   Creating a database

❑   Entering, updating, and deleting data using SQL

❑   Extracting data using SQL — more specifically, how to answer the sort of questions often posed of databases in real-life situations

By the time you've completed Chapter 3, you'll be ready to go out and create your own databases and write your own SQL code to a sufficient standard for many real-life programming situations. You may want to go and create a few databases of your own before returning to the second part of the book.

The second half of the book, Chapters 4 onward, goes into more detail and looks at more advanced topics. Its aim is to provide a fairly wide and thorough grounding in many aspects of SQL programming. The sort of topics covered include the following:

❏   Advanced database design, taking a look at the theory and practical application of normalization, and how to improve a database's efficiency and reliability

❏   Using and manipulating data with SQL's built-in data manipulation and calculation functions

❏   Selecting data from lots of different tables

❏   Database security

❏   Database optimization

The book also includes three appendixes. Appendix A contains the answers to the exercise questions in each chapter, so no peeking until you've given the questions a go. Appendix B covers how to download, install, and use each of the five supported database systems used by this book. Appendix C includes the initial data for the example database, which is available to download from www.wrox.com if you want to avoid aching fingers!

What You Need to Use This Book

To really make use of this book and run the examples, you need to have a database system on which to practice. This book's code has been thoroughly tested on the following five commonly available database systems:

❏   MySQL

❏   Microsoft SQL Server

❏   IBM DB2

❏   Microsoft Access

❏   Oracle 10g

The good news is that almost all of those can be downloaded free off the Internet as full or trial versions. In Appendix B, you'll learn where to download them, how to install them, and how to use them.

It's not a problem if you're using a different database system, because as often as possible, I've avoided database system-specific code and have kept to standard SQL supported by most database systems. Where it's impossible to have the same code for all the database systems, I've listed the ways around as well as alternative syntax. You'll likely find that one of the variations of syntax will work on your system, possibly with a little modification.

Conventions

To help you get the most from the text and keep track of what's happening, this book uses a number of conventions throughout.

Try It Out

The *Try It Out* is an exercise that you should work through, following the text in the book.

1. They usually consist of a set of steps.
2. Each step has a number.
3. Follow the steps through with your copy of the database.

How It Works

After each Try It Out, the code you've typed will be explained in detail.

> **Boxes like this one hold important, not-to-be-forgotten information that is directly relevant to the surrounding text.**

Tips, hints, tricks, and asides to the current discussion are offset and placed in italics like this.

As for styles in the text:

❑ New terms and important words are *italicized* as they are introduced.

❑ Keyboard strokes are shown like this: Ctrl+A.

❑ Filenames, URLs, and code within the text are shown like so: `persistence.properties`.

❑ Code is presented in two different ways:

```
In code examples, new and important code is highlighted with a gray background.
```

```
The gray highlighting is not used for code that's less important in the present
context or that has been shown before.
```

Source Code

As you work through the examples in this book, you may choose either to type in all the code manually or to use the source code files that accompany the book. All of the source code used in this book is available for download at `http://www.wrox.com`. Once at the site, simply locate the book's title (either by using the Search box or by using one of the title lists) and click the Download Code link on the book's detail page to obtain all the source code for the book.

Because many books have similar titles, you may find it easiest to search by ISBN; for this book, the ISBN is 0-7645-7732-8.

Once you download the code, just decompress it with your favorite compression tool. Alternatively, you can go to the main Wrox code download page at http://www.wrox.com/dynamic/books/download.aspx to see the code available for this book and all other Wrox books.

Errata

We make every effort to ensure that there are no errors in the text or in the code. However, no one is perfect, and mistakes do occur. If you find an error in one of our books, like a spelling mistake or faulty piece of code, we would be very grateful for your feedback. By sending in errata, you may save another reader hours of frustration, and at the same time you will be helping us provide even higher-quality information.

To find the errata page for this book, go to http://www.wrox.com and locate the title using the Search box or one of the title lists. Then, on the Book Details page, click the Book Errata link. On this page, you can view all errata that has been submitted for this book and posted by Wrox editors. A complete book list including links to each book's errata is also available at www.wrox.com/misc-pages/booklist.shtml.

If you don't spot "your" error on the Book Errata page, go to www.wrox.com/contact/techsupport.shtml and complete the form there to send us the error you have found. We'll check the information and, if appropriate, post a message to the book's errata page and fix the problem in subsequent editions of the book.

p2p.wrox.com

For author and peer discussion, join the P2P forums at p2p.wrox.com. The forums are a Web-based system for you to post messages relating to Wrox books and related technologies and interact with other readers and technology users. The forums offer a subscription feature to email you topics of interest of your choosing when new posts are made to the forums. Wrox authors, editors, other industry experts, and your fellow readers are present on these forums.

At http://p2p.wrox.com you will find a number of different forums that will help you not only as you read this book but also as you develop your own applications. To join the forums, just follow these steps:

1. Go to p2p.wrox.com and click the Register link.
2. Read the terms of use and click Agree.
3. Complete the required information to join as well as any optional information you wish to provide and click Submit.
4. You will receive an email with information describing how to verify your account and complete the joining process.

You can read messages in the forums without joining P2P, but in order to post your own messages, you must join.

Introduction

Once you join, you can post new messages and respond to messages that other users post. You can read messages at any time on the Web. If you would like to have new messages from a particular forum emailed to you, click the Subscribe to this Forum icon by the forum name in the forum listing.

For more information about how to use the Wrox P2P, be sure to read the P2P FAQs for answers to questions about how the forum software works as well as many common questions specific to P2P and Wrox books. To read the FAQs, click the FAQ link on any P2P page.

Introduction to SQL

A nice, gentle introductory chapter, this chapter begins by looking at databases in terms of what they are and why and when you want to use them. Then the chapter turns to SQL and discovers how it links in with databases and how it can be useful. After tackling the basics of SQL and how it works in theory, you examine how to use it to create a database. This chapter also walks you through creating the structure of the example database used throughout the book.

By the end of the chapter, you should understand how a database enables you to efficiently organize and retrieve the information you want, as well as how to create a fully functional database, all ready and waiting to accept add data. But before diving headlong into writing lines of SQL code, it's helpful to know a little bit of background about databases.

A Brief History of Databases

Modern databases emerged in the 1960s thanks to research at IBM, among other companies. The research mainly centered around office automation, in particular automating data storage and indexing tasks that previously required a great deal of manual labor. Computing power and storage had become much cheaper, making the use of computers for data indexing and storage a viable solution. A pioneer in the database field was Charles W. Bachman, who received the Turing Award in 1973 for pioneering work in database technology. In 1970, an IBM researcher named Ted Codd published the first article on relational databases.

Although IBM was a leader in database research, Honeywell Information Systems, Inc., released a commercial product in 1976 based on the same principles as the IBM information system, but it was designed and implemented separately from IBM's work.

In the early 1980s, the first database systems built upon the SQL standard appeared from companies such as Oracle, with Oracle Version 2, and later SQL/DS from IBM, as well as a host of other systems from other companies.

Now that you have a brief idea of where databases came from, you can turn to the more practical task of what databases are and why and when to use them.

Identifying Databases

What is a database, you ask?

The Free On-Line Dictionary of Computing (`http://foldoc.doc.ic.ac.uk`) defines a database as "one or more large structured sets of persistent data, usually associated with software to update and query the data. A simple database might be a single file containing many records, each of which contains the same set of fields where each field is a certain fixed width."

Breaking this definition down into something more manageable, first it says that a database consists of structured sets of data, which means that a database contains collections of data. For example, the database might contain the details of Uncle Bob's golf scores or data about all the books in a library. You probably wouldn't want to mix these two collections of data, or else when you want to find data about a book you'd have to look through irrelevant data on golf scores. In short, databases help you organize your data. A database stores its collections of data in *tables*, a concept explored further in Chapter 2.

The definition goes on to say that databases are usually associated with software that allows the data to be updated and queried. Real-life examples of database software include Microsoft's Access, Oracle's 10g, IBM's DB2, MySQL AB's MySQL, and Microsoft's SQL Server 2000. Often these programs are referred to as databases, but strictly speaking, they are database management systems (DBMS). A database is the *sets* (collections of related data) grouped into one entity. You could, for example, create an Access database, call it MyDatabase, include various data collections inside that one database, and manage the whole thing with the MS Access software.

Finally, the definition states that, as with the Access database example, a simple database might be just one file with many records with each record broken down into *fields*. But what are records and fields? A field is a single item of data about a specific thing. A thing could be a person, and a single item of data about a person could be their date of birth. Or the thing might be the address of a house and the specific item of data might be its street. Using the book example, the year a book was published is a specific piece of data that can be stored in a field. Another field might be the book's title; yet another could be the author's name. For this book, the fields would contain 2005 for the Year Published field, *Beginning SQL* for the Title field, and Paul Wilton and John Colby for the Author field. All these fields refer to one specific thing, a book called *Beginning SQL*. Collectively these fields are known as a *record*. Each book has its own record, and all the records are stored collectively in a database in something called a *table*. A single database can contain one or more tables. If all this information is a bit too much to absorb at once, don't worry: I'll be revisiting the concepts of fields and records later in this chapter.

By now, hopefully you get the idea that a database helps you store, organize, and retrieve data. One last thing to mention is the term *relational database,* which is a database containing data organized and linked (related) to each other. All records in a database are organized into tables. Related data, such as details of sales persons, are grouped in one table. You could put the details of cars they have sold in another table and then specify a relationship between which salesperson sold which cars—for example, salesperson X sold car Y on date Z. Figure 1-1 shows a table from the example database. On first glance, you may notice its resemblance to a spreadsheet with rows being your records and columns containing the fields for the records. In Chapter 3 you discover that you really need to think in terms of sets of data.

> *Most database management systems these days are relational, termed relational database management system (RDBMS). These systems make storing data and returning results easier and more efficient. They allow different questions to be posed of the database—even questions the original designer of the database didn't expect to be asked.*

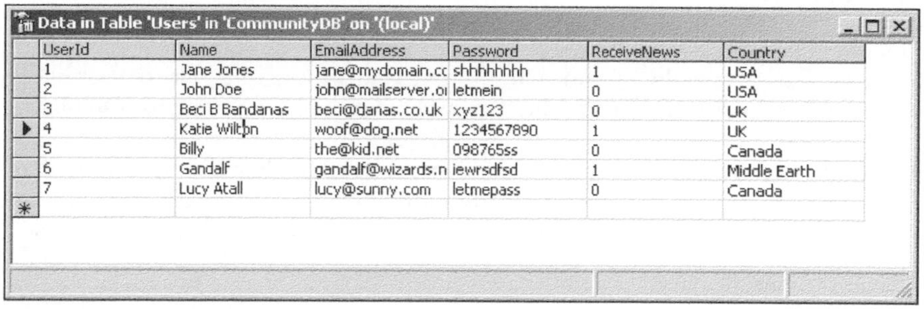
Data in Table 'Users' in 'CommunityDB' on '(local)'

UserId	Name	EmailAddress	Password	ReceiveNews	Country
1	Jane Jones	jane@mydomain.cc	shhhhhhhh	1	USA
2	John Doe	john@mailserver.oı	letmein	0	USA
3	Beci B Bandanas	beci@danas.co.uk	xyz123	0	UK
4	Katie Wilton	woof@dog.net	1234567890	1	UK
5	Billy	the@kid.net	098765ss	0	Canada
6	Gandalf	gandalf@wizards.n	iewrsdfsd	1	Middle Earth
7	Lucy Atall	lucy@sunny.com	letmepass	0	Canada

Figure 1-1

Why and When to Use a Database

When there are a huge number of alternative ways to store data, why should you trouble yourself creating a database? What advantages does a database hold?

The main advantage is fast and efficient data retrieval. A database helps you to organize your data in a logical manner. Database management systems are fine-tuned to rapidly retrieve the data you want in the way you want it. Databases also enable you to break data into specific parts. Retrieving data from a database is called *querying*. You'll often see the term *SQL query*, which briefly means any SQL code that extracts data from the database. This topic is covered in more depth later in this chapter.

Relational databases have the further advantage of allowing you to specify how different data relates to each other, as you saw in the car sales database example. If you store sales details and salesperson data in related databases, the question "How many cars has salesperson X sold in January?" becomes very easy to answer. If you just shoved all the information into a large text file, you'd find it one enormous task to question, or query, the data and find out specific answers.

Databases also allow you to set up rules that ensure that data remains consistent when you add, update, or delete data. Imagine that your imaginary car sales company has two salespeople named Julie Smith. You can set up a database to ensure that each salesperson has a unique ID, called a unique identifier (so that the Julies don't get mixed up); otherwise, telling who sold which cars would prove impossible. Other data storage systems, such as text files or spreadsheets, don't have these sorts of checks and quite happily allow you to store erroneous data. In later chapters you learn how to set up other rules to limit the risk of data becoming corrupted. For example, you might specify that an employee's social security number must be unique in the database. Or if a car is sold and it's listed as being sold by the employee with an ID of 123, you might add a check to see that full details of employee 123 are held in one of the database tables.

A properly set-up database minimizes data redundancy. Again using the car sales example, you can store all the details of a salesperson just once in the database and then use a unique ID to identify each salesperson. When you have other data that relates to a particular salesperson (for example, which cars they've sold), you can use the unique ID to search for the data. The unique ID is often a number that takes up less storage space than the person's full name.

Databases store raw data—just the facts, so to speak, and no intelligence. A car sales database might contain the make, model, and price of each car, but you wouldn't normally store the average number of cars sold in a month, because you can calculate that from the car sales information, the raw data.

A spreadsheet, however, may contain processed data, such as averages and statistical analysis. A database simply stores the data and generally leaves data processing to a *front-end* program, or the interface the user sees. Examples of front-end programs include a Web page that draws its data from a database or a program that hooks into the database's data and allows the user to view it.

Sharing data is also much easier using a database. You can share data among a number of users on the same computer or among users on different computers linked via a network or the Internet. If the example car sales company has branches in New York, Washington, and Boston, you could set up a computer containing a database in one location that is accessible by all of the offices via a network. This is not only possible but also safe because databases have a clearly defined structure and also enforce rules that protect the data contained. They also allow more than one person to access the database at the same time and change the data stored; the database management system handles simultaneous changes. Imagine the potential chaos if you used an Excel spreadsheet, and two salespeople change data simultaneously. You want to keep both sets of changes, but whoever saves the spreadsheet last is the person whose changes are stored, overwriting any earlier changes.

Databases also make sharing data between different systems much easier than using proprietary data formats — that is, a format specific to a particular program, manufacturer, or operating system. An Excel spreadsheet, for example, is easily read on a Windows machine with MS Office, but it is more of a challenge to read on a UNIX, Macintosh, or Linux machine because those computers handle data in a different way. Even on a Windows machine, you need to have MS Office installed. You can house a database on a central computer, put the database management system on there, and then enable access via a local network or the Internet.

As an alternative to databases, text files and spreadsheets have one big advantage, which is also their weakness: flexibility. Text files have no real rules. You can insert whatever text data you like wherever you like. To a large extent, spreadsheets are the same. You can ask users to add data in a predefined structure, but you have no real way to enforce such a request. Using databases limits user access to just the data and does not allow users to change the structure.

One final significant advantage of databases is security. Most database management systems allow you to create users in order to specify various levels of security. Before someone accesses the database, he or she must log on as a specific user. Each user has various rights and limits. Someone who maintains the database has full ability to edit data, change the database's structure, add and delete users, and so on. Other users may only have the ability to view data but not change it, or you may even want to limit what data they can view. Many database management systems provide a granular level of security, that is, they are very specific as to what a user can do. They are not just an all-or-nothing approach in which the user either has access or has no access.

Databases are used pretty much everywhere. Data processing played a big part in the development of computers, and even today it is one of their main roles. Nearly every walk of life or business requires a database somewhere along the way. Databases are commonly used on personal computers to store data used locally, and on company networks databases store and share company-wide information. The Internet has seen a big rise in databases used to share information; most online shops of a reasonable size use databases. When you visit online stores of any significant size, a database usually provides all the information on the goods being sold. Rather than every page being created by hand, large merchants use a template for book or CD details, and SQL retrieves the book information from the database. Imagine how much work it'd be if Amazon created every single page by hand!

Databases are great at dealing with large amounts of data that need to be searched, sorted, or regularly updated. As you find out in the next few chapters, databases combined with SQL allow you to get the answers you want in the order you want.

Database Management Systems Used in This Book

Databases are great for storing data, the database management system provides ways of looking at the data, and usually software provided allows you to view the data. But how do you use the data outside of the database management software? The operating system, whether it's Windows, UNIX, Linux, or the Macintosh, provides ways of hooking into the database management system and extracting the data. You need to write programming code to put inside a stand-alone application that the user runs on their computer, or you could set up a Web page to extract data. You're not restricted to certain languages, so long as the language allows you to hook into the database management software.

You can buy any number of different relational database management systems off the shelf, but this book's aim is to present SQL that is standards compliant (more on the standards in the next section) and that works with as wide a range of RDBMSs as possible. However, there are times when the standards don't allow you to do what you want. Other times, you may find that the various DBMS vendors haven't implemented them consistently. This book provides details specific to MS Access, MS SQL Server 2000, IBM DB2, MySQL, and Oracle 10.

Structured Query Language (SQL)

The first questions to ask are what is SQL and how do you use it with databases? SQL has three main roles:

❑   Creating a database and defining its structure

❑   Querying the database to obtain the data necessary to answer questions

❑   Controlling database security

Defining database structure includes creating new database tables and fields, setting up rules for data entry, and so on, which is expressed by a SQL sublanguage called Data Control Language (DCL), covered later in this chapter. The next section discusses querying the database.

Finally, DCL deals with database security. Generally, database security is something that database administrators handle.

Creating SQL every time you want to change the database structure or security sounds like hard work, and it is! Most modern database systems allow you to execute changes via a user-friendly interface without a single line of SQL.

Introducing SQL Queries

SQL queries are the most common use of SQL. A SQL sublanguage called Data Manipulation Language (DML) deals with queries and data manipulation. SQL allows you to pose a query (basically a question)

to the database, and the database then provides the data that answers your query. For example, with a database that stores details of salespersons, car sales, type of cars sold, and so on, you might want to know how many cars each salesperson sold in each month and how much money they made the company. You could write a SQL query that asks this question and the database goes away and gets the data that answers it. A SQL query consists of various statements, clauses, and conditions. A *statement* is an instruction or a command. For example, "Get me some data" is a statement. A *clause* specifies limits to a statement, the limits being specified using *conditions*. For example, instead of "Get some data," you might say, "Get data only for the sales that were in the month of May," where "only for" is the clause that specifies which data to retrieve. The condition is "were in the month of May." If the data doesn't meet the condition's criteria, in this case, "month of May," then you don't want it. Written as actual SQL code, this could be something like the following:

```
SELECT CarModel
FROM CarSales
WHERE CarSoldDate BETWEEN 'May 1 2005' AND 'May 31 2005';
```

The SELECT statement tells the database system that you want to select some data from the database. You then list the data you want, in this case CarModel data, which is a field name. You then specify the place the data needs to be taken from, in this case a table called CarSales. Finally, you have a condition. The statement above specifies that you want only the data where certain conditions are true. In this case, the condition is that the CarSoldDate is between the first and thirty-first of May 2005. Lots of SQL code like that above is covered in Chapter 3's discussion of statements, clauses, and conditions.

Comparing SQL to Other Programming Languages

Now that you know what SQL can be used for, you can compare it to other programming languages. To be honest, SQL is quite different from the *procedural* languages such as C++, Visual Basic, Pascal, and other third-generation programming languages, which allow the programmer to write step-by-step instructions telling the computer exactly what to do to achieve a specified goal. Taking the car sales example, your goal might be to select all the information about sales made in July from the New York car showroom. Very roughly, your procedural language might be along the lines of the following:

1. Load the sales data into the computer's memory.
2. Extract the individual items of data from the sales data.
3. Check to see if each item of data is from the month of July and from the New York showroom.
4. If it is, then make a note of the data.
5. Go to the next item of data and keep going until all items have been checked.
6. Loop through the data results and display each one.

SQL, however, is a *declarative* language, which means that instead of telling it what to do to get the results you want, you simply tell it what you want, and it figures out what to do and comes back with the results. In the car sales example, if you were using SQL, you'd specify the results you want, something like this:

SELECT all the data from the sales table WHERE the sales were in July and made at the New York showroom.

The SQL language is actually fairly easy to read. The actual SQL could look like this:

```
SELECT * FROM SalesMade WHERE SaleDate = "July 2005" AND SalesOffice = "New York"
```

The asterisk simply means return the data from all the fields in the record.

You learn a lot more about how the SQL SELECT statement works in Chapter 3.

Understanding SQL Standards

As with databases, IBM did a lot of the original SQL work. However, a lot of other vendors took the IBM standard and developed their own versions of it. Having so many differing dialects causes quite a headache for the developer, and in 1986 it was adopted by the standards body the American National Standards Institute (ANSI) and in 1987 by the International Standards Organization (ISO), who created a standard for SQL. Although this has helped minimize differences between the various SQL dialects, there are still differences between them.

The following table gives a brief summary of the various standards and updates to those standards.

Year	Name	Also Known As	Changes
1986	SQL-86	SQL-87 (date when adopted by ISO)	First publication of the ANSI/ISO standard
1989	SQL-89		Only small revision of the original standard
1992	SQL-92	SQL2	Major update of the original standard and still the most widely supported standard
1999	SQL-99	SQL3	Update of the 1992 standard adding new ways of selecting data and new rules on data integrity and introducing object orientation
2003	SQL-2003		Introduced XML support and fields with autogenerated values

This book concentrates on SQL-92, SQL-99, and SQL-2003 because most of their features have been implemented by most relational database management systems (RDBMSs). The SQL you write works on most RDBMSs with only minor modifications. There are times when the various RDBMSs do things so differently that compatible code is impossible without big changes; however, these instances are few and far between in this book.

Although standards are important to help bring some sort of commonality among the various RDBMSs' implementation of SQL, at the end of the day what works in practice is what really counts. Instead of endlessly debating standards, this book provides information to help you in the real world of databases. That said, the next section shows you how to create your own SQL database.

Database Creation

So far, this chapter has examined what a database is and where you might use one. This section takes a more in-depth look at the components of a database, its structure, and the accompanying terminology. Finally, you put the theory into action and set up your own sample database.

Once you grasp the basics, this section discusses how to structure your database in an efficient and easy-to-use manner. Good database design simplifies data extraction and reduces wastage by avoiding data duplication.

By the end of this chapter, you'll have a fully functioning database all ready to go for the next chapter when you use SQL to insert, update, and delete data in a database. Not only that, but you'll have the knowledge to experiment on your own and create your own databases. Before any of that happens, however, you need to know more about organizing and structuring a database.

Organizing a Relational Database

This section examines how database systems are organized and what structures they are made up of. These structures include, among other things, databases, tables, and fields. In database terminology, these structures are called *objects*.

The database management system is the overall program that manages one or more databases. Within each database are the tables, which consist of fields. A field contains a specific item of data about something — for example, the age of a person, their height, their eye color, and so on. A table contains one or more fields, and it's usual for a table to contain information about a specific thing or at least data that is related in some way. For example, data about a person could be stored in the Person table. If the information is about a type of person, for example, employee, you might call your table Employees.

As illustrated by the heading, this section is about relational databases, the key word being *relational*. This concept is explained in more detail shortly, but briefly stated, it means that there is some sort of link between data in one table and data in another table, indicating some sort of relationship. For example, the relationship between car sales and car sales employees could be that a particular salesperson sold a particular car.

Figure 1-2 illustrates the basic structure of a relational database.

At the top of the diagram is the RDBMS. This is the application software that manages the various databases. In Figure 1-2, the RDBMS creates two databases, but a RDBMS can be in control of as few as one database to many, many thousands of databases. The RDBMS is the intelligence behind the database system. The RDBMS does all the work involved in creating and maintaining databases and the structures inside them. Additionally, the RDBMS controls security; performs the actual data insertion, deletion, and retrieval; and allows users to interact with the database system via a management console.

Below the RDBMS itself are the actual databases contained therein. Each database contains a collection of one or more tables. Strictly speaking, your database could contain zero tables, but that would make for a pretty useless database! Databases are self-contained, which means that what happens in one table doesn't affect another table. For example, you can create tables with the same names in each database if you wish, and the database system doesn't complain. Each database you create receives its own specific name or identifier. How a database system manages databases and tables varies depending on your RDBMS. Microsoft Access, for example, works on only one database at a time, although there are ways of linking one database to another. Each Access database is contained in its own file. Other RDBMSs allow you to manage more than one database from the same console.

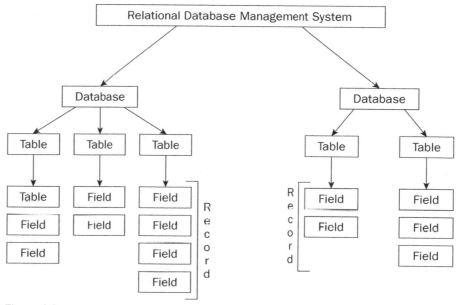

Figure 1-2

Within each database is a collection of tables that contain the records, which hold the data. A good real-world analogy is a train or bus timetable, for example. A simple train timetable could look something like the table shown below:

Start	Destination	Departs	Arrives
London	Manchester	10:15	11:45
Cambridge	Newcastle	9:30	13:55
Lands End	John O'Groats	4:15	23:50
Chester	Liverpool	15:45	16:30
Penzance	Bristol	11:40	18:00

If this were an actual table in your database, you could create a table to hold this data and perhaps call it something stunningly original like `train_times`. The rules as to what you can name tables are fairly flexible but vary a little among RDBMSs. Generally, though, as long as the name doesn't contain punctuation (except things like underscores) and isn't more than 128 characters or so, you are fairly safe.

From the preceding timetable, you can see that it contains four categories of information: start, destination, time of departure, and time of arrival. In database terminology, these categories are called *fields*, and each field has its own unique name within the table.

Each line in the timetable contains data specific to one aspect of a train schedule. The row contains data pertaining to the train leaving London at 10:15 and arriving in Manchester at 11:45. In a database, the data collectively provided by the fields is called a *record*. The preceding table contains five records. A *column* is all the instances of a particular field from all records in a table. So, in the timetable example, the start column is all the data from the start field for all the records in the table: London, Cambridge, Lands End, Chester, Penzance.

To sum up relational database structure, a RDBMS manages one or more databases, each database contains a collection of one or more tables, and each table contains zero or more records, each record being a collection of fields.

Take what you've learned so far and use SQL to create a database and tables.

SQL Syntax

In programming, *syntax* is the rules to be followed when writing code and the terminology used. Syntax is very much like rules of grammar in languages. For example, the rules of English grammar state that a sentence should end with a period (or full stop as it's known in British English). Of course, there are exceptions to this rule. For example, if you end a sentence with a question, then you use a question mark rather than a period. In SQL there are no sentences; instead there are statements. A statement is a self-contained action. For example, you can use a statement to select certain data, to change the database by adding a new table, and so on. A statement should end with a semicolon; even though many database systems let you get away with leaving it off, it's good practice to include the semicolon.

This book refers to three categories of syntax term: identifiers, literals, and keywords. An *identifier* is something that uniquely identifies something in a database system, using an object such as a database, a table, or field name. If you create a database called MyDatabase, then you would say that its identifier is MyDatabase. If you create a table called SalesPeople, then its identifier is SalesPeople. If you need to refer to the SalesPeople table, then you use its identifier:

```
SELECT PersonFirstName
FROM SalesPeople;
```

The previous statement selects data from the SalesPeople table. The database system knows from which table to retrieve data because you used its identifier, SalesPeople.

A *literal* is an actual value, such as 120, Paul, or January 10, 2007. If, for example, you want a list of all salespeople with a first name of Bob, you'd write the following statement:

```
SELECT PersonFirstName, PersonLastName
FROM SalesPeople
WHERE PersonFirstName = 'Bob';
```

This statement uses the literal value of Bob in its comparison. Don't worry if the SQL is still a bit unclear — you take an in-depth look at SELECT statements in Chapter 3.

A *keyword* is a word that has some meaning to the database system. For example, if you say, "flob-badob," people would no doubt wonder what on earth you were talking about! But if you use the word "stop," it's a word you know and it has a certain meaning for you. So to the database system, "flob-badob" means nothing, but SELECT has a special meaning that the database system acts on. It means, "I want to select some data." Each keyword has its own rules. If you use SELECT, then the database system expects as a minimum a list of data you want to select and where that data is coming from. It also has optional keywords, such as a WHERE clause, specifying what sort of results you want. As you meet each new keyword in this book, you also meet what the database system expects as a minimum and what optional parts can be added.

If you've come from other programming languages, you might be wondering about code layout. Some languages allow only one statement per line. SQL, however, allows you to spread your statements over one or more lines. For example, both of the following statements are valid:

```
SELECT CarModel FROM Cars WHERE CarMake = 'Ford';

SELECT CarModel;
FROM Cars
WHERE CarMake = 'Ford';
```

Spacing code over more than one line tends to make it more readable, if it's done logically. The preceding example puts the individual parts of the SELECT statement on their own lines.

Well, that's enough boring syntax for now. You get more detailed syntax discussions on an as-needed basis as you progress through the book. The discussion now turns to creating a database.

Creating a Database

The first step in databases is creating the database. There are two main ways to create a database.

First, many RDBMSs come with a nice, user-friendly front-end interface, which makes the task of creating a new database very easy. In fact, all it takes is a few mouse clicks, entering a name for the database, and away you go. Systems such as MS Access, MS SQL Server, Oracle, and IBM DB2 all provide a front-end interface. MySQL, however, doesn't come with a default front end, but there are plenty of free ones available, such as MySQL Control Center.

In the case of MS Access, using the program to create a database is the only way to do so. However, other RDBMSs allow you to use SQL to create a database. Each RDBMS has its own way of allowing you to enter and run SQL statements. For example, SQL Server has the Query Analyzer tool, DB2 has the Command Center, and MySQL has the MySQL Control Center (among many other similar tools). Regardless of the tool you choose to use, the SQL required to create a new database is as follows:

```
CREATE DATABASE myFirstDatabase;
```

It really is that easy! Once you become more advanced, you discover a plethora of options you can play with, but for the purposes of this book, the default options used by the CREATE DATABASE statement are fine.

The database is called myFirstDatabase, but you could have called it pretty much anything. Some restrictions on the name exist, on its length, for example. DB2 limits name length to eight characters, and

SQL Server limits it to 123 characters. It's safer to stick to letters, numbers, and the underscore character and to avoid any punctuation in the name. For example, My_db is fine, but £$%^my&&&db is unlikely to work or (and be honest) be easy to pronounce! Numbers are usually fine to include, but most RDBMSs don't allow a database's name to begin with a number. Finally, and it may seem obvious, a database name must be unique within the RDBMS. If you call two databases myDB, the RDBMS won't know which one you're referring to when you're writing your SQL code.

What if you want to delete the database? Again, most RDBMSs have a nice and easy user console that allows you do that, but you can also drop a database using SQL. You don't use *delete database* as you might expect; instead you use the DROP DATABASE statement followed by the database's name.

So to drop the myFirstDatabase you write the following:

```
DROP DATABASE myFirstDatabase
```

This isn't a command to be used lightly, though! Dropping the database removes it from the RDBMS and you could potentially lose all your data.

Oracle is a bit of an exception when it comes to dropping databases. Instead of the DROP DATABASE command, you create the database again! If you already have a database called myFirstDatabase, the RDBMS deletes it if you write

```
CREATE DATABASE myFirstDatabase
```

This is something to be very careful of.

After creating a database, the next stage is to add tables to it. However, before you can add tables, you need to look at the concept of data types.

Understanding Data Types

Outside of the world of information technology, you categorize various bits of information into different types quite naturally. You think of the price of goods in a shop as being numerical data. If you ask for directions from New York to Washington, you expect to receive verbal instructions such as "turn left at...." In databases, a *data type* is the classification of different sorts of data being stored, whether the data are numbers, characters, or dates. It helps the database system make sense of the values being inserted into a database. So just as in the world outside databases, you categorize different types of data, but you do so in a more formal way. Returning to the train timetable example, the following table outlines what type of data each field holds:

Field	Data Type	Example
Start	Character data	London, Chester
Destination	Character data	Manchester, Bristol
Departs	Time	10:15, 11:40
Arrives	Time	11:45, 18:00

A perfectly valid question to ask is, "Why have different data types?" Why not just treat everything as text? The main reason is efficiency. The amount of storage space and the speed of access improve when the database knows what sort of data it's dealing with. For example, the number 243787452 can be stored in as little as 4 bytes of computer memory. Storing the same number as text takes 9 bytes of memory for the character data.

In addition, the data type determines what the RDBMS expects users to do with the data. If you have numerical data, then 123 + 123 calculates as addition with the answer being 246. If it were text data, the RDBMS would interpret the plus sign as meaning that you want to join the two character strings together to form 123123.

So what are the various data types available? Unfortunately, data type varies among RDBMSs. Added to this conundrum is the problem that while the ANSI SQL standards such as SQL-92, SQL-99, and SQL-2003 define standards for data types, they are far from fully and universally implemented by the various RDBMS manufacturers. However, all is not lost. There's enough support of the standards for the purposes of this book. Once you have a handle on the basic ANSI SQL data types, researching the data types that your particular RDBMS uses is fairly easy. You can then use them in addition to the data types examined here.

The following table contains a subset of the more commonly used ANSI SQL data types and the name of the same data type in other RDBMSs such as SQL Server, IBM DB2, and so on.

ANSI SQL	MS Access	SQL Server 2000	IBM DB2	MySQL	Oracle 10
Character	char	char	char	char	char
Character varying	varchar	varchar	varchar	varchar	varchar
National character	char	nchar	graphic	char	nchar
National character varying	varchar	nvarchar	vargraphic	varchar	nvarchar
Integer	number (long integer)	int	int	int	int
Smallint	number (integer)	smallint	smallint	smallint	smallint
Real	number (double)	real	real	real	real
Decimal	number (decimal)	decimal	decimal	decimal	decimal
Date	date	datetime	date	date	date
Time	time	datetime	time	time	date

Although this table includes only a small subset of all the possible data types for all the RDBMSs out there, it's more than enough to get you started. Note that although Oracle does support the `nchar` and `nvarchar` types, it does so only if you create a new database and specify that the character set is a Unicode character set such as `AL16UTF16`. Otherwise, by default it doesn't support `nchar` and `nvarchar`.

The following table describes each data type, roughly how much storage space it uses, and an example of its use. The ANSI names have been used for the data type.

Data Type	Description	Storage Used	Example
character	Stores text data. A character can be any letter, number, or punctuation. You must specify how many characters you want to store in advance. If you actually store fewer than you allow for, the RDBMS adds spaces to the end to pad it out.	One byte per character allocated.	`char(8)` allocates space for eight characters and takes up approximately 8 bytes of space.
character varying	Similar to character except the length of the text is variable. Only uses up memory for the actual number of characters stored.	One byte per character stored.	`varchar(8)` allocates space for up to eight characters. However, storing only one character consumes only 1 byte of memory, storing two characters consumes 2 bytes of memory, and so on; up to 8 bytes allocated.
national character	Similar to character, except it uses two bytes for each character stored. This allows for a wider range of characters and is especially useful for storing foreign characters.	Two bytes per character allocated.	`nchar(8)` allocates space for eight characters and consumes 16 bytes of memory regardless of the number of characters actually stored.
national character varying	Similar to character varying, except it uses 2 bytes to store each character, allowing for a wider range of characters. Especially useful for storing foreign characters.	Two bytes per character stored.	`nvarchar(8)` allocates space for eight characters. How much storage is used depends on how many characters

Data Type	Description	Storage Used	Example
integer	A whole number between −2,147,483,648 and 2,147,483,647.	Four bytes.	int consumes 4 bytes regardless of the number stored.
smallint	A whole number between −32,768 and 32,767.	Two bytes.	smallint consumes 2 bytes of memory regardless of the number stored.
real	A floating-point number; range is from −3.40E+38 through 3.40E+38. It has up to eight digits after its decimal point, for example, 87.12342136.	Four bytes.	real consumes 4 bytes of memory regardless of the number stored.
decimal	A floating-point number. Allows you to specify the maximum number and how many digits after the decimal place. Range is from $-10\wedge38 + 1$ through $10\wedge38 - 1$.	5–17 bytes.	decimal(38,12) sets a number that is up to 38 digits long with 12 digits coming after the decimal point.
date	Stores the date.	Four bytes.	date, for example, 1 Dec 2006 or 12/01/2006. Be aware of differences in date formats. In the U.K., for example, "12/01/2006" is actually January 12, 2006, whereas in the U.S. it's December 1, 2006.
time	Stores the time.	Three bytes.	time, for example, 17:54:45.

Note that the storage requirements pertain only to the actual data. The RDBMS usually requires a little bit of extra storage to make a note of where in its memory the data is stored. However, these internal workings are not something you need to worry about unless you're involved in very advanced database work. Also, details may vary depending on the RDBMS system you use.

Although some of the data types are self-explanatory, some of them need a little more explanation. The following sections explain some data types in greater depth, starting with character data types.

Characters

When you want to store text, you use one of the character data types. Note that the term *string* means one or more characters together. There are four possible variations of character data type selection:

- ❏ Fixed length
- ❏ Variable length
- ❏ Standard 1 byte per character (char and varchar types)
- ❏ Standard 2 bytes per character (nchar or nvarchar types)

I'll examine the difference between the fixed- and variable-length data types first. Note the following code:

```
char(127)
```

If you use the preceding code, the RDBMS allocates enough memory to hold 127 characters. If you store only 10 characters, then the other 117 allocated places in memory are filled with spaces, which is fairly wasteful. If you're using only 10 characters, you might wonder whether you can just write

```
char(10)
```

That's fine, but sometimes you may fill all 127 character places.

By contrast, varchar(127) doesn't allocate any memory; it simply says to the RDBMS, "I might want to store up to 127 characters but I don't know yet." So if you store only 10 characters, you use only the memory space required for 10 characters. Storing 127 characters is fine, too, though that uses memory required for 127 characters.

At this point, it may seem like a bother to use the fixed character type. Why not always use varchar? There are two main reasons. First, inserting and updating fixed character data types is quicker — not by a huge amount, but some databases might be updating tens of thousands of records a second, in which case very small differences can add to one big difference. So where you're storing only a few characters and where speed is of the essence, then the fixed data type wins out.

Second, if you store only a few characters, the memory savings between the two methods is fairly insignificant.

The next variation is between the char/varchar data types that use just one byte to store a character and the nchar/nvarchar that use 2 bytes. The 1-byte system originates from the ASCII character set. ASCII (or American Standard Code for Information Interchange) was developed in the early 1960s as a universal way of representing characters on a computer. Computers work only on bits and understand only binary numbers, so characters are stored as numbers, where a number between 0 and 255 represents each letter. For example, the letter A has a numerical value of 65, B has a value of 66, and so on. While this is more than enough to cover letters of the alphabet, numbers, and some punctuation, there are plenty of other characters, especially ones common in foreign languages, that ASCII just can't cope with. To overcome this problem, the Unicode character set was developed. Unicode uses 2 bytes to represent each character and allows you to specify 65,536.

The `char` and `varchar` data types use the one-byte ASCII-based storage. The `nchar` and `nvarchar` support the 2-byte Unicode character set. Which data type you use depends on whether your database requires compatibility with foreign characters. Whichever character set you choose, the usage in SQL code is generally the same, unless the database system has a specific feature designed to work differently based on Unicode or ASCII. The obvious downside of `nchar` and `nvarchar` is that they use twice as much memory to store characters, because they use 2 bytes per character.

Before moving on, you should note something about maximum character storage. MS Access and MySQL can store only a maximum of 255 characters in a character field. To get around this, use the memo *data type for MS Access, which can store up to 65,535 characters—more than enough for most purposes. For MySQL, if you want to store large amounts of text, use the* text *data type, which also stores a maximum of 65,535 characters. You don't need to specify the maximum number of characters either the* memo *or* text *data type can hold—it's preset by the database system itself.*

Numerical Data

The easiest numbers to understand and deal with are the integers: whole numbers rather than numbers with decimal points. They are particularly useful as unique identifiers for a record, something you learn more about later in this chapter when you create the example database and look at primary keys. Fractional numbers are subject to rounding errors and therefore are best avoided if you want a unique identifier for a record. Integer numbers are also less work for the RDBMS, and less work means more speed. Therefore, they are more efficient unless you really do need the fractional part. For example, you'd need the fractional part if you're dealing with money and want to store dollars and cents.

The two integer data types used in this book are `int` and `smallint`. The difference between the two is simply in the size of number they can store and in how many bytes of memory they require to store a number. `smallint` can deal with a range between –32,768 and 32,767, whereas `int` can handle a range between –2,147,483,648 and 2,147,483,647.

The final two numerical data types covered in this chapter can store the fractional parts of numbers: `real` and `decimal`. The `real` data type can store a range of numbers between –3.40E+38 through 3.40E+38, though this varies from RDBMS to RDBMS. Note that 3.40E+38 is an example of scientific notation. It means the same as 3.4×10 to the power of 38. For example, 539,000,000 could be stated in scientific notation as 5.39E+8. This data type is very useful if you have huge numbers but are not too concerned about preciseness. When you store numbers in a `real` data type, you can use either the scientific notation or just the number itself. If the number is too large to store precisely in a `real` data type, the database system converts it to the scientific notation for you, but quite possibly with some loss of accuracy. It's not a data type you'll find yourself using particularly often.

The `decimal` data type is similar to `real` in that it allows you to store floating-point numbers as opposed to whole numbers. A floating-point number is a number with a fractional part—numbers after a decimal point—and that decimal point is not fixed in any particular position (123.445 or 4455.4, for example). Whole numbers, or integers as they are also known, can't store fractional numbers, meaning that they don't store a decimal point. `decimal` is more accurate and flexible than the `real` data type. How can the `decimal` data type be more accurate than the `real` data type, you ask? Surely the answer is either right or wrong. After all, this is math and not sociology, so there's no room for debate. Actually, while the `real` data type can store huge numbers, it does so using scientific notation, so not all the digits are actually stored if the data is over a certain size.

Look at an example to make this clearer. If you have the number 101236.8375 and try to store it as a `real` data type, the RDBMS stores 101236.84. Why did the 75 at the end disappear? On some RDBMSs, such as SQL Server and DB2, `real` can store only eight digits. The number above is 10 digits long, so the RDBMS rounds off the number and chops off the last 2 digits. Say you have a very large number, such as 101249986.8375. Even after rounding off, the number is still larger than 8 digits, so the RDBMS uses scientific notation and displays 1.0124998E+8.

The `decimal` data type differs from the `real` data type in that it stores all the digits it can. If you store a number larger than it can handle, the RDBMS throws an error saying that there is an overflow. Therefore, the digits on the left of the decimal point are always correct. The `decimal` data type, however, rounds up any digits to the right of the decimal point if it doesn't have enough spare space to display them.

The `decimal` data type's flexibility comes into play when it allows you to specify how many digits you want to store, as well as how many digits can appear on the right side of the decimal point. The following code tells the RDBMS to allocate space for 38 digits, with space reserved for 12 digits after the decimal point:

```
decimal(38,12)
```

This means that the RDBMS stores 101249986.8375 correctly, though it adds zeros after the 8375 to fill in 12 reserved spaces.

The maximum number of digits many RDBMSs allow for the `decimal` data type is 38. The more digits you ask the RDBMS to store, the more storage space you require. So `decimal(9,2)` requires 5 bytes, whereas `decimal(38,2)` requires 17 bytes!

Date and Time

Time is fairly easy to deal with. You simply store the time in the format hours:minutes:seconds. For example, 17:56:22 translates to 5:56 P.M. and 22 seconds.

Most RDBMSs uses the 24-hour clock, so to store 5:36 P.M., you write 17:36:00.

Some RDBMSs don't have a separate date and time, but instead combine them into one, in which case the date goes first and then the time in the format just mentioned of hh:mm:ss. For example, you may encounter a date and time similar to the following: 1 Mar 2006 10:45:55.

Whereas the format for time is fairly standard, dates can have many possible variations. For example, all of the following are valid in either the United States or Europe:

❑   12 Mar 2006

❑   Mar 12, 2006

❑   12 March 2006

❑   12/03/2006

❑   03/12/2006

❑   03-12-2006

Most RDBMSs handle the most common variations, like the preceding examples. However, the biggest problem arises when you specify the month by number instead of name — 03/12/2006, for example. An American would read this as the 12th day of March 2006, and a resident of the United Kingdom would see the date as the 3rd day of December 2006 — quite a difference! There is little else in database development that produces bigger headaches than dates!

Even worse is when the computer the RDBMS is running is set to the American format and the computer accessing the data from the database is set to the U.K. format. And with many companies having U.S. and foreign-based offices, this can often happen.

Whenever possible, avoid the number format, such as 12/07/2006, and instead use the month's name or at least the abbreviation of its name (12 Jul 2006, for example). Unfortunately many RDBMSs return the date format as 12/07/2006 even if you stored it as 12 Jul 2006. In this case, use formatting commands, which are covered in Chapter 5, to circumvent this problem. Also try to make sure you know the format that the RDBMS server is using.

Now that the brief introduction to data types is over with, you can move on to something a bit more interesting and hands-on — creating tables!

Creating, Altering, and Deleting Tables

This section discusses the basics of creating a table using SQL. It shows you how to create a new table, how to modify existing tables, and finally, how to delete tables that you no longer need. After that, using what you've learned, you create the tables for the book's example database.

Creating a Table

To create a table, use SQL's CREATE TABLE statement. Creating a basic table involves naming the table and defining its columns and each column's data type.

More advanced table options and constraints are covered in Chapter 4.

The following is the basic syntax for creating a table:

```
CREATE TABLE name_of_table
(
    name_of_column column_datatype
)
```

CREATE TABLE is the keyword telling the database system what you want to do — in this case, you want to create a new table. The unique name or identifier for the table follows the CREATE TABLE statement. Then in brackets comes the list defining each column in the table and what sort of data type it is. The syntax becomes clearer with an example.

The following SQL creates a table based on the earlier train timetable example:

```
CREATE TABLE Train_Times
(
    start_location varchar(75),
    destination varchar(75),
    departs time,
    arrives time
);
```

> *MS SQL Server doesn't have the* time *data type, so you need to change the data type to* datetime. *For Oracle, you need to change the data type to* date *rather than* time, *because Oracle's* date *data type stores both date and time.*
>
> *For this and all of the examples in this book, load up the tool that came with your RDBMS that allows SQL code to be written and run. You can find installation details in Appendix B at the end of the book.*

Examining the code line by line, first you specify that you want to create a table called Train_Times:

```
CREATE TABLE Train_Times
```

Then, inside brackets, you specify the four fields that make up each record. For each record, you need to identify the field name and data type:

```
(
    start_location varchar(75),
    destination varchar(75),
    departs time,
    arrives time
)
```

A comma must separate each field definition. Notice the SQL's neat layout, with the CREATE TABLE statement and each field definition on separate lines. Such layout is not compulsory. In fact, you could cram the whole lot on one line. However, laying out the code on separate lines makes the code a lot more readable and therefore easier to write and makes it easier for you to fix errors, or *debug*, if things go wrong.

You can see that creating tables is pretty easy. There are more complexities with table creation than listed here, and these are examined in Chapter 4. The next issue is how to alter tables. Say you want to add a new field, delete an existing one, or perform other routine table maintenance. The good news is that SQL allows you to perform all of these functions with one statement: ALTER TABLE.

Altering an Existing Table

The key to changing an existing table is the ALTER TABLE statement. This one statement allows you to add and delete columns in an existing table. What the ANSI SQL standard ALTER TABLE statement doesn't let you do, however, are things like changing the data type of an existing column. However, many RDBMSs have extended the ALTER TABLE statement and include their own way of changing column definitions.

To add a new column, use the basic syntax shown below:

```
ALTER TABLE name_of_table
  ADD name_of_field data_type
```

ALTER TABLE is the keyword that tells the database system what to do. After the ALTER TABLE statement, you supply the name of the table being altered. Finally, the syntax above tells the database system that you want to add a new column and then supplies the name of the column and its data type — in much the same way that you define column name and data type when creating a table.

To delete an existing column, the syntax is identical except you now tell the database system that you want to delete a column and supply that column's name:

```
ALTER TABLE name_of_table
  DROP COLUMN name_of_field
```

A couple of examples make this a bit clearer. In order to add a column called runs_at_weekend with the data type char(1) to the Train_Times table, use the following SQL:

```
ALTER TABLE Train_Times
  ADD runs_at_weekend char(1);
```

To delete the same column, you write the following:

```
ALTER TABLE Train_Times
  DROP COLUMN runs_at_weekend;
```

> IBM DB2 doesn't support the DROP COLUMN statement.

Remember, as with dropping a table, dropping a column most likely permanently deletes the data in that column. Use the DROP COLUMN statement carefully!

Finally, the next section discusses how to delete an existing table.

Deleting an Existing Table

By now you're probably seeing a pattern emerge when it comes to deleting things, so yes, you guessed it, deleting a table involves using the DROP TABLE statement. The basic syntax is

```
DROP TABLE name_of_table
```

To delete the Train_Times table, you write

```
DROP TABLE Train_Times
```

This section only scratches the surface of adding and altering tables and columns. Chapter 4 identifies potential complications that may arise when dropping a table that contains data that another table relies upon.

You should now know enough fundamentals to begin creating usable databases and tables. The final section of this chapter walks you through creating the example database that you use throughout the book. First, though, you need to know how to use good database design techniques to create an effective database.

Good Database Design

This section examines some basic rules and ideas that help you develop an effective and well-designed database. While Chapter 4 takes a more in-depth look, this chapter provides enough of the fundamentals to get you started. Begin with the all-important first step: consider why you even need a database.

Obtaining and Analyzing Your Data Needs

Before you create the database and write a single SQL statement, you need to sit down and think about why you're creating the database in the first place. This doesn't only mean because someone just paid you huge piles of cash to do so, though that is a nice benefit! It means to ask yourself, or whomever the database is for, what sort of data will be stored and what sort of answers the data needs to provide. For example, imagine that you decide to set up a film club, and being a high-tech sort of person, you decide that keeping membership details on the back of an old envelope is just too low-tech! So you decide that you need a database to help run the club. First of all, you need to sit down and think about why you need the database and what data you need to store. The club membership database may need to store details of club members. You might also like to know how popular the club is by keeping details of meetings and attendance. A good start would be to write a list of all the information you want to store.

Say you want to be able to contact each member to send out information by post and email. You also want to send them a birthday card each birthday (how nice are you!). Finally, you want to make sure that members pay their annual memberships fees, so you need to keep track of when they joined. The following list summarizes what you want to store:

❑   Full name

❑   Date of birth

❑   Address

❑   Email address

❑   Date member joined club

The aim with meetings is to keep track of how popular meetings are at various locations and who attends regularly. The following is the sort of data to store in order to keep track of such information:

❑   Meeting date

❑   Location

❑   Who attended the meeting

Now that you know what you want to store, the next step is to divide the data logically to get some idea of your table structure.

Dividing Data Logically

For now, don't worry about table names, column names, or data types; rather, just get a rough idea of what table structure you want to use.

In a first attempt, you might decide to just lump the whole lot into one huge table, including the following information:

❑ Full name

❑ Date of birth

❑ Address

❑ Email address

❑ Date member joined club

❑ Meeting date

❑ Location

❑ Whether member attended meeting

If you were to use the preceding example data, your records could look like the following table:

Name	Date of Birth	Address	Email	Date of Joining	Meeting Date	Location	Did Member Attend?
Martin	Feb 27, 1972	1 The Avenue, NY	martin@some.com	Jan 10, 2005	Mar 30, 2005	Lower West Side, NY	Y
Jane	Dec 12, 1967	33 Some Road, Washington	Jane@server.net	Jan 12, 2005	Mar 30, 2005	Lower West Side, NY	N
Kim	May 22, 1980	19 The Road, New Townsville	kim@mail.com	Jan 23, 2005	Mar 30, 2005	Lower West Side, NY	Y

Seems like a reasonable start. However, you do have one problem: How do you store details of more than one meeting? One option would be to simply create a new record for each meeting, something akin to the following table:

Name	Date of Birth	Address	Email	Date of Joining	Meeting Date	Location	Did Member Attend?
Martin	Feb 27, 1972	1 The Avenue, NY	martin@some. com	Jan 10, 2005	Mar 30, 2005	Lower West Side, NY	Y
Martin	Feb 27, 1972	1 The Avenue, NY	martin@some. com	Jan 10, 2005	April 28, 2005	Lower North Side, NY	Y
Jane	Dec 12, 1967	33 Some Road, Washington	Jane@server. net	Jan 12, 2005	Mar 30, 2005	Lower West Side, NY	N
Jane	Dec 12, 1967	33 Some Road, Washington	Jane@server. net	Jan 12, 2005	April 28, 2005	Upper North Side, NY	Y
Kim	May 22, 1980	19 The Road, New Townsville	kim@mail. com	Jan 23, 2005	Mar 30, 2005	Lower West Side, NY	Y
Kim	May 22, 1980	19 The Road, New Townsville	kim@mail. com	Jan 23, 2005	April 28, 2005	Upper North Side, NY	Y

Although that method seems to work fine, it's bad news in terms of efficiency and becomes unmanageable later on as more members join and more meetings are held.

What's so wrong with it?

First, you have unnecessary data duplication. Each time you hold a new meeting, you need to store not only the meeting details, but also, because they are in the same record, the members' details again. Your database would become huge in size quite quickly. Additionally, a lot of work is involved in actually updating the data. If Jane, for example, moves into a new house, then you need to update not just one record, but every single record relating to her. Another problem arises when you try to retrieve member details. Choosing which of the members' records to retrieve the data from would be extremely difficult; after all, you can choose from more than one record.

Rethinking your organization, you need to store details of more than one meeting, so instead of having more than one record per person, instead create new columns for each meeting so that your fields include the following:

- ❑ Full name
- ❑ Date of birth
- ❑ Address
- ❑ Email address
- ❑ Date member joined club
- ❑ Meeting date 1
- ❑ Location 1
- ❑ Whether member attended meeting 1

- ❑ Meeting date 2
- ❑ Location 2
- ❑ Whether member attended meeting 2
- ❑ Meeting date 3
- ❑ Location 3
- ❑ Whether member attended meeting 3

Organizing your columns like this saves some data duplication but results in inflexibility. Say you want to keep records of the last 10 meetings. To do so, you need a total of 30 columns in the table, and you would have to redesign the database every time you want to record more meetings. Such organization also makes writing SQL statements to extract the data harder and more long-winded.

What you need to do is split apart the data into logical parts. In this case, you are collecting data about two distinct things: club members and meeting attendance. An obvious relationship exists between the two. After all, without any members, there is no point in having meetings! That said, split your data into club member details in one table and meeting attendance data in a second table.

In the MemberDetails table, include the following:

- ❑ Full name
- ❑ Date of birth
- ❑ Address
- ❑ Email address
- ❑ Date member joined club

In the meeting attendance details table, include the following:

- ❑ Full name
- ❑ Date of the meeting
- ❑ Location
- ❑ Whether member attended meeting

Now the MemberDetails table might look something like this:

Name	Date of Birth	Address	Email	Date of Joining
Martin	Feb 27, 1972	1 The Avenue, NY	martin@some.com	Jan 10, 2005
Jane	Dec 12, 1967	33 Some Road, Washington	Jane@server.net	Jan 12, 2005
Kim	May 22, 1980	19 The Road, New Townsville	kim@mail.com	Jan 23, 2005

The Attendance table could look like this:

Name	Meeting Date	Location	Did Member Attend?
Martin	Mar 30, 2005	Lower West Side, NY	Y
Martin	April 28, 2005	Lower North Side, NY	Y
Jane	Mar 30, 2005	Lower West Side, NY	N
Jane	April 28, 2005	Upper North Side, NY	Y
Kim	Mar 30, 2005	Lower West Side, NY	Y
Kim	April 28, 2005	Upper North Side, NY	Y

Splitting member details and meeting details into two tables saves a lot of data redundancy. Member details are stored only once, and the only redundant data is the name, which links the two tables together. This is a reasonable start to database table design, so now turn your attention to defining the data types.

Selecting Correct Data Types

After getting a rough idea of the table design, the next step is to choose the data types for each field. Sometimes this is fairly obvious. For example, storing a person's name in a numerical field doesn't make sense!

However, there are times when perhaps the data type is less obvious. For example, although a telephone number is a number, you store it in a character field for a couple of reasons. First, telephone numbers are rarely involved in mathematical calculations. Second, sometimes telephone numbers start with zeros. For example, 077123333 would be stored as 77123333 in a numerical field; the RDBMS removes the leading zero because it's not important to the number's value as a number, though the zero is important to the number's value as a telephone number.

Consider these factors when choosing a data type to use:

❏   **The data's use:** Is the data intended for mathematical calculations? Does the data represent date or time situations? Does the data simply display text-based information?

❏   **The data's size:** Choose a data type that covers the largest value you reasonably expect to store. For example, if you expect people with names 100 characters long, then ensure that the character field could handle it. If the data is a number, ensure that the largest number fits into the field.

❏   **Correct information storage:** For example, if you use an integer data type to store a monetary value, then you lose any fractional parts. So, the integer data type stores $2.99 as 2. Even with data types that store the fractional parts, you may find that the database rounds them up or down, resulting in incorrect values—especially with the real data type. Use a field specific to money if your RDBMS supports it, or at least use DECIMAL(10,2).

❏   **Non-English characters:** If you need to store non-English characters, choose one of the nchar or nvarchar data types for your text data.

Generally speaking, picking a data type is common sense. Using the Film Club database's MemberDetails table, pick some names and data types:

Field Name	Data Type
Name	varchar(75)
DateOfBirth	date
Address	varchar(200)
Email	varchar(200)
DateOfJoining	date

As you can see, it's mostly common sense when choosing data types. A name, a street address, or an email address are text-based information, so you would choose the text data type. Likewise, date of birth, a date, is stored in the date data type. The size of the fields, however, contains an element of guesswork. You can't be 100% sure that there isn't someone out there with a name longer than 75 characters, but a good guess is that they are few and far between. To be on the safe side, go for an estimate that holds more characters than you ever expect to be stored.

The data types for the Attendance table are the following:

Field Name	Data Type
Name	varchar(75)
MeetingDate	date
Location	varchar(200)
MemberAttended	char(1)

Again it's fairly easy to choose, with Name and Location being text-based data — so a character data type, here varchar, is the best choice. MeetingDate is a date field, so the date data type has been chosen. MemberAttended is unusual. You just want to store whether a member did or did not attend. To do this, you can go for a yes or no choice, with *yes* represented by a Y, and *no* represented by an N. A character data type is best, and because you only ever plan to store one character, it's more efficient to use the fixed char data type and specify that the field can hold just one character.

Using a Primary Key

A *primary key* is a field or fields that uniquely identify a record from the other records in the database table. Continuing with the film club example, you might consider yourself the first club member, so keeping a database record of membership is pretty easy. As a few more people join, you decide to create a database and store their details as well, including name, age, address, and so on. When there are just a few people in the club, and, hence, just a few records in the database, using members' names to identify people in the database is probably going to work fine. Imagine, though, that the club expands massively to thousands of members. Suddenly the risk of there being two, three, or more identical names gets ever higher, and your ability to select the right person from the database gets lower! In such cases, you need some sort of unique identification. You could use name and age in combination, but the problem is that people age, so the unique identifier changes, which makes keeping track of people quite hard. There's also the small risk of two people with the same name and age. You could use name and address, but again, addresses change, and also addresses are quite long, which slows down the database in terms of searching and sorting data.

You may have already guessed that the answer to the problem is to give everyone a unique identifier that only they have. In a club, you might call the unique identifier something like the MemberId. And this is all a primary key is — a unique identifier. You know that MemberId 1234432 applies to just one person, and if you select that data from the database, you are guaranteed to get the record you want.

Primary keys also link one table to another. For example, if you have one table with member details in it and a second table that contains details of meeting attendance, you could link the two tables together with a primary key. For example, the MemberDetails table could look like this:

Field Name	Data Type
MemberId	integer
Name	varchar(75)
DateOfBirth	date
Address	varchar(200)
Email	varchar(200)
DateOfJoining	date

Note that the MemberId column is the primary key column for this table.

Your Attendance table could look like this:

Field Name	Data Type
MeetingDate	date
Location	varchar(200)
MemberAttended	char(1)
MemberId	integer

Note that the MemberId column is the *foreign key* column for this table. A foreign key contains the value of a primary key in another table, allowing the second table to reference the first. In the film club example, the MemberId field links the member in the Attendance table with their full details in the MemberDetails table.

You have a primary key for the MemberDetails table, MemberId, but what about for the Attendance table? The Attendance table has a unique identifier — the combination of MeetingDate and MemberId, because it's not possible for a member to attend the same meeting twice! Therefore, using those two columns in combination to provide unique identification is safe. This provides a nice segue to the second point about primary keys: They don't have to be composed of just one column, as in the case of the Attendance table. If you wanted to, you could create a unique meeting ID, but in this situation a unique meeting ID is not necessary and wastes storage space. If speed of data retrieval were a vital issue, you might consider using a primary key, but most of the time it's not necessary.

A primary key simply involves having a column to store a unique value and then generating that value. However, most RDBMSs also allow you to specify a column as a primary key, and in doing so, the RDBMS manages data entry. In particular, you can apply constraints to exactly what data can go in the field. For example, constraints prevent you from having two records with the same primary key value. After all, the point of a primary key is that it's unique. Chapter 4 delves deeper into the more advanced and tricky aspects of primary keys and constraints, but now you have the requisite knowledge to create your first full-fledged database. The database you create in the next section is the one you use throughout the book.

Creating the Example Database

The example database continues the previous discussion of the Film Club database. You need to create a database to store the tables. You can call your database something like Film Club, though for the purposes of this book, the database's name is not important. Appendix B has all the specifics needed for creating a blank example database in either Access, SQL Server, DB2, MySQL, or Oracle. Once you've created the Film Club database, it's time to start populating it with tables.

The basic premise is that you're running a film club, and you want a database that stores the following information:

❑ Club member details, such as name, address, date of birth, date they joined, and email address

❑ Meeting attendance details

❑ Film details

❑ Members' film category preferences

These are the requirements now, though later in the book, you develop and expand the database.

You've already established the club membership's details, but notice the additional fields in the following table:

Field Name	Data Type	Notes
MemberId	integer	Primary key.
FirstName	nvarchar(50)	Change data type to vargraphic(50) in IBM DB2 and to varchar(50) in MySQL and MS Access. In Oracle nvarchar is not available with the default character set; change to varchar. You must have selected Unicode character set when creating the database to use nvarchar.
LastName	nvarchar(50)	Change data type to vargraphic(50) in IBM DB2 and to varchar(50) in MySQL and MS Access. In Oracle nvarchar is not available with the default character set; change to varchar. You must have selected Unicode character set when creating the database to use nvarchar.
DateOfBirth	date	Change data type to datetime in MS SQL Server.
Street	varchar(100)	
City	varchar(75)	
State	varchar(75)	
ZipCode	varchar(12)	
Email	varchar(200)	
DateOfJoining	date	Change data type to datetime in MS SQL Server.

Notice that the name and address fields are split into smaller parts. Name is split into FirstName and LastName; address is split into Street, City, State, and ZipCode. Splitting name and address data makes searching for specific data more efficient. If you want to search for all members in New York City, then you simply search the City field. If you store street, city, state, and zip code in one address field, searching by city is very difficult.

Create the SQL table creation code. If you prefer, you can use your RDBMS's management console to create the table.

```
CREATE TABLE MemberDetails
(
    MemberId integer,
    FirstName nvarchar(50),
    LastName nvarchar(50),
    DateOfBirth date,
    Street varchar(100),
    City varchar(75),
    State varchar(75),
    ZipCode varchar(12),
    Email varchar(200),
    DateOfJoining date

);
```

Depending on which RDBMS you're using, you need to change some of the data types as outlined in the preceding table. Also, if you're using IBM's DB2 then varchar type is vargraphic. If you're using MS SQL then date is datetime. In MYSQL and MS Access nvarchar needs to be varchar.

The next table to create is the Attendance table, which contains the following fields and data types:

Field Name	Data Type	Notes
MeetingDate	date	Change data type to datetime if using MS SQL Server
Location	varchar(200)	
MemberAttended	char(1)	
MemberId	integer	Foreign key linking to MemberDetails table

The Attendance table is unchanged from the previous discussion of the Film Club database. The SQL to create the Attendance table is as follows:

```
CREATE TABLE Attendance
(
    MeetingDate date,
    Location varchar(200),
    MemberAttended char(1),
    MemberId integer
);
```

What could the unique primary key be for this table? If you assume that you have only one meeting a day in any one location, then a combination of the meeting date and meeting location provides a unique reference. If it were possible, there could be one or more meetings on the same day in the same location, but at different times. In such an instance, you need to store meeting time as well as the meeting date—by having an extra column called MeetingTime. You could then use MeetingDate, MeetingTime, and Location to provide a unique key, or you could create a column called MeetingId containing a unique integer for each meeting to use as the primary key. This sort of situation requires you to go back and ask whomever the database is for what their requirements are and then design your database based on the information they provide, because it's better to get it right from the start.

You still have to add tables to store the following information:

❏ Film details

❏ Members' film category preferences

A new table called Films needs to be created. The information to be stored in the Films table is as follows:

❏ Film name

❏ Year of release

❏ Brief plot summary

❏ Film's availability on DVD

❏ User film ratings (for example, 1–5, where 1 is awful beyond belief and 5 is an all-time classic)

Finally, you need to assign each film a category—for example, horror, action, romance, and so on.

The following table outlines the Films table's contents:

Field Name	Data Type	Notes
FilmId	`integer`	Primary key
FilmName	`varchar(100)`	
YearReleased	`integer`	
PlotSummary	`varchar(2000)`	Change to `memo` data type if using MS Access or to the `text` data type if using MySQL
AvailableOnDVD	`char(1)`	
Rating	`integer`	
CategoryId	`integer`	Foreign key

Before going further, there are two points to note regarding the field definitions. First, the PlotSummary field is a `varchar` data type, except when used in MS Access, which only supports `varchar` with a size of up to 255 characters. Because you need to store up to 2000 characters, you must use Access's `memo` field, which allows you to store up to 65,536. You can't specify length; it's set at a maximum of 65,536 characters, which is equivalent to a `varchar(65536)` data type.

The second point to note pertains to the CategoryId field. It is a foreign key field, which means that its value is the primary key field in another table, and it provides a way of relating the two tables. The table containing the primary key to which the Films table links is the FilmCategory table, which you will create shortly. First, though, the SQL to create the Films table is as follows:

```
CREATE TABLE Films
(
    FilmId integer,
    FilmName varchar(100),
    YearReleased integer,
    PlotSummary varchar(2000),
    AvailableOnDVD char(1),
    Rating integer,
    CategoryId integer
);
```

After creating the Films table, you can create the FilmCategory table, which contains the following data:

Field Name	Data Type	Notes
CategoryId	`integer`	Primary key
Category	`varchar(100)`	

The FilmCategory table is very small and simple. The SQL you need to create it is likewise very simple:

```
CREATE TABLE Category
(
    CategoryId integer,
    Category varchar(100)
);
```

The final table you need to create is called FavCategory, and it stores each member's favorite film categories:

Field Name	Data Type	Notes
CategoryId	integer	Foreign key
MemberId	integer	Foreign key

As you can see, it's a very simple table! Both CategoryId and MemberId are foreign keys, the first from the Category table and the second from the MemberDetails table. Combined, they make up a unique primary key. The SQL to create the FavCategory table is as follows:

```
CREATE TABLE FavCategory
(
    CategoryId integer,
    MemberId integer
);
```

Creating the FavCategory table completes the basic database structure. As you can see, creating a database is actually fairly easy! Chapter 4 covers more complex examples and options, but what you learned in this chapter lays a good foundation of database creation.

Summary

This chapter walked you through the fundamentals of SQL and database design and provided you with instruction on how to write the SQL code necessary to create a database's structure. You now have enough knowledge to start designing your own databases.

In this chapter, you discovered the following:

❑   Databases are an efficient way to store large amounts of raw data. They don't process the data; that's left to the application that uses the data.

❑   Databases make sharing data easier than do other means, such as text files, spreadsheets, or other documents. They also allow secure data sharing and allow you to define the levels of user access. You can limit what you let others do to your database's data.

❑   Relational databases contain tables and fields and provide ways of relating data in different tables and ways of ensuring that any data entered is valid and doesn't corrupt the database.

❏ Databases are part of a larger software application called a database management system (DBMS).

❏ SQL is a declarative programming language, that is, you use it to specify the answers you want and leave the DBMS to work out how to get them.

After getting the basics under your belt, you got down to some practical work. In particular, you created a database and learned the basics of SQL and table creation. In doing so, you found out the following:

❏ How databases are organized. You saw that databases are composed of tables, which themselves are composed of records, and that each record is split into fields or columns.

❏ How to create a database. You learned that you can create a database either with the RDBMS's management tools or with SQL statements.

❏ Different types of data are stored differently. You learned that databases support a number of different data types for storing text (char and varchar), numbers (integer, real, and decimal), and time and dates (time and date). These are just the basic data types, and most RDBMSs support many more data types.

❏ The principles of good database design.

Finally, at the end of the chapter, you created the book's example database using the techniques and code covered earlier in the chapter. In the next chapter, you learn how to add, update, and delete data using SQL. Don't forget to have a go at the exercises!

Exercises

1. As it happens, the film club holds meetings regularly in several different locations, which means a lot of redundancy in the Attendance table. What changes could you make to the database table structure?

2. Write the necessary SQL to complete the changes required by Exercise 1 and at the same time split the location's address details into street, city, and state.

Entering Information

The last chapter examined creating a database and adding tables, so now you're ready to start adding data. Most RDBMSs provide management tools that allow you to view tables and the records they hold, as well as allowing you to add, modify, and delete the data. These tools are very convenient when you have small amounts of data or when you're just testing the database. However, you don't generally enter data using the management tools. Much more common is some sort of program or Web page that acts as a pleasant front end into which the user enters and views data. This chapter's focus is on how to use SQL statements to insert, update, or delete data contained in a database.

This chapter covers the three SQL statements that deal with altering data. The first is the INSERT INTO statement, which inserts new data. The UPDATE statement updates existing data in the database. Finally, this chapter covers the DELETE statement, which (surprise, surprise) deletes records.

Inserting New Data

The INSERT INTO statement makes inserting new data into the database very easy. All you need to do is specify into which table you want to insert data, into which columns to insert data, and finally what data to insert. The basic syntax is as follows:

```
INSERT INTO table_name (column_names) VALUES (data_values)
```

This line of code adds a record to the Category table:

```
INSERT INTO Category (CategoryId, Category) VALUES (1, 'Thriller');
```

You can see that inserting data is simply a matter of listing each column name (separated by a comma) in the brackets after the table name. In the brackets after the VALUES statement, simply list each item of data to go into the matching column and separate each with a comma. Character and date data must be wrapped up inside single quotes. Delimiters are unnecessary around numerical data; simply insert them as is. If you load your RDBMS's SQL editor, connect to your Film Club database, and then enter and execute the statement, the following record is added to the Category table:

CategoryId	Category
1	Thriller

To check whether it worked, either use your RDBMS's management tools to view table data or use the following SQL statement:

```
SELECT * FROM Category
```

This statement displays all the records in the Category table. Chapter 3 covers the full details of the SELECT statement. For now, just use it to ensure that the INSERT INTO statement worked.

Once you make sure the first INSERT statement works, you can insert more values into your Category table:

```
INSERT INTO Category (CategoryId, Category) VALUES (2, 'Romance');
INSERT INTO Category (CategoryId, Category) VALUES (3, 'Horror');
INSERT INTO Category (CategoryId, Category) VALUES (4, 'War');
INSERT INTO Category (CategoryId, Category) VALUES (5, 'Sci-fi');
```

Now your Category table should contain the following values:

CategoryId	Category
1	Thriller
2	Romance
3	Horror
4	War
5	Sci-fi

Check whether yours does by using the following SELECT statement:

```
SELECT * FROM Category
```

You can specify the column names in any order you like, so you could also write the above SQL as follows:

```
INSERT INTO Category (Category, CategoryId) VALUES ('Historical', 6);
```

Regardless of category order, SQL performs exactly the same way, as long as you match column names in the first set of brackets with the correct data in the second set.

If you want to, you can leave off the column names altogether. You can write the code:

```
INSERT INTO Category (CategoryId, Category) VALUES (6, 'Historical')
```

like this:

```
INSERT INTO Category VALUES (6, 'Historical')
```

The RDBMS interprets it as meaning the following:

```
INSERT INTO Category (CategoryId, Category) VALUES (6, 'Historical')
```

The RDBMS decides the columns' order based on their order when you defined the table. Remember that you defined the Category table with CategoryId first and Category second, like this:

```
CREATE TABLE Category
(
    CategoryId integer,
    Category varchar(100)
)
```

You defined your MemberDetails table like this:

```
CREATE TABLE MemberDetails
(
    MemberId integer,
    FirstName nvarchar(50),
    LastName nvarchar(50),
    DateOfBirth date,
    Street varchar(100),
    City varchar(75),
    State varchar(75),
    ZipCode varchar(12),
    Email varchar(200),
    DateOfJoining date

)
```

Based on this information, the column order is MemberId, FirstName, LastName, DateOfBirth, Street, City, State, ZipCode, Email, DateOfJoining.

Writing the following INSERT INTO statement:

```
INSERT INTO MemberDetails
VALUES
  (
  1,
  'Katie',
  'Smith',
  '1977-01-09',
  'Main Road',
  'Townsville',
  'Stateside',
  '123456',
  'katie@mail.com',
  '2004-02-23'
  );
```

makes the MemberDetails table look like this:

Member Id	First Name	Last Name	Date OfBirth	Street	City	State	Zip Code	Email	Date OfJoining
1	Katie	Smith	1977-01-09	Main Road	Townsville	Stateside	123456	Katie@ mail.com	2004-02-23

Notice that dates in the preceding table are specified in the form year-month-day, so February 23, 2004, is entered as 2004-02-23. The exact format acceptable to each database system varies not only with the database system but also with the way the database was first created and installed, as well as the date/time format specified by the computer itself. However, the format year-month-day works in most circumstances. However, the year-month-day format doesn't work on the default installation of Oracle. For Oracle, use the format day-month_name-year. So you would write January 9, 1977, as 9 January 1977 and February 23, 2004, as 23 Feb 2004.

The advantages of not naming the columns in your INSERT statement are that it saves typing and makes for shorter SQL. The disadvantage is that it's not as easy to see what data goes into which columns. For example, in the following INSERT statement, it's easy to match up column names to data being inserted without having to use the management tool to remind yourself of the column names.

```
INSERT INTO MemberDetails
(
  MemberId,
  FirstName,
  LastName,
  DateOfBirth,
  Street,
  City,
  State,
  ZipCode,
  Email,
  DateOfJoining
)
VALUES
(
  2,
  'Bob',
  'Robson',
  '1987-01-09',
  'Little Street',
  'Big City',
  'Small State',
  '34565',
  'rob@mail.com',
  '2004-03-13'
);
```

Of course, while it's all fresh in your mind it's not that hard to match column name and data. However, how about in six months or a year's time when you're asked to change the database structure or even to identify bugs? Your code is a little more readable if the column names are in there.

That's pretty much all there is to the INSERT INTO statement, so now you can finish it off by inserting data into the Film Club database.

Inserting Data into the Case Study Database

You've already inserted six records into the Category table and two records into the MemberDetails table. For the rest of the data to be inserted, you can turn to Appendix C to add the remaining data. Note that Appendix C and the book's downloadable files include for completeness the six records you already added to the Category table and the two MemberDetails records, so if you've already added them, don't add them a second time. Note that some RDBMSs allow you to insert all the data at once; others, such as MS Access, require you to insert one SQL statement at a time.

Now that you've got some data in the database, take a look at how you can alter it.

Updating Data

Not only do you need to add new records, but at some point you also need to change the records. To update records, you use the UPDATE statement. Specifying which records to change is the main difference between inserting new data and updating existing data. You specify which records to update with the WHERE clause, which allows you to specify that the only records to update are those where a certain condition is true. For example, say film club member Steve Gee has changed his address. His MemberId is 4, so you could tell the database to update the address where the MemberId is 4.

You don't, however, have to update all the details in a record. As in the example of Steve's change of address, only his address changes, not his name, date of birth, and so on. The UPDATE statement allows you to set which fields to update and with what data to update the field. The basic syntax of the UPDATE statement is as follows:

```
UPDATE table_name
SET column_name = value
WHERE condition
```

Start with a simple example, where film club member Steve Gee's new address is the following:

45 Upper Road
New Town
New State
99112

Keep in mind that Steve's MemberId is 4. The SQL needed to make the changes is shown below:

```
UPDATE MemberDetails
SET
Street = '45 Upper Road',
City = 'New Town',
State = 'New State',
ZipCode = '99112'
WHERE MemberId = 4;
```

Now Steve's record looks like this:

Member Id	First Name	Last Name	Date OfBirth	Street	City	State	Zip Code	Email	Date Of Joining
4	Steve	Gee	Oct 5, 1967	45 Upper Road	New Town	New State	99112	steve@ gee.com	Feb 22 2004

Looking at the code, first you specified which table to update with the following UPDATE statement:

```
UPDATE MemberDetails
```

In the SET clause, you specified each column name and the new value each should hold:

```
Street = '45 Upper Road',
City = 'New Town',
State = 'New State',
ZipCode = '99112'
```

As you can see in the example, with the UPDATE statement, you can use the SET clause to specify one or more columns to be updated; you just need to separate each column and name/value pair with a comma. Finally, you have the WHERE clause:

```
WHERE MemberId = 4
```

This clause says to update all records where the MemberId column has a value equal to 4. Because the MemberId is the unique primary key value in the MemberDetails table, this means that only one record is changed. However, if there is more than one match, then every matching record's column values are updated. For example, say the people of Big Apple City get bored with their city's name and want to change it to Orange Town. To make this update in your database, you'd write the following SQL:

```
UPDATE MemberDetails
SET City = 'Orange Town'
WHERE City = 'Big Apple City';
```

Execute this SQL in your RDBMS's SQL tool, and the two records in the MemberDetails table that have a City column with the value Big Apple City are changed to Orange Town. However, it would be easy to forget that the Location table also contains City names, one of which is Big Apple City. You also need to update the Location table with this query:

```
UPDATE Location SET City = 'Orange Town' WHERE City = 'Big Apple City';
```

The ability to update more than one record at once is very powerful, but watch out! If you get your WHERE clause wrong, you could end up corrupting your database's data. And if you leave out the WHERE clause altogether, all records are updated in the specified table.

For the most part, the UPDATE statement is pretty simple. However, you need to examine the WHERE clause in more detail, because it's significantly more complicated.

The WHERE Clause

So far you've seen only a situation in which the database system performs an update if a column is equal to a certain value, but you can use other comparisons as well. The following table details a few of the fundamental comparison operators.

Comparison Operator	Name	Example	Example Matches All Records in Film Table Where Rating Is...
=	Equals	WHERE Rating = 5	5
<>	Not equal to	WHERE Rating <> 1	2, 3, 4, or 5
>	Greater than	WHERE Rating > 2	3, 4, or 5
<	Less than	WHERE Rating < 4	1, 2, or 3
>=	Greater than or equal to	WHERE Rating >= 3	3, 4, or 5
<=	Less than or equal to	WHERE Rating <= 2	1 or 2

The preceding table uses the Film table's Rating column in the Example and Example Matches columns. The comparison operators work with numerical fields, date fields, and text fields. In fact, they work with most data types, though there are exceptions. For example, some RDBMSs support the Boolean data type, which can be one of two values — true or false. It doesn't make sense to use operators other than the "equals" or "not equal to" operators with that data type.

With text-based data types, the operators >, <, >=, and <= make a comparison that equates to alphabetical order. For example, *a* is less than *b* in the alphabet, so to select all values in the column field where the first letter is lower than *f* in the alphabet, you use the following clause:

```
UPDATE SomeTable SET SomeColumn = 'SomeValue' WHERE Column < 'f';
```

The same principle applies to dates: January 1, 2005, is less than February 1, 2005.

Continuing the film club example, imagine that Sandra Jakes marries Mr. William Tell and that you need to update her surname to Tell.

```
UPDATE MemberDetails SET LastName = 'Tell' WHERE MemberId = 3;
```

This code fragment tells the database to update the MemberDetails table, changing the LastName field to the text value Tell for all records where the MemberId is equal to 3. In this case, because the MemberId field stores a unique number for each record, only one record is changed. Alternatively, you could have used the following SQL to update the record:

```
UPDATE MemberDetails SET LastName = 'Tell' WHERE LastName = 'Jakes';
```

This would work fine with the records currently in the MemberDetails table, because at the moment only one person has the surname Jakes, though there's no guarantee that it will remain the only one. If you have two or more member with the surname Jakes, the SQL would update each record to match the WHERE statement.

So far your WHERE statement has just checked for one condition, such as LastName = 3. However, as you see in the next section, you can check more than one condition.

The Logical Operators AND and OR

The AND and OR logical operators allow you to test more than one condition in a WHERE statement. Their meanings in SQL and their meanings in English are almost identical. The AND operator means that both the condition on the left-hand side of the operator and the condition on the right-hand side must be true.

```
WHERE MyColumn = 132 AND MyOtherColumn = 'TEST'
```

The condition on the left-hand side of the operator is as follows:

```
MyColumn = 132
```

The following condition is on the right-hand side of the AND operator:

```
MyOtherColumn = 'TEST'
```

For the overall WHERE statement to be true, both conditions must also be true. For example, MyColumn must equal 132 and MyOtherColumn must equal TEST.

Returning to the example database and the MemberDetails table, the street New Lane in Big Apple City has changed its name to Newish Lane. To update all the appropriate records in the MemberDetails table, you need to check for records where the street name is New Lane and the city is Big Apple (after all, there could be another New Lane in another city). Use this SQL to update the records:

```
UPDATE MemberDetails SET Street = 'Newish Lane' WHERE Street = 'New Lane'
                               AND City = 'Orange Town';
```

Notice that the AND clause is on its own separate line. That's not necessary; it's done here simply to improve readability. When the SQL is executed, any cities with the name Orange Town and the street name New Lane have their Street column updated and set to the value Newish Lane. There are two records in the MemberDetails table that match the criteria, and hence they are updated.

The other logical operator mentioned is the OR operator, which means that the condition is true and the record updates where one or both of the expressions are true. For example,

```
WHERE MyColumn = '10' OR MyOtherColumn = 'TEST'
```

The WHERE clause is true and the record updates if MyColumn equals 10, MyOtherColumn equals TEST, or both MyColumn equals 10 and MyOtherColumn equals TEST.

Now that you're familiarized with the AND and OR logical operators, you can use them to update records in your database.

Try It Out   Using Logical Operators to Update Database Records

A new president has decided that Small State and Stateside states should merge into one new state called Mega State. You need to update the database to reflect these changes. Remember that you store details of states in the Location and the MemberDetails tables, so you need to update both tables.

1.   Enter this SQL to update the two records in the MemberDetails table:

```
UPDATE MemberDetails
SET State = 'Mega State'
WHERE
State = 'Small State'
OR
State = 'Stateside';
```

This statement updates the two records in the MemberDetails table. The SQL to do the same for the Location table is identical except that the name of the table being updated has to be changed.

2.   Enter the following SQL to update the records in the Location table:

```
UPDATE Location
SET State = 'Mega State'
WHERE
State = 'Small State'
OR
State = 'Stateside';
```

How It Works

The only difference between these two statements is the name of the table affected by the UPDATE statements; otherwise, they are identical. The first bit of SQL tells the database to update the MemberDetails table where the State column holds a value of either Small State or Stateside. The second SQL fragment tells the database to update the Location table where the State column holds a value of either Small State or Stateside. The State field in both tables should now be Mega State.

So far you've used only one AND or OR operator in each WHERE clause, but you can include as many, within reason, as you like. You can also mix AND and OR operators in the same WHERE clause.

The WHERE clause is vital to selecting data from the database, something covered in great detail in Chapter 3. Everything that applies to the WHERE clause in Chapter 3 also applies to the WHERE clause of an UPDATE statement.

Deleting Data

So far in this chapter, you've learned how to add new data and update existing data, so all that remains to learn is how to delete data. The good news is that deleting data is very easy. You simply specify which table to delete the records from, and if required, you add a WHERE clause to specify which records to delete.

If you want to delete all the records from a table, you simply leave out the WHERE clause, as shown in the following statement:

```
DELETE FROM MemberDetails;
```

The preceding SQL fragment deletes all the records in the MemberDetails table. Don't execute it or else you'll have to enter the records again. If you want to delete some of the records, you use the WHERE clause to specify which ones:

```
DELETE FROM MemberDetails WHERE MemberId = 3;
```

Enter and execute this SQL. This SQL deletes all records from the MemberDetails table where the MemberId column has a value of 3. Because it holds a unique value, only the details of Sandra Tell are deleted — she is the only person whose MemberId is 3. Now that Sandra is gone from the membership, you also need to delete her details from the FavCategory and Attendance tables. Use the following statements to do so:

```
DELETE FROM Attendance WHERE MemberId = 3;
DELETE FROM FavCategory WHERE MemberId = 3;
```

Everything that applies to the WHERE clause when used with the UPDATE statement also applies to the DELETE statement.

Summary

For now, that completes your introduction to adding, updating, and deleting data. This chapter covered the following:

❑ How to add new records to a database using the INSERT INTO statement. To add a new record, you must specify which table the record should go into, which fields you assign values to, and finally the values to be assigned.

❑ Next you looked at how to update data already in the database using the UPDATE statement, which specifies which table's records receive updates, as well as the fields and new values assigned to each record. Finally, you learned that the WHERE clause specifies which records in the table receive updates. If you don't use a WHERE clause, all records in the table receive updates.

❑ The final statement covered in this chapter was the DELETE statement, which allows you to delete records from a table. You can either delete all records or use a WHERE clause to specify which records you want to delete.

This chapter only touched on the basics; Chapter 3 shows you how to take data from one table and use it to insert data from one table into a second table. Chapter 3 also examines the WHERE clause in greater depth.

Exercises

1. Three new members have joined the film club. Add the following details to the database:

Member ID: 7
First Name: John
Last Name: Jackson
Date of Birth: May 27, 1974
Street: Long Lane
City: Orange Town
State: New State
Zip Code: 88992
Email: jjackson@mailme.net
Date of Joining: November 21, 2005

Member ID: 8
First Name: Jack
Last Name: Johnson
Date of Birth: June 9, 1945
Street: Main Street
City: Big City
State: Mega State
Zip Code: 34566
Email: jjohnson@me.com
Date of Joining: June 2, 2005

Member ID: 9
First Name: Seymour
Last Name: Botts
Date of Birth: October 21, 1956
Street: Long Lane
City: Windy Village
State: Golden State
Zip Code: 65422
Email: Seymour@botts.org
Date of Joining: July 17, 2005

You need to ensure that the date format matches the format expected by your database system. Remember that Oracle accepts day-month-year format (23 January 2004), whereas the other four databases expect the format year-month-day, such as 2004-01-23.

2. Bob Robson, MemberId 2, took a job in Hollywood and left the club. Delete his details from the database. Remember to delete not only his membership details but also his film category preferences.

3. The government has decided to reorganize the boundaries of Orange Town. All residents living on Long Lane in Orange Town now live in Big City. Update the database to reflect this change.

Extracting Information

So far you've learned how to set up a database and how to insert data into it, so now you can learn how to extract data from your database. Arguably, SQL's most powerful feature is its ability to extract data, and extracting data can be as simple or complex as you require. You can simply extract data in the same form in which it was entered into the database, or you could query the database and obtain answers to questions that are not obvious from the basic data. In your example database, you can use SQL to find out which meeting locations are most popular, or you could find out which meeting locations are most popular for which film category. It might turn out that Windy Village has a particularly large number of sci-fi fans. If the film club decides to show a film at that location, you would be aware that a sci-fi film is likely to be popular. The ability to ask the database questions and get answers via SQL queries makes SQL so popular and useful.

The key to getting data out is the SELECT statement, which in its basic form is very simple and easy to use. However, as you go through this chapter and then the advanced chapters, you see lots of extra options that make the SELECT statement very powerful. Before getting too complicated, however, you need to familiarize yourself with the SELECT statement.

The SELECT Statement

At its simplest, the SELECT requires you to tell it which columns and from what table you want to obtain data. The basic syntax is as follows:

```
SELECT column1, column2,.....columnx FROM table_name
```

Using the basic syntax, the SQL required to select the MemberId and FirstName columns from all records in the MemberDetails table is

```
SELECT MemberId, FirstName FROM MemberDetails;
```

The order in which you list the columns in the SELECT statement determines the order in which they are returned in the results. The preceding query returns this order:

MemberId	FirstName
1	Katie
3	Sandra
4	Steve
5	John
6	Jenny
7	John
8	Jack
9	Seymour

The order of the results in the example database table usually reflects on the order in which the records were first entered into the database, but the order is not guaranteed, so don't worry if your order looks different from what appears in the preceding table. Chapter 4 shows you how to create a columns index on columns to determine the order of results. Later in this chapter, you learn how to use the ORDER BY clause to specify the order in which records are returned.

Specifying which columns you want returned is fine, but sometimes you may want all of the columns, which is a lot of typing if your table has many fields. The good news is that SQL provides a shorthand way of selecting all the columns without having to type out all their names. Instead of typing the column names, just type an asterisk:

```
SELECT * FROM Location;
```

The preceding code fragment is the same as writing the following:

```
SELECT LocationId, Street, City, State FROM Location;
```

Both lines of code return the following results:

LocationId	Street	City	State
1	Main Street	Orange Town	New State
2	Winding Road	Windy Village	Golden State
3	Tiny Terrace	Big City	Mega State

However, use shorthand only when you need all the columns, otherwise you make the database system provide information you don't need, which wastes CPU power and memory. Memory and CPU power may not matter on a small database, but they make a huge difference on a large database being accessed by many people.

Returning Only Distinct Rows

If you want to know all the unique values in a record, how would you go about retrieving them? The answer is by using the DISTINCT keyword. The DISTINCT keyword is added to the SELECT statement's column listing, directly after the SELECT keyword. For example, if someone asks you which cities members come from, you could try a query similar to the following:

```
SELECT City FROM MemberDetails;
```

Executing the query gives you the following results:

City
Townsville
Orange Town
New Town
Orange Town
Orange Town
Big City
Windy Village

As you can see, Orange Town is listed three times because there are three members from that city. But if you simply want a list of the unique places that members live in, you could add the DISTINCT keyword:

```
SELECT DISTINCT City FROM MemberDetails;
```

Executing the modified query gives these results:

City
Big City
New Town
Orange Town
Townsville
Windy Village

This time, Orange Town is mentioned just once. The DISTINCT keyword works on all columns in combination; all the columns listed in the SELECT statement must be unique. If you change the previous query to include MemberId, which is unique for every single row, and rerun the query, you end up with all the rows:

```
SELECT DISTINCT City, MemberId FROM MemberDetails;
```

The results are as follows:

City	MemberId
Big City	8
New Town	4
Orange Town	5
Orange Town	6
Orange Town	7
Townsville	1
Windy Village	9

Orange Town appears three times because MemberId is unique on each row. In fact, using the DISTINCT keyword where one of the columns is always unique is pointless.

Using Aliases

Just as James Bond is also known by the alias 007, you can give column names an alias in the results. An *alias* is simply a secondary or symbolic name for a collection of data. If, for example, instead of LastName you want your results to return an alias called Surname, you would write the following query:

```
SELECT LastName AS Surname FROM MemberDetails;
```

Specifying Surname with the AS keyword tells the database system that you want the results to be known as the alias Surname. Using an alias doesn't change the results returned in any way, nor does it rename the LastName in the MemberDetails tables. It affects only the name of the column in the results set. Using aliases may not seem that useful right now, but later on in the book you use aliases as a short-hand way of referring to table names, among other uses.

So far all the data from tables has been returned, but what if you just want specific data — for example, details of members older than 60 years old? In such a case, you need to use a WHERE clause, which is the topic of the next section.

Filtering Results with the WHERE Clause

Although you may occasionally have to select all the records in a table, it's much more common to filter results so that you get only the information you want. For example, you could filter query results to find out all the names of members living in New State. In Chapter 2 you saw how you can use the WHERE clause to update or delete specific records. You can also use the WHERE clause with SELECT statements to filter results so that you get back only the data you want.

The good news is that everything you learned in Chapter 2 about the WHERE clause can be applied to WHERE clauses used with SELECT statements. This chapter delves even deeper into WHERE clauses and looks at some of the more sophisticated stuff not covered in Chapter 2.

To recap briefly, the WHERE clause allows you to set one or more conditions that must be satisfied by each record before it can form part of the results. So if you were asked for a list of members who live in Big City, you would need to specify that the column City must be equal to Big City. The SQL for such a request appears below:

```
SELECT FirstName + ' ' + LastName AS [Full Name]
FROM MemberDetails
WHERE City = 'Big City';
```

The query provides the following results:

Full Name
John Jackson
Jack Johnson

You can also use the operators you saw in Chapter 2 to find out the names of all the films released before 1977:

```
SELECT FilmName
FROM Films
WHERE YearReleased < 1977
```

This query gives these results:

FilmName
On Golden Puddle
Planet of the Japes
The Maltese Poodle
Soylent Yellow

However, if you want to find out which films were released in or before 1977, then change the "less than" operator (<) to a "less than or equal to" (<=) operator:

```
SELECT FilmName
FROM Films
WHERE YearReleased <= 1977
```

The results to this query also include *The Lion, the Witch, and the Chest of Drawers*, a film released in 1977:

FilmName
On Golden Puddle
The Lion, the Witch, and the Chest of Drawers
Planet of the Japes
The Maltese Poodle
Soylent Yellow

Before moving on, you should note that while MS Access is happy inserting dates delimited (enclosed by single quotes), when it comes to SELECT statements and WHERE clauses, Access requires any date literals to be enclosed by the hash (#) symbol. For example, consider the following code:

```
WHERE DateOfBirth < #2005-12-23#
```

SQL queries are all about finding answers to questions. The following Try It Out provides a few questions and shows you how SQL can provide answers.

Try It Out   Querying Your Database

Five new members have joined the club, so their details need to be added to the database. The following steps detail how you would add the new members to the Film Club database:

1. Enter the SQL code into your database or download the code from www.wrox.com and then execute it. Included are the new members' information and INSERT statements to record their favorite category of films. Note that if you're using Oracle, the date formats must be changed from their current format of year-month-day to the day-month-year format.

```
INSERT INTO
MemberDetails (MemberId,
FirstName,LastName,DateOfBirth,Street,City,State,ZipCode,Email,DateOfJoining)
VALUES
(
  10, 'Susie','Simons','1937-1-20','Main Road','Townsville',
  'Mega State','123456','susie@mailme.com','2005-08-20'
);

INSERT INTO
FavCategory (CategoryId, MemberId)
VALUES ( 1, 10 );

INSERT INTO
FavCategory (CategoryId, MemberId)
VALUES ( 3, 10 );

INSERT INTO
FavCategory (CategoryId, MemberId)
VALUES ( 6, 10 );

INSERT INTO
```

```
  MemberDetails (MemberId,
FirstName,LastName,DateOfBirth,Street,City,State,ZipCode,Email,DateOfJoining)
VALUES
(
  11, 'Jamie','Hills','1992-07-17','Newish Lane','Orange Town',
  'New State','88776','jamie@the_hills.com','2005-08-22'
);

INSERT INTO
FavCategory (CategoryId, MemberId)
VALUES ( 4, 11 );

INSERT INTO
FavCategory (CategoryId, MemberId)
VALUES ( 3, 11 );

INSERT INTO
FavCategory (CategoryId, MemberId)
VALUES ( 5, 11 );

INSERT INTO
MemberDetails (MemberId,
FirstName,LastName,DateOfBirth,Street,City,State,ZipCode,Email,DateOfJoining)
VALUES
(
  12, 'Stuart','Dales','1956-08-07','Long Lane','Windy Village',
  'Golden State','65422','sdales@mymail.org','2005-08-27'
);

INSERT INTO
FavCategory (CategoryId, MemberId)
VALUES ( 1, 12 );

INSERT INTO
FavCategory (CategoryId, MemberId)
VALUES ( 4, 12 );

INSERT INTO
FavCategory (CategoryId, MemberId)
VALUES ( 6, 12 );

INSERT INTO
MemberDetails (MemberId,
FirstName,LastName,DateOfBirth,Street,City,State,ZipCode,Email,DateOfJoining)
VALUES
(
  13, 'William','Doors','1994-05-28','Winding Road','Big City',
  'Mega State','34512','knockon@thedoors.com','2005-08-29'
);

INSERT INTO
FavCategory (CategoryId, MemberId)
VALUES ( 3, 13 );

INSERT INTO
```

```
FavCategory (CategoryId, MemberId)
VALUES ( 5, 13 );

INSERT INTO
MemberDetails (MemberId,
FirstName,LastName,DateOfBirth,Street,City,State,ZipCode,Email,DateOfJoining)
VALUES
(
  14, 'Doris','Night','1997-05-28','White Cliff Street','Dover',
  'Golden State','68122','dnight@whitecliffs.net','2005-09-02'
);

INSERT INTO
FavCategory (CategoryId, MemberId)
VALUES ( 2, 14 );

INSERT INTO
FavCategory (CategoryId, MemberId)
VALUES ( 6, 14 );
```

2. Query the database to find the names and addresses of members who joined in January 2005 using this SQL:

```
SELECT FirstName, LastName, Street, City, State, ZipCode
FROM MemberDetails
WHERE DateOfJoining >= '2005-01-01' AND DateOfJoining <= '2005-01-31';
```

Remember to change the date format for Oracle. Also, for MS Access, you need to enclose date literals inside the hash sign (#) rather than single quotes. Use the following statement for Access:

```
SELECT FirstName, LastName, Street, City, State, ZipCode
FROM MemberDetails
WHERE DateOfJoining >= #2005-01-01# AND DateOfJoining <= #2005-01-31#;
```

3. Query the database to find the names of members over 16 years of age who live in New State using this SQL:

```
SELECT FirstName, LastName
FROM MemberDetails
WHERE DateOfBirth <= '1989-05-01' AND State = 'New State';
```

Again, remember to change the date format for Oracle and the single quotes around the date value to the hash (#) symbol.

How It Works

In the first step, you inserted new data into the database using a series of INSERT INTO statements. You added five new members, plus details of their favorite film categories. Next came the SQL SELECT statements required to answer each of the three questions.

Begin your SELECT statement by choosing which columns and from what table it obtains its data. The MemberDetails table contains information on members' names, addresses, and joining dates. Within the

MemberDetails table, the columns FirstName, LastName, Street, City, State, and ZipCode contain all the information you need. So the SELECT statement begins with the following:

```
SELECT FirstName, LastName, Street, City, State, ZipCode
FROM MemberDetails
```

As it stands, that statement returns all the records, but now add a WHERE clause to select only those records where the joining date falls between January 1, 2005, and January 31, 2005. You need to check the DateOfJoining column to see if the value is greater than January 1 but less than or equal to January 31:

```
WHERE DateOfJoining >= '2005-01-01' And DateOfJoining <= '2005-Jan-31'
```

Adding the WHERE clause to the SELECT statement generates the following results:

FirstName	LastName	Street	City	State	Zip
John	Jones	Newish Lane	Orange Town	New State	88776
Jenny	Jones	Newish Lane	Orange Town	New State	88776

The next query asks for the names of all members older than 16 years of age who live in New State. This time the data you want is first name and last name, again from the MemberDetails table:

```
SELECT FirstName, LastName
FROM MemberDetails
```

Next comes the WHERE clause, which must specify that the member's age is greater than 16 and that he or she lives in New State. Assuming that today's date is May 31, 2005, anyone born after that date is less than 16 years old. So far, the WHERE clause looks like this:

```
WHERE DateOfBirth <= '1989-05- 31'
```

However, for the record to be included in the results, its State column must equal New State. So the final query looks like this:

```
SELECT FirstName, LastName
FROM MemberDetails
WHERE DateOfBirth <= '1989-05- 31' AND State = 'New State';
```

Both DateOfBirth and State conditions must be true; hence the use of the AND operator. The results of the query are as follows:

FirstName	LastName
John	Jackson
Steve	Gee
John	Jones
Jenny	Jones

Logical Operators and Operator Precedence

With the AND and OR operators out of the way, this section introduces a few more useful operators. This section also examines *operator precedence*, or the rules that determine the order in which operators are evaluated when there is more than one operator in a condition.

The effects of incorrect operator precedence are numerous, so you need to be familiar with operator precedence before you can manipulate SQL to its full advantage.

Introducing Operator Precedence

The American Declaration of Independence states that all men are created equal, but it fails to mention anything about operators. If it did, it would have to say that all operators are definitely not created equal. A hierarchy of operators determines which operator is evaluated first when a condition has multiple operators. If all the operators have equal precedence, then the conditions are interpreted from left to right. If the operators have different precedence, then the highest ones are evaluated first, then the next highest, and so on. The following table details all the logical operators. Their order in the table mirrors their order of precedence from highest to lowest. Operators contained in the same row have the same order of precedence; for example, OR has the same precedence as ALL.

Operator
Brackets ( )
NOT
AND
ALL, ANY, BETWEEN, IN, LIKE, OR, SOME

So far, you've experienced only the AND and OR operators. The next section details NOT, BETWEEN, LIKE, and IN operators, and the remaining operators are covered in Chapter 7.

Remembering that the AND operator has precedence over the OR operator, can you guess how the following SQL would be evaluated?

```
SELECT State, DateOfJoining
FROM MemberDetails
WHERE State = 'New State' OR State = 'Golden State'
AND DateOfJoining >= '2005-08-01';
```

If the AND and OR operators were of equal precedence, the preceding code would be evaluated as follows: State is equal to New State OR Golden State, AND the DateOfJoining must be greater than or equal to August 1, 2005.

If such an interpretation were true, then it would give the following results:

State	DateOfJoining
New State	2005-11-21
New State	2005-08-22
Golden State	2005-08-27
Golden State	2005-09-02

However, you won't see the preceding results, because the AND operator has a higher precedence than the OR operator, which is found in the WHERE clause of the SQL statement:

```
WHERE State = 'New State' OR State = 'Golden State'
AND DateOfJoining >= '2005-08-01';
```

The WHERE clause is actually evaluated like this: Is the State column equal to Golden State AND is the DateOfJoining on or after August 1, 2005, OR is the State column equal to New State?

This interpretation gives quite different results:

State	DateOfJoining
New State	2004-02-22
New State	2005-01-02
New State	2005-01-02
New State	2005-11-21
New State	2005-08-22
Golden State	2005-08-27
Golden State	2005-09-02

If you want the database to provide a list of members in New State or Mega State who joined on or after August 1, 2005, then clearly the query results are wrong. To solve this problem, use brackets to increase the precedence of the operators inside them, just as you would in math to differentiate between $(1 + 1) \_ 2$ and $1 + 1 \_ 2$. Brackets are right at the top of the precedence hierarchy, so they are always evaluated first. If you add brackets to the SQL statement, the condition inside the brackets is evaluated first:

```
SELECT State, DateOfJoining
FROM MemberDetails
WHERE (State = 'New State' OR State = 'Golden State')
AND DateOfJoining >= '2005-08-01';
```

Because brackets are the highest precedence, the SQL statement now reads as follows: State is equal to New State OR Golden State, AND the DateOfJoining must be greater than or equal to August 1, 2005.

The statement returns these results, which are exactly what you want:

State	DateOfJoining
New State	2005-11-21
New State	2005-08-22
Golden State	2005-08-27
Golden State	2005-09-02

Using brackets is the key to ensuring operator precedence. Additionally, brackets can make the SQL easier to read because they make it clear which conditions are evaluated first, which is quite handy if the conditions are quite complex. Otherwise you have to remember the order of operator precedence.

To illustrate operator precedence, try out a more complex WHERE statement where lots of brackets are necessary. What's required this time is a list of all the names, cities, and dates of birth of members who live in either Townsville or Big City and are either older than 60 or younger than 16. Again, assume that today's date is May 31, 2005. Members under 16 years of age must have been born after May 31, 1989, and members over 60 years of age must have been born on or before May 31, 1945.

Try It Out   Increasing Operator Precedence Using Brackets

1. The film club chairperson wants to know which members live in either Townsville or Big City and were born either before May 31, 1945, or after May 31, 1989. The SQL to answer this question is as follows:

```
SELECT FirstName, LastName, City, DateOfBirth
FROM MemberDetails
WHERE
( City = 'Townsville' OR City = 'Big City' )
AND
(DateOfBirth > '1989-05-31' OR DateOfBirth <= '1945-05-31')
```

If you're using MS Access, then the date literals in the last line of code must be enclosed in hash characters (#) rather than single quotes, as shown below. All other components of the statement remain the same:

```
(DateOfBirth > #1989-05-31# OR DateOfBirth <= #1945-05-31#)
```

If you're using Oracle, you may find that you need to change the date format in the last line of code to day-month-year, as shown below. All other components of the statement remain the same:

```
(DateOfBirth > '31 May 1989' OR DateOfBirth <= '31 May 1945')
```

How It Works

The SELECT part of the query is fairly straightforward:

```
SELECT FirstName, LastName, City, DateOfBirth
FROM MemberDetails
```

It simply tells the database system to retrieve the values from the FirstName, LastName, City, and DateOfBirth columns of the MemberDetails table.

The WHERE clause is slightly trickier. This time, you're looking for records where the member lives in Townsville or Big City and is younger than 16 or older than 60. There are two main conditions: the city the person lives in and their date of birth. You can start with the city condition:

```
( City = 'Townsville' OR City = 'Big City' )
```

The other condition checks their ages:

```
( 'DateOfBirth' > '1989-05-31' OR DateOfBirth <= '1945-05-31' )
```

Both of the main conditions must be true for the record to be part of the results, so an AND operator is required:

```
( City = 'Townsville' OR City = 'Big City' )
AND
( 'DateOfBirth' > '1989-05-31' OR DateOfBirth <= '1945-05-31' )
```

You must enclose the conditions in brackets because the AND operator is of higher precedence than the OR operator. If you don't include brackets, SQL evaluates the AND operator first.

Putting the whole query together results in the final SQL shown below:

```
SELECT FirstName, LastName, City, DateOfBirth
FROM MemberDetails
WHERE
( City = 'Townsville' OR City = 'Big City' )
AND
(DateOfBirth > '1989-05-31' OR DateOfBirth <= '1945-05-31')
```

Executing the query provides the following results:

FirstName	LastName	City	DateOfBirth
Susie	Simons	Townsville	Jan 20 1937
William	Doors	Big City	May 28 1994

The next section examines the NOT, BETWEEN, LIKE, and IN logical operators in turn. The remaining operators are covered later in Chapter 7.

Using Logical Operators

Now that you know how to use the AND and OR logical operators, you can learn how to use a few new ones, starting with the NOT operator.

NOT Operator

Examples thus far have been filtered based on true conditions. The NOT operator, however, selects a record if the condition is false. The following SQL selects records where the State field is not equal to Golden State.

```
SELECT FirstName
FROM MemberDetails
WHERE NOT State = 'Golden State';
```

The preceding example is the same as this example:

```
SELECT FirstName
FROM MemberDetails
WHERE State <> 'Golden State';
```

The only difference is the use of the "not equal to" operator (<>) instead of the NOT operator. In this situation, the "not equal to" operator (<>) reads easier than the NOT operator.

You can also use the NOT operator with brackets:

```
SELECT City
FROM MemberDetails
WHERE NOT (City = 'Townsville' OR City = 'Orange Town' OR City = 'New Town');
```

The preceding SQL selects all records where the conditions inside the brackets are not true. In this case, the condition inside the brackets is that the City is equal to Townsville or it is equal to Orange Town or it is equal to New Town. Using the NOT operator is the same as saying "is not true," which is the same as saying "is false." So, you could rephrase the explanation to say that the query is looking for values that are false, that do not equal Townsville, Orange Town, or New Town. The results returned are shown here:

City
Big City
Windy Village
Windy Village
Big City
Big City

As you see shortly, you can use the NOT operator in combination with other operators such as BETWEEN, ANY, SOME, AND, OR, or LIKE.

BETWEEN Operator

The BETWEEN operator allows you to specify a range, where the range is between one value and another. Until now, when you needed to check for a value within a certain range, you used the "greater than or equal to" operator (>=) or the "less than or equal to" operator (<=).

The BETWEEN operator functions exactly the same way, except it's shorter — it saves on typing and also makes the SQL more readable. The following SQL uses the BETWEEN operator to select films with a rating between 3 and 5:

```
SELECT FilmName, Rating
FROM Films
WHERE Rating BETWEEN 3 AND 5
```

If you use the BETWEEN operator, you see that it provides exactly the same results as the "greater than or equal to" (>=) and "less than or equal to" (<=) operators do. It is extremely important to remember that the BETWEEN operator is inclusive, meaning that in the preceding code, 3 and 5 are also included in the range.

You can use BETWEEN with data types other than numbers, such as text and dates. You can also use the BETWEEN operator in conjunction with the NOT operator, in which case SQL selects a value that is not in the range specified, as you see in the following Try It Out.

Try It Out   Using the NOT and BETWEEN Operators

1. The film club has added more films to its database. The SQL to add the films is listed below and must be executed against the database.

```
INSERT INTO Films
    (FilmId, FilmName, YearReleased, PlotSummary, AvailableOnDVD, Rating, CategoryId)
VALUES
    (9, 'One Flew Over the Crow''s Nest',1975,
    'Life and times of a scary crow.', 'Y',2,3);

INSERT INTO Films
    (FilmId, FilmName, YearReleased, PlotSummary, AvailableOnDVD, Rating, CategoryId)
VALUES
    (10, 'Raging Bullocks',1980,
    'A pair of bulls get cross with each other.', 'N',4,1);

INSERT INTO Films
    (FilmId, FilmName, YearReleased, PlotSummary, AvailableOnDVD, Rating, CategoryId)
VALUES
    (11, 'The Life Of Bob',1984,
    'A 7 hour drama about Bob''s life. What fun!', 'Y',1,1);

INSERT INTO Films
    (FilmId, FilmName, YearReleased, PlotSummary, AvailableOnDVD, Rating, CategoryId)
VALUES
    (12, 'Gone With the Window Cleaner',1988,
    'Historical documentary on window cleaners. Thrilling', 'Y',3,6);

INSERT INTO Films
    (FilmId, FilmName, YearReleased, PlotSummary, AvailableOnDVD, Rating, CategoryId)
VALUES
    (12, 'The Good, the Bad, and the Facially Challenged',1989,
    'Joe seeks plastic surgery in this spaghetti Western.', 'Y',5,6);
```

Remember to commit the data if you're using Oracle.

2. Using the following SQL, query the database to produce a list of all the films released in the 1980s that have a rating between 2 and 4 and are available on DVD. The answer should detail the film name, date of release, rating, and availability on DVD.

```
SELECT FilmName, YearReleased, Rating, AvailableOnDVD
FROM Films
WHERE ( YearReleased BETWEEN 1980 AND 1989 )
AND
( Rating BETWEEN 2 AND 4 )
AND
( AvailableOnDVD = 'Y' );
```

3. Query the database to produce a list of films of any decade except the 1960s whose names are between *P* and *T*. The answer should detail the film names. Use the following SQL to execute the query:

```
SELECT FilmName
FROM Films
WHERE ( YearReleased NOT BETWEEN 1960 AND 1969 )
AND
( FilmName BETWEEN 'P' AND 'T' );
```

How It Works

You begin by inserting five new films into the Films table using INSERT INTO statements. Remember to commit the data if you're using Oracle using the COMMIT command, unless you've already set the auto-commit to on.

The SELECT clause of the first query is fairly straightforward. It simply asks the database to select FilmName, YearReleased, Rating, and AvailableOnDVD from the Films database.

```
SELECT FilmName, YearReleased, Rating, AvailableOnDVD
FROM Films
```

Next comes the query's WHERE clause. First, it requires that the film be from the 1980s, and therefore it requires a range between 1980 and 1989. The BETWEEN operator is ideal for such a requirement:

```
WHERE YearReleased BETWEEN 1980 AND 1989
```

The next requirement is that the film must have a rating between 2 and 4. Again, a BETWEEN operator is the obvious choice. Because both conditions (YearReleased and Rating) must be true, an AND operator is required to link the two:

```
WHERE ( YearReleased BETWEEN 1980 AND 1989 )
AND
( Rating BETWEEN 2 AND 4 )
```

Notice that each condition appears inside brackets. Using brackets is not strictly necessary, but it does make things more readable: Brackets make it clear that an AND operator joins two unrelated conditions.

The final condition required is a check to see if the film is available on DVD. Again, the compulsory condition is matched. If you want the right answer to the question, an AND statement must be used. This condition is fairly simple, just a check if the AvailableOnDVD column contains a single character Y:

```
WHERE ( YearReleased BETWEEN 1980 AND 1989 )
AND
( Rating BETWEEN 2 AND 4 )
AND
AvailableOnDVD = 'Y'
```

Putting it all together, you have the following SQL:

```
SELECT FilmName, YearReleased, Rating, AvailableOnDVD
FROM Films
WHERE ( YearReleased BETWEEN 1980 AND 1989 )
AND
( Rating BETWEEN 2 AND 4 )
AND
( AvailableOnDVD = 'Y' )
```

Execute the SQL and the result is just one record:

FilmName	YearReleased	Rating	AvailableOnDVD
Gone with the Window Cleaner	1988	3	Y

The SELECT clause of the second query is also quite straightforward. It simply asks the database system to retrieve records from the FilmName column of the Films table:

```
SELECT FilmName FROM Films
```

The query's first condition requires that the film must not have been released in the 1960s, or to rephrase it, the film's year of release must not be between 1960 and 1969. This condition requires a BETWEEN operator:

```
WHERE ( YearReleased NOT BETWEEN 1960 AND 1969 )
```

The next condition requires that film's name must begin with a letter in the range of *P* to *T*:

```
WHERE ( YearReleased NOT BETWEEN 1960 AND 1969 )
AND
( FilmName BETWEEN 'P' AND 'T' )
```

Putting it all together provides the following SQL:

```
SELECT FilmName
FROM Films
WHERE ( YearReleased NOT BETWEEN 1960 AND 1969 )
AND
( FilmName BETWEEN 'P' AND 'T' )
```

When you execute the query, you get the following results:

FilmName
Sense and Insensitivity
Raging Bullocks

Continuing the look at logical operators, the next section takes you through the LIKE operator.

LIKE Operator

The LIKE operator allows you to use *wildcard characters* when searching a character field. A wildcard character is one that doesn't match a specific character but instead matches any one character or any of one or more characters. One example of its use would be finding out details of all members in the film club whose surname begins with *J*.

The following table details the two available wildcard characters.

Wildcard	Description
%	Matches one or more characters. Note that MS Access uses the asterisk (*) wildcard character instead of the percent sign (%) wildcard character.
_	Matches one character. Note that MS Access uses a question mark (?) instead of the underscore (_) to match any one character.

The SQL to match all names beginning with a *J* is as follows:

```
SELECT LastName FROM MemberDetails
WHERE LastName LIKE 'J%';
```

Remember, if you're using MS Access you need to change the percent sign (%) to an asterisk (*):

```
SELECT LastName FROM MemberDetails
WHERE LastName LIKE 'J*';
```

The preceding code fragment produces these results:

LastName
Jackson
Jones
Jones
Johnson

In some database systems, the LIKE *operator is case-sensitive; in others it is not. Oracle, for example, is case-sensitive, so* LIKE 'J%' *matches only an uppercase J followed by one or more characters. In SQL Server,* LIKE 'J%' *matches an uppercase or lowercase J followed by one or more characters.*

You can use as many or as few wildcard characters as you wish, and you can mix percent signs and underscores (if required) when searching your database as well, as shown in the following code:

```
SELECT LastName FROM MemberDetails
WHERE LastName LIKE 'D___s';
```

The preceding SELECT statement matches any last name that starts with a *D*, ends with an *s*, and has any three characters in between. The results from the example database are as follows:

LastName
Dales
Doors

Remember, on some database systems, the LIKE *operator is case-sensitive, so* LIKE D___s *matches only strings starting with a capital D. On other systems, it matches uppercase and lowercase Ds. Oracle and DB2 are case-sensitive; MS SQL Server, MySQL, and MS Access are not. Also remember that on MS Access you need to use a question mark instead of the underscore.*

You can also use the NOT operator in concert with the LIKE operator, which produces a match when the character and wildcard combination is not found. For example, the condition in the following WHERE clause is true if the LastName column doesn't start with a *J* followed by one or more characters:

```
SELECT LastName FROM MemberDetails
WHERE LastName NOT LIKE 'J%';
```

Executing the WHERE clause provides reverse results of what you saw in the earlier example:

LastName
Smith
Simons
Gee
Botts
Hills
Dales
Doors
Night

Now that you're acquainted with LIKE and NOT LIKE, you can use them to query your Film Club database to find specific information about your members. In the following Try It Out, see if you can answer two questions.

Querying a Database with LIKE and NOT LIKE

1. Using the following SQL, query the database to draw up a list of all members' names and zip codes where their zip code starts with 65.

```
SELECT FirstName, LastName, ZipCode
FROM MemberDetails
WHERE ZipCode LIKE '65%'
```

2. Use the following SQL to query the database to find out which people don't live on a street called Road or Street.

```
SELECT FirstName, LastName, Street
FROM MemberDetails
WHERE Street NOT LIKE '% Road' AND Street NOT LIKE '% Street'
```

How It Works

Specify that the database provide results from the FirstName, LastName, and ZipCode fields from the MemberDetails database:

```
SELECT FirstName, LastName, ZipCode
FROM MemberDetails
```

The LIKE clause is ideal to filter records that have a ZipCode column starting with 65 and ending with any numbers:

```
WHERE ZipCode LIKE '65%'
```

The 65 matches the numbers 6 and 5, and the percent sign (%) is the wildcard that matches one or more characters after the 65.

Putting all the elements together provides this SQL:

```
SELECT FirstName, LastName, ZipCode
FROM MemberDetails
WHERE ZipCode LIKE '65%';
```

When you execute the SQL, the results are as follows:

FirstName	LastName	ZipCode
Seymour	Botts	65422
Stuart	Dales	65422

The second query is a negative, in that it requires that the Street field should not end in either Road or Street. Using the NOT and LIKE operators in conjunction with one another is the obvious choice. Another obvious choice is to use the AND operator, which tells the database to search the Street field for streets that don't end in Street and don't end in Road.

```
SELECT FirstName, LastName, Street
FROM MemberDetails
WHERE Street NOT LIKE '% Road' AND Street NOT LIKE '% Street';
```

Executing the SQL provides the results you want:

FirstName	LastName	Street
John	Jackson	Long Lane
John	Jones	Newish Lane
Jenny	Jones	Newish Lane
Seymour	Botts	Long Lane
Jamie	Hills	Newish Lane
Stuart	Dales	Long Lane

IN Operator

So far you've used the OR operator to check whether a column contains one of two or more values. For example, if you want to check whether a member lives in Townsville, Windy Village, Dover, or Big City, you'd write the following:

```
SELECT City
FROM MemberDetails
WHERE
City = 'Townsville'
OR
City = 'Windy Village'
OR
City = 'Dover'
OR
City = 'Big City';
```

That query is a bit long-winded, and that's where the IN operator helps: it functions exactly like the OR operator but requires much less typing!

Using the IN operator, you can rewrite the preceding SQL like this:

```
SELECT City
FROM MemberDetails
WHERE
City IN ('Townsville', 'Windy Village', 'Dover', 'Big City');
```

It's as simple as that! The IN operator checks the database to see if the specified column matches one or more of the values listed inside the brackets. You can use the IN operator with any data type, not just text as shown above. The preceding SQL produces the following results:

City
Townsville
Townsville
Big City
Windy Village
Windy Village
Big City
Dover

Chapter 8 shows you how to use a SQL SELECT statement instead of a list of literal values. In the following Try It Out, however, you stick with the IN operator and literal values.

Try It Out   Using the IN Operator

1. Using the following SQL, query the Film Club database to see which films were released in 1967, 1977, or 1987 and have a rating of either 4 or 5. Include FilmName, YearReleased, and Rating in the search.

```
SELECT FilmName, YearReleased, Rating
FROM Films
WHERE
YearReleased IN (1967, 1977, 1987)
AND
Rating IN (4,5);
```

2. Execute the SQL.

How It Works

The SELECT statement simply specifies the database and the fields to search:

```
SELECT FilmName, YearReleased, Rating
FROM Films
```

The WHERE clause employs the IN operator to search for a film's year of release:

```
YearReleased IN (1967, 1977, 1987)
```

Use the IN operator again to search for films with a rating of either 4 or 5:

```
Rating IN (4,5)
```

Because both conditions (YearReleased and Rating) must be true, an AND statement is required to link them:

```
YearReleased IN (1967, 1977, 1987)
AND
Rating IN (4,5)
```

Putting the whole statement together gives you the following SQL:

```
SELECT FilmName, YearReleased, Rating
FROM Films
WHERE
YearReleased IN (1967, 1977, 1987)
AND
Rating IN (4,5);
```

Executing the SQL statement provides the following results:

FilmName	YearReleased	Rating
On Golden Puddle	1967	4
Planet of the Japes	1967	5
Soylent Yellow	1967	5

That completes the look at logical operators for this chapter. Chapter 8 discusses logical operators in greater depth. The next section focuses on how to order your query's results.

Ordering Results with ORDER BY

So far, query results have come in whatever order the database decides, which is usually based on the order in which the data was entered, unless the database is designed otherwise (as you see in later chapters). However, listing query results in a certain order (a list of names in alphabetical order or a list of years in numerical order) often comes in handy. SQL allows you to specify the order of results with the ORDER BY clause.

The ORDER BY clause goes right at the end of the SELECT statement. It allows you to specify the column or columns that determine the order of the results and whether the order is ascending (smallest to largest) or descending (largest to smallest). For example, the following SQL statement displays a list of film years, ordered from earliest to latest:

```
SELECT YearReleased
FROM Films
ORDER BY YearReleased;
```

By default, ORDER BY sorts into ascending order, which is why the results of the preceding SQL sort from lowest to highest number:

YearReleased
1947
1967
1967
1967
1975
1977
1980
1984
1987
1988
1989
1989
1997
2001
2005

If you require descending order, however, you must add DESC after the list of columns in the ORDER BY clause:

```
SELECT YearReleased
FROM Films
ORDER BY YearReleased DESC;
```

If you execute the preceding SELECT statement, the results are displayed from highest to lowest number, as shown in the following table:

YearReleased
2005
2001
1997
1989
1989
1988
1987

YearReleased
1984
1980
1977
1975
1967
1967
1967
1947

Because ascending order is the default for ORDER BY, specifying ascending order is not necessary in the SQL, but for completeness, adding ASC after the ORDER BY clause ensures that results display in ascending order:

```
SELECT YearReleased
FROM Films
ORDER BY YearReleased ASC;
```

The column used to order the results, however, doesn't have to form part of the results. For example, in the following SQL, the SELECT statement returns the FilmName and Rating, but the YearReleased column determines order:

```
SELECT FilmName, Rating
FROM Films
ORDER BY YearReleased;
```

The preceding SQL produces the following results:

FilmName	Rating
The Maltese Poodle	1
On Golden Puddle	4
Soylent Yellow	5
Planet of the Japes	5
One Flew over the Crow's Nest	2
The Lion, the Witch, and the Chest of Drawers	1
Raging Bullocks	4
The Life of Bob	1
The Dirty Half Dozen	2

Table continued on following page

FilmName	Rating
Gone with the Window Cleaner	3
The Good, the Bad, and the Facially Challenged	5
15th Late Afternoon	5
Nightmare on Oak Street, Part 23	2
Sense and Insensitivity	3
The Wide Brimmed Hat	1

So far, you've sorted results with just one column, but you can use more than one column to sort results. To sort by more than one column, simply list each column by which to sort the results and separate each column with a comma, just as in the column list for a SELECT statement. The order in which the columns are listed determines the order of priority in sorting. For example, the SQL to obtain a list of film names, ratings, and years of release and to order them by rating, year of release, and name is as follows:

```
SELECT FilmName, Rating, YearReleased
FROM Films
ORDER BY Rating, YearReleased, FilmName;
```

The preceding SQL produces the following results set:

FilmName	Rating	YearReleased
The Maltese Poodle	1	1947
The Lion, the Witch, and the Chest of Drawers	1	1977
The Life of Bob	1	1984
The Wide Brimmed Hat	1	2005
One Flew over the Crow's Nest	2	1975
The Dirty Half Dozen	2	1987
Nightmare on Oak Street, Part 23	2	1997
Gone with the Window Cleaner	3	1988
Sense and Insensitivity	3	2001
On Golden Puddle	4	1967
Raging Bullocks	4	1980
Planet of the Japes	5	1967
Soylent Yellow	5	1967
15th Late Afternoon	5	1989
The Good, the Bad, and the Facially Challenged	5	1989

First, the database system orders the results by the first column specified in the ORDER BY clause, in this case the Rating column. You can see that the Rating column is in complete order from highest to lowest. If multiple records in the Rating column contain two or more identical values, the database system looks at the next column specified in the ORDER BY clause (YearReleased, in this case) and orders results by that column.

Look at the results where the rating is 1. You can also see that the YearReleased column is in ascending order for that rating. The same is true for the other ratings.

Finally, if the values for the first and second columns specified in the ORDER BY clause have the same value as one or more other records, the final column specified in the clause determines order. In the preceding example, the FilmName column is the final column specified in the clause. If you look at the results with a rating of 5, you notice that two of the films were released in 1967 and two were released in 1989. You also see that the two 1967 films appear in alphabetical order based on the FilmName column, which is specified as the final sort column in the event that the other two columns are of the same value. The same is true of the 1989 films, which again are ordered by FilmName.

You can use WHERE clauses in conjunction with the ORDER BY clause without any problem. You must ensure that the ORDER BY clause goes after the WHERE clause. The following example produces a list of films released in the 1960s and orders the results by FilmName:

```
SELECT FilmName, Rating, YearReleased
FROM Films
WHERE YearReleased BETWEEN 1960 AND 1969
ORDER BY FilmName;
```

The preceding SQL produces the results set shown here:

FilmName	Rating	YearReleased
On Golden Puddle	4	1967
Planet of the Japes	5	1967
Soylent Yellow	5	1967

Notice that the FilmName column appears in ascending alphabetical order. Curiously, the rating column is in order as well, but this is just a fluke, a coincidence. When you don't specify order, you can't rely on results being in any particular order, unless you set up the database to produce specific results. Chapter 3 explores such database setup in greater depth. In the meantime, use the following Try It Out to generate a list of all film club members sorted in alphabetical order by last name, then by date of birth, and finally by first name.

Try It Out   **Generating Ordered Results**

1. Query the database to produce a list of all members ordered alphabetically by last name, ordered next by date of birth, and finally by first name. Use the following SQL:

```
SELECT LastName, FirstName, DateOfBirth
FROM MemberDetails
ORDER BY LastName, DateOfBirth, FirstName;
```

2. Add a WHERE clause to the preceding SQL to filter the list so that it includes only those members who joined in 2005.

```
SELECT LastName, FirstName, DateOfBirth
FROM MemberDetails
WHERE DateOfJoining BETWEEN '2005-01-01' AND '2005-12-31'
ORDER BY LastName, DateOfBirth, FirstName;
```

3. Finally, query the database with the following SQL to produce a list of members' names and dates of birth sorted in descending order by date of birth.

```
SELECT LastName, FirstName, DateOfBirth
FROM MemberDetails
ORDER BY DateOfBirth DESC;
```

How It Works

Write the SELECT statement to select the LastName, FirstName, and DateOfBirth fields from the MemberDetails table:

```
SELECT LastName, FirstName, DateOfBirth
FROM MemberDetails ;
```

To return the results in the order you want, an ORDER BY clause is required. Because the ORDER BY clause determines priority of ordering, be sure to list the columns in the order LastName, DateOfBirth, FirstName:

```
SELECT LastName, FirstName, DateOfBirth
FROM MemberDetails
ORDER BY LastName, DateOfBirth, FirstName;
```

When you execute the preceding SQL, you get the results you want:

LastName	FirstName	DateOfBirth
Botts	Seymour	1956-10-21
Dales	Stuart	1956-08-07
Doors	William	1994-05-28
Gee	Steve	1967-10-05
Hills	Jamie	1992-07-17
Jackson	John	1974-05-27
Johnson	Jack	1945-06-09
Jones	John	1952-10-05
Jones	Jenny	1953-08-25

LastName	FirstName	DateOfBirth
Night	Doris	1997-05-28
Simons	Susie	1937-01-20
Smith	Katie	1977-01-09

To filter the results to include only members who joined in 2005, simply add a WHERE clause before the ORDER BY clause. Using a BETWEEN clause is the easiest way to include only dates in 2005. Currently the database contains only dates in 2004 and 2005, so it might be tempting to filter all dates with a >= 2005 operator, but if you add data later that includes 2006 dates and beyond, the SQL would no longer return valid results. With the WHERE clause added, the SQL is now as follows:

```
SELECT LastName, FirstName, DateOfBirth
FROM MemberDetails
WHERE DateOfJoining BETWEEN '2005-01-01' AND '2005-12-31'
ORDER BY LastName, DateOfBirth, FirstName;
```

Remember that Oracle's date format is day-month-year. Also remember that MS Access needs the hash sign (#) rather than single quotes around the dates.

When executed, the preceding SQL provides these results:

LastName	FirstName	DateOfBirth
Botts	Seymour	1956-10-21
Dales	Stuart	1956-08-07
Doors	William	1994-05-28
Hills	Jamie	1992-07-17
Jackson	John	1974-05-27
Johnson	Jack	1945-06-09
Jones	John	1952-10-05
Jones	Jenny	1953-08-25
Night	Doris	1997-05-28
Simons	Susie	1937-01-20

Previously, results have appeared in ascending order, which is the ORDER BY clause's default order. This time, however, you want results to appear in descending order, so you must add DESC at the end of the ORDER BY clause's list of columns:

```
SELECT LastName, FirstName, DateOfBirth
FROM MemberDetails
ORDER BY DateOfBirth DESC;
```

Executing this SQL provides the following results:

LastName	FirstName	DateOfBirth
Night	Doris	1997-05-28
Doors	William	1994-05-28
Hills	Jamie	1992-07-17
Smith	Katie	1977-01-09
Jackson	John	1974-05-27
Gee	Steve	1967-10-05
Botts	Seymour	1956-10-21
Dales	Stuart	1956-08-07
Jones	Jenny	1953-08-25
Jones	John	1952-10-05
Johnson	Jack	1945-06-09
Simons	Susie	1937-01-20

The next section looks at how columns in the results set can be joined together, for example, returning FirstName and LastName columns as one column called FullName.

Joining Columns — Concatenation

Not only does SQL allow you to query various columns, but it also allows you to combine one or more columns and give the resulting column an alias. Note that using an alias has no effect on the table itself; you're not really creating a new column in the table, only one for the results set. When you join columns together, you *concatenate* them. For example, if you have the data ABC and concatenate it to DEF, you get ABCDEF.

This chapter only attempts to concatenate text literals or columns that have the char or varchar data type. Joining text with a number can cause errors. Chapter 5 shows you how to convert data types and use this to convert numbers to text and then concatenate.

So how do you go about concatenating text? Unfortunately, concatenating text varies depending on the database system you're using. Because there are significant differences among the five database systems covered in this chapter, each is taken in turn, starting with SQL Server and MS Access. You simply need to read the section relevant to the database system you're using — feel free to skip over the others.

MS SQL Server and MS Access

Both SQL Server and Access concatenate columns and data in the same manner — with the concatenation operator, which on these systems is the plus (+) sign. So, in order to return the full name, that is first and last name, of members, you'd write the following:

```
SELECT FirstName + ' ' + LastName AS FullName FROM MemberDetails;
```

The preceding SQL returns the following results:

FullName
Katie Smith
Susie Simons
John Jackson
Steve Gee
John Jones
Jenny Jones
Jack Johnson
Seymour Botts
Jamie Hills
Stuart Dales
William Doors
Doris Night

Notice that not only can you join columns, but you can also join text. In the preceding example, you added a space between the first name and last name to make it more readable; otherwise, results would have been KatieSmith, SandraTell, and so on. When you join columns, you can add whatever text you wish. Consider the following query:

```
SELECT 'First name is ' + FirstName + ', last name is ' + LastName FullName
FROM MemberDetails;
```

The preceding code produces these results:

FullName
First name is Katie
First name is Susie
First name is John
First name is Steve
First name is John
First name is Jenny
First name is Jack
First name is Seymour
First name is Jamie

Table continued on following page

FullName
First name is Stuart
First name is William
First name is Doris

Likewise, you can assign more than one alias in the SELECT statement, as in the following code:

```
SELECT LastName AS Surname, FirstName AS ChristianName
FROM MemberDetails;
```

The results of the preceding SELECT statement are as follows:

Surname	ChristianName
Smith	Katie
Simons	Susie
Jackson	John
Gee	Steve
Jones	John
Jones	Jenny
Johnson	Jack
Botts	Seymour
Hills	Jamie
Dales	Stuart
Doors	William
Night	Doris

Finally, if you want to use an alias that contains spaces or any other characters normally not permitted for column names or aliases, then you must enclose the alias name inside square brackets, as shown in the following statement:

```
SELECT LastName AS Surname, FirstName AS [Christian Name]
FROM MemberDetails;
```

Using this SQL, the alias Christian Name has a space, so it's enclosed inside the square brackets. Square brackets allow you to use names for columns or aliases that contain characters not normally considered legal. For example, you would receive an error if you tried to use the alias One***Two, as in the following query:

```
SELECT DateOfBirth AS One***Two FROM MemberDetails;
```

If you put square brackets around it (as shown below), the database system is happy:

```
SELECT DateOfBirth AS [One***Two] FROM MemberDetails;
```

That covers concatenation in MS Access and SQL Server; now it's time to look at Oracle and DB2's way of concatenating.

Oracle and IBM DB2

There are two ways of concatenating text data or text-based columns in Oracle and DB2. The first is to use the concatenation operator, which in these systems is two vertical pipe (||) characters (see the following statement). The second is to use the CONCAT() function, which is covered later in this section.

```
SELECT FirstName || ' ' || LastName AS FullName FROM MemberDetails;
```

The preceding SQL returns the following results:

FullName
Katie Smith
Susie Simons
John Jackson
Steve Gee
John Jones
Jenny Jones
Jack Johnson
Seymour Botts
Jamie Hills
Stuart Dales
William Doors
Doris Night

As with SQL Server, not only can you join columns, but you can also join text. In the preceding example, you added a space between the first name and last name to improve readability; otherwise, results would have been KatieSmith, SandraTell, and so on. When you join columns, you can add whatever text you wish, as shown in the following statement:

```
SELECT 'First name is ' || FirstName || ', last name is ' || LastName FullName
FROM MemberDetails;
```

The preceding code produces these results:

FullName
First name is Katie, last name is Smith
First name is Susie, last name is Simons
First name is John, last name is Jackson
First name is Steve, last name is Gee
First name is John, last name is Jones
First name is Jenny, last name is Jones
First name is Jack, last name is Johnson
First name is Seymour, last name is Botts
First name is Jamie, last name is Hills
First name is Stuart, last name is Dales
First name is William, last name is Doors
First name is Doris, last name is Night

Likewise, you can assign more than one alias in the SELECT statement. For example, the following statement uses the aliases Surname and ChristianName:

```
SELECT LastName AS Surname, FirstName AS ChristianName
FROM MemberDetails;
```

The results of the preceding SELECT statement are as follows:

Surname	ChristianName
Smith	Katie
Simons	Susie
Jackson	John
Gee	Steve
Jones	John
Jones	Jenny
Johnson	Jack
Botts	Seymour
Hills	Jamie
Dales	Stuart
Doors	William
Night	Doris

Finally, if you want to use an alias that contains spaces or any other characters normally not permitted for column names or aliases, then you must enclose the alias name inside square brackets, as shown below:

```
SELECT LastName AS Surname, FirstName AS [Christian Name]
FROM MemberDetails;
```

Using this SQL, the alias `Christian Name` has a space, so it's enclosed inside the square brackets. Square brackets allow you to use names for columns or aliases that contain characters not normally considered legal. For example, you would receive an error if you tried to use the alias `One***Two`, as shown in the following statement:

```
SELECT DateOfBirth AS One***Two FROM MemberDetails;
```

But if you put square brackets around the alias, the database system is happy:

```
SELECT DateOfBirth AS [One***Two] FROM MemberDetails;
```

Both Oracle and DB2 support a second way of concatenating: the `CONCAT()` function. You pass the two things you want to join, either columns or literal strings, as arguments to the function, and the function returns them joined. For example, to join FirstName and LastName columns, you would write the following query:

```
SELECT CONCAT(FirstName, LastName) FROM MemberDetails;
```

Executing this query produces the following results:

KatieSmith
SusieSimons
JohnJackson
SteveGee
JohnJones
JennyJones
JackJohnson
SeymourBotts
JamieHills
StuartDales
WilliamDoors
DorisNight

Although `CONCAT()` does the same thing in Oracle and DB2, there are plenty of subtle differences. One difference is that Oracle does its best to convert values into text. Although the following statement works on Oracle, it produces an error in DB2:

```
SELECT CONCAT(DateOfBirth, LastName) FROM MemberDetails;
```

Even though DateOfBirth is a date column and not a `character` data type, if you try to execute the same query in DB2, you get an error. For most of this book, you'll find it easier to use the double vertical pipe (||) to concatenate data.

That covers concatenation in Oracle and DB2. Now it's time to look at MySQL's way of concatenating.

MySQL

MySQL concatenates using one of two functions. The first is the `CONCAT()` function, which works in a way similar to `CONCAT()` used with Oracle and DB2. However, unlike under those database systems, it can take two or more arguments. So, if you want to join three columns, you would write a query similar to the following:

```
SELECT CONCAT(MemberId,FirstName,LastName) FROM MemberDetails;
```

Executing the query gives these results:

1KatieSmith

4SteveGee

5JohnJones

6JennyJones

7JohnJackson

8JackJohnson

9SeymourBotts

10SusieSimons

11JamieHills

12StuartDales

13WilliamDoors

14DorisNight

Notice that a numeric data type column is concatenated. MySQL's `CONCAT()` function will, if possible, convert numeric data types to string values before concatenating.

As well as columns, `CONCAT()` can also join string literals. Consider the following code:

```
SELECT CONCAT('The member is called ',FirstName,' ',LastName) AS 'Member Name' FROM
MemberDetails;
```

Executing the preceding query creates the following results:

Member Name
The member is called Katie Smith
The member is called Steve Gee
The member is called John Jones
The member is called Jenny Jones
The member is called John Jackson
The member is called Jack Johnson
The member is called Seymour Botts
The member is called Susie Simons
The member is called Jamie Hills
The member is called Stuart Dales
The member is called William Doors
The member is called Doris Night

Notice that the results returned by CONCAT() are given an alias of Member Name. Notice also that the alias is enclosed in single quotes because there are spaces in the alias. The same is true if you want to use characters such as punctuation in the alias.

In the preceding example, you can see that spaces are added to ensure that the sentence reads correctly. A space should appear between a member's first name and a member's last name: "The member is called Katie Smith," not "The member is called KatieSmith."

The second concatenation option provided by MySQL is the CONCAT_WS() function, which adds a separator between each of the columns or literals to be concatenated. If you want a single space between each column, you could write a query similar to the following:

```
SELECT CONCAT_WS(' ', 'The member is called',FirstName,LastName) AS 'Member Name'
FROM MemberDetails;
```

Executing the query with the CONCAT_WS() function provides exactly the same results as the previous example:

Member Name
The member is called Katie Smith
The member is called Steve Gee
The member is called John Jones
The member is called Jenny Jones
The member is called John Jackson

Table continued on following page

Member Name
The member is called Jack Johnson
The member is called Seymour Botts
The member is called Susie Simons
The member is called Jamie Hills
The member is called Stuart Dales
The member is called William Doors
The member is called Doris Night

That completes the look at concatenation. The next section shows you how to select data from more than one table at a time.

Selecting Data from More Than One Table

Using the SQL you've learned so far, you can extract data from only one table in the database, which is quite limiting because often answers require data from more than one table. The developers of SQL realized this limitation and implemented a way of joining data from more than one table into one results set. Using the word *joining* is no accident: in SQL the JOIN keyword joins one or more tables together in a results set. Chapter 8 examines all the different types of joins, but this chapter covers the most commonly used (and also the easiest to use) join: the inner join.

To see why joins are necessary and useful, begin with a problem. Say that you want a list of all the film names, years of release, and ratings for the Historical film category. Assume that you know the category name but don't know what the CategoryId value is for Historical.

If SQL didn't support joins, your first task would be to look in the Category table for the CategoryId for the category with a value Historical:

```
SELECT CategoryId
FROM Category
WHERE Category = 'Historical';
```

The preceding SQL returns just one result: 6. Now you know that the CategoryId for Historical is 6, and that can be used with the CategoryId column in the Films table to get a list of films in the Historical category:

```
SELECT FilmName, YearReleased, Rating
FROM Films
WHERE CategoryId = 6;
```

Running the preceding SQL returns the following results:

FilmName	YearReleased	Rating
Sense and Insensitivity	2001	3
15th Late Afternoon	1989	5
Gone with the Window Cleaner	1988	3
The Good, the Bad, and the Facially Challenged	1989	5

You might argue that if your database has only six categories, looking up each category is not that hard or time-consuming. It's a different story altogether, though, if your database contains 50 or 100 categories. Also, while computers might be more at home with numbers, most humans prefer names. For example, imagine that you create a film club Web site that contains a page allowing users to choose a category and then display all the films for that category. It's unlikely that the Web site user would want to choose categories based on category IDs. What's more likely is that users would choose by name and allow the database to work out the ID and display the results.

That said, how can you use a join to obtain a list of films in the `Historical` category?

First, you need to determine which table contains category names and allows you to look up the CategoryId. From the previous example, it's clearly the Category table that provides this information. Second, you need to determine which table or tables provide the results you want. Again, based on the preceding example, you know that the Films table contains the data needed. The task now is to join the two tables together. To join the tables, you need to find a link between the two tables. No prizes for guessing that the CategoryId field, which is present in both tables, links the two!

The type of join to use in this case is an *inner join*. An inner join combines two tables and links, or joins, them based on columns within the tables. The inner join allows you to specify which columns form the join and under what conditions. For example, you could specify a condition that says the MemberId column in the MemberDetails table matches a value from the MemberId column in the FavCategory table. Then only records where there is a matching MemberId in both tables are included in the results. To create an inner join, you must specify the two tables to be joined and the column or columns on which the join is based. The syntax looks like this:

```
table1 INNER JOIN  table2 ON column_from_table1 = column_from_table2
```

Applying the syntax to the problem at hand yields the following code:

```
SELECT FilmName, YearReleased, Rating
FROM Films INNER JOIN Category
ON Films.CategoryId = Category.CategoryId
WHERE Category.CategoryId = 6;
```

At the top is the SELECT statement's list of the columns required to form the results. On the following line are the tables from which the results are drawn. Specify them as normal, except this time the INNER JOIN keyword specifies that the two tables should be joined. The ON keyword that follows specifies what joins the tables; in this case, the CategoryId field joins them. Note that you must specify the table names in front of the CategoryId, otherwise the database doesn't know if you mean the CategoryId in the Films table or the CategoryId in the Category table. In fact, the two columns don't actually need to have the same name, depending on the database's design. Designing a database that way doesn't make sense, though; when someone looks at the database design, they should be able to see that CategoryId in each table relates to the same set of values.

91

The preceding SQL produces the same results as before:

FilmName	YearReleased	Rating
Sense and Insensitivity	2001	3
15th Late Afternoon	1989	5
Gone with the Window Cleaner	1988	3
The Good, the Bad, and the Facially Challenged	1989	5

The INNER part of INNER JOIN is actually optional in most database systems: INNER JOIN is the default join because it's the most common. That said, you can write the SQL as follows:

```
SELECT FilmName, YearReleased, Rating
FROM Films JOIN Category
ON Films.CategoryId = Category.CategoryId
WHERE Category.CategoryId = 6;
```

Using INNER JOIN or simply JOIN to create an inner join between tables is not, in fact, the only way to join tables. You may prefer it, though, because INNER JOIN and JOIN make explicit which tables are being joined, and that in turn makes the SQL easier to read and understand. The alternative way of creating an inner join is simply to specify the link in the WHERE clause. Rewriting the preceding SQL by specifying the link looks like this:

```
SELECT FilmName, YearReleased, Rating
FROM Films, Category
WHERE Films.CategoryId = Category.CategoryId AND
Category.CategoryId = 6;
```

The WHERE clause specifies that Films.CategoryId should equal Category.CategoryId, which creates the join.

So far, you've used the equals operator (=) to join tables, which is termed *equijoin*. Equijoin is the most common join type, but using any of the other operators is fine.

As mentioned earlier, you're not limited to joining just two tables together in one SELECT statement; within reason, it's possible to join as many tables as you like. You are sure to encounter a problem that requires joining multiple tables. For example, say you want to produce a list of each film club member's name and all the films they enjoy based on their favorite film category. In the results, you want to display the members' first and last names, the name of each film, each film's year of release, and finally the category in which each film belongs.

Now this might seem like a fairly simple problem, but it actually involves the most complex SQL so far in the book. When illustrated step-by-step, however, it's not so bad at all.

Having a diagram of the database tables and their fields often helps when it comes to the more tricky SQL queries. Shown in Figure 3-1 is a diagram of the Film Club database.

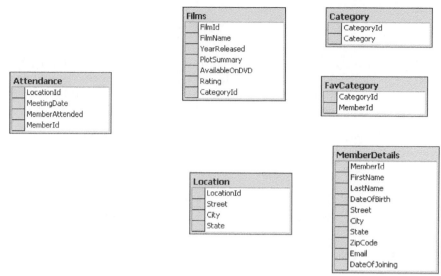

Figure 3-1

The first task when tackling tricky SQL problems is to work out what information is required and which tables contain that information. The preceding scenario specifies that the results must contain the following information:

- ❑ Members' names
- ❑ All the films that are in the members' favorite categories
- ❑ Film names
- ❑ Films' year of release
- ❑ Category to which each film belongs

You can obtain the members' first and last names from the MemberDetails table. Details of the film names come from the Films table. The category each film belongs to is slightly trickier. Although the Films table contains a CategoryId for each record of a film, this is just a number — the results need to display the category's name. Looking at the table diagram, you can see that the Category table contains the category name, so the Category table provides the category name. But you need to link the Category table to the Films table. The CategoryId field is in both tables, so the CategoryId field provides the link between the two. Remember that when you set up the database, the CategoryId field was a primary key field in the Category table and a foreign key field in the Films table; this field provides the link between the two data sets they hold. Finally, the results ask for each film in a member's favorite category. The FavCategory table contains this information, but again it just contains MemberId and CategoryId, so in order to get the information in a human-friendly format, you need to link these two tables to the MemberDetails and Category tables.

Below is a list summing up the tables you need to use to get the results you want:

- ❑ MemberDetails
- ❑ Films

❑   Category

❑   FavCategory

Now you need to work out how to link them all up. The results you're after comprise a list of films in each member's favorite category, and the FavCategory table is central to the results, so the first step is to link that table. You don't need to use a WHERE clause in this SQL because you want all the results. Begin with a simple SELECT statement to return all the results from the FavCategory table:

```
SELECT FavCategory.CategoryId, FavCategory.MemberId
FROM FavCategory;
```

That's simple enough and returns the following results:

CategoryId	MemberId
1	3
1	5
1	10
2	1
2	3
3	3
4	6
4	1
3	10
5	3
5	4
6	10
4	11
3	11
5	11
1	12
4	12
6	12
3	13
5	13
2	14
6	14
1	3

That's all well and good, but so far your results are only numbers; you're after the category's name. To get the category's name, you need to link to the Category table via the CategoryId column, which links both tables. To link them, use an INNER JOIN:

```
SELECT Category.Category, FavCategory.MemberId
FROM FavCategory INNER JOIN Category
ON FavCategory.CategoryId = Category.CategoryId;
```

The SQL produces the following results:

Category	MemberId
Thriller	3
Thriller	5
Thriller	10
Thriller	3
Romance	1
Romance	3
Horror	3
War	6
War	1
Horror	10
Sci-fi	3
Sci-fi	4
Historical	10
War	11
Horror	11
Sci-fi	11
Thriller	12
War	12
Historical	12
Horror	13
Sci-fi	13
Romance	14
Historical	14

You're one step further, but now you need to get rid of the MemberId and replace it with the members' first and last names. To do this, you need to link to the MemberDetails table and get the data from there, which involves a second INNER JOIN:

```
SELECT Category.Category, MemberDetails.FirstName, MemberDetails.LastName
FROM FavCategory INNER JOIN Category
ON FavCategory.CategoryId = Category.CategoryId
INNER JOIN MemberDetails
ON FavCategory.MemberId = MemberDetails.MemberId
ORDER BY MemberDetails.LastName, MemberDetails.FirstName;
```

The preceding code includes a second INNER JOIN statement after the first one. The ON statement links to the first INNER JOIN by linking the FavCategory and MemberDetails tables. The ORDER BY statement orders the results by last name and then first name to identify which member likes which categories. Note that if you're using MS Access, you must change the SQL slightly. Access is happy with just one join but insists that you put brackets around each additional join. So the preceding code needs to be rewritten as follows:

```
SELECT Category.Category, MemberDetails.FirstName, MemberDetails.LastName
FROM (FavCategory INNER JOIN Category
ON FavCategory.CategoryId = Category.CategoryId)
INNER JOIN MemberDetails
ON FavCategory.MemberId = MemberDetails.MemberId
ORDER BY MemberDetails.LastName, MemberDetails.FirstName;
```

Notice the brackets around the first inner join. The second inner join, which joins to the results of the first, doesn't need brackets. Note that this code works on the other database systems but that the brackets aren't required around the additional joins.

The results so far are as follows:

Category	FirstName	LastName
Thriller	Stuart	Dales
War	Stuart	Dales
Historical	Stuart	Dales
Horror	William	Doors
Sci-fi	William	Doors
Sci-fi	Steve	Gee
War	Jamie	Hills
Horror	Jamie	Hills
Sci-fi	Jamie	Hills

Category	FirstName	LastName
War	Jenny	Jones
Thriller	John	Jones
Romance	Doris	Night
Historical	Doris	Night
Thriller	Susie	Simons
Horror	Susie	Simons
Historical	Susie	Simons
Romance	Katie	Smith
War	Katie	Smith

What you have at the moment is a results set that details each member's favorite film categories. What you need, though, is a list of all the films under each category for each member. To produce such a list, you need to link to the Films table where all the film data is stored. The field that links the two tables is the CategoryId field, which was a primary key field in the Category table and a foreign key field in the Films table when you designed the database. You need to add the following INNER JOIN to the bottom of the current INNER JOIN list:

```
INNER JOIN Films
ON Films.CategoryId = Category.CategoryId
```

This is the final link needed. It joins the Films table to the results and allows details such as FilmName and YearReleased to be included in the results:

```
SELECT MemberDetails.FirstName, MemberDetails.LastName, Category.Category,
FilmName, YearReleased
FROM ((FavCategory INNER JOIN Category
ON FavCategory.CategoryId = Category.CategoryId)
INNER JOIN MemberDetails
ON FavCategory.MemberId = MemberDetails.MemberId)
INNER JOIN Films
ON Films.CategoryId = Category.CategoryId
ORDER BY MemberDetails.LastName, MemberDetails.FirstName;
```

Note the brackets around the joins, which ensures that the code works with MS Access. The other database systems don't need the brackets, and they can be left off. Notice also that the results of each join are bracketed. The first join is bracketed on its own, then this is bracketed together with the second join, and finally the third join links to these results and doesn't need brackets

The final SQL provides the following results set that details all the films in each member's favorite film category:

FirstName	LastName	Category	FilmName	YearReleased
Stuart	Dales	Thriller	The Maltese Poodle	1947
Stuart	Dales	Thriller	Raging Bullocks	1980
Stuart	Dales	Thriller	The Life Of Bob	1984
Stuart	Dales	War	The Dirty Half Dozen	1987
Stuart	Dales	War	Planet of the Japes	1967
Stuart	Dales	Historical	Sense and Insensitivity	2001
Stuart	Dales	Historical	15th Late Afternoon	1989
Stuart	Dales	Historical	Gone with the Window Cleaner	1988
Stuart	Dales	Historical	The Good, the Bad, and the Facially Challenged	1989
William	Doors	Horror	The Lion, the Witch, and the Chest of Drawers	1977
William	Doors	Horror	Nightmare on Oak Street, Part 23	1997
William	Doors	Horror	One Flew over the Crow's Nest	1975
William	Doors	Sci-fi	The Wide Brimmed Hat	2005
William	Doors	Sci-fi	Soylent Yellow	1967
Steve	Gee	Sci-fi	The Wide Brimmed Hat	2005
Steve	Gee	Sci-fi	Soylent Yellow	1967
Jamie	Hills	War	The Dirty Half Dozen	1987
Jamie	Hills	War	Planet of the Japes	1967
Jamie	Hills	Horror	The Lion, the Witch, and the Chest of Drawers	1977
Jamie	Hills	Horror	Nightmare on Oak Street, Part 23	1997
Jamie	Hills	Horror	One Flew over the Crow's Nest	1975
Jamie	Hills	Sci-fi	The Wide Brimmed Hat	2005
Jamie	Hills	Sci-fi	Soylent Yellow	1967
Jenny	Jones	War	The Dirty Half Dozen	1987
Jenny	Jones	War	Planet of the Japes	1967
John	Jones	Thriller	The Maltese Poodle	1947
John	Jones	Thriller	Raging Bullocks	1980
John	Jones	Thriller	The Life of Bob	1984

FirstName	LastName	Category	FilmName	YearReleased
Doris	Night	Romance	On Golden Puddle	1967
Doris	Night	Historical	Sense and Insensitivity	2001
Doris	Night	Historical	15th Late Afternoon	1989
Doris	Night	Historical	Gone with the Window Cleaner	1988
Doris	Night	Historical	The Good, the Bad, and the Facially Challenged	1989
Susie	Simons	Thriller	The Maltese Poodle	1947
Susie	Simons	Thriller	Raging Bullocks	1980
Susie	Simons	Thriller	The Life of Bob	1984
Susie	Simons	Horror	The Lion, the Witch, and the Chest of Drawers	1977
Susie	Simons	Horror	Nightmare on Oak Street, Part 23	1997
Susie	Simons	Horror	One Flew over the Crow's Nest	1975
Susie	Simons	Historical	Sense and Insensitivity	2001
Susie	Simons	Historical	15th Late Afternoon	1989
Susie	Simons	Historical	Gone with the Window Cleaner	1988
Susie	Simons	Historical	The Good, the Bad, and the Facially Challenged	1989
Katie	Smith	Romance	On Golden Puddle	1967
Katie	Smith	War	The Dirty Half Dozen	1987
Katie	Smith	War	Planet of the Japes	1967

If you want only one member's list of films based on their favorite film categories, all you need to do is add a WHERE clause and specify their MemberId. The following SQL specifies Jamie Hills's ID, which is 11:

```
SELECT MemberDetails.FirstName, MemberDetails.LastName, Category.Category,
FilmName, YearReleased
FROM (( FavCategory INNER JOIN Category
ON FavCategory.CategoryId = Category.CategoryId)
INNER JOIN MemberDetails
ON FavCategory.MemberId = MemberDetails.MemberId)
INNER JOIN Films
ON Films.CategoryId = Category.CategoryId
WHERE MemberDetails.MemberId = 11
ORDER BY MemberDetails.LastName, MemberDetails.FirstName;
```

This time, you achieve more specific results:

FirstName	LastName	Category	FilmName	YearReleased
Jamie	Hills	War	The Dirty Half Dozen	1987
Jamie	Hills	War	Planet of the Japes	1967
Jamie	Hills	Horror	The Lion, the Witch, and the Chest of Drawers	1977
Jamie	Hills	Horror	Nightmare on Oak Street, Part 23	1997
Jamie	Hills	Horror	One Flew over the Crow's Nest	1975
Jamie	Hills	Sci-fi	The Wide Brimmed Hat	2005
Jamie	Hills	Sci-fi	Soylent Yellow	1967

As you created the query, you probably noticed that each time you ran the query it produced a unique set of results. That happens because each additional INNER JOIN linked to the results set created by the previous SQL. Before moving on to the section that explains the set-based nature of SQL, you should gain more familiarity with the use of brackets in MS Access.

Using Brackets around Inner Joins in MS Access

You can skip over this section if you're not using MS Access. As mentioned previously, MS Access requires brackets around joins when there's more than one join. Each join creates a set of data, which is discussed later. Each set of data needs to be enclosed in brackets, unless there's only one set.

For example, the following statement involves only one join and therefore only one source set of data:

```
SELECT MemberDetails.MemberId
FROM MemberDetails INNER JOIN FavCategory
ON MemberDetails.MemberId = FavCategory.MemberId;
```

However, if you then join that set of data to another table, creating a second set of data, you must enclose the first set of data inside brackets, like so:

```
SELECT MemberDetails.MemberId
FROM (MemberDetails INNER JOIN FavCategory
ON MemberDetails.MemberId = FavCategory.MemberId)
INNER JOIN Category
ON Category.CategoryId = FavCategory.CategoryId;
```

The following excerpt illustrates how the original join is enclosed inside its own brackets:

```
FROM (MemberDetails INNER JOIN FavCategory
ON MemberDetails.MemberId = FavCategory.MemberId)
```

If you take this further and join the current sets of data to yet another table, then the first two joins must be enclosed in brackets. The following is the original join:

```
FROM (MemberDetails INNER JOIN FavCategory
ON MemberDetails.MemberId = FavCategory.MemberId)
```

Then add the join to the Category table. Note that the first join is enclosed in brackets:

```
FROM ((MemberDetails INNER JOIN FavCategory
ON MemberDetails.MemberId = FavCategory.MemberId)
INNER JOIN Category
ON Category.CategoryId = FavCategory.CategoryId)
```

Now you can add the third join:

```
FROM ((MemberDetails INNER JOIN FavCategory
ON MemberDetails.MemberId = FavCategory.MemberId)
INNER JOIN Category
ON Category.CategoryId = FavCategory.CategoryId)
INNER JOIN Films
ON Category.CategoryId = Films.CategoryId;
```

The full SQL is as follows:

```
SELECT MemberDetails.MemberId
FROM ((MemberDetails INNER JOIN FavCategory
ON MemberDetails.MemberId = FavCategory.MemberId)
INNER JOIN Category
ON Category.CategoryId = FavCategory.CategoryId)
INNER JOIN Films
ON Category.CategoryId = Films.CategoryId;
```

If you add a fourth join, you need to enclose the first three joins in brackets:

```
SELECT MemberDetails.MemberId
FROM (((MemberDetails INNER JOIN FavCategory
ON MemberDetails.MemberId = FavCategory.MemberId)
INNER JOIN Category
ON Category.CategoryId = FavCategory.CategoryId)
INNER JOIN Films
ON Category.CategoryId = Films.CategoryId)
INNER JOIN Attendance
ON MemberDetails.MemberId = Attendance.MemberId;
```

And so it would continue if you add a fifth join, a sixth join, and so on.

None of this adding of brackets is necessary for the other database systems, so the extra brackets aren't included in every example; be sure to add them if you're using Access.

SQL Is Set-Based

You might remember from your high school math days the concept of the set, which is simply a collection, in no particular order, of items of the same type. SQL is set-based, the sets being sets of records. As with sets in math, there is no particular order to SQL data sets unless you specify the order, using the ORDER BY clause, for example. With the more straightforward queries (like the ones earlier in the chapter), considering the set-based nature of SQL queries isn't really necessary. However, with trickier queries, especially those involving more than one table, thinking in terms of sets is helpful.

Taking the example from the previous section, examine how the first step looks as a set. The first step's SQL is as follows:

```
SELECT FavCategory.CategoryId, FavCategory.MemberId
FROM FavCategory;
```

Represented as a set diagram, the first step looks like Figure 3-2.

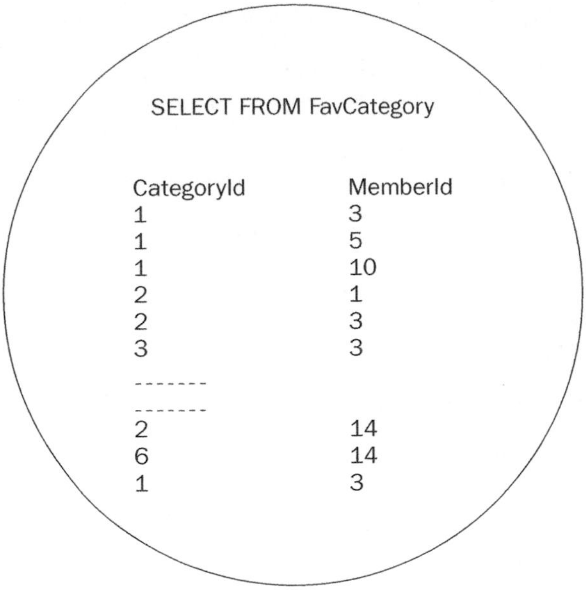

SELECT FROM FavCategory

CategoryId	MemberId
1	3
1	5
1	10
2	1
2	3
3	3

2	14
6	14
1	3

Figure 3-2

The set simply contains all the records and columns from the FavCategory table.

The next step joins the Category and FavCategory tables with this SQL:

```
SELECT Category.Category, FavCategory.MemberId
FROM FavCategory INNER JOIN Category
ON FavCategory.CategoryId = Category.CategoryId;
```

Figure 3-3 shows a set diagram of the SQL.

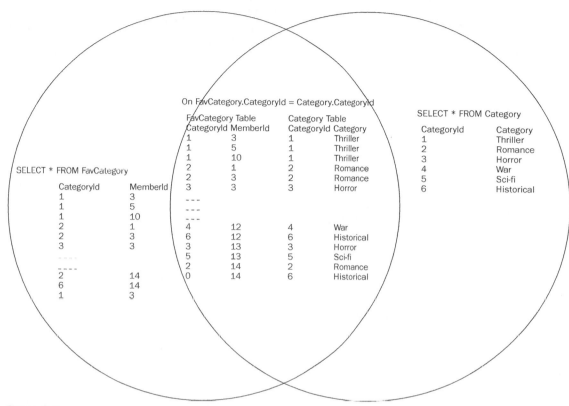

Figure 3-3

The circle on the left represents the set of records from the FavCategory table. Because the set isn't filtered (for example, with a WHERE clause), it includes all the FavCategory records, though the diagram shows only a handful. The circle on the right is the set of records from the Category table, again unfiltered to include all the records. In the center is the overlap between the two sets, defined by the ON clause in the INNER JOIN. The results set in the overlap is the final results obtained. It includes all the records from the other two results sets, where there is a matching CategoryId in each table for each record. As it happens, the CategoryId in every record in the FavCategory table finds a matching CategoryId in the CategoryId column, so every record from the FavCategory table is included. The SQL statement selects only two columns, Category and MemberId, to be returned in the results. However, when the database performs the join, all the fields listed in the ON statement are also considered.

In order to demonstrate that only records with matching CategoryId's in both tables are included in the joined results set, add another record to the Category table. First, though, here are the results without the new record added:

Category	MemberId
Thriller	5
Thriller	10
Romance	1
War	6
War	1
Horror	10
Sci-fi	4
Historical	10
War	11
Horror	11
Sci-fi	11
Thriller	12
War	12
Historical	12
Horror	13
Sci-fi	13
Romance	14
Historical	14

Note that there are 18 rows.

Now execute the following SQL to add a new record to the Category table:

```
INSERT INTO Category (CategoryId, Category)
VALUES (7, 'Comedy');
```

Next, re-execute the query:

```
SELECT Category.Category, FavCategory.MemberId
FROM FavCategory INNER JOIN Category
ON FavCategory.CategoryId = Category.CategoryId;
```

The re-execution provides the following results:

Category	MemberId
Thriller	5
Thriller	10
Romance	1
War	6
War	1
Horror	10
Sci-fi	4
Historical	10
War	11
Horror	11
Sci-fi	11
Thriller	12
War	12
Historical	12
Horror	13
Sci-fi	13
Romance	14
Historical	14

Notice the difference? That's right, there is no difference; even though you added an extra record to the Category table, the addition doesn't affect the results because no records exist in the FavCategory results set that match the new CategoryId of 7. Now add a few new favorite categories to the FavCategory table that have a CategoryId of 7:

```
INSERT INTO FavCategory (CategoryId, MemberId)
VALUES (7, 6);

INSERT INTO FavCategory (CategoryId, MemberId)
VALUES (7, 4);


INSERT INTO FavCategory (CategoryId, MemberId)
VALUES (7, 12);
```

Execute the SQL and then rerun the SELECT query:

```
SELECT Category.Category, FavCategory.MemberId
FROM FavCategory INNER JOIN Category
ON FavCategory.CategoryId = Category.CategoryId;
```

You should see the following results:

Category	MemberId
Thriller	5
Thriller	10
Thriller	12
Romance	1
Romance	14
Horror	10
Horror	11
Horror	13
War	6
War	1
War	11
War	12
Sci-fi	4
Sci-fi	11
Sci-fi	13
Historical	10
Historical	12
Historical	14
Comedy	6
Comedy	4
Comedy	12

Because three new records appear in the FavCategory table with a matching record in the Category table, the results appear in the resulting join.

The next stage joins the MemberDetails table to the current results set:

```
SELECT Category.Category, MemberDetails.FirstName, MemberDetails.LastName
FROM FavCategory INNER JOIN Category
ON FavCategory.CategoryId = Category.CategoryId
INNER JOIN MemberDetails
ON FavCategory.MemberId = MemberDetails.MemberId
ORDER BY MemberDetails.LastName, MemberDetails.FirstName;
```

Remember to add brackets around the first join if you're using MS Access:

```
SELECT Category.Category, MemberDetails.FirstName, MemberDetails.LastName
FROM (FavCategory INNER JOIN Category
ON FavCategory.CategoryId = Category.CategoryId)
INNER JOIN MemberDetails
ON FavCategory.MemberId = MemberDetails.MemberId
ORDER BY MemberDetails.LastName, MemberDetails.FirstName;
```

Figure 3-4 shows the resulting diagram.

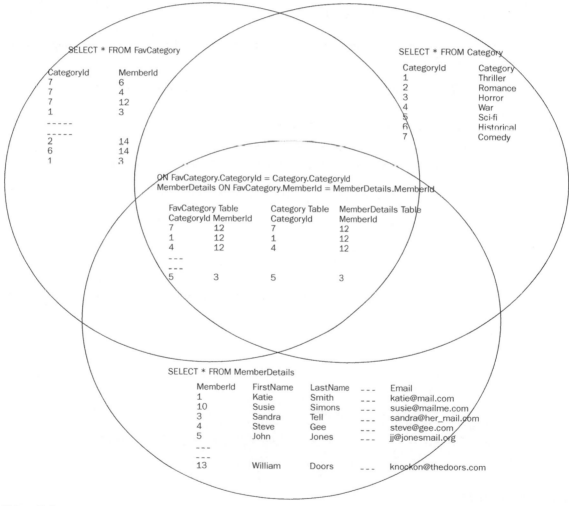

Figure 3-4

The overlapping portions of the three data sets form the final results set. The ON statements define the overlap area, which is summarized as follows:

❑ Every record in the FavCategory table must have a matching record in the Category table with the same value in the CategoryId field.

❑ Every record in the Category table must have a matching record in the FavCategory table with the same value in the CategoryId field.

❑ Every record in the FavCategory table must have a matching record in the MemberDetails table with the same value in the MemberId field.

❑ Every record in the MemberDetails table must have a matching record in the Category table with the same value in the MemberId field.

Documenting the remaining steps in the SQL in diagram form would consume precious pages, so hopefully SQL's set-based nature is clear.

By now, you should be familiar enough with sets and inner joins to try out a few.

Try It Out   Using Inner Joins to Form Sets

1. Using the following SQL, generate a list for the film club chairperson of all the members who don't live in a city in which the club holds meetings. Don't forget to create a set diagram.

```
SELECT MemberDetails.FirstName, MemberDetails.LastName,
       MemberDetails.City, MemberDetails.State
FROM MemberDetails INNER JOIN Location
ON (MemberDetails.City <> Location.City AND MemberDetails.State = Location.State)
OR (MemberDetails.City = Location.City AND MemberDetails.State <> Location.State)
ORDER BY MemberDetails.LastName;
```

2. The club's chairperson also wants a list of all the members who have attended meetings, the date of attendance, and where the meeting was held. To create the list, use the following SQL:

```
SELECT
  MemberDetails.MemberId,
  MemberDetails.FirstName,
  MemberDetails.LastName,
  Attendance.MeetingDate,
  Location.City
FROM
(MemberDetails INNER JOIN Attendance
ON MemberDetails.MemberId = Attendance.MemberId)
INNER JOIN Location ON Location.LocationId = Attendance.LocationId
WHERE Attendance.MemberAttended = 'Y'
ORDER BY MeetingDate, Location.City, LastName, FirstName;
```

How It Works

First, you need to create a list of all members not living in a city in which club meetings are held. The data for meeting locations resides in the Location table. This information provides one results set. Not surprisingly, the MemberDetails table holds member details, the second results set. Now it's necessary to combine the two sets to get the result you want: a list of all members whose city is not listed in the Location table. More than one city may have the same name, so assume that such cities in the same state are the same. Therefore, you joined the MemberDetails table to the Location table using an INNER JOIN based on the City and State columns:

```
FROM MemberDetails INNER JOIN Location
ON (MemberDetails.City <> Location.City AND MemberDetails.State = Location.State)
OR (MemberDetails.City = Location.City AND MemberDetails.State <> Location.State)
ORDER BY MemberDetails.LastName;
```

The ON clause is the key to this query, so you need results where the cities don't match but the states do (same state but different city name). You also want to include records where the city name is the same but the state name is different (same city name but in a different state). It seems obvious when written down, but oftentimes looking at the two results sets and making the comparison in your mind first is helpful. The key fields in both tables are City and State, so you need to make your comparison with those fields. Figure 3-5 shows the set diagram.

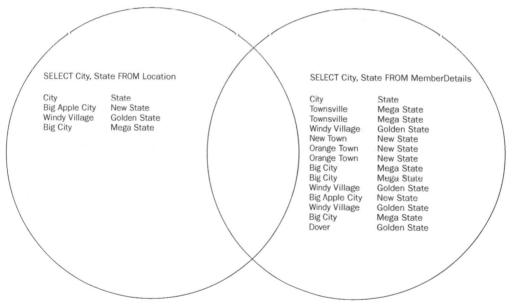

Figure 3-5

Check if the Townsville record at the top of the MemberDetails table appears in the City field in any of the records in the Location set. Townsville doesn't appear, so you know that Townsville is not a valid meeting location, and therefore it should form part of the results. You also need to take into account data that isn't there but should be. For example, say that a city called Big City in Sunny State appears in the Location table. In this case, simply comparing the City columns in each table means that Big City, Sunny State, would not be included in the results even though clearly Big City, Mega State, and Big City, Sunny State, are totally different cities.

More than one condition exists in your ON clause. ON clauses are very similar to a SELECT statement's WHERE clause in that you can use the same operators and OR and AND logical operators are allowed. The ON clause in the preceding SQL contains two conditions linked with an OR operator. The first condition states

```
MemberDetails.City <> Location.City AND MemberDetails.State = Location.State
```

It matches a record where the City columns in MemberDetails and Location are not the same. Remember, you want a list of members in cities that don't match in the Location table. The states must be the same, and only the City column must differ. This works so long as each state has cities with unique names!

The second part of the ON clause, joined with the OR statement, checks for cities where the name is the same but the state is different:

```
MemberDetails.City = Location.City AND MemberDetails.State <> Location.State
```

The final SQL is as follows:

```
SELECT MemberDetails.FirstName, MemberDetails.LastName,
       MemberDetails.City, MemberDetails.State
FROM MemberDetails INNER JOIN Location
ON (MemberDetails.City <> Location.City AND MemberDetails.State = Location.State)
OR (MemberDetails.City = Location.City AND MemberDetails.State <> Location.State)
ORDER BY MemberDetails.LastName;
```

Executing the final SQL provide the results shown in the following table:

FirstName	LastName	MemberDetails.City	MemberDetails.State
Steve	Gee	New Town	New State
Doris	Night	Dover	Golden State
Susie	Simons	Townsville	Mega State
Katie	Smith	Townsville	Mega State

Phew! That's quite a query, but hopefully it helps to underline SQL's set-based nature.

To find out which members attended which meetings and the dates and locations of attendance, you need to decide which tables hold that data. In this case, the MemberDetails, Attendance, and Location tables hold the data you need. Next, consider how to link the tables together. The Attendance table is central to this query because it contains the LocationId field needed to find out location details, as well as the MemberId field needed to find out member information.

Figure 3-6 shows the set diagram for this problem.

Note that the set in the left circle doesn't contain all the records from a particular table; it contains only records from the Attendance table where the MemberAttended column contains a Y. It reminds you that *set* is not simply another word for *table*; sets contain a selection of a table's records.

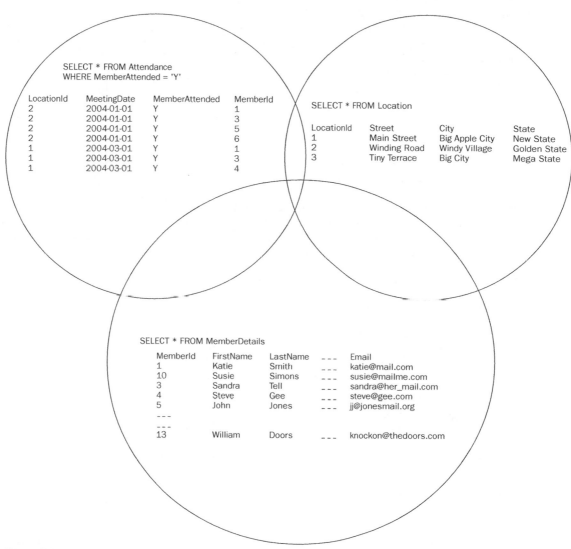

Figure 3-6

Start by linking the Location and Attendance tables:

```
SELECT
Attendance.MeetingDate,
Location.City
FROM Attendance
INNER JOIN Location ON Location.LocationId = Attendance.LocationId
```

Next, link the MemberDetails table:

```
SELECT
   MemberDetails.MemberId,
   MemberDetails.FirstName,
   MemberDetails.LastName,
   Attendance.MeetingDate,
   Location.City
FROM
   (MemberDetails INNER JOIN Attendance
   ON MemberDetails.MemberId = Attendance.MemberId)
   INNER JOIN Location ON Location.LocationId = Attendance.LocationId
ORDER BY MeetingDate, Location.City, LastName, FirstName
```

Order the results by meeting date, location, last name, and finally, first name. Remember, however, that you require a list of members who have attended a meeting. Your results set from the Attendance table should include only those records where the MemberAttended field contains a Y. So, to finalize your query, add a WHERE clause:

```
SELECT
   MemberDetails.MemberId,
   MemberDetails.FirstName,
   MemberDetails.LastName,
   Attendance.MeetingDate,
   Location.City
FROM
(MemberDetails INNER JOIN Attendance
ON MemberDetails.MemberId = Attendance.MemberId)
INNER JOIN Location ON Location.LocationId = Attendance.LocationId
WHERE Attendance.MemberAttended = 'Y'
ORDER BY MeetingDate, Location.City, LastName, FirstName;
```

Executing the final query provides the results shown in the following table:

MemberId	FirstName	LastName	MeetingDate	City
6	Jenny	Jones	2004-01-01	Windy Village
5	John	Jones	2004-01-01	Windy Village
1	Katie	Smith	2004-01-01	Windy Village
4	Steve	Gee	2004-03-01	Orange Town
1	Katie	Smith	2004-03-01	Orange Town

One final note before moving on: The vital point to remember is that SQL doesn't compare just one record in one set to just one record in the second set; SQL compares each record in one set to *every* record in the other set, and vice versa. If the ON condition is true for a particular record, then the final results set includes that record. You should always remember that SQL is set-based and compares all records in each set to all the records in the other sets. Reducing set size in WHERE clauses is also worthwhile, because smaller sets compare fewer records, which increases the efficiency of queries.

That's it for this section. The next section delves into the unknown!

Introducing NULL Data

In the sections leading up to this one, you've dealt strictly with known data, but often that's not possible. Given that statement, you might assume that data with no specified value has no value at all. SQL, however, doesn't allow for data to hold no value. Fields with no specified value actually do have a value: NULL. NULL is not the same thing as nothing; NULL represents the unknown. If you were asked how many hairs there are on your head, unless you're bald, you'd have to say that you don't currently know. There is a value, and one day you might know it and be able to store it in a database, but right know it's unknown. This is where NULL comes into play. NULL represents, and allows you to search for, unknown values.

The following is a SQL statement that inserts a new record into the MemberDetails table. Execute the statement in your own database:

```
INSERT INTO MemberDetails
(MemberId, FirstName, LastName, Email, DateOfJoining)
VALUES (15, 'Catherine','Hawthorn', 'chawthorn@mailme.org', '2005-08-25')
```

The MemberDetails table contains DateOfBirth, Street, City, and State fields, yet the SQL doesn't specify any values for these fields. This is perfectly acceptable, so the question is, what values are contained in the fields where no value is specified? You might suggest that because you specified no values, the values in those fields are no value, or nothing at all. In fact, the database system considers the value not to be nothing but instead to be unknown, or NULL.

You might be wondering why you should care about all this.

First of all, NULLs can lead to unexpected and overlooked results. For example, you might think that the following SQL would return all the records in the MemberDetails database:

```
SELECT FirstName, LastName, DateOfBirth
FROM MemberDetails
WHERE DateOfBirth <= '1970-01-01' OR DateOfBirth > '1970-01-01';
```

After all, the statement selects all dates of birth on or before January 1, 1970, and also after January 1, 1970, and yet the record just added to the database for Catherine Hawthorn is not there because the date of birth is NULL (see the following table). Don't forget to change the date format for Oracle and the single quotes to hash marks (#) for Access in the preceding SQL.

FirstName	LastName	DateOfBirth
Katie	Smith	1977-01-09
Steve	Gee	1967-10-05
John	Jones	1952-10-05
Jenny	Jones	1953-08-25
John	Jackson	1974-05-27
Jack	Johnson	1945-06-09
Seymour	Botts	1956-10-21
Susie	Simons	1937-01-20
Jamie	Hills	1992-07-17
Stuart	Dales	1956-08-07
William	Doors	1994-05-28
Doris	Night	1997-05-28

When the database looks at the records, it says for Catherine's record, "Is NULL (unknown) less than January 1, 1970, or is it greater than January 1, 1970?"

Well, the answer is unknown! Records that contain NULL values are always excluded from a results set. The same principle applies to any comparison and to inner joins as well. Additionally, most database systems consider unknowns equal when using an ORDER BY clause, so all NULL values are grouped together.

In order to check for NULL values, you must use the IS NULL operator. To ensure that a value is not NULL, use the IS NOT NULL operator, as in the following code:

```
SELECT FirstName, LastName, DateOfBirth
FROM MemberDetails
WHERE DateOfBirth <= '1970-01-01' OR DateOfBirth > '1970-01-01'
OR DateOfBirth IS NULL;
```

The preceding SQL returns all records, shown in the following table:

FirstName	LastName	DateOfBirth
Katie	Smith	1977-01-09
Susie	Simons	1937-01-20
John	Jackson	1974-05-27
Steve	Gee	1967-10-05
John	Jones	1952-10-05

FirstName	LastName	DateOfBirth
Jenny	Jones	1953-08-25
Jack	Johnson	1945-06-09
Seymour	Botts	1956-10-21
Jamie	Hills	1992-07-17
Stuart	Dales	1956-08-07
William	Doors	1994-05-28
Doris	Night	1997-05-28
Catherine	Hawthorn	

Depending on your database system, it might list DateOfBirth for Catherine as NULL or it may just show nothing at all, as in the preceding table.

Generally speaking, you are better off avoiding the NULL data type and instead using some default value. For example, if you query for a numerical field, use a number that is never normally part of the results, such as –1 for an age field. For a text field, use an empty string, and so on. Chapter 5 revisits the NULL data type when looking at SQL math.

Summary

This chapter covered a lot of topics, some of which were quite challenging, but they all dealt with how to get answers out of a database. At the end of the day, that's what SQL and databases are all about—getting answers. The key to extracting data with SQL is the SELECT query, which allows you to select which columns and from what tables to extract data.

The chapter also discussed the following:

❑ How to filter results so that you get only the data you require. The WHERE clause allows you to specify any number of conditions in order to filter your results to suit your particular query. Only if your specific conditions are met does a record appear in the final results set.

❑ The logical operators AND, OR, NOT, BETWEEN, IN, and LIKE. Coverage of the AND and OR operators was a rehash from the previous chapter, but the rest were introduced in this chapter. NOT allows you to reverse a condition. The BETWEEN operator allows you to specify a range of values and proves a condition true when a column value is within the specified range. When you have a list of potential values, the IN operator comes in handy. It proves a condition true when the column has a value that is in the list of given values. Finally, you learned how to use the LIKE operator with text. The LIKE operator allows the use of wildcard characters.

❑ After you learned how to get the results set you want, you learned how to use the ORDER BY clause, which allows you to list the order of results in ascending or descending order, based on one or more columns.

❑ The slightly tricky topic of selecting data from more than one table. Up to that point, you could use only one table to create the final results set. However, using the INNER JOIN statement allows you to link two or more tables to form a new results set.

❑ The NULL value, which is not the same as no value or zero but in fact signifies an unknown value. The NULL value can cause problems when selecting data, however, because when comparing an unknown value to any other value, the result is always unknown and not included in the final results. You must use the IS NULL or IS NOT NULL operators in order to check for a NULL value.

The next chapter returns to database design, this time looking at it in more depth and covering some of the issues not yet covered. This chapter, however, completes the introductory portion of this book; you're now ready to get out there and create your own databases and get your own results! The second half of the book covers more advanced topics, with the aim of developing your SQL skills.

Exercises

For each of the following exercise questions, write the SQL to list the answers:

1. What is William Doors's (MemberId 13) address?

2. Which members have a surname beginning with the letter *J*?

3. Which members joined before December 31, 2004? Order the results by last name and then by first name.

4. List all the members who attended meetings in Windy Village, Golden State.

Advanced Database Design

This chapter is all about improving the design of a database in terms of ease of management, efficiency, and limiting the risks of entering invalid data. The chapter begins with a bit of theory and relates it to the practical, in particular the Film Club database. This covers improving efficiency in terms of data storage and minimizing wasted space.

Next, the chapter covers various ways of ensuring that only valid data enters the database. The database can't check the accuracy of what you enter, but it can ensure that what you enter doesn't cause the database to stop working as expected. For example, the Attendance table in the Film Club database relies on its relationship with the Location table. The Attendance table doesn't store the full address details of meetings; it just stores a unique ID that matches a record in the Location table. If, however, no matching record exists in the Location table, then queries return incorrect results. This chapter shows you, among other things, how to enforce the relationship between tables and prevent such a situation from occurring.

You use the things you learn throughout the chapter to update and improve the Film Club database. The chapter finishes off with some tips on things to look out for and things to avoid when designing your database.

Normalization

Chapter 1 discussed how to design the database structure using tables and fields in order to avoid problems such as unnecessary duplication of data and the inability to uniquely identify records. Although not specifically called *normalization* in Chapter 1, that was the concept used. This section explains normalization in more detail and how to use it to create well-structured databases.

Normalization consists of a series of guidelines that help guide you in creating a good database structure. Note that they are guidelines and not rules to follow blindly. Database design is probably as much art as it is science, and your own common sense is important, too.

Normalization guidelines are divided into *normal forms*; think of *form* as the format or the way a database structure is laid out. Quite a lot of normal forms exist, but this chapter examines only the first three, because that's as far as most people need to go in normalizing a database. Taken too far, normalization can make database access slower and more complex. The aim of normal forms is to organize the database structure so that it complies with the rules of first normal form, then second normal form, and finally third normal form. It's your choice to take it further and go to fourth normal form, fifth normal form, and so on, but generally speaking, third normal form is enough.

First Normal Form

Chapter 1 walked you through some basic steps for creating a well-organized database structure. In particular, it said that you should do the following:

❑ Define the data items required, because they become the columns in a table. Place related data items in a table.

❑ Ensure that there are no repeating groups of data.

❑ Ensure that there is a primary key.

These rules are those of first normal form, so you've covered first normal form without even knowing it. The Film Club database already complies with first normal form, but to refresh your memory, here is a brief summary of first normal form.

First, you must define the data items. This means looking at the data to be stored, organizing the data into columns, defining what type of data each column contains, and finally putting related columns into their own table. For example, you put all the columns relating to locations of meetings in the Location table, those relating to members in the MemberDetails table, and so on.

This gives a rough idea of table structures. The next step is ensuring that there are no repeating groups of data. If you remember from Chapter 1, when you created the Film Club database, you began by defining a table that held members' details and also details of meetings they had attended. An example of how the table and records might look is shown below:

Name	Date of Birth	Address	Email	Date Joined	Meeting Date	Location	Did Member Attend?
Martin	Feb 27, 1972	1 The Avenue, NY	martin@some.com	Jan 10, 2005	Mar 30, 2005	Lower West Side, NY	Y
Jane	Dec 12, 1967	33 Some Road, Washington	Jane@server.net	Jan 12, 2005	Mar 30, 2005	Lower West Side, NY	N
Kim	May 22, 1980	19 The Road, New Townsville	kim@mail.com	Jan 23, 2005	Mar 30, 2005	Lower West Side, NY	Y

You find, though, that each time you want to add a record of details of another meeting you end up duplicating the members' details:

Name	Date of Birth	Address	Email	Date Joined	Meeting Date	Location	Did Member Attend?
Martin	Feb 27, 1972	1 The Avenue, NY	martin@ some.com	Jan 10, 2005	Mar 30, 2005	Lower West Side, NY	Y
Martin	Feb 27, 1972	1 The Avenue, NY	martin@ some.com	Jan 10, 2005	April 28, 2005	Lower North Side, NY	Y
Jane	Dec 12, 1967	33 Some Road, Washington	Jane@ server.net	Jan 12, 2005	Mar 30, 2005	Lower West Side, NY	N
Jane	Dec 12, 1967	33 Some Road, Washington	Jane@ server.net	Jan 12, 2005	April 28, 2005	Upper North Side, NY	Y
Kim	May 22, 1980	19 The Road, New Townsville	kim@mail. com	Jan 23, 2005	Mar 30, 2005	Lower West Side, NY	Y
Kim	May 22, 1980	19 The Road, New Townsville	kim@mail. com	Jan 23, 2005	April 28, 2005	Upper North Side, NY	Y

There are a number of problems with this approach. First, it wastes a lot of storage space. You only need to store the members' details once, so repeating the data is wasteful. What you have is repeating groups, something that the second rule of first normal form tells you to remove. You can remove duplicated data by splitting the data into tables: one for member details, another to hold location details, and a final table detailing meetings that took place. Another advantage of splitting data into tables is that it avoids something called the *deletion anomaly*, where deleting a record results in also deleting the data you want to keep. For example, say you want to delete details of meetings held more than a year ago. If your data isn't split into tables and you delete records of meetings, then you also delete members' details, which you want to keep. By separating member details and meeting data, you can delete one and not both.

After you split data into tables, you need to link the tables by some unique value. The final rule of the first normal form — create a primary key for each table — comes into play. For example, you added a new column, MemberId, to the MemberDetails table and made it the primary key. You don't have to create a new column, however; you could just use one or more of the existing columns, as long as, when taken together, the data from each column you combine makes for a unique key. However, having an ID column is more efficient in terms of data retrieval.

Second Normal Form

First normal form requires every table to have a primary key. This primary key can consist of one or more columns. The primary key is the unique identifier for that record, and second normal form states that there must be no partial dependences of any of the columns on the primary key. For example, imagine that you decide to store a list of films and people who starred in them. The data being stored is film ID, film name, actor ID, actor name, and date of birth.

You could create a table called ActorFilms using those columns:

Field Name	Data Type	Notes
FilmId	integer	Primary key
FilmName	varchar(100)	
ActorId	integer	Primary key
ActorName	varchar(200)	
DateOfBirth	date	

This table is in first normal form, in that it obeys all the rules of first normal form. In this table, the primary key consists of FilmId and ActorId. Combined they are unique, because the same actor can hardly have starred in the same film twice!

However, the table is not in second normal form because there are partial dependencies of primary keys and columns. FilmName is dependent on FilmId, and there's no real link between a film's name and who starred in it. ActorName and DateOfBirth are dependent on ActorId, but they are not dependent on FilmId, because there's no link between a film ID and an actor's name or their date of birth. To make this table comply with second normal form, you need to separate the columns into three tables. First, create a table to store the film details, somewhat like the Films table in the example database:

Field Name	Data Type	Notes
FilmId	integer	Primary key
FilmName	varchar(100)	

Next, create a table to store details of each actor:

Field Name	Data Type	Notes
ActorId	integer	Primary key
ActorName	varchar(200)	
DateOfBirth	date	

Finally, create a third table storing just FilmIds and ActorIds to keep track of which actors starred in which films:

Field Name	Data Type	Notes
FilmId	integer	Primary key
ActorId	integer	Primary key

Now the tables are in second normal form. Look at each table and you can see that all the columns are tied to the primary key, except that both columns in the third table make up the primary key.

Third Normal Form

Third normal form is the final step this book illustrates. More normal forms exist, but they get more complex and don't necessarily lead to an efficient database. There's a trade-off in database design between minimizing data redundancy and database efficiency. Normal forms aim to reduce the amount of wasted storage and data redundancy. However, they can do so at the cost of database efficiency, in particular, the speed of getting data in and out. Good practice is to ensure that your database tables are in second normal form. Third normal form is a little more optional, and its use depends on the circumstances.

A table is in third normal form when the following conditions are met:

- ❑   It is in second normal form.

- ❑   All nonprimary fields are dependent on the primary key.

The dependency of nonprimary fields is between the data. For example, street name, city, and state are unbreakably bound to the zip code. For example, New Street, New City, Some State, has an assigned and unique zip code. If you mail a letter, in theory supplying the street address and zip code is enough for someone to locate the house. Another example is social security number and a person's name. No direct dependency exists, however, between zip code and a person's name. The dependency between social security number and name and between zip code and address is called a *transitive dependency*.

Take a look at the Film Club database. Can you see any tables not in third normal form?

Check out the MemberDetails table:

Field Name	Data Type
MemberId	integer
FirstName	nvarchar(50)
LastName	nvarchar(50)
DateOfBirth	date
Street	varchar(100)
City	varchar(75)
State	varchar(75)
ZipCode	varchar(12)
Email	varchar(200)
DateOfJoining	date

The Street, City, and State fields all have a transitive dependency on the ZipCode field. To comply with third normal form, all you need to do is move the Street, City, and State fields into their own table, which you can call the ZipCode table:

Field Name	Data Type
ZipCode	varchar(12)
Street	varchar(100)
City	varchar(75)
State	varchar(75)

Then alter the MemberDetails table and remove the Street, City, and State fields, leaving the ZipCode field as a way of matching the address details in the ZipCode table:

Field Name	Data Type
MemberId	integer
FirstName	nvarchar(50)
LastName	nvarchar(50)
DateOfBirth	date
ZipCode	varchar(12)
Email	varchar(200)
DateOfJoining	date

The advantages of removing transitive dependencies are mainly twofold. First, the amount of data duplication is reduced and therefore your database becomes smaller. Two or more people living on the same street in the same city in the same town have the same zip code. Rather than store all that data more than once, store it just once in the ZipCode table so that only the ZipCode is stored more than once.

The second advantage is data integrity. When duplicated data changes, there's a big risk of updating only some of the data, especially if it's spread out in a number of different places in the database. If address and zip code data were stored in three or four different tables, then any changes in zip codes would need to ripple out to every record in those three or four tables. However, if it's all stored in one table, then you need to change it in only one place.

There is a downside, though: added complexity and reduced efficiency. Before changing the database, the query for a member's name and address would be as follows:

```
SELECT FirstName, LastName, Street, City, State, ZipCode
FROM MemberDetails;
```

After changing the database so that the MemberDetails table is in third normal form, the same query looks like this:

```
SELECT FirstName, LastName, Street, City, State, ZipCode.ZipCode
FROM MemberDetails INNER JOIN ZipCode
ON ZipCode.ZipCode = MemberDetails.ZipCode;
```

In addition to being a little more complex, the code is also less efficient. The database takes longer to retrieve the data. In a small database with a few records, the difference in speed is minimal, but in a larger database with more records, the difference in speed could be quite significant.

Leave the Film Club database's structure intact for now, and make any necessary changes in the section later in this chapter that re-examines the database's structure.

Ensuring Data Validity with Constraints

When creating database tables and fields, you can specify *constraints* that limit what data can go in a field. It might sound a bit odd — why constrain things? Imagine that a database user is working late, entering data into the database. He's all bleary-eyed and kind of keen to get home. When entering primary key data, he accidentally enters the same value twice. Now the unique primary key is no longer unique, causing data corruption in the database and causing queries, which rely on the uniqueness of the primary key, to fail. Sorting out corrupted data can be quite tricky, especially if you're dealing with a huge database and lots of records. Preventing data corruption in the first place is much better — for example, by defining a constraint when creating the table that specifies that a column must contain unique values. If someone tries to add two identical values, the database throws an error and stops them.

Using the DBMS to protect data integrity is not the only way, but it's probably the best. An alternative is having an external program ensure that the data is valid, as most databases are not accessed directly by the user but via some third-party front-end interface. For example, if you buy a program off the shelf to help catalog and organize your CD and record collection, it's quite unlikely that all you'd get is a database! Instead, the program installs a nice, easy-to-use front-end program on the user's computer that accesses a database in the background without the user ever seeing it. This program can control the data and ensure that no data corruption occurs. However, preventing data corruption using the DBMS has its advantages. For example, the check has to be done in only one place: in the database itself. Additionally, the DBMS can run the check more efficiently than can an external program.

This section covers the following constraints:

❑   NOT NULL

❑   UNIQUE

❑   CHECK

❑   PRIMARY KEY

❑   FOREIGN KEY

MySQL versions prior to 5.0.2 support the constraints mentioned here but don't enforce them, which somewhat reduces their effectiveness. The code described in the following sections works in MySQL, but when you enter data prohibited by a particular constraint, MySQL won't reject it as other database systems would. Discussion of constraints and invalid data as they relate to MySQL is beyond the scope of this book. Be sure to check the MySQL product documentation for specific information.

NOT NULL Constraint

Chapter 3 briefly covered the NULL data type. If you recall, NULL is not the same as no data; rather, it represents unknown data. However, the NULL data type can cause problems with query results. It makes sorting columns with NULL values difficult, because one NULL is the same as the next, so all the NULLs appear at the start of any sorted results set. You may also want to ensure that a particular column has a value — that it's a compulsory column when inserting a new record. This is where the NOT NULL constraint comes in. It ensures that the column must have a value or else the record cannot be inserted.

Whether a column in a table can contain NULLs is something that you need to define when you first create the table. SQL allows NULLs by default, so only when you don't want NULLs do you need to specify such in the table creation SQL. Add the constraint to the column definition, immediately after the data type. For example, the following SQL creates a new table called MyTable and adds three columns, two of which, Column1 and Column3, specify not to accept NULLs:

```
CREATE TABLE MyTable
(
Column1 int NOT NULL,
Column2 varchar(20),
Column3 varchar(12) NOT NULL
)
```

What if you decide later on, after you create a table, that you want to make one or more of the columns subject to a NOT NULL constraint? Answering this question is a little trickier, and this is another good reason for planning database table creation in advance of creating the tables. Some DBMSs, such as Oracle, allow users to modify columns in an existing table with the ALTER TABLE MODIFY statement. For example, to add a NOT NULL constraint to Column1 in Oracle and MySQL, you would write a statement similar to the following:

```
ALTER TABLE MyTable
MODIFY Column2 varchar(20) NOT NULL;
```

However, many database systems don't allow this statement, so you must take a different approach: alter the column definition itself and re-create it with the NOT NULL constraint:

```
ALTER TABLE MyTable
ALTER COLUMN Column2 varchar(20) NOT NULL;
```

The ALTER COLUMN statement changes Column2, specifying the same data type but adding the NOT NULL constraint.

IBM's DB2 doesn't allow you to alter a column so that it doesn't allow NULLs. You can either delete the table and redefine it, this time making sure the column has a NOT NULL constraint, or add a CHECK constraint. The CHECK constraint is covered later in this chapter, but to add a NOT NULL CHECK constraint in DB2, the syntax is as follows:

```
ALTER TABLE table_name
ADD CONSTRAINT constraint_name
CHECK (column_name IS NOT NULL)
```

So, to add a NOT NULL CHECK constraint for Column2 of MyTable, you would write the following code:

```
ALTER TABLE MyTable
ADD CONSTRAINT Column2_NotNull
CHECK (Column2 IS NOT NULL);
```

With the NOT NULL constraint added to the database systems, test it out by executing the following SQL:

```
INSERT INTO MyTable(Column1,Column3)
VALUES (123,'ABC');
```

You should get an error message similar to Cannot insert the value NULL into column 'Column2'. The new record isn't added to the table.

Consider this final issue. What if the column in your table that you want to make subject to a NOT NULL constraint already contains NULL records? You can easily deal with that by using a bit of SQL, (like that shown in the following example) to update all those records containing NULLs and set them to whatever default value you think best:

```
UPDATE MyTable
SET Column2 = ''
WHERE Column2 IS NULL;
```

You must do this prior to adding a NOT NULL clause in order to avoid error messages.

If you ran the examples against the Film Club database, delete MyTable from the database, as it's not needed:

```
DROP TABLE MyTable;
```

UNIQUE Constraint

The UNIQUE constraint prevents two records from having identical values in a particular column. In the MemberDetails table, for example, you might want to prevent two or more people from having identical email addresses.

You can apply the UNIQUE constraint in two ways: add it when creating the table, or add it after creating the table.

Except for IBM's DB2, when creating a table, add the UNIQUE constraint to the table definition immediately after the column's type definition:

```
CREATE TABLE MyUniqueTable
(
  Column1 int,
  Column2 varchar(20) UNIQUE,
  Column3 varchar(12) UNIQUE
);
```

The preceding SQL creates a new table called MyUniqueTable and adds the UNIQUE constraint to Column2 and Column3. If you're using DB2, you can't create a UNIQUE constraint unless the column is also defined as NOT NULL. For DB2, make the following changes to the code:

```
CREATE TABLE MyUniqueTable
(
  Column1 int,
  Column2 varchar(20) NOT NULL UNIQUE,
  Column3 varchar(12) NOT NULL UNIQUE
);
```

Execute the SQL that's right for your database system, and then try to insert the following values with the SQL shown here:

```
INSERT INTO MyUniqueTable(Column1,Column2, Column3)
VALUES (123,'ABC', 'DEF');

INSERT INTO MyUniqueTable(Column1,Column2, Column3)
VALUES (123,'XYZ','DEF');
```

You should find that the first INSERT INTO executes just fine and adds a new record, but the second INSERT INTO tries to add a second record where the value of Column3 is DEF, violating the UNIQUE constraint that you added to the column definition. An error message should appear, which says something like Violation of UNIQUE KEY constraint 'UQ__MyUniqueTable__3A81B327'. Cannot insert duplicate key in object 'MyUniqueTable'. The statement has been terminated.

The error message's text varies between database systems, but the message is the same: If the value is not unique, you can't add it.

Setting the UNIQUE constraint by simply adding UNIQUE after a column is nice and easy, but there's another way that has two advantages. In this alternative, you add the constraint at the end of the column listing in the table definition, which allows you to specify that two or more columns must in combination be unique. The other advantage is that you can give the constraint a name and you can delete the constraint using SQL. You're done with MyUniqueTable, so you can delete it:

```
DROP TABLE MyUniqueTable;
```

The following code creates a new table, AnotherTable, and adds a unique constraint called `MyUniqueConstraint`. Remember that it needs to be changed on IBM's DB2. This constraint specifies that Column2 and Column3 must in combination be unique:

```
CREATE TABLE AnotherTable
(
  Column1 int,
  Column2 varchar(20),
  Column3 varchar(12),
  CONSTRAINT MyUniqueConstraint UNIQUE(Column2, Column3)
);
```

On DB2 you need to ensure that the column doesn't accept NULLs:

```
CREATE TABLE AnotherTable
(
  Column1 int,
  Column2 varchar(20) NOT NULL,
  Column3 varchar(12) NOT NULL,
  CONSTRAINT MyUniqueConstraint UNIQUE(Column2, Column3)
);
```

Try running the preceding SQL for your database system to create the table and then try inserting data with the following INSERT INTO statements:

```
INSERT INTO AnotherTable (Column1, Column2, Column3)
VALUES (1,'ABC','DEF');

INSERT INTO AnotherTable (Column1, Column2, Column3)
VALUES (2,'ABC','XYZ');

INSERT INTO AnotherTable (Column1, Column2, Column3)
VALUES (3,'DEF','XYZ');

INSERT INTO AnotherTable (Column1, Column2, Column3)
VALUES (4,'ABC','DEF');
```

The first three INSERT INTO statements execute and insert the records. Even though the first two INSERT statements add records where Column2 has the value ABC, the record is allowed because the value is unique in combination with Column3. The final INSERT statement fails because the first INSERT statement already entered the combination of ABC for Column2 and DEF for Column3 into the table. Therefore, the combination is no longer unique and violates the constraint MyUniqueConstraint, which states that the combination of Column2 and Column3 must be unique. Delete AnotherTable:

```
DROP TABLE AnotherTable;
```

You can add more than one constraint to a table, so long as each constraint has a different name and is separated by a comma:

```
CREATE TABLE AnotherTable
(
  Column1 int,
  Column2 varchar(20),
  Column3 varchar(12),
  CONSTRAINT MyUniqueConstraint UNIQUE(Column2, Column3),
  CONSTRAINT AnotherConstraint UNIQUE(Column1, Column3)
);
```

If you're using DB2, you would write the following statement:

```
CREATE TABLE AnotherTable
(
  Column1 int NOT NULL,
  Column2 varchar(20) NOT NULL,
  Column3 varchar(12) NOT NULL,
  CONSTRAINT MyUniqueConstraint UNIQUE(Column2, Column3),
  CONSTRAINT AnotherConstraint UNIQUE(Column1, Column3)
);
```

You can delete AnotherTable from the database:

```
DROP TABLE AnotherTable;
```

So far you've learned how to add a UNIQUE constraint at the time of a table's creation. However, using the ALTER TABLE statement, you can add and remove a UNIQUE constraint after the table's creation. Chapter 1 discussed the ALTER TABLE statement in relation to adding and removing columns in a table. To add a constraint, you specify which table to alter and then state that you want to ADD a constraint. The SQL code required to define a constraint with an ALTER TABLE statement is identical to how you create a constraint at table creation.

The following code demonstrates how to add a constraint called MyUniqueConstraint to a table called YetAnotherTable:

```
CREATE TABLE YetAnotherTable
(
  Column1 int,
  Column2 varchar(20),
  Column3 varchar(12)
);

ALTER TABLE YetAnotherTable
ADD CONSTRAINT MyUniqueConstraint UNIQUE(Column2, Column3);
```

If you're using DB2, the code is as follows:

```
CREATE TABLE YetAnotherTable
(
  Column1 int,
  Column2 varchar(20) NOT NULL,
  Column3 varchar(12) NOT NULL
);

ALTER TABLE YetAnotherTable
ADD CONSTRAINT MyUniqueConstraint UNIQUE(Column2, Column3);
```

This constraint is identical to the one created earlier for AnotherTable. Again, you can add more than one constraint to a table, just as you did with the constraint definition when you defined the table.

Use ALTER TABLE to delete the constraint, and simply drop it as shown below, unless you're using MySQL:

```
ALTER TABLE YetAnotherTable
DROP CONSTRAINT MyUniqueConstraint;
```

If you're using MySQL, the code is as follows:

```
ALTER TABLE YetAnotherTable
DROP INDEX MyUniqueConstraint;
```

You can also use the preceding code to drop constraints created at the time of a table's creation, as long as the constraint has a name.

The table YetAnotherTable can be deleted:

```
DROP TABLE YetAnotherTable;
```

CHECK Constraint

The CHECK constraint enables a condition to check the value being entered into a record. If the condition evaluates to false, the record violates the constraint and isn't entered into the table. For example, allowing a column storing an age to contain a negative value doesn't make sense. After all, how many people do you know who are minus 35 years old? The CHECK condition can be any valid SQL condition, similar to those found in a WHERE clause, although SQL can check only the table into which you insert a record. Note that although MS Access supports the CHECK constraint, its implementation is outside the scope of this book, and the code examples can't be executed from the main MS Access query designer.

You can add a CHECK constraint either at the time of a table's creation or when you alter a table. The following Try It Out shows you how to use the CHECK constraint.

Try It Out   Adding a CHECK Constraint

1. Using the following SQL, add a CHECK clause to the Age column:

```
CREATE TABLE NamesAges
(
  Name varchar(50),
  Age int CHECK (Age >= 0)
);
```

2. Execute the table creation SQL from Step 1, and then execute the following INSERT INTO statements:

```
INSERT INTO NamesAges (Name, Age)
VALUES ('Jim', 30);

INSERT INTO NamesAges (Name)
VALUES ('Jane');

INSERT INTO NamesAges (Name, Age)
VALUES ('Will', -22);
```

How It Works

Whenever you add a record to the table, the condition on the Age column must evaluate to true or unknown for the database to accept the record. If Age is 22, the condition is true and the database inserts the record. If you try to insert -22, the record violates the CHECK clause and is not inserted. If you insert no value, the clause evaluates to unknown and is valid.

The first INSERT INTO statement works because the CHECK condition evaluates to true. Indeed, 30 is greater than or equal to zero.

The second INSERT INTO is successful because the CHECK condition evaluates to unknown, or NULL, because NULL >= 0 is unknown.

The final INSERT INTO fails because the CHECK condition evaluates to false: -22 >=0 is false because Age values can't be negative numbers.

Given that NULL data types are always considered valid, you can prevent them by adding a NOT NULL constraint. Drop the NamesAges table:

```
DROP TABLE NamesAges;
```

Now that you're through with the Try It Out, consider the following table definition:

```
CREATE TABLE NamesAges
(
  Name varchar(50),
  Age int NOT NULL CHECK (Age >= 0)
);
```

The NOT NULL constraint prevents this INSERT INTO statement from being considered valid:

```
INSERT INTO NamesAges (Name)
VALUES ('Jane');
```

The statement is considered invalid because only the Name column is having data inserted into it; the Age column is left off, so NULL is inserted, causing an error because it conflicts with the NOT NULL constraint. Drop the table:

```
DROP TABLE NamesAges;
```

A problem with adding a CHECK clause to an individual column definition is that the condition can check only that column. For example, the CHECK clause added to AvgMonthlyWage below is invalid and causes the DBMS to throw an error because it contains the column HourlyRate in the condition:

```
CREATE TABLE Employee
(
  EmployeeName varchar(50),
  AvgMonthlyWage decimal(12,2) CHECK (AvgMonthlyWage > HourlyRate),
  HourlyRate decimal(12,2)
);
```

If you want your CHECK condition clause (the clause defined following the CHECK statement) to include multiple columns from the table, you need to define it at the end of the column definitions. Rewrite the preceding SQL like this:

```
CREATE TABLE Employee
(
  EmployeeName varchar(50),
  AvgMonthlyWage decimal(12,2),
  HourlyRate decimal(12,2),
  CONSTRAINT HourlyLess CHECK (AvgMonthlyWage > HourlyRate)
);
```

This SQL creates a table constraint called HourlyLess, which contains a condition that checks that AvgMonthlyWage is greater than HourlyRate.

You can see that adding a CHECK constraint is nearly identical to adding a UNIQUE constraint. Another similarity is the way in which you add a CHECK constraint after you create a table. As with the UNIQUE constraint, you use the ALTER TABLE statement along with ADD CONSTRAINT, the constraint's name, the type of constraint, and in this case, the CHECK constraint's condition.

The following code adds an HourlyLess constraint to the Employee table, though its name conflicts with the constraint of the same name defined when the table was created:

```
ALTER TABLE Employee
ADD CONSTRAINT HourlyLess CHECK (AvgMonthlyWage > HourlyRate);
```

Obviously, if the table included a constraint called HourlyLess, which it does in this case, the DBMS will throw an error. To delete an existing constraint, simply use the DROP statement as shown below. Unfortunately, this won't work on MySQL:

```
ALTER TABLE Employee
DROP CONSTRAINT HourlyLess;
```

With the old constraint gone, you can now run the ALTER TABLE code and add the constraint with the name HourlyLess. You can now drop the Employee table:

```
DROP TABLE Employee;
```

The constraint covered in the next section is the very important PRIMARY KEY constraint.

Primary Key and PRIMARY KEY Constraint

Of all the constraints, PRIMARY KEY is the most important and most commonly used. In fact, every table should have a primary key because first normal form requires it. A primary key provides a link between tables. For example, MemberId is the primary key in the Film Club database's MemberDetails table and is linked to the FavCategory and Attendance tables.

In order for the relationship to work, the primary key must uniquely identify a record, which means that you can include only unique values and no NULLs. In fact, the PRIMARY KEY constraint is essentially a combination of the UNIQUE and NOT NULL constraints.

Whereas you can have more than one UNIQUE or CHECK constraint on a table, only one PRIMARY KEY constraint per table is allowed.

Given its importance, you should decide on a primary key at the database design state, before you create any tables in the database. Creating the PRIMARY KEY constraint is usually easiest when writing the table creation SQL. The format is very similar to the UNIQUE and CHECK constraints. You can specify the primary key as either a single column or more than one column. To specify a single column, simply insert PRIMARY KEY after its definition, like this:

```
CREATE TABLE HolidayBookings
(
  CustomerId int PRIMARY KEY,
  BookingId int,
  Destination varchar(50)
);
```

Note that with IBM DB2, the primary key column must also be defined as NOT NULL. The following code works on the other database systems but isn't strictly necessary:

```
CREATE TABLE HolidayBookings
(
  CustomerId int NOT NULL PRIMARY KEY,
  BookingId int,
  Destination varchar(50)
);
```

In the preceding code, CustomerId is the primary key. Alternatively, more than one column can act as the primary key, in which case you need to add the constraint at the end of the table, after the column definitions.

The following Try It Out shows you how to use the PRIMARY KEY constraint.

Try It Out   Establishing a PRIMARY KEY Constraint

1.   Execute the following SQL to create the MoreHolidayBookings table:

```
CREATE TABLE MoreHolidayBookings
(
  CustomerId int NOT NULL,
  BookingId int NOT NULL,
  Destination varchar(50),
  CONSTRAINT booking_pk PRIMARY KEY (CustomerId, BookingId)
);
```

2.   Now try executing the following SQL to insert data into the MoreHolidayBookings table:

```
INSERT INTO MoreHolidayBookings (CustomerId, BookingId, Destination)
VALUES (1,1,'Hawaii');

INSERT INTO MoreHolidayBookings (CustomerId, BookingId, Destination)
VALUES (1,2,'Canada');

INSERT INTO MoreHolidayBookings (CustomerId, BookingId, Destination)
VALUES (2,2,'England');

INSERT INTO MoreHolidayBookings (CustomerId, BookingId, Destination)
VALUES (1,1,'New Zealand');

INSERT INTO MoreHolidayBookings (CustomerId, Destination)
VALUES (3,'Mexico');
```

How It Works

In Step 1, the booking_pk constraint is a PRIMARY KEY constraint, and the columns CustomerId and BookingId are the primary key columns. Remember that the PRIMARY KEY constraint is a combination of the UNIQUE and NOT NULL constraints, which means that the CustomerId and BookingId columns cannot contain NULL values. They must also be unique in combination. Thus, you can have the same value a number of times in CustomerId as long as BookingId is different each time, and vice versa. Note that the NOT NULL constraint following the primary key columns is strictly necessary only with DB2, but the code works fine on the other database systems even though NOT NULL isn't needed.

The first three INSERT INTO statements work fine, but the fourth one doesn't because it tries to insert the same combination of values for CustomerId and BookingId, which the first INSERT INTO statement already inserted. Because the primary key constraint doesn't allow duplicates, you receive an error message.

The final INSERT INTO also fails because it doesn't assign a value for BookingId when inserting a new record, so BookingId is NULL. Likewise, you receive an error message because the primary key constraint does not allow NULL values.

Drop the MoreHolidayBookings table:

```
DROP TABLE MoreHolidayBookings;
```

Returning to the regular discussion, although good practice is to create the primary key upon table creation, it's also possible to add a primary key to an existing table. The method of doing so is very similar to adding a UNIQUE constraint: you use the ALTER TABLE statement. However, there is one proviso: The columns forming part of the primary key must already contain the NOT NULL constraint. If you try to add a primary key to a column that allows NULLs, you receive an error message.

With that in mind, if theCustomerId and BookingId columns of the MoreHolidayBookings table already defined the NOT NULL constraint when the table was created:

```
CREATE TABLE MoreHolidayBookings
(
  CustomerId int NOT NULL,
  BookingId int NOT NULL,
  Destination varchar(50)
);
```

Then with the NOT NULL constraint already defined, you can add the PRIMARY KEY constraint:

```
ALTER TABLE MoreHolidayBookings
ADD CONSTRAINT more_holiday_pk PRIMARY KEY (CustomerId, BookingId);
```

The constraint is called more_holiday_pk and it defines CustomerId and BookingId as the primary key columns. If the NOT NULL constraint weren't defined prior to altering the table, you would receive an error.

If you have an existing table without a column or columns to which you want to add a primary key, but that weren't created with the NOT NULL constraint, then you must add the NOT NULL constraint, as shown earlier in the chapter. As an alternative to adding the NOT NULL constraint, simply save the data in a temporary table and then re-create the table with a PRIMARY KEY constraint. Your RDBMS may have other ways around the problem that are specific to that system.

Finally, deleting a PRIMARY KEY constraint is the same as deleting the UNIQUE and CHECK constraints. Except on MySQL, use an ALTER TABLE statement coupled with a DROP statement:

```
ALTER TABLE MoreHolidayBookings
DROP CONSTRAINT more_holiday_pk;
```

On MySQL, the code is as follows:

```
ALTER TABLE MoreHolidayBookings
DROP PRIMARY KEY;
```

The MoreHolidayBookings table is no longer needed, so you should drop it:

```
DROP TABLE MoreHolidayBookings;
```

Foreign Key

Foreign keys are columns that refer to primary keys in another table. Primary and foreign keys create relations between data in different tables. Chapter 1 very briefly covered foreign keys, and the Film Club database was designed with a number of tables with primary and foreign keys. When you designed the Film Club database, you didn't set up any PRIMARY KEY constraints, but they link tables nevertheless. For example, the MemberDetails table contains all the personal data about a member, their name, address, and so on. It also has a primary key column, MemberId. Other tables, such as Attendance and FavCategory, also contain data about members, but rather than repeat personal details about the member, you created a foreign key, MemberId, that links a record in one table to a record containing a member's personal details in the MemberDetails table. Figure 4-1 illustrates this relationship.

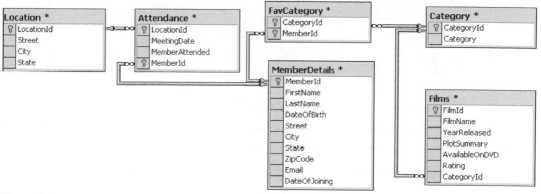

Figure 4-1

Each of the lines linking the tables represents a relationship between the tables. For example, Attendance doesn't store all the location details; it simply stores the primary key value from the Location table for that particular location. LocationId in Attendance is therefore a foreign key, and LocationId in the Location table contains the primary key to which the foreign key refers.

When discussing the primary key, you learned how important it is for it not to contain NULLs and for it to contain unique values; otherwise you lose the relationship, and queries return invalid data. The PRIMARY KEY constraint helps ensure that duplicate primary key values never occur and prevents NULLs being entered. But so far there's nothing stopping someone from entering a value in a foreign key table that doesn't have a matching value in the primary key table. For example, in the Film Club database, the Location table's primary key column is LocationId. Currently the Location table holds only three records, with the values in the records' primary key column having the values 1, 2, and 3:

LocationId	Street	City	State
1	Main Street	Orange Town	New State
2	Winding Road	Windy Village	Golden State
3	Tiny Terrace	Big City	Mega State

If you want to return a results set detailing meeting dates, the MemberId of each member who attended, and the street, city, and state of the meeting, you need to get the information from the MemberDetails and Location tables. To ensure that the data is linked — that the member who attended and the location where they attended are correctly matched in each row — you need to join the Location and Attendance tables with an INNER JOIN:

```
SELECT MemberId, MeetingDate, Street, City, State
FROM Location INNER JOIN Attendance
ON Attendance.LocationId = Location.LocationId;
```

Doing so returns the results in the following table:

MemberId	MeetingDate	Street	City	State
1	2004-01-01	Winding Road	Windy Village	Golden State
4	2004-01-01	Winding Road	Windy Village	Golden State
5	2004-01-01	Winding Road	Windy Village	Golden State
6	2004-01-01	Winding Road	Windy Village	Golden State
1	2004-03-01	Main Street	Orange Town	New State
4	2004-03-01	Main Street	Orange Town	New State
5	2004-03-01	Main Street	Orange Town	New State
6	2004-03-01	Main Street	Orange Town	New State

The following SQL inserts a record into the Attendance table where the LocationId has no matching LocationId in the Location table:

```
INSERT INTO Attendance (LocationId, MeetingDate, MemberAttended, MemberId)
VALUES (99,'2005-12-01','Y',3);
```

Running the preceding query again produces the results in the following table:

MemberId	MeetingDate	Street	City	State
1	2004-01-01	Winding Road	Windy Village	Golden State
4	2004-01-01	Winding Road	Windy Village	Golden State
5	2004-01-01	Winding Road	Windy Village	Golden State
6	2004-01-01	Winding Road	Windy Village	Golden State
1	2004-03-01	Main Street	Orange Town	New State

MemberId	MeetingDate	Street	City	State
4	2004-03-01	Main Street	Orange Town	New State
5	2004-03-01	Main Street	Orange Town	New State
6	2004-03-01	Main Street	Orange Town	New State

Notice the difference? That's right, there is no difference! The new attendance record doesn't show up in the results because the added data is invalid, and the relationship between the Location and Attendance tables has been broken for that record. How can you prevent the relationship between tables from breaking? SQL has the FOREIGN KEY constraint for this very purpose. It allows you to specify when a column in a table is a foreign key from another table — when a column in one table is really just a way of referencing rows in another table. For example, you can specify that LocationId in the Attendance table is a foreign key and that it's dependent on the primary key value existing in the Location table's LocationId column.

The basic syntax to create a foreign key is shown in the following code:

```
ALTER TABLE name_of_table to add foreign_key
ADD CONSTRAINT name of_foreign_key
FOREIGN KEY (name_of_column_that_is_foreign_key_column)
REFERENCES name_of_table_that_is_referenced(name_of_column_being_referenced)
```

The following Try It Out walks you through the process of creating a FOREIGN KEY constraint. Unfortunately, the code won't work on IBM's DB2, as before a primary key constraint can be added, the column must have the NOT NULL constraint. This can be added in DB2 only at the time the table is created, not after it. Although a CHECK clause can be added to stop NULLs, it's not the same as a NOT NULL constraint. The only option is to delete a table and re-create it, this time with the appropriate columns with a NOT NULL constraint. However, deleting and re-creating the table will result in the loss of the data in the dropped table, unless you transfer it to another table, something not covered until Chapter 5. The code is included here, but it is more fully explained in the next chapter.

Try It Out   Creating a FOREIGN KEY Constraint

1. First, delete the invalid record in the Attendance table:

```
DELETE FROM Attendance
WHERE LocationId = 99;
```

2. Add the NOT NULL constraint:

```
ALTER TABLE Location
ALTER COLUMN LocationId int NOT NULL;
```

If you're using Oracle or MySQL, the SQL code is as follows:

```
ALTER TABLE Location
MODIFY LocationId  int NOT NULL;
```

If you're using IBM DB2, you need to use the following code:

```
CREATE TABLE TempLocation
(
    LocationId integer NOT NULL,
    Street varchar(100),
    City varchar(75),
    State varchar(75)
);

INSERT INTO TempLocation SELECT * FROM Location;

DROP TABLE Location;

CREATE TABLE Location
(
    LocationId integer NOT NULL,
    Street varchar(100),
    City varchar(75),
    State varchar(75)
);

INSERT INTO Location SELECT * FROM TempLocation;
DROP TABLE TempLocation;
```

You must add a NOT NULL constraint before any attempt to add a primary key, lest you receive an error message.

3. Next, add the primary key:

```
ALTER TABLE Location
ADD CONSTRAINT locationid_pk PRIMARY KEY (LocationId);
```

4. Finally, add the FOREIGN KEY constraint:

```
ALTER TABLE Attendance
ADD CONSTRAINT locationid_fk
FOREIGN KEY (LocationId)
REFERENCES Location(LocationId);
```

How It Works

In the first step, you simply deleted the erroneous record in the Attendance table, the record with a LocationId of 99.

Next, you specified which table you want to alter, much as with the other constraints. Before you can create a FOREIGN KEY constraint, however, you need to ensure that the column you specify as the primary key is actually subject to a PRIMARY KEY constraint. However, you can add a PRIMARY KEY constraint to only a column that has a NOT NULL constraint, and the LocationId column has no such constraint. Therefore, the second step added the ADD CONSTRAINT followed by the constraint name and set the primary key. The IBM DB2 syntax is particularly convoluted. It creates a temporary table identical in structure to the Location table. Then data from the existing Location table is copied to this temporary table. After that, the Location table is dropped and then re-created, but with a NOT NULL constraint on the LocationId column, the one to which you want to add a primary key. Finally, the temporary table is dropped.

The third step had you create the primary key on the Location table's LocationId column.

The third line of the fourth step stated the type of constraint, FOREIGN KEY, and the brackets following contain all the columns that in combination make up the foreign key. On the final line of code, the REFERENCES statement established which table the foreign key references. Following that is the name of the table that holds the primary key and, in brackets, a list of the primary key columns that the foreign key references.

In the preceding example, the primary key, and therefore the matching foreign key, consists of just one column; however, they can consist of more than one column. For example, three columns form the primary and foreign keys in the following SQL:

```
ALTER TABLE SomeTable
ADD CONSTRAINT SomeTable_fk1
FOREIGN KEY (EmployeeName, EmployeeId, MemberShipId)
REFERENCES SomePrimaryKeyTable(EmployeeName, EmployeeId, MemberShipId)
```

Now that the FOREIGN KEY constraint is in place, try the INSERT INTO statement from earlier:

```
INSERT INTO Attendance (LocationId, MeetingDate, MemberAttended, MemberId)
VALUES (99,'2005-12-01','Y',3);
```

It isn't entered into the database, and you receive an error message.

So far, you've learned how to add a FOREIGN KEY constraint to an existing table, but it can be defined at the time the table is created, in a similar manner to the CHECK and UNIQUE constraints. As demonstrated in the following code, you add the constraint definition at the end of the table definition, just after the column definitions:

```
CREATE TABLE Attendance
(
    LocationId integer,
    MeetingDate date,
    MemberAttended char(1),
    MemberId integer,
    CONSTRAINT SomeTable_fk1
    FOREIGN KEY (LocationId)
    REFERENCES Location(LocationId)
);
```

Those are all the constraints covered in this book. The next section examines how to speed up results using an index.

Speeding Up Results with Indexes

Indexes are special lookup tables that the database search engine can use to speed up data retrieval. They also organize the way in which the database stores data. A good real-world example is a book, much like this one, that has an index at the back that helps you find where the important information is. It saves a lot of flicking through the pages randomly trying to find the topic you want. Given that an index helps speed up SELECT queries and WHERE clauses, why not always have one? First of all, while it speeds up data retrieval, it slows down data input, with UPDATE and INSERT statements, for example. Additionally, it adds to a database's size, albeit not massively, though it is a consideration. Using indexes is good practice, but it is best done judiciously — for example, using them to help your most common queries.

Creating an index involves the CREATE INDEX statement, which allows you to name the index, to specify the table and which column or columns to index, and to indicate whether the index is in ascending or descending order. Indexes can also be unique, similar to the UNIQUE constraint, in that the index prevents duplicate entries in the column or combination of columns on which there's an index. The basic format of the statement is as follows:

```
CREATE INDEX <index_name>
ON <table_name> (<column_names>)
```

The following code adds an index called member_name_index on the MemberDetails table, and it indexes the FirstName and LastName columns:

```
CREATE INDEX member_name_index
ON MemberDetails (FirstName, LastName);
```

If you execute the following SELECT statement, you notice something interesting:

```
SELECT FirstName, LastName
FROM MemberDetails;
```

The results, shown in the following table, appear in ascending order, by first name and then last name, even though you did not add an ORDER BY clause:

FirstName	LastName
Catherine	Hawthorn
Doris	Night
Jack	Johnson
Jamie	Hills
Jenny	Jones
John	Jackson
John	Jones
Katie	Smith
Seymour	Botts
Steve	Gee
Stuart	Dales
Susie	Simons
William	Doors

The results are ordered because, by default, the index orders results in ascending order. The default order is based on the order in which you list the columns in the index definition's SELECT statement. To delete the index, you need to use the DROP INDEX statement, specifying the index name in the statement. Note that in some RDBMSs, such as MS SQL Server, you need to specify the table name in addition to the index name. So, the SQL to drop the index just created in MS SQL Server is as follows:

```
DROP INDEX MemberDetails.member_name_indx;
```

In IBM DB2 and Oracle, the DROP INDEX statement simply requires the index name without the table name prefixed:

```
DROP INDEX member_name_indx;
```

In MySQL, the code to drop the index is as follows:

```
ALTER TABLE MemberDetails
DROP INDEX member_name_indx;
```

MS Access has yet another way of dropping the index:

```
DROP INDEX member_name_indx ON MemberDetails;
```

After dropping the index, run the same SELECT statement:

```
SELECT FirstName, LastName
FROM MemberDetails;
```

You find that the results are no longer necessarily in order:

FirstName	LastName
Katie	Smith
Susie	Simons
John	Jackson
Steve	Gee
John	Jones
Jenny	Jones
Jack	Johnson
Seymour	Botts
Jamie	Hills
Stuart	Dales
William	Doors
Doris	Night
Catherine	Hawthorn

The results you get may be in a slightly different order, depending on your DBMS. When results are not ordered, there's no real guarantee of what the order might be.

You can set two other options when creating an index. The first, the UNIQUE option, prevents duplicate values from being entered and works very much like the UNIQUE constraint. The second option determines the column order. Recall that the default results order is ascending, but you can also order results in descending order.

The following SQL creates a unique index that orders results by last name in descending order and then by first name. Using the DESC keyword, execute the following SQL:

```
CREATE UNIQUE INDEX member_name_indx
ON MemberDetails (LastName DESC, FirstName);
```

After executing the preceding code, execute this query:

```
SELECT LastName, FirstName
FROM MemberDetails;
```

Query results are provided in the following table:

LastName	FirstName
Botts	Seymour
Dales	Stuart
Doors	William
Gee	Steve
Hawthorn	Catherine
Hills	Jamie
Jackson	John
Johnson	Jack
Jones	Jenny
Jones	John
Night	Doris
Simons	Susie
Smith	Katie

You can see that LastName now goes in order from the lowest to the highest — from *a* to *z* in the alphabet.

The index is no longer needed, so delete it with the following code. If using MS SQL Server, write the following DROP INDEX statement:

```
DROP INDEX MemberDetails.member_name_indx;
```

In IBM DB2 and Oracle, the DROP INDEX statement simply requires the index name without the table name prefixed:

```
DROP INDEX member_name_indx;
```

In MySQL, the code to drop the index is as follows:

```
ALTER TABLE MemberDetails
DROP INDEX member_name_indx;
```

MS Access has yet another way of dropping the index:

```
DROP INDEX member_name_indx ON MemberDetails;
```

You've learned a lot of useful stuff for improving the design and efficiency of your databases. The next section takes that knowledge and applies it to the Film Club database.

Improving the Design of the Film Club Database

This section revisits the Film Club database, taking into account the topics discussed in this chapter: normalization, ensuring data integrity with constraints, and using indexes to speed up data retrieval.

The discussion begins with an examination of the database structure and then turns to constraints and indexes.

Reexamining the Film Club Database Structure

Generally speaking, the database is in third normal form, with the exception of the MemberDetails table. The Street, City, and State columns are all transitively dependent on the ZipCode column. Therefore, the MemberDetails table is still in second normal form. The question now, however, is one of common sense, because the amount of duplication reduced by going to third normal form is going to be quite small. It's unlikely that many people from the same street would join the club, and with a small database, storage size is not usually an issue. In addition, changing the table to comply with third normal form involves creating another table, and as a result any SELECT queries require another JOIN statement, which impinges on database efficiency. Therefore, in this instance, the database is fine as it is, and moving the MemberDetails table to third normal form is probably unnecessary and only adds complexity without really saving any storage space.

However, one area of the database design needs altering: the Attendance table. Consider the following query:

```
SELECT * FROM Attendance;
```

The results of the query are shown in the following table:

MeetingDate	MemberAttended	MemberId	LocationId
2004-01-01	Y	1	2
2004-01-01	N	4	2
2004-01-01	Y	5	2
2004-01-01	Y	6	2
2004-03-01	Y	1	1
2004-03-01	Y	4	1
2004-03-01	N	5	1
2004-03-01	N	6	1

For each meeting, the Attendance table stores each film club member and their attendance status. Rather than store a record regardless of whether a member attended or not, you can save space by storing a record only if a member actually attends a meeting. Getting a list of members who attended a meeting is simple enough. The SQL to find out who didn't attend, however, is a little more involved and is covered in greater detail in Chapter 7.

To make the changes, delete all the records where the member didn't attend, that is, where MemberAttended equals N. Then delete the MemberAttended column.

Use this SQL to delete all the records where MemberAttended equals N:

```
DELETE FROM Attendance
WHERE MemberAttended = 'N';
```

Once you delete those records, you can drop the whole column:

```
ALTER TABLE Attendance
DROP COLUMN MemberAttended;
```

Dropping the column deletes all the data stored in that column for all rows. Unfortunately, IBM's DB2 doesn't support dropping a column. The only option, as you saw earlier, is to delete the whole table and re-create it from scratch, having first saved the data:

```
CREATE TABLE TempAttendance
(
    MeetingDate date,
    LocationId integer,
    MemberId integer
);

INSERT INTO TempAttendance (MeetingDate, LocationId, MemberId)
SELECT MeetingDate, LocationId, MemberId FROM Attendance
```

```
    WHERE MemberAttended = 'Y';

    DROP TABLE Attendance;

    CREATE TABLE Attendance
    (
        MeetingDate date NOT NULL,
        LocationId integer NOT NULL,
        MemberId integer NOT NULL
    );

    INSERT INTO Attendance (MeetingDate, LocationId, MemberId)
    SELECT MeetingDate, LocationId, MemberId FROM Attendance;
    DROP TABLE TempAttendance;
```

As in the earlier example, the data from the table that you need to change is saved in a temporary table. The MemberAttended column is being deleted, so there's no need to save data from that. The original table is deleted and then re-created, but without the MemberAttended column. The data is then copied back from the TempAttendance table, which is then dropped.

The changes made to the Attendance table have an additional consequence as far as SELECT queries go. Displaying all members who attended is now easier. You don't need to include a WHERE clause specifying that MemberAttended equals Y; a basic SELECT * FROM Attendance statement now suffices. However, finding out lists of members who didn't attend meetings is harder and involves subqueries, a topic covered in Chapter 7.

Often, however, the downside to more efficient data storage is more complex SQL queries, covered in more detail in Chapter 7. The next section deals with ensuring data validation in your more efficient database.

Improving Data Validation and Efficiency

This section employs the various constraints discussed earlier to help reduce the risk of data corruption. A good first step is to enforce the primary keys in each table by adding a PRIMARY KEY constraint.

The Location table already has a PRIMARY KEY constraint, added when you learned about the FOREIGN KEY constraint. Begin by adding a PRIMARY KEY constraint to the MemberDetails table. First, however, you need to add a NOT NULL constraint because the PRIMARY KEY constraint can't be added to a column that allows NULLs:

```
    ALTER TABLE MemberDetails
    ALTER COLUMN MemberId int NOT NULL;
```

If using Oracle or MySQL, you need to change the code to the following:

```
    ALTER TABLE MemberDetails
    MODIFY MemberId int NOT NULL;
```

Remember, IBM DB2 doesn't support adding NOT NULL after the table has been created, so you have to go the long-winded route of copying the data to a temporary table, dropping the MemberDetails table, and then re-creating it with the NOT NULL constraint, as shown in the following code:

```
CREATE TABLE TempMemberDetails
(
    MemberId integer,
    FirstName vargraphic(50),
    LastName vargraphic(50),
    DateOfBirth date,
    Street varchar(100),
    City varchar(75),
    State varchar(75),
    ZipCode varchar(12),
    Email varchar(200),
    DateOfJoining date

);

INSERT INTO TempMemberDetails
SELECT * FROM MemberDetails;

DROP TABLE MemberDetails;

CREATE TABLE MemberDetails
(
    MemberId integer NOT NULL,
    FirstName vargraphic(50),
    LastName vargraphic(50),
    DateOfBirth date,
    Street varchar(100),
    City varchar(75),
    State varchar(75),
    ZipCode varchar(12),
    Email varchar(200),
    DateOfJoining date

);

INSERT INTO MemberDetails
SELECT * FROM TempMemberDetails;

DROP TABLE TempMemberDetails;
```

Having added the NOT NULL constraint, via whichever means your database system requires, now execute the following code, which adds the actual PRIMARY KEY:

```
ALTER TABLE MemberDetails
ADD CONSTRAINT memberdetails_pk PRIMARY KEY (MemberId);
```

Primary keys must be unique and cannot contain NULLs, so if by accident your table contains NULLs or duplicate values for the MemberId column, then you need to edit and correct them before the statement can work.

Next, add a PRIMARY KEY constraint to the Films table. First, you need to add a NOT NULL constraint. Use the following code for MS Access and SQL Server:

```
ALTER TABLE Films
ALTER COLUMN FilmId int NOT NULL;
```

If you're using Oracle or MySQL, use the following statement:

```
ALTER TABLE Films
MODIFY FilmId int NOT NULL;
```

Again, with IBM's DB2, you need to add the NOT NULL constraint by re-creating the whole table:

```
CREATE TABLE TempFilms
(
    FilmId integer,
    FilmName varchar(100),
    YearReleased integer,
    PlotSummary varchar(2000),
    AvailableOnDVD char(1),
    Rating integer,
    CategoryId integer
);

INSERT INTO TempFilms
SELECT * FROM Films;

DROP TABLE Films;

CREATE TABLE Films
(
    FilmId integer NOT NULL,
    FilmName varchar(100),
    YearReleased integer,
    PlotSummary varchar(2000),
    AvailableOnDVD char(1),
    Rating integer,
    CategoryId integer
);

INSERT INTO Films
SELECT * FROM TempFilms;
DROP TABLE TempFilms;
```

Be sure to check all columns for duplicate entries in order to avoid errors in creating the PRIMARY KEY constraint. In this case, the FilmId column contains duplicate values. It's surprisingly easy for invalid data to occur, which makes defining a PRIMARY KEY constraint essential. To rid the FilmId column of duplicates, execute the following three UPDATE statements:

```
UPDATE Films
SET FilmId = 13
WHERE FilmId = 12 AND
FilmName = 'The Good, the Bad, and the Facially Challenged';

UPDATE Films
SET FilmId = 14
WHERE FilmId = 2 AND
FilmName = '15th Late Afternoon';

UPDATE Films
SET FilmId = 15
WHERE FilmId = 2 AND
FilmName = 'Soylent Yellow';
```

Execute the following SQL to create the PRIMARY KEY constraint:

```
ALTER TABLE Films
ADD CONSTRAINT films_pk PRIMARY KEY (FilmId);
```

Next, add a PRIMARY KEY constraint to the Category table. The steps are identical to those described previously. First, add a NOT NULL constraint. If you're using MS Access or SQL Server, the code is as follows:

```
ALTER TABLE Category
ALTER COLUMN CategoryId int NOT NULL;
```

If you're using MySQL or Oracle, use the following statement:

```
ALTER TABLE Category
MODIFY CategoryId int NOT NULL;
```

Once again, with IBM's DB2, you need to re-create the table:

```
CREATE TABLE TempCategory
(
    CategoryId integer,
    Category varchar(100)
);

INSERT INTO TempCategory
SELECT * FROM Category;

DROP TABLE Category;

CREATE TABLE Category
(
    CategoryId integer NOT NULL,
    Category varchar(100)
);
INSERT INTO Category
SELECT * FROM TempCategory;
DROP TABLE TempCategory;
```

Then add the PRIMARY KEY constraint:

```
ALTER TABLE Category
ADD CONSTRAINT category_pk PRIMARY KEY (CategoryId);
```

Just two more tables to go to an efficient database. First, update the FavCategory table. This time, though, the primary key is based on two columns, CategoryId and MemberId, so you need to make sure to add both to the list of columns defining the PRIMARY KEY constraint. First, add the NOT NULL constraint to both columns. In MS Access and SQL Server, the code is as follows:

```
ALTER TABLE FavCategory
ALTER COLUMN CategoryId int NOT NULL;

ALTER TABLE FavCategory
ALTER COLUMN MemberId int NOT NULL;
```

If you're using Oracle or MySQL, the preceding code should read as follows:

```
ALTER TABLE FavCategory
MODIFY CategoryId int NOT NULL;

ALTER TABLE FavCategory
MODIFY MemberId int NOT NULL;
```

In IBM DB2, you should use the following statement:

```
CREATE TABLE TempFavCategory
(
    CategoryId integer,
    MemberId integer
);

INSERT INTO TempFavCategory
SELECT * FROM FavCategory;

DROP TABLE FavCategory;

CREATE TABLE FavCategory
(
    CategoryId integer NOT NULL,
    MemberId integer NOT NULL
);
INSERT INTO FavCategory
SELECT * FROM TempFavCategory;

DROP TABLE TempFavCategory;
```

Now you can add the PRIMARY KEY constraint:

```
ALTER TABLE FavCategory
ADD CONSTRAINT favcategory_pk PRIMARY KEY (CategoryId, MemberId);
```

Finally, you do the same thing for the Attendance table, beginning with the NOT NULL constraint:

```
ALTER TABLE Attendance
ALTER COLUMN LocationId int NOT NULL;

ALTER TABLE Attendance
ALTER COLUMN MemberId int NOT NULL;
```

Again, for Oracle or MySQL, change the code to the following:

```
ALTER TABLE Attendance
MODIFY LocationId int NOT NULL;

ALTER TABLE Attendance
MODIFY MemberId int NOT NULL;
```

Then you add the PRIMARY KEY constraint:

```
ALTER TABLE Attendance
ADD CONSTRAINT attendance_pk PRIMARY KEY (LocationId, MemberId);
```

Your next objective in improving the database is to prevent columns containing NULL values where necessary. Good practice is to add the NOT NULL constraint when creating the table. For example, if the FilmName column contains no value, it makes the whole record rather pointless, as the name is so essential. On the other hand, having a missing rating is not as much of a problem. Begin by adding a NOT NULL constraint to the FilmName column. In MS Access or SQL Server, use the following code:

```
ALTER TABLE Films
ALTER COLUMN FilmName varchar(100) NOT NULL;
```

In Oracle or MySQL, type this statement:

```
ALTER TABLE Films
MODIFY FilmName varchar(100) NOT NULL;
```

Finally, in IBM DB2, use the following SQL:

```
CREATE TABLE TempFilms
(
    FilmId integer NOT NULL,
    FilmName varchar(100),
    YearReleased integer,
    PlotSummary varchar(2000),
    AvailableOnDVD char(1),
    Rating integer,
    CategoryId integer
);

INSERT INTO TempFilms
SELECT * FROM Films;

DROP TABLE Films;

CREATE TABLE Films
```

```
(
    FilmId integer NOT NULL,
    FilmName varchar(100) NOT NULL,
    YearReleased integer,
    PlotSummary varchar(2000),
    AvailableOnDVD char(1),
    Rating integer,
    CategoryId integer
);

INSERT INTO Films
SELECT * FROM TempFilms;
DROP TABLE TempFilms;
```

Next up is the MemberDetails table. Again, the person's first and last names are pretty much essential to track the person, and therefore these columns should not remain incomplete.

Add the NOT NULL constraints in MS SQL Server or Access with this code:

```
ALTER TABLE MemberDetails
ALTER COLUMN FirstName varchar(50) NOT NULL;

ALTER TABLE MemberDetails
ALTER COLUMN LastName varchar(50) NOT NULL;
```

Change the code in Oracle or MySQL to the following:

```
ALTER TABLE MemberDetails
MODIFY FirstName varchar(50) NOT NULL;

ALTER TABLE MemberDetails
MODIFY LastName varchar(50) NOT NULL;
```

In DB2, use the following statement:

```
CREATE TABLE TempMemberDetails
(
    MemberId integer,
    FirstName vargraphic(50),
    LastName vargraphic(50),
    DateOfBirth date,
    Street varchar(100),
    City varchar(75),
    State varchar(75),
    ZipCode varchar(12),
    Email varchar(200),
    DateOfJoining date

);

INSERT INTO TempMemberDetails
```

```
SELECT * FROM MemberDetails;

DROP TABLE MemberDetails;

CREATE TABLE MemberDetails
(
    MemberId integer NOT NULL,
    FirstName vargraphic(50) NOT NULL,
    LastName vargraphic(50) NOT NULL,
    DateOfBirth date,
    Street varchar(100),
    City varchar(75),
    State varchar(75),
    ZipCode varchar(12),
    Email varchar(200),
    DateOfJoining date

);

INSERT INTO MemberDetails
SELECT * FROM TempMemberDetails;
DROP TABLE TempMemberDetails;
```

Once the NOT NULL constraints are in place, you can add the index again:

```
CREATE UNIQUE INDEX member_name_indx
ON MemberDetails (LastName DESC, FirstName);
```

Finally, define the relationships between tables by adding FOREIGN KEY constraints. Figure 4-1 shows the foreign key links, and the following list reiterates them.

❑   The CategoryId column in the Films table is a foreign key linking to the CategoryId column in the Category table.

❑   The CategoryId column in the FavCategory table is a foreign key linking to the CategoryId column in the Category table.

❑   The MemberId column in the FavCategory table is a foreign key linking to the MemberId column in the MemberDetails table.

❑   The LocationId column in the Attendance table is a foreign key linking to the LocationId column in the Location table.

❑   The MemberId column in the Attendance table is a foreign key linking to the MemberId column in the MemberDetails table.

In an earlier Try It Out, you defined the relationship between the Attendance and Location tables. The Location table is the primary table to which the Attendance table links via the LocationId column. The Attendance table also links to the MemberDetails table, so you need to define that relationship as well.

If you've already added the constraint in the earlier Try It Out, then don't execute the code again or you'll receive an error. If you didn't execute the code, then the SQL used in an earlier Try It Out to add the constraint was as follows:

```
ALTER TABLE Attendance
ADD CONSTRAINT attend_loc_fk
FOREIGN KEY (LocationId)
REFERENCES Location(LocationId);
```

The Attendance table is the one being altered; the FOREIGN KEY constraint doesn't affect the Location table. This constraint, for example, is named attend_loc_fk, a mixture of the two tables involved in the relationship, where fk denotes its status as a foreign key. You can name your constraints anything you like; just make sure the name is something that identifies the relationship between tables. Finally, the statement specifies the table and the column or columns being referenced.

The following SQL adds a second FOREIGN KEY constraint to the Attendance table, this time for the relationship between the Attendance and MemberDetails tables:

```
ALTER TABLE Attendance
ADD CONSTRAINT attend_memdet_fk
FOREIGN KEY (MemberId)
REFERENCES MemberDetails(MemberId);
```

The next table that contains a foreign key is the FavCategory table, but defining that relationship is one of the exercise questions at the end of the chapter. That leaves just one more relationship to define: between the Category and Film tables. The Category table is the primary table to which the Films table links. The link is between the CategoryId columns present in both tables. The following code formally defines this relationship:

```
ALTER TABLE Films
ADD CONSTRAINT films_cat_fk
FOREIGN KEY (CategoryId)
REFERENCES Category(CategoryId);
```

That completes the changes to the database. Innumerable ways to improve a database exist, and these depend on how you intend to use the database. Apart from the index on the MemberDetails table's FirstName and LastName fields, you didn't create any new indexes. If in live use you find that some queries take too long to return results, simply review the database structure again and look at changing tables or adding an index to speed things up. Quite a lot of RDBMSs have tools that help monitor performance and tweak settings to ensure the best possible results.

Now that you can design a relatively complex normalized database, complete with constraints and primary and foreign keys, here are some things to keep in mind any time you design or modify a database.

Tips for Designing a Better Database

Keeping the following subjects in mind helps ensure that your database design and updates go smoothly.

❑ **Don't design a database that copes with the norm.** Tempting as it is to design a database that covers most situations, doing so is dangerous. The unexpected happens just when you least expect it, so make sure you design your database to cover all situations that could arise, or at least ensure that it can cope with the unusual situations. Even if a client tells you not to worry about the possibility of two people attempting to reserve the same holiday cottage at the same time, assume that it will happen.

❑ **Choose meaningful names for tables and fields.** Try to use field and table names that help give an idea of what data they store. For example, the MemberDetails table stores members' details, which makes it fairly obvious without further explanation what the table holds. Name tables so that further explanation or looking into the table is unnecessary. The same applies to column names.

❑ **Try to keep names simple.** Maybe this seems to contradict the previous point, but it doesn't: Names should be as descriptive as possible, but they shouldn't be overly long or complex. Long names increase the likelihood of errors.

❑ **Be consistent in your naming and choice of data type.** To prevent confusion, don't call a field ZipCode in one table and PostalCode in another if they refer to the same data. Also make sure that both fields are the same data type and can store the same width of data. If you define one as varchar(12) in one table and varchar(8) in another, you risk truncation if you ever insert from one table into another.

❑ **Analyze your data needs on paper first.** It's very tempting when asked to create a database to rush off and start designing on the fly, as it were. However, take time out first to sit down with pen and paper and consider what data needs to be stored and, most importantly, what answers the database is expected to supply. If the person needing the database already operates some other system (for example, a paper-based storage system), take a look at that and use it as your starting point for the data input.

❑ **Pick your primary key carefully.** Choose a field that is unlikely to change and preferably one that is a whole-number-based field. The primary key must always be unique. If no field is obvious, then create your own whole-number field for the purpose of creating a unique primary key.

❑ **Create an index.** Indexes help speed up searches, so adding them to fields that are regularly used in searches or joins is worthwhile. Indexes are especially worthwhile where you have lots of different values — for example, the ZipCode field in the MemberDetails table. Including an index is not a good idea, however, if you have only a few values, such as the MemberAttended column in the Attendance table. Indexes also slow down data entry, something particularly important to note if the column is likely to have lots of inserts or updates.

❑ **Add a multicolumn index.** Multicolumn indexes come in particularly handy in fields where users often search more than one column. For example, if you often search for City and State together, add an index based on both columns.

❑ **Avoid using reserved words as table or field names.** Reserved words are words used by the SQL language and are therefore reserved for its use only. For example, words such as *select*, *join*, and *inner* are exclusive to SQL. Although you can sometimes use reserved words by putting square brackets around them, avoiding them altogether is easier.

❑ **Consider storage space requirements.** When selecting a field's data type, allow for the maximum storage space likely to be required, and then add a little bit! If you think the greatest number of characters to be stored is probably 8, make your definition 10, or varchar(10). Doing so adds a little bit of a safety net. The same goes with numbers.

Summary

This chapter covered all facets of improving your database designing skills. It looked at normalization and the ways in which it provides steps to follow to minimize redundant data storage, as well as the following topics:

❑ You learned the importance of ensuring that data in a database remains valid — for example, ensuring that there are no duplicated values in primary key columns. The mechanism that disallows duplicate data is the constraint, which includes NOT NULL, UNIQUE, CHECK, PRIMARY KEY, and FOREIGN KEY.

❑ You learned how to speed up query results by using indexes.

❑ Using the chapter's topics, you improved the Film Club database's design, making it leaner, more efficient, and less likely to fall afoul of invalid data.

The next chapter examines how to manipulate data returned by a query and covers such subjects as arithmetic in SQL.

Exercises

1. Your friend runs a bookstore and uses a simple database to store details of books, authors, and booksellers. She thinks the database might need a bit of a tune-up. Figure 4-2 shows its current structure, which consists of just one table containing two columns: Column Name and Data Type. Using what you learned about normalization, see if you can improve the current structure.

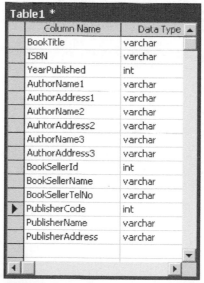

Table1 *	
Column Name	Data Type
BookTitle	varchar
ISBN	varchar
YearPublished	int
AuthorName1	varchar
AuthorAddress1	varchar
AuthorName2	varchar
AuhtorAddress2	varchar
AuthorName3	varchar
AuthorAddress3	varchar
BookSellerId	int
BookSellerName	varchar
BookSellerTelNo	varchar
PublisherCode	int
PublisherName	varchar
PublisherAddress	varchar

Figure 4-2

2. When improving the Film Club database, you added various constraints as well as primary and foreign keys. You didn't, however, add a FOREIGN KEY constraint to the FavCategory table. Create and execute the SQL required to enforce all its relationships with the other tables.

Manipulating Data

In Chapter 3, you looked simply at getting raw data from the database using SQL queries. This chapter, however, examines how to use, alter, and manipulate data using SQL. It starts off with a look at math in SQL, though don't worry if math isn't your favorite subject, as SQL math is fairly basic! The chapter then turns to the manipulation of character data and takes you through a whole host of functions that cover everything from reversing the order of characters in a string to matching columns based on words that sound alike. After that, coverage dives into another look at NULL, in particular how it can alter results in unexpected ways and how to deal with those altered results. Finally, this chapter finishes with a look at copying data from one table to another using INSERT INTO and SELECT statements.

Understanding SQL Arithmetic

The available math functions in SQL are fairly limited, which reflects SQL's use as a tool for pulling out the raw data to answer questions. Any actual processing of the answers is really something left to high-level programming languages in middleware or front-end applications. For example, a Web server might connect to a database to pull back a customer's name and credit card details, but you wouldn't expect the database to process the card details.

You start by looking at the four basic math functions supported by all flavors of SQL, and then you look at some more sophisticated math functions, which, although not part of the SQL standards, are commonly available on most database systems.

Basic Math Operators

It's no great surprise to learn that the four basic math operators are multiplication, division, subtraction, and addition, which are listed in the following table, along with the operators SQL uses to represent them:

Function	Operator
Multiply	*
Divide	/
Add	+
Subtract	-

What's not obvious from this list is the order of precedence of the operators. If you remember back to Chapter 3, you'll recall the discussion of the order of precedence of logical operators and that some operators are evaluated first.

You can see the effects of operator precedence in the following SQL:

```
SELECT MemberId, MemberId + 2 * 3
FROM MemberDetails
WHERE MemberId < 10;
```

Running this query gives the following results:

MemberId	MemberId + 2 * 3
1	7
4	10
5	11
6	12
7	13
8	14
9	15

Rather than adding the MemberId to the number 2 and multiplying the sum by 3, the multiplication operator has higher precedence, so 2 is multiplied by 3 and the result of this, 6, is then added to the value in MemberId. This is very similar to the order of operations in algebra, where multiplication and division take precedence over addition and subtraction when they appear in the same equation. So if you want MemberId + 2 to be evaluated first and then multiplied by 3, you need to raise the order of precedence of that part by using brackets:

```
SELECT MemberId, ( MemberId + 2 ) * 3
FROM MemberDetails
WHERE MemberId < 10;
```

The results of this query are as follows:

MemberId	(MemberId + 2) * 3
1	9
4	18
5	21
6	24
7	27
8	30
9	33

As you can see, this time the operations inside the brackets are evaluated first, so for the first row in the preceding table, the equation reads as follows:

(MemberId + 2) = (1 + 2) = 3

Then the results of the operations inside the brackets are multiplied by 3, as evidenced in the following equation:

(1 + 2) * 3 = (3) * 3 = 9

So far you've used only whole numbers, and nothing with a decimal point. Fractional numbers present the potential problem of rounding errors. These occur when the number of digits after the decimal point exceeds either the limitations of a field's storage type or simply the limitations of the database itself.

Before dealing with fractional numbers, however, you need to have a basic understanding of SQL's four basic math functions.

Common Math Functions

The SQL standard (and almost every SQL implementation) contains four basic math functions. However, a number of other math functions exist, which, while not in the ANSI SQL standard, are found in enough database implementations that it's worth listing them here, although you have to find out for yourself which functions your database system supports. While the basic math functions are not earth-shattering in their extent, you should remember that SQL and databases are suppliers of raw data and are not intended to do significant data processing.

The ABS() Function

The ABS() function returns the *absolute value* of a number—a number without any positive or negative sign. Basically, it makes negative numbers positive but leaves positive numbers as they are. The function's basic format is shown below, where x is the expression to be converted to its absolute value:

```
ABS(x)
```

Consider the following SQL query:

```
SELECT MemberId, MemberId - 10, ABS(MemberId - 10)
FROM MemberDetails;
```

Executing the query provides the results shown in the following table:

MemberId	MemberId - 10	ABS(MemberId - 10)
1	-9	9
4	-6	6
5	-5	5
6	-4	4
7	-3	3
8	-2	2
9	-1	1
10	0	0
11	1	1
12	2	2
13	3	3
14	4	4
15	5	5

Look at the first row in the preceding table (remember that the order of your results may well be different). The way the equation is worked out for the second column is as follows: `MemberId - 10 = 1 - 10 = -0`.

Results for the third column are worked out as shown here: `ABS(MemberId - 10) = ABS(1 - 10) = ABS(-9) = 9`.

In the third column, the negative result has its sign removed, and therefore `-9` becomes simply `9`.

The POWER() Function

The `POWER()` function is an exponential function that raises a number by the power of a second number. For example, it could be used to find the square of a number—a number multiplied by itself. The function takes two parameters. The first is the expression to be raised to a power, and the second is the power to which it is raised. The basic syntax is as follows:

```
POWER(expression, power_raise_to)
```

You can raise a number to any power, from 1 to whatever the database system can handle; some huge numbers, however, will be too large for the database system to handle. For example, if you want to know what the results are when the MemberId is squared (raised to the power of 2), cubed (raised to the power of 3), and raised to the power of 7, you'd write the following SQL

```
SELECT MemberId, POWER(MemberId,2), POWER(MemberId, 3) , POWER(MemberId, 7)
FROM MemberDetails
ORDER BY MemberId;
```

Executing the statement gives the results in the following table:

MemberId	POWER(MemberId,2)	POWER(MemberId, 3)	POWER(MemberId, 7)
1	1	1	1
4	16	64	16384
5	25	125	78125
6	36	216	279936
7	49	343	823543
8	64	512	2097152
9	81	729	4782969
10	100	1000	10000000
11	121	1331	19487171
12	144	1728	35831808
13	169	2197	62748517
14	196	2744	105413504
15	225	3375	170859375

For the first and second rows in the preceding table, the columns were calculated as shown in the following table:

MemberId	POWER(MemberId,2)	POWER(MemberId, 3)	POWER(MemberId, 7)
1	1 * 1 = 1	1 * 1 * 1 = 1	1 * 1 * 1 * 1 * 1 * 1 * 1 = 1
4	4 * 4 = 16	4 * 4 * 4 = 64	4 * 4 * 4 * 4 * 4 * 4 * 4 = 16384

Now that you've learned how to raise to the power of 2, you can put that in reverse and find the square root of a number.

The SQRT() Function

The SQRT() function finds the square root of an expression, the opposite of what the POWER() function does. It takes just one parameter, the expression that you want to find the square root of, as shown in the basic syntax:

```
SQRT(expression_to_square_root)
```

So, in order to find the square root of the MemberId column of the Films table, you would use the following SQL:

```
SELECT MemberId, SQRT(MemberId)
FROM MemberDetails
ORDER BY MemberId;
```

Executing the query gives the following results:

MemberId	SQRT(MemberId)
1	1
4	2
5	2.236068
6	2.44949
7	2.645751
8	2.828427
9	3
10	3.162278
11	3.316625
12	3.464102
13	3.605551
14	3.741657
15	3.872983

The SQRT() function is simple enough. Now you can move on to a more complex SQL math function.

The RAND() Function

The RAND() function, which is short for *random*, generates a fractional random number between 0 and 1. It's the sort of thing computer game writers love, but perhaps it's a bit less essential in SQL. Be very wary of using the RAND() function to generate unique primary keys, because there's no guarantee that they'll generate a unique number.

Note that in MS Access the function is called RND(). Oracle, however, doesn't support the RAND() function, but it does support a function RANDOM inside an additional package called DBMS_RANDOM. It's more sophisticated than the RAND() function, and its scope is beyond this chapter.

To demonstrate the sort of results `RAND()` gives, execute the following SQL:

```
SELECT MemberId, MemberId + RAND(), RAND() FROM MemberDetails
ORDER BY MemberId;
```

The code returns MemberId, MemberId plus a random number, and finally a random number that the database system generates on its own.

The query produces 13 results, one for each record in the table:

MemberId	MemberId + RAND()	RAND()
1	1.133239	0.142173
4	4.311148	0.129218
5	5.712648	0.175588
6	6.739993	0.173202
7	7.64603	0.710545
8	8.614636	0.941545
9	9.863819	0.494457
10	10.88083	0.920768
11	11.96136	0.044484
12	12.33835	0.558281
13	13.77636	0.206976
14	14.70579	0.908012
15	15.4227	0.389447

Because it's random, your results will be different from the ones shown here. Note that in MS SQL Server, the `RAND()` function generates the fractional part, and it also generates only one random number for each `RAND()` used in a results set. Most databases (IBM's DB2, for example) create a new random number for each record. Such long fractional numbers are not really that useful, but you can make them whole numbers by multiplying them and then using one of the rounding functions (discussed in the next section) to cut off the fractional part.

Rounding Numbers

The final three math functions covered here are all related, the relationship being that they all remove all or part of the fractional part of a floating-point number. The difference among the three is how they decide to remove the part after the decimal point. The three rounding functions are `CEILING()`, `FLOOR()`, and `ROUND()`, each covered in its own section.

Before continuing with the discussion of the rounding functions, you need to add some data to the Film Club database. In addition to keeping track of whether a film is available on DVD, the film club chairperson now also requires that you store the price of the DVD. This requires a new column in the Films table, to be called DVDPrice. Executing the following SQL creates this column:

```
ALTER TABLE Films
ADD DVDPrice DECIMAL(12,2);
```

In MS Access, use the following ALTER TABLE statement:

```
ALTER TABLE Films
ADD DVDPrice NUMBER DECIMAL;
```

After executing the ALTER TABLE statement, add the prices of DVDs with the following UPDATE statements:

```
UPDATE Films
SET DVDPrice = 12.99
WHERE FilmId = 2;

UPDATE Films
SET DVDPrice = 9.99
WHERE FilmId = 4;

UPDATE Films
SET DVDPrice = 15.99
WHERE FilmId = 6;

UPDATE Films
SET DVDPrice = 12.99
WHERE FilmId = 7;

UPDATE Films
SET DVDPrice = 2.99
WHERE FilmId = 8;

UPDATE Films
SET DVDPrice = 8.95
WHERE FilmId = 9;

UPDATE Films
SET DVDPrice = 12.99
WHERE FilmId = 11;

UPDATE Films
SET DVDPrice = 9.99
WHERE FilmId = 12;

UPDATE Films
SET DVDPrice = 12.99
WHERE FilmId = 15;

UPDATE Films
SET DVDPrice = 8.95
WHERE FilmId = 13;
```

With all the proper information in place, you can follow along with all the examples in this section. The first function covered here is the CEILING() function.

The CEILING() Function

The CEILING() function removes all the numbers after the decimal point and rounds up to the next highest integer. For example, 3.35 would be rounded up to 4, 5.99 rounded up to 6, and -3.35 rounded up to -3. If the rounding of negative numbers seems strange (why not -4 rather than -3?), just remember that the CEILING() function rounds up to the next highest integer; negative numbers that are closer to 0 are higher in value, so -3 is higher than -4.

> *In Oracle, the* CEILING() *function is called* CEIL(), *but it works the same way — only the name is different. Note also that the* CEILING() *function isn't supported in MS Access.*

The CEILING() function's basic syntax is as follows:

```
CEILING(number_to_be_rounded)
```

The following SQL shows the CEILING() function used in practice:

```
SELECT DVDPrice, CEILING(DVDPrice)
FROM Films
ORDER BY DVDPrice;
```

Executing the query provides the following results:

DVDPrice	CEILING(DVDPrice)
NULL	NULL
NULL	NULL
NULL	NULL
NULL	NULL
NULL	NULL
2.99	3
8.95	9
8.95	9
9.99	10
9.99	10
12.99	13
12.99	13
12.99	13
12.99	13
15.99	16

Some of the values in the DVDPrice column are NULL, and so the CEILING() function returns NULL as a result. After all, NULL is simply an unknown value, so there's no way of knowing what to round up to! Note that MySQL may show only one digit after the decimal point in the DVDPrice column.

The FLOOR() Function

The FLOOR() function works in the opposite way as CEILING() in that it rounds down to the next lowest integer value. For example, 3.35 would be rounded down to 3, 5.99 rounded down to 5, and –3.35 rounded down to –4, as –4 is lower than –3. Again, the FLOOR() function is not supported by MS Access's version of SQL.

The following is the basic syntax for the FLOOR() function:

```
FLOOR(number_to_be_floored)
```

Rewrite the SQL used in the previous section and replace CEILING() with FLOOR():

```
SELECT DVDPrice, FLOOR(DVDPrice)
FROM Films
ORDER BY DVDPrice;
```

Running the SQL provides the results shown in the following table:

DVDPrice	FLOOR(DVDPrice)
NULL	NULL
NULL	NULL
NULL	NULL
NULL	NULL
NULL	NULL
2.99	2
8.95	8
8.95	8
9.99	9
9.99	9
12.99	12
12.99	12
12.99	12
12.99	12
15.99	15

This time, the FLOOR() function has removed the decimal point but reduced the number to the next lowest integer; so 2.99 becomes 2, whereas with CEILING() it would become 3.

The ROUND() Function

The last of the rounding functions rounds in a more traditional way: to the nearest whole-number value. Rather than always rounding up like CEILING() or down like FLOOR(), the ROUND() function rounds based on the digits after the decimal point. If the digit after the decimal point is 4 or less, then it's simply removed. If the digit after the decimal point is 5 or more, then the number is rounded up to the next highest whole number and the digit is removed. For example, 3.55 rounded to a whole number using the ROUND() function would be 4, whereas 3.42 rounded to a whole number would be 3. It's important to remember that with negative numbers, lower means a higher number (-5 is lower in value than -4). So, -4.6 rounded to the next highest integer is -5. Unlike CEILING() and FLOOR(), the ROUND() function is supported by MS Access.

> *Many implementations of the* ROUND() *function in SQL work along these lines: If the number to be truncated, or cut off, is 4 or less, then it's removed and the remaining number isn't changed; if the number is 5 or more, then the remaining number is rounded up. This method of rounding is called the scientific method. An alternative but less common method is the commercial method of rounding. In the commercial method, if the digit to be removed is 4 or less, then it is rounded down. If the digit is 6 or more, then it is rounded up. However, if the digit is 5, then it's rounded up half the time and rounded down the other half to prevent rounding errors. All the databases in this book use the scientific method of rounding.*

One more difference exists between the ROUND() function and the CEILING() and FLOOR() functions. The ROUND() function allows you to specify how many digits are permitted after the decimal point, whereas the FLOOR() and CEILING() functions remove all digits. The ROUND() function, therefore, requires two values to be passed to it: first, the number to be rounded, and second, the number of digits allowed after the decimal point. The ROUND() function's basic syntax is as follows:

```
ROUND(number_to_be_rounded, number_of_decimal_places)
```

If you want to limit the results from the DVDPrice field to one decimal place, you would write the following SQL:

```
SELECT DVDPrice, ROUND(DVDPrice,1)
FROM Films
ORDER BY DVDPrice;
```

Executing the preceding query produces the following results:

DVDPrice	ROUND(DVDPrice,1)
NULL	NULL
NULL	NULL
NULL	NULL
NULL	NULL
NULL	NULL
2.99	3.00
8.95	9.00
8.95	9.00
9.99	10.00

Table continued on following page

DVDPrice	ROUND(DVDPrice,1)
9.99	10.00
12.99	13.00
12.99	13.00
12.99	13.00
12.99	13.00
15.99	16.00

You might wonder why all the values have been rounded up to the nearest whole number. That's because all the amounts end in either .99 or .95. The query specifies that the first digit after the decimal point should remain, so the second digit is removed. In every case, the second digit is either 5 or 9, and therefore the remaining digit is rounded up. Because 9 is as high as you can go in decimal math, the first digit before the decimal point is rounded up.

That covers manipulation of numbers. The next section covers manipulation of character data.

Introducing String Functions

This section walks you through a number of very useful functions that enable you to manipulate and search string-based data. *String* data is a collective name for a group of characters, such as a person's name or a group of numbers. Although each character is stored in its own memory location, the database allows you to manipulate a column of characters at the same time. Human beings tend to think and work in terms of words and sentences, rather than individual characters, and the database system's support of string functions reflects that. This section also touches on powerful functions that allow you to match words that sound alike, such as *Smith* and *Smythe*, even though the spellings are different.

The SUBSTRING() Function

The SUBSTRING() function allows you to obtain just part of a string—one or more characters out of the whole string of characters. When using this function, it's important to remember that a string is simply a chain of individual characters. For example, Wrox Press is a string, and the individual characters are as follows:

Character Position in the String	1	2	3	4	5	6	7	8	9	10
Character	W	r	o	x		P	r	e	s	s

The preceding table shows how characters in a column are stored, and although the column's data is usually treated as a whole, each character can be identified by its position inside the string of characters. So, if you have a varchar column and store the characters Wrox Press, you would call Wrox Press your string. The first character in that string is W, so when you want to refer to it on a character level, it is known by its position in the string: 1. The P in Wrox Press is the sixth character in the string, so its *character index* (its position within the string) is 6.

The SUBSTRING() function works at the character level. The function takes three parameters: the string out of which the substring is obtained, the first character to be obtained, and how many total characters are required. Consider the following syntax:

```
SUBSTRING(string, start_character_position, length_of_string_to_obtain)
```

MS Access doesn't utilize the SUBSTRING() function. Instead, it employs the MID() function, which has exactly the same syntax and works in the same way as does the SUBSTRING() function. So if you're using MS Access, wherever you see SUBSTRING(), simply replace it with MID(). Oracle and IBM's DB2 support SUBSTRING(), but they call it SUBSTR(). If you're using DB2 or Oracle, wherever you see SUBSTRING(), replace it with SUBSTR().

As previously stated, the position of each character within the string is often called the character index. If you want to extract the substring rox from the string Wrox Press, you would write the following function:

```
SUBSTRING('Wrox Press',2,3)
```

Wrox Press is the string from which the substring is extracted. 2 is the character index for the first character to be extracted, in this case the letter r. Finally, 3 is the number of characters to be extracted, in this case rox.

The following code uses SUBSTRING() to find out the first letter of each member's last name and the first two letters of the name of their state of residence:

```
SELECT LastName, SUBSTRING(LastName,1,1), State, SUBSTRING(State,1,2)
FROM MemberDetails;
```

Executing the query provides the following results:

LastName	SUBSTRING(LastName,1,1)	State	SUBSTRING(State,1,2)
Smith	S	Mega State	Me
Gee	G	New State	Ne
Jones	J	New State	Ne
Jones	J	New State	Ne
Jackson	J	New State	Ne
Johnson	J	Mega State	Me
Botts	B	Golden State	Go
Simons	S	Mega State	Me
Hills	H	New State	Ne
Dales	D	Golden State	Go
Doors	D	Mega State	Me
Night	N	Golden State	Go
Hawthorn	H	NULL	NULL

Note that, as with all the string functions, if the string passed is NULL, the result returned by the function is always NULL.

Some database systems, such as earlier versions of MySQL, support a different version of SUBSTRING(). The syntax for this version is shown here:

```
SUBSTRING(string FROM start_character_position)
```

You can specify only the start of the substring, not how many characters will be returned. Consider the following SQL:

```
SUBSTRING("ABC123456789" FROM 4)
```

This function would return 123456789, all the characters from the fourth character to the last character. Earlier versions of MySQL support only this more limited syntax version of the SUBSTRING() function.

The next section looks at converting the character case of strings.

Case Conversion Functions

This section covers two functions, UPPER() and LOWER(), which change the case of a string. Both are very simple to use and work only with character-based data types. All you need to do is pass the string that needs its case converted, and the function returns the same string, but with all uppercase or lower-case letters. For example, UPPER('abc') returns ABC, and LOWER('ABC') returns abc.

Note that MS Access doesn't support the UPPER() or LOWER() functions. Instead, they are called UCASE() *and* LCASE(), *respectively.*

The following code uses the UPPER() and LOWER() functions to change the case of the results from the LastName column:

```
SELECT LastName, UPPER(LastName), LOWER(LastName)
FROM MemberDetails;
```

Executing the code provides these results:

LastName	UPPER(LastName)	LOWER(LastName)
Smith	SMITH	smith
Simons	SIMONS	simons
Night	NIGHT	night
Jones	JONES	jones
Jones	JONES	jones
Johnson	JOHNSON	johnson
Jackson	JACKSON	jackson
Hills	HILLS	hills

LastName	UPPER(LastName)	LOWER(LastName)
Hawthorn	HAWTHORN	hawthorn
Gee	GEE	gee
Doors	DOORS	doors
Dales	DALES	dales
Botts	BOTTS	botts

Now that you know how to change a string's case, the next section looks at how to turn a string backward.

The REVERSE() Function

The REVERSE() function reverses the order of the characters in a string. For example, ABC becomes CBA. It takes just one argument, the string to be reversed. MS Access calls its REVERSE() function the StrReverse() function, and it works the same. IBM DB2 doesn't support the REVERSE() function.

The following SQL returns LastName and LastName reversed:

```
SELECT LastName, Reverse(LastName)
FROM MemberDetails;
```

The results of the query appear in the following table:

LastName	REVERSE(LastName)
Smith	htimS
Simons	snomiS
Night	thgiN
Jones	senoJ
Jones	senoJ
Johnson	nosnhoJ
Jackson	noskcaJ
Hills	slliH
Hawthorn	nrohtwaH
Gee	eeG
Doors	srooD
Dales	selaD
Botts	sttoB

The TRIM() Functions

Trimming involves removing unwanted characters from the beginning or end of a string. In most database implementations, the only character that can be trimmed is the space. However, trimming spaces is very useful with a `character` data type column. A variable character column stores only the number of characters you ask it to store; however, a nonvarying character column pads out the string with spaces if the string being stored is less than the maximum number of characters the column can store.

For example, define a new table using the following SQL:

```
CREATE TABLE MyTable
(
    first_column char(80)
);
```

The column `first_column` can hold up to 80 characters. Now, consider this `INSERT` statement:

```
INSERT INTO MyTable (first_column)
VALUES ('ABC');
```

`ABC` plus seven blank spaces is stored. If you want the results to return only the characters you inserted and no spaces, you can trim off the spaces with one of the two trim functions: `LTRIM()` or `RTRIM()`. `LTRIM()` removes any spaces on the left of the characters, while `RTRIM()` removes any spaces on the right of the characters. So, if you want to remove the trailing spaces from the example table defined previously, you would use `RTRIM()`:

```
SELECT first_column, RTRIM(first_column)
FROM MyTable;
```

The results for this are as follows:

first_column	RTRIM(first_column)
ABC	ABC

Notice that `first_column` is a lot wider than `RTRIM(first_column)` due to the extra spaces. Note also that some database systems don't display the spaces even when they're there. You no longer need MyTable, so delete it by running the following code:

```
DROP TABLE MyTable;
```

Your next stop on the tour of string functions is the function to find how many characters there are in a string — finally, a definitive answer to the question, "How long is a piece of string?"

The LENGTH() Function

Sometimes it can be very useful to find out how many characters there are in a string. Oracle, IBM, and MySQL use the `LENGTH()` function to find out how long a string is. MS Access and MS SQL Server use the `LEN()` function, which does the same thing and works the same way.

The LENGTH() function takes just one argument, the string for which the length is required. So to find out how long each member's last name is, use the following query:

```
SELECT LastName, LENGTH(LastName)
FROM MemberDetails;
```

Remember to use LEN(), and not LENGTH(), if your database system is MS Access or SQL Server.

The query's results are as follows:

LastName	LENGTH(LastName)
Smith	5
Simons	6
Night	5
Jones	5
Jones	5
Johnson	7
Jackson	7
Hills	5
Hawthorn	8
Gee	3
Doors	5
Dales	5
Botts	5

The LENGTH() function is especially useful when used in combination with other functions. For example, you can use it to make sure that the members' surnames start with a capital letter. As it happens, all the last names are correctly entered with capital letters, so you won't see any difference. The following example demonstrates the code converting strings to lowercase by using the LOWER() function so that you can see the LENGTH() function actually working. In SQL Server, the code is as follows:

```
SELECT LastName, LOWER(SUBSTRING(LastName,1,1)) +
                 SUBSTRING(LastName,2,LEN(LastName) - 1)
FROM MemberDetails;
```

If you're using MySQL, use the following code:

```
SELECT LastName, CONCAT(LOWER(SUBSTRING(LastName,1,1)),
              SUBSTRING(LastName,2,LENGTH(LastName) - 1))
FROM MemberDetails;
```

In Oracle and IBM's DB2, the following SQL is correct:

```
SELECT LastName, CONCAT(LOWER(SUBSTR(LastName,1,1)),
                 SUBSTR(LastName,2,LENGTH(LastName) - 1))
FROM MemberDetails;
```

Although the function names are different among the different database systems, the principles are the same, so the examples here concentrate on the SQL Server version. The tricky part of the SQL is the line shown below, so it's helpful to break it down into parts:

```
LOWER(SUBSTRING(LastName,1,1)) + SUBSTRING(LastName,2,LEN(LastName) - 1)
```

The first part is as follows:

```
LOWER(SUBSTRING(LastName,1,1))
```

This is the bit that changes the case of the first letter to lowercase. SUBSTRING(LastName,1,1) extracts the first character, and then the LOWER() function converts that character to lowercase.

The second part is as follows:

```
SUBSTRING(LastName,2,LEN(LastName) - 1)
```

This part extracts all the characters from the string except the first one. The code uses the function to find out how many characters there are and passes as its argument of the SUBSTRING() function that value minus 1 as the number of characters to be extracted.

The two parts are then concatenated, or joined together, using the + concatenation operator.

Executing the query yields the following results:

LastName	LOWER(SUBSTRING(LastName,1,1)) + SUBSTRING(LastName,2,LEN(LastName) - 1)
Smith	smith
Simons	simons
Night	night
Jones	jones
Jones	jones
Johnson	johnson
Jackson	jackson
Hills	hills
Hawthorn	hawthorn
Gee	gee

LastName	LOWER(SUBSTRING(LastName,1,1)) + SUBSTRING(LastName,2,LEN(LastName) - 1)
Doors	doors
Dales	dales
Botts	botts

The SOUNDEX() and DIFFERENCE() Functions

So far, all searching and matching with strings have been based on their actual characters. The following SQL, for example, matches only the FirstName Jack:

```
SELECT FirstName
WHERE FirstName = 'Jack';
```

Sometimes, however, the exact spelling of a name might not be known; you might have only an idea of what it sounds like. It's exactly this problem that the SOUNDEX() and DIFFERENCE() functions are designed to conquer. Unfortunately MS Access doesn't support SOUNDEX() or DIFFERENCE(). MySQL, on the other hand, supports SOUNDEX() but doesn't support DIFFERENCE().

The SOUNDEX() function converts a string into a special four-character code representing the way the string sounds rather than how it is spelled. Its basic syntax is as follows:

```
SOUNDEX(name_to_be_converted_to_code);
```

Note that MS Access doesn't support the SOUNDEX() function.

The first character in the code is always the first character of the original string. Following that is a three-digit number representing how the word sounds based on the SOUNDEX() guidelines. SOUNDEX() was actually first developed long before database systems, for use with the U.S. census and patented in 1918. For example, the following SQL returns the SOUNDEX() values for first names in the MemberDetails table:

```
SELECT FirstName,SOUNDEX(FirstName)
FROM MemberDetails;
```

The query results are as follows:

FirstName	SOUNDEX(FirstName)
Katie	K300
Susie	S200
Doris	D620
Jenny	J500
John	J500
Jack	J200

Table continued on following page

FirstName	SOUNDEX(FirstName)
John	J500
Jamie	J500
Catherine	C365
Steve	S310
William	W450
Stuart	S363
Seymour	S560

Note that you may get slightly difference results because different database systems implement slightly different versions of the SOUNDEX() algorithm.

Admittedly, the results are perhaps not that useful without an in-depth understanding of SOUNDEX() and the algorithm, whose rules are fairly complex. You can learn all about the SOUNDEX() system at www.archives.gov/research_room/genealogy/census/soundex.html.

However, the good news is that the DIFFERENCE() function interprets SOUNDEX() values and returns a number between 0 and 4 comparing how two strings sound. The more similar they sound, the higher the number. DIFFERENCE() takes two arguments: the two strings to be compared. The DIFFERENCE() function's syntax is as follows:

```
DIFFERENCE(some_name, comparison_name)
```

Note that Oracle, MySQL, and MS Access don't support the DIFFERENCE() function.

Say, for example, that you want the details of all members whose first name sounds like *Katherine* or *Johnny*. You could use the DIFFERENCE() function to help you find those details. The following is a SQL statement that returns the difference value for Katherine and Johnny compared to values from the FirstName column:

```
SELECT FirstName,DIFFERENCE(FirstName, 'Katherine'),
       DIFFERENCE(FirstName, 'Johnny')
FROM MemberDetails;
```

The query results are shown in the following table:

FirstName	DIFFERENCE(FirstName, 'Katherine')	DIFFERENCE(FirstName, 'Johnny')
Katie	2	2
Susie	0	2
Doris	1	1
Jenny	1	4

FirstName	DIFFERENCE(FirstName, 'Katherine')	DIFFERENCE(FirstName, 'Johnny')
John	1	4
Jack	0	3
John	1	4
Jamie	1	4
Catherine	3	1
Steve	1	1
William	1	2
Stuart	2	0
Seymour	1	2

From the results, you can see that a difference value of 3 or 4 means that the two strings sound either identical or quite similar. For example, a comparison of John and Johnny gives a difference value of 4, but a comparison of Johnny and Stuart gives a value of 0.

Using the DIFFERENCE() function in the WHERE clause makes more sense, because doing so limits results to just those names that sound the most similar. Consider the following query:

```
SELECT FirstName
FROM MemberDetails
WHERE
DIFFERENCE(FirstName, 'Katherine') >= 3 OR DIFFERENCE(FirstName, 'Johnny') >= 3
```

The preceding code compares the value returned by DIFFERENCE() functions, if the value returned is greater than or equal to 3, with the assumption that the names are reasonably similar.

On SQL Server, the query provides the following results:

FirstName
Jenny
John
Jack
John
Jamie
Catherine

The results have returned names that are similar, or at least vaguely similar, to either Johnny or Katherine. For example, Katherine is very similar to Catherine. All these results are due to the comparison made by the DIFFERENCE() function returning a value of 3 or more. You may get different results depending on which database system you use.

Date Functions

Sometimes it's quite useful to be able to extract individual parts of a date, such as day of the month, month, or year. To do this, SQL provides the DAY(), MONTH(), and YEAR() functions. These are supported by all of the database systems except Oracle.

These functions perform in the same manner, and the syntax for each is as follows:

```
DAY(date)
```

```
MONTH(date)
```

```
YEAR(date)
```

The following code displays the DateOfBirth of each film club member, as well as the day of the month, month, and year of their birth:

```
SELECT DateOfBirth, DAY(DateOfBirth), MONTH(DateOfBirth), YEAR(DateOfBirth)
FROM MemberDetails
ORDER BY YEAR(DateOfBirth);
```

Executing the preceding statement provides the following results:

DateOfBirth	DAY(DateOfBirth)	MONTH(DateOfBirth)	YEAR(DateOfBirth)
1937-01-20	20	1	1937
1945-06-09	9	6	1945
1952-10-05	5	10	1952
1953-08-25	25	8	1953
1956-08-07	7	8	1956
1956-10-21	21	10	1956
1967-10-05	5	10	1967
1974-05-27	27	5	1974
1977-01-09	9	1	1977
1992-07-17	17	7	1992
1994-05-28	28	5	1994
1997-05-28	28	5	1997

Notice the use of a date function in the ORDER BY clause, which allows you to order the results (by year in this case). The first row of the results is empty because the DateOfBirth column in one of the rows contains a NULL value.

Most database systems contain a large number of date- and time-related functions, so it's worth checking the database help files or product documentation to see what particular functions your system has.

Converting Different Data Types

This section examines how to convert from one data type to another, such as from characters to numbers or from dates to strings, and so on. For example, if you want to form a sentence that includes a column defined as a numerical data type, then you should convert the data from numerical to character. Often the database system converts data types without needing to be asked. Take a look at the following example:

```
SELECT ZipCode, MemberId, ZipCode / MemberId
FROM MemberDetails;
```

Given that ZipCode is actually a string, dividing it by MemberId surely shouldn't work, right? In fact, it does, as the following results show:

ZipCode	MemberId	ZipCode / MemberId
123456	1	123456
65423	3	21807
99112	4	24778
88776	5	17755
88776	6	14796
88992	7	12713
34566	8	4320
65422	9	7269
123456	10	12345
88776	11	8070
65422	12	5451
34512	13	2654
68122	14	4865
NULL	15	NULL

The query works because although the ZipCode column was defined as a character data type, the values stored in ZipCode are digits, and the database system can convert them into a number. It does this conversion without being told to.

However, there are times when you might want to specify the conversion yourself, where, for example, it's not obvious what data type the system should convert to. Alternatively, the system could fail to convert; for example, if you're using IBM's DB2, the preceding SQL example fails because you need to tell it to convert ZipCode into a number. Some database systems are more helpful and convert the data for you. Others, like DB2, require you to do the conversion yourself. In this situation, you need to convert to a specific data type using the CAST() function.

The syntax for the CAST() function consists of the expression to be cast and what data type you want to cast it as:

```
CAST(expression AS data_type)
```

The code example at the beginning of this section doesn't work with DB2 because ZipCode is a character data type column, and DB2 doesn't automatically try to convert the data type to a number, unlike other systems such as SQL Server.

In order to rewrite the earlier example so that it works with IBM's DB2, you need to cast the ZipCode column as an int data type, as illustrated in the following SQL, which will work with all the database systems including DB2:

```
SELECT ZipCode, MemberId, CAST(ZipCode AS int) / MemberId
FROM MemberDetails;
```

Note that CAST() works only with later versions of MySQL, from 4.02 onward, and that only some of the data types can be cast. To make the preceding code work in MySQL, you need to change it to the following:

```
SELECT ZipCode, MemberId, CAST(ZipCode AS signed integer) / MemberId
FROM MemberDetails;
```

You can convert most data types to another data type, so long as the data can be converted. For example, ZipCode contains digits, so conversion to an integer data type works fine. If you try converting ZipCode to a date data type, as shown in the following SQL, you would receive errors because the values contained in ZipCode simply can't be converted to a date:

```
SELECT ZipCode, MemberId, CAST(ZipCode AS date)
FROM MemberDetails;
```

MS Access SQL doesn't support CAST(), but its Visual Basic language does have a number of conversion functions, which are beyond the scope of this book.

This section covered how to convert values of a specific data type to another data type. The next section returns to the problematic question of the NULL data type.

Re-examining NULL

NULLs can be a bit problematic and can lead to unexpected results when used with functions, in comparisons, or in math. Whereas Chapter 3 covered the concept of NULL being unknown data, this section covers some of the issues that NULLs can throw up when used with math functions, string functions, and concatenation. The section also introduces the NULLIF() and COALESCE() functions.

NULLs and Math

If NULL appears in any of your SQL math, then the result is always NULL. To illustrate this point, use the following SQL to create a temporary table called MyTable and insert a few NULL values:

```
CREATE Table MyTable(FirstColumn int, SecondColumn int);

INSERT INTO MyTable(FirstColumn,SecondColumn)
VALUES (3,2);

INSERT INTO MyTable(FirstColumn)
VALUES (5);

INSERT INTO MyTable(SecondColumn)
VALUES (7);
```

Now try the following query:

```
SELECT FirstColumn, SecondColumn, 10 + (SecondColumn * 1.175) + FirstColumn - 5
FROM MyTable;
```

The query calculates SecondColumn * 1.175, then adds 10, and then adds the value of FirstColumn minus 5. You get results that are mostly NULL because of NULL values in FirstColumn or SecondColumn:

FirstColumn	SecondColumn	10 + (SecondColumn * 1.175) + FirstColumn - 5
3	2	10.350
5	NULL	NULL
NULL	7	NULL

The last column in the first row of the table is calculated like this: 10 + (SecondColumn * 1.175) + FirstColumn - 5 = 10 + (2 * 1.175) + 3 - 5 = 10 + (2.35) + 3 - 5 = 10.35.

The third column in the second row is calculated like this: 10 + (SecondColumn * 1.175) + FirstColumn - 5 = 10 + (NULL * 1.175) + 5 - 5 = 10 + (NULL) + 5 - 5 = NULL.

The final answer is NULL because any time NULL data is involved the answer comes out NULL. If you were asked to compute 1 plus 1, the answer is obviously 2. However, if you were asked to add 1 to some unknown number, all you can say is that you don't know — the answer is unknown. Remember, NULL represents unknown data rather than any specific value.

It's easy to forget that if NULL is involved at any point in a math calculation, the result always comes out NULL, so you need to make sure the program using the data can handle NULLs. Otherwise, if the data is displayed directly to a user, they may wonder what NULL means!

To circumvent these problems, you can choose either to filter out NULL results or to use one of the functions (discussed shortly) to change NULL to something the end user can understand.

The same problem of unexpected NULL results applies if you use the math functions, such as POWER(), ABS(), and so on. A NULL value causes the function to return NULL, which propagates to the whole expression, leaving a final result of NULL.

MyTable is no longer needed and can be dropped from the database:

```
DROP TABLE MyTable;
```

NULLs and Strings

NULL data causes unexpected results in strings just as it does in math calculations. This section takes you through some of the effects of NULL data as it relates to string functions, and the following section looks at how to deal with it. For example, the following SQL uses the CONCAT() function to detail which city a person lives in:

```
SELECT FirstName, LastName, City, CONCAT( CONCAT(FirstName,' '),
CONCAT(CONCAT(LastName,  ' lives in '), City))
FROM MemberDetails;
```

If you're using MS SQL Server or MS Access, the SQL is as follows:

```
SELECT FirstName, LastName, City, FirstName + ' ' + + LastName + ' lives in ' +
City
FROM MemberDetails;
```

Either statement provides the same results, shown here:

FirstName	LastName	City	CONCAT(CONCAT(FirstName,' '), CONCAT(CONCAT(LastName, ' lives in '), City))
Katie	Smith	Townsville	Katie Smith lives in Townsville
Steve	Gee	New Town	Steve Gee lives in New Town
John	Jones	Orange Town	John Jones lives in Orange Town
Jenny	Jones	Orange Town	Jenny Jones lives in Orange Town
John	Jackson	Orange Town	John Jackson lives in Orange Town
Jack	Johnson	Big City	Jack Johnson lives in Big City
Seymour	Botts	Windy Village	Seymour Botts lives in Windy Village
Susie	Simons	Townsville	Susie Simons lives in Townsville
Jamie	Hills	Orange Town	Jamie Hills lives in Orange Town
Stuart	Dales	Windy Village	Stuart Dales lives in Windy Village
William	Doors	Big City	William Doors lives in Big City
Doris	Night	Dover	Doris Night lives in Dover
Catherine	Hawthorn	NULL	NULL

Everything's fine with the results until you hit the last one, which just says NULL, despite the other text and the fact that FirstName and LastName contain values. The NULL value in City has propagated, resulting in the whole result being NULL.

The next section looks at how to deal with this problem of NULL propagation to produce a more acceptable result.

The COALESCE() Function

The COALESCE() function returns the first non-NULL value from the list of values passed to it as arguments. If all the arguments are NULL, then the function passes back NULL. Note that MS Access does not support the COALESCE() function.

The following is the basic syntax for the COALESCE() function:

```
COALESCE(first_expression, second_expression,.....,last_expression)
```

Note that each argument passed to COALESCE() must be either the same data type (a string or number) or one that can be converted. If you get an error when passing different data types as arguments, then use the CAST() function discussed earlier in the chapter to explicitly convert to the same data type.

For example, to return either a city name or Not Known, you would use COALESCE() as shown below:

```
SELECT City, COALESCE(City, 'Not Known')
 FROM MemberDetails;
```

Executing the query provides the following results:

City	COALESCE(City,'Not Known')
Townsville	Townsville
New Town	New Town
Orange Town	Orange Town
Orange Town	Orange Town
Orange Town	Orange Town
Big City	Big City
Windy Village	Windy Village
Townsville	Townsville
Orange Town	Orange Town
Windy Village	Windy Village
Big City	Big City
Dover	Dover
NULL	Not Known

If you use the COALESCE() function with the earlier example, instead of getting NULL results, you get something a little more user-friendly — that is, a sentence rather than just Not Known. The MS SQL Server version of the query is as follows:

```
SELECT FirstName,
LastName, City,
COALESCE(FirstName + ' ' + LastName + ' lives in ' +  City,
         'We have no details for ' + FirstName + ' ' + LastName,
         'No data available')
FROM MemberDetails;
```

For the other database systems—IBM DB2, MySQL, and Oracle—the query should read as follows:

```
SELECT FirstName, LastName, City,
COALESCE(
  CONCAT( CONCAT(FirstName,' '), CONCAT(CONCAT(LastName,  ' lives in '), City)),
          CONCAT('We have no details for ',CONCAT(CONCAT(FirstName,' '),LastName)),
          'No data available')
FROM MemberDetails;
```

Running either query gives the following results:

FirstName	LastName	City	COALESCE(CONCAT(CONCAT(FirstName,' '), CONCAT(CONCAT(LastName, ' lives in '), City)), CONCAT('We have no details for ',CONCAT(CONCAT(FirstName,' '),LastName)), 'No data available')
Katie	Smith	Townsville	Katie Smith lives in Townsville
Steve	Gee	New Town	Steve Gee lives in New Town
John	Jones	Orange Town	John Jones lives in Orange Town
Jenny	Jones	Orange Town	Jenny Jones lives in Orange Town
John	Jackson	Orange Town	John Jackson lives in Orange Town
Jack	Johnson	Big City	Jack Johnson lives in Big City
Seymour	Botts	Windy Village	Seymour Botts lives in Windy Village
Susie	Simons	Townsville	Susie Simons lives in Townsville
Jamie	Hills	Orange Town	Jamie Hills lives in Orange Town
Stuart	Dales	Windy Village	Stuart Dales lives in Windy Village
William	Doors	Big City	William Doors lives in Big City
Doris	Night	Dover	Doris Night lives in Dover
Catherine	Hawthorn	NULL	We have no details for Catherine Hawthorn

To explain this relatively complex SQL, consider the three arguments passed to the COALESCE() function. The first argument appears below:

```
CONCAT( CONCAT(FirstName,' '), CONCAT(CONCAT(LastName,  ' lives in '), City)),
```

Ideally, this first argument is the result you want returned. If it turns out to be NULL, however, then you want the next argument to be the value that COALESCE() returns:

```
CONCAT('We have no details for ',CONCAT(CONCAT(FirstName,' '),LastName))
```

This argument won't return NULL so long as FirstName and LastName don't contain NULL values. However, if they do, then the final argument you pass is returned, and because the argument is a literal string, it's guaranteed to not be NULL:

```
'No data available'
```

You can pass a considerable number of arguments to COALESCE(), though obviously each system has an upper limit to the number of arguments that can be passed. That limit is fairly high, however.

Using INSERT INTO with the SELECT Statement

This final section details how a SELECT statement can supply the data to be inserted into a table using the INSERT INTO statement. Using these two statements in conjunction with one another is useful for copying data from one table to another. For example, if you decide to restructure a database's table design but need to retain all the data, you would use the combination of INSERT INTO and SELECT statements. You could create your new tables and then use INSERT INTO with SELECT to copy the data over. The combination is also useful if you want to create a new identical copy of a database — for example, for backup purposes or if you need to move the database to a new computer.

The basic syntax is as follows:

```
INSERT INTO destination_table_name
SELECT column_list FROM
source_table_name
WHERE condition
```

If you use this syntax, the destination columns and source columns must match. The number of columns and appropriate data types must match, although there's no need for column names to match. The WHERE clause is optional and is needed only if you don't want to copy over all records. For example, if you want to create a copy of the Location table, first you need to create the table:

```
CREATE TABLE AnotherLocation
( LocationId int,
  Street varchar(50),
  City varchar(50),
  State varchar(50)
);
```

After creating the table, you can copy over the data:

```
INSERT INTO AnotherLocation
SELECT LocationId, Street, City, State
FROM Location
WHERE State IN ('New State' ,'Golden State');
```

This SQL copies over all records where State equals either `New State` or `Golden State`. You can check it for yourself by using the following `SELECT` statement:

```
SELECT * FROM AnotherLocation;
```

You should see results similar to the following:

LocationId	Street	City	State
1	Main Street	Orange Town	New State
2	Winding Road	Windy Village	Golden State

Note that the table receiving the data must have columns defined that can accept the size of the data being transferred. For example, imagine that you defined your table as outlined in the following `CREATE TABLE` definition, with the Street column accepting a maximum of only five characters:

```
CREATE TABLE AnotherLocation
( LocationId int,
  Street varchar(5),
  City varchar(50),
  State varchar(50)
);
```

You might find in this instance that your database system reports an error saying something like, "String or binary data would be truncated. The statement has been terminated."

You receive this error because you made the definition of Street `varchar(5)`, so it can hold only five characters, and yet the data you're trying to insert is more than five characters long. Some database systems, such as MySQL, don't report an error but simply store the first five characters and get rid of the rest. The important point to learn from this is to make sure that the table being copied to can handle the data being copied. With strings, this means making sure there's enough space for all the characters; with numbers, this means making sure they are not too large to fit.

If you want to copy across only some of the columns, you need to specify which columns you want to copy in the `INSERT INTO` statement, making sure the order in the `INSERT INTO` matches the order in the `SELECT` column list. To copy over only data from the LocationId and State columns, include those columns in parentheses after the table:

```
INSERT INTO AnotherLocation(LocationId, State)
SELECT LocationId, State
FROM Location
WHERE State = 'Mega State';
```

Specifying the columns means that the AnotherLocation table contains the following records (note the change to the `WHERE` clause in the preceding code to prevent data duplication):

LocationId	Street	City	State
1	Main Street	Orange Town	New State
2	Winding Road	Windy Village	Golden State
3	NULL	NULL	Mega State

AnotherTable isn't used again, so you can delete it from the database:

```
DROP TABLE AnotherLocation;
```

That's it for INSERT INTO with SELECT for this chapter, though it returns in Chapter 8 when you learn about subqueries.

Summary

This chapter covered a number of topics relating to manipulating the results returned by SQL queries. Specifically you discovered that SQL has the basic four math functions dealing with addition, subtraction, multiplication, and division. Although SQL's mathematical ability is fairly basic, it also includes a number of other math functions in addition to the fundamental four. These additional functions vary considerably among various database systems, but this chapter covered a few of the more common ones including the following:

- ❏ ABS(), which finds the absolute value of a number
- ❏ POWER(), which raises a number to a specified power (for example, *squared* means that a number is raised to the power of 2)
- ❏ SQRT(), which finds the square root of a number
- ❏ RAND(), which produces a fractional random number between 0 and 1

In addition to math functions, you learned that SQL also contains functions such as CEILING, FLOOR, and ROUND, which all deal with rounding up or down fractional numbers either to create a whole number or, in the case of ROUND, to reduce the number of decimal places.

Furthermore, you learned that SQL has a number of functions that enable you to manipulate character-based data. Each database system usually has a huge number of these functions, and this chapter covered the ones most commonly found in database systems including the following:

- ❏ SUBSTRING(), which allows you to extract part of a string from a larger string
- ❏ CASE() functions, which change the case of a string
- ❏ REVERSE(), which reverses the order of characters in a string
- ❏ LTRIM() and RTRIM() functions, which trim off spaces from the start or end of a string
- ❏ LENGTH(), which counts how many characters there are in a string
- ❏ SOUNDEX() and DIFFERENCE() functions, which deal with matching based on how a word sounds rather than its exact spelling

You also learned that math and string functions can throw up unexpected results when dealing with NULL values. In particular, NULL propagates so that if a query finds just one occurrence of NULL in an expression, the whole expression evaluates to NULL. The COALESCE function can help deal with that by returning a different value if NULL is found.

Finally, this chapter covered copying a whole table, or selected columns in a table, to another table by using INSERT INTO in conjunction with SELECT statements.

That's it for this chapter. The next chapter looks at more complex joins.

Exercises

1.   The film club chairperson wants a list of members' names and addresses. She needs only the street and zip code. If either the Street column or the ZipCode column is NULL, make sure that the address is listed as No address details available for this member.

2.   This question is for MS SQL Server and IBM DB2 users. After speaking to a member at a club meeting last night, the film club chairperson wants to contact the member again but can't quite remember her name. She thinks it sounds something like *Jilly Johns*. Can you help track down the person using a SQL query?

Grouping and Aggregating Data

So far, results returned by SELECT queries have been a list of records, that is, specific data rather than summaries or overviews. This chapter examines two main things: sorting data into groups and returning the data for that group as a whole, and aggregation functions available in SQL. *Aggregation* is another way of saying *a summary of data*. For example, aggregating data might involve finding the average age of film club members or counting how many members live in a particular state. What you've learned so far allows you to answer questions pertaining to which film categories each member likes or what John Jones's favorite film category is. However, by the end of this chapter, using a combination of groups and aggregation will enable you to answer questions such as how many members like thrillers. The difference between grouping and aggregation is that grouping finds out information about a particular record, whereas aggregation summarizes more than one record.

Specifically, this chapter covers the GROUP BY clause, which groups results according to the parameters set forth in the clause. Additionally, this chapter examines the COUNT() function, which counts records; the SUM() function, which adds the value of records together; the AVG() function, which finds averages; and finally, the MAX() and MIN() functions, which find the lowest and highest values in a set of records, respectively. The chapter begins by looking at grouping results with the GROUP BY clause.

Grouping Results

This section examines the GROUP BY clause, which is used in conjunction with the SELECT statement. It allows you to group identical data into one subset rather than listing each record. The GROUP BY clause is at its most powerful when used with SQL's summarizing and aggregating functions, which are covered in the next section. The GROUP BY clause is also very useful with subqueries, a concept examined in Chapter 7. The aim of this section is to get a handle on how GROUP BY works; the next section shows you how to use it more effectively.

Chapter 6

Begin by looking at how GROUP BY can answer the question, "Which states do members of the film club live in?"

The answer doesn't require a list of every member and the state they live in; you simply want a list of the specific different states. Use the GROUP BY clause to answer this question, even though strictly speaking SELECT DISTINCT would work just as well:

```
SELECT State
FROM MemberDetails
GROUP BY State;
```

The GROUP BY clause must go after any FROM or WHERE clauses in the SELECT statement. All the columns you want to be grouped must be listed in the GROUP BY column list. For example, the preceding code groups by the State column. If you want to include more than one column in the GROUP BY clause, then separate the columns with commas, in the same way that you would separate columns in a SELECT statement's column list.

The preceding SQL produces the results shown in the following table. One of the values in the table is NULL, so you end up with one group that is NULL:

State
NULL
Golden State
Mega State
New State

When dealing with a GROUP BY clause, the database system first creates a temporary results set based on the FROM and WHERE clauses. So, in the preceding example, the results set is created from the following SELECT statement:

```
SELECT State
FROM MemberDetails;
```

The DBMS then uses these results and looks for groups of identical records based on the column or columns specified in the GROUP BY clause. In this case, State is the only column, so it's just a matter of grouping all the identical states into one row. If your query includes a WHERE clause, like the one shown below, the grouping is based on the results returned by the WHERE clause:

```
SELECT State
FROM MemberDetails
WHERE State IN ('Mega State', 'Golden State','New State')
GROUP BY State;
```


190

Running the query, complete with a WHERE clause, produces the following final results:

State
Golden State
Mega State
New State

The GROUP BY clause isn't limited to just one column; it can be two or more as the following query shows:

```
SELECT City, State
FROM MemberDetails
WHERE State IN ('Mega State', 'Golden State','New State')
GROUP BY City, State;
```

Executing the query produces the results in the following table:

City	State
Big City	Mega State
Dover	Golden State
New Town	New State
Orange Town	New State
Townsville	Mega State
Windy Village	Golden State

The order of the columns in the GROUP BY clause affects the order of results, but it doesn't change the results as a whole, just the order in which they arrive.

Both examples include the same columns in the SELECT results set, as in the GROUP BY clause, and this is no accident. Most DBMSs don't allow the columns that appear in the results to differ from the columns in the GROUP BY clause. The reason for this is that if you specify no group for a column in the SELECT statement, then the DBMS has no way of deciding which value to include for a particular group. Remember, your results can include only one identical record per group; each row represents the results from a group of records and not the individual records themselves. You can't include an ungrouped column; otherwise there may be more than one row for each group, which isn't allowed.

Summarizing and Aggregating Data

Until now, results obtained from the database have all consisted of a set of individual records rather than records that have been summarized by, say, including an average or counting records. Queries have answered questions such as "Who are the members of the film club and which state do they live in?"

This section covers queries that provide more of a summary, or *aggregation*, of results. You learn how to use SQL to answer questions such as "How many members come from each state?" "What's the average film rating of all the films in the Film Club database?" and "How old is the oldest person in the club?"

The section begins by looking at the COUNT() aggregate function.

Counting Results

You can use the COUNT() function to count the number of records in the results. It's used in the SELECT statement along with the column list. Inside the brackets, insert the name of the column you want counted. The value returned in the results set is the number of non-NULL values in that column. Alternatively, you can insert an asterisk (*), in which case all columns for all records in the results set are counted regardless of whether the value is NULL or not. The COUNT() function can also accept expressions, for example COUNT(MemberId + CategoryId).

Execute the following SQL:

```
SELECT COUNT(*)
FROM MemberDetails;
```

You get the answer 14, which is how many records the SQL returns, which, given the lack of a WHERE clause, represents all the records in the MemberDetails table. However, if you execute the following SQL, you get the answer 13:

```
SELECT COUNT(Street)
FROM MemberDetails;
```

Why 13 and not 14? After all, it's the same SQL with no WHERE clause, so surely it has the same number of records regardless of which column is counted. The difference is that when a column name is specified in the COUNT() function's arguments, only the columns where the value is not NULL are counted. As you can see from the following table, which is the result of SELECT MemberId, Street,City,State FROM MemberDetails, one of the records in the Street, City, and State columns contains a NULL value:

MemberId	Street	City	State
1	Main Road	Townsville	Mega State
4	45 Upper Road	New Town	New State
5	Newish Lane	Orange Town	New State
6	Newish Lane	Orange Town	New State
7	Long Lane	Orange Town	New State
8	Main Street	Big City	Mega State
9	Long Lane	Windy Village	Golden State
10	Main Road	Townsville	Mega State

MemberId	Street	City	State
11	Newish Lane	Orange Town	New State
12	Long Lane	Windy Village	Golden State
13	Winding Road	Big City	Mega State
14	White Cliff Street	Dover	Golden State
15	NULL	NULL	NULL

You can also see that the MemberId column contains no NULLs, so if you change the column counted to MemberId (by including `MemberId` inside parentheses), you get the value 13, because 13 records in the MemberId column contain values that are not NULL.

You can include more than one aggregate function in the SELECT statement. Consider the following statement:

```
SELECT COUNT(City), COUNT(LastName)
FROM MemberDetails;
```

Executing the preceding SQL returns the following results:

COUNT(City)	COUNT(MemberId)
12	13

Remember, the City column does contain one record with a NULL value; hence the value above is 12. The MemberId column contains no NULLs in any of the records, so its value is 13, or all the records in the results set.

Trying to combine an aggregate function and a nonaggregate column is not allowed by the rules of SQL. For example, the following SQL results in an error:

```
SELECT City, COUNT(MemberId)
FROM MemberDetails;
```

The reason for this rule is that City might return more than one row, whereas COUNT() only ever returns one row.

In this situation, the GROUP BY clause comes in quite handy. For example, if you want to know how many members live in each state based on information from the MemberDetails table, run the following query:

```
SELECT State, COUNT(LastName)
FROM MemberDetails
GROUP BY State;
```

This query gives the results in the following table:

State	Count(State)
NULL	1
Golden State	3
Mega State	4
New State	5

A GROUP BY clause essentially splits off results into groups, each being a subset of the full results. The COUNT() function in this case counts the results from each subset of the main results. Things might be a bit clearer if you look at the following table, which contains a list of States and LastNames returned by the FROM MemberDetails clauses:

State	LastName	Notes
NULL	Hawthorn	*Null group*
Golden State	Botts	*Golden State group*
Golden State	Dales	
Golden State	Night	
Mega State	Doors	*Mega State group*
Mega State	Johnson	
Mega State	Simons	
Mega State	Smith	
New State	Gee	
New State	Hills	*New State group*
New State	Jackson	
New State	Jones	
New State	Jones	

The different groups in the preceding table are highlighted with different shading. If you count each group, you'll find that they match the results from the COUNT(State) results table.

Just as the SELECT statement has a DISTINCT option, so do aggregate functions. The DISTINCT option counts only the number of unique records; any duplicates are counted just once. Also, NULLs are not counted at all. For example, the following SQL counts how many distinct values the CategoryId column of the FavCategory table contains. Note that MS Access doesn't support the DISTINCT keyword:

```
SELECT COUNT(DISTINCT CategoryId)
FROM FavCategory;
```

Executing the SQL returns seven distinct values. The following Try It Out puts your knowledge of counting and grouping results to the test.

Try It Out   **Counting and Grouping Results**

The film club's chairperson wants to know which film categories are most popular among club members. The list must be in order from the most popular category to the least popular category.

1.   Execute the following SQL to obtain the grouped results:

```
SELECT Category, COUNT(FavCategory.CategoryId) AS Popularity
FROM FavCategory INNER JOIN Category
ON FavCategory.CategoryId = Category.CategoryId
GROUP BY Category
ORDER BY Popularity DESC;
```

Note that the preceding code won't work in MS Access unless you change the ORDER BY clause as shown here:

```
ORDER BY COUNT(FavCategory.CategoryId) DESC;
```

How It Works

This SQL statement is a little trickier than what you've seen so far. Perhaps the hardest part with SQL is not the actual code but rather working out how to get the information you want, determining where it's coming from, and then translating that into SQL. If you find that the SQL necessary to answer a particular question is a little bit tricky, it's best to start simple and build the code up. For example, a good start in answering the film club chairperson's query could be simply to select all the CategoryIds in the FavCategory table:

```
SELECT FavCategory.CategoryId
FROM FavCategory;
```

After selecting the categories, you can count the categories:

```
SELECT COUNT(FavCategory.CategoryId)
FROM FavCategory;
```

This query returns 21, which tells you nothing except that there are 21 rows in the table. However, you want to know how many rows there are in each category, so you need to group the results by CategoryId:

```
SELECT COUNT(FavCategory.CategoryId)
FROM FavCategory
GROUP BY FavCategory.CategoryId;
```

Executing this code gives a count for each category, but it contains only the CategoryId, so you need to join the FavCategory and Category tables together to get the names of the category groups:

```
SELECT Category, COUNT(FavCategory.CategoryId) AS Popularity
FROM FavCategory INNER JOIN Category
ON FavCategory.CategoryId = Category.CategoryId
GROUP BY Category;
```

You're almost there. You have the right results, but the categories aren't ordered from most popular to least popular. You need to add an ORDER BY clause. ORDER BY clauses can order on aggregate functions as well as on columns, so you just need to add the clause and the alias you gave the aggregate function in the SELECT list:

```
SELECT Category, COUNT(FavCategory.CategoryId) AS Popularity
FROM FavCategory INNER JOIN Category
ON FavCategory.CategoryId = Category.CategoryId
GROUP BY Category
ORDER BY Popularity DESC;
```

The preceding code gives the final results with the data ordered as required:

Category	Popularity
War	4
Sci-fi	3
Thriller	3
Comedy	3
Historical	3
Horror	3
Romance	2

Note, however, that using an alias for the COUNT(FavCategory.CategoryId) in the SELECT clause isn't essential. You could have achieved the same results with this SQL, which is in fact the only SQL that MS Access will accept:

```
SELECT Category.Category, COUNT(FavCategory.CategoryId)
FROM FavCategory INNER JOIN Category
ON FavCategory.CategoryId = Category.CategoryId
GROUP BY Category.Category
ORDER BY COUNT(FavCategory.CategoryId)
```

However, giving a meaningful name to the aggregate function's results makes the code more readable. If you return to this SQL statement in a year's time, you'll know exactly what the COUNT(FavCategory.CategoryId) represents.

Adding Results

The SUM() function adds up all the values for the expression passed to it as an argument, either a column name or the result of a calculation. The basic syntax is as follows:

```
SUM(expression_to_be_added_together)
```

For example, the following code adds up all the values in the CategoryId column for all records in the Category table:

```
SELECT SUM(CategoryId)
FROM Category;
```

The result of the statement is 28. Given that the CategoryId column is simply a primary key column, the result is not that meaningful. SUM() can also contain expressions and calculations:

```
SELECT SUM(CategoryId * MemberId)
FROM FavCategory
WHERE CategoryId < 4;
```

The preceding code sums up CategoryId multiplied by MemberId for each record and then sums up the results for all records where CategoryId is less than 4; the final answer is 159.

You can use SUM() only with numerical fields. The SUM() function counts only actual values; NULL values are ignored. As with COUNT(), the SUM() function contains a DISTINCT option, so that your results include the sum of only distinct values. The Try It Out that follows shows you how to use the SUM() function.

Try It Out   **Using the SUM() Function**

1. The club chairperson is feeling quite generous and has decided to buy a copy of all the films available on DVD. Use the following SQL to calculate the total cost, including sales tax of 10%:

```
SELECT SUM(DVDPrice * 1.1) FROM Films
WHERE AvailableOnDVD = 'Y';
```

2. After seeing how much each DVD costs, the chairperson has a change of mind and wants to buy only the films available on DVD that cost less than $10. Using the following SQL, calculate the total cost, including sales tax of 10%:

```
SELECT SUM(DVDPrice * 1.1) FROM Films
WHERE AvailableOnDVD = 'Y' AND DVDPrice < 10;
```

How It Works

First, you created the SQL to extract the total price for all DVDs in the database:

```
SELECT SUM(DVDPrice * 1.1) FROM Films
WHERE AvailableOnDVD = 'Y';
```

Running the query provides the result 119.702, except on MySQL, where it returns 118.80.

The SUM() function is used in the SELECT clause and a calculation passed as an argument, which is the DVDPrice column multiplied by the value 1.1, which increases the value of DVDPrice by 10% to reflect sales tax. The WHERE clause includes only those records where the AvailableOnDVD column contains a value of Y. After all, there's no point adding up the cost of a DVD where it's not even available. Strictly speaking, the WHERE clause is not necessary because NULL values are not included by the SUM() function, but it's better to make it explicit that DVDs that are unavailable are not included. After all, perhaps a DVD is due for release in a few months' time, the expected price being known and therefore entered into the database even though the DVD isn't currently available for purchase. Limiting the number of unnecessary results that the database has to deal with is also good practice. It's worth mentioning once again that aggregate functions take their records from the results set as a whole, including the effect of WHERE clauses, not just from the tables specified.

The second SQL query (shown again below) finds out the total cost of all DVDs under $10:

```
SELECT SUM(DVDPrice * 1.1) FROM Films
WHERE AvailableOnDVD = 'Y' AND DVDPrice < 10;
```

This query is identical to the previous SQL, except you added an extra condition to the WHERE clause that states that only records where the DVDPrice is less than $10 are included when doing the SUM() calculation.

Now that you have a grasp of the SUM() function, you can move on to the next aggregate function, AVG(), which allows you to average results.

Averaging Results

If you want to find out the average for a column or expression in a results set, you need to use the AVG() function. This works in the same way as the SUM() function, with the obvious difference that it obtains an average value.

If you want to find out the average price of a DVD, write the following SQL:

```
SELECT AVG(DVDPrice)
FROM Films
WHERE AvailableOnDVD = 'Y';
```

Executing this query gives the result 10.882. The AVG() function, as with the SUM() function, ignores NULL values. So if you remove the WHERE clause in the preceding SQL so that NULL values appear in DVDPrice where the DVD is not available, you get exactly the same result.

As with COUNT() and SUM() functions, you can use the DISTINCT keyword so that only unique values are counted. The DBMS ignores values that appear twice or more in the results set. Change the preceding code and add DISTINCT:

```
SELECT AVG(DISTINCT DVDPrice)
FROM Films
WHERE AvailableOnDVD = 'Y'
```

Executing this query provides the answer 10.182 because values such as 12.99, 9.99, and 8.95 appear more than once in the results.

As well as columns, the AVG() function takes expressions. For example, the following SQL finds out the average price of DVDs with sales tax of 10% added:

```
SELECT AVG(DISTINCT DVDPrice * 1.1)
FROM Films
WHERE AvailableOnDVD = 'Y'
```

Running the query gives the answer 11.2002. The following Try It Out puts the AVG() function to practical use.

Using the AVG() Function

1. Produce a list of categories and average prices for DVDs in each category.

```
SELECT Category, AVG(DVDPrice)
FROM Films
INNER JOIN Category
ON Films.CategoryId = Category.CategoryId
WHERE AvailableOnDVD = 'Y'
GROUP BY Category;
```

How It Works

With more complex queries, it's often better to start simple. First, work out where the data comes from. In this case, DVD prices are in the Films table, and category names are in the Category table. Start by joining the two tables:

```
SELECT Category
FROM Films
INNER JOIN Category
ON Films.CategoryId = Category.CategoryId
WHERE AvailableOnDVD = 'Y';
```

The query so far provides only a list of categories for each film in the Films table:

Category
Romance
Horror
Historical
War
Thriller
Horror
Thriller
Historical
Historical
Sci-fi

You now need to group them by category and find out the average price for the films in each group, which leads you to the final step of adding a GROUP BY clause and AVG() function to the SELECT list:

```
SELECT Category, AVG(DVDPrice)
FROM Films
INNER JOIN Category
ON Films.CategoryId = Category.CategoryId
WHERE AvailableOnDVD = 'Y'
GROUP BY Category;
```

The AVG price result receives the alias Average Price, which although not strictly needed, does help identify what the result means.

Executing this query produces the results in the following table:

Category	Average Price
Historical	11.643333
Horror	9.470000
Romance	12.990000
Sci-fi	12.990000
Thriller	7.990000
War	12.990000

MAX() and MIN() in Results

The MAX() and MIN() aggregate functions return the lowest and highest values found in a results set, respectively. Basically, it's the same as if the results were ordered and the first and last results were picked from the list. Unlike the SUM() and AVG() functions, you can use MAX() and MIN() with data types other than numerical data types. For example, you can use MAX() and MIN() to find the earliest or latest date or time in a date or time field.

The following SQL finds the youngest and oldest members in the MemberDetails table:

```
SELECT MAX(DateOfBirth), MIN(DateOfBirth)
FROM MemberDetails;
```

It provides the following results:

MAX(DateOfBirth)	MIN(DateOfBirth)
1997-05-28	1937-01-20

In addition to a date or time field, you can also choose a character field. Again, the MIN() and MAX() are the values for the specified column for the first and last records in an ordered results set. For example, the following SQL finds the MIN() and MAX() values for the LastName column in the MemberDetails table where MemberId is less than 3:

```
SELECT MAX(LastName), MIN(LastName)
FROM MemberDetails
WHERE MemberId > 3;
```

Executing the code gives the results in the following table:

MAX(LastName)	MIN(LastName)
Simons	Botts

In the following SQL, the MAX() and MIN() functions have been removed, and executing the code will show only the results set ordered using an ORDER BY clause

```
SELECT LastName
FROM MemberDetails
WHERE MemberId > 3
ORDER BY LastName;
```

You can see that MAX(LastName) is simply the last item in the list and MIN(LastName) is the first item in the list:

LastName
Botts
Dales
Doors
Gee
Hawthorn
Hills
Jackson
Johnson
Jones
Jones
Night
Simons

You can also see that generally ORDER BY, and therefore MAX() and MIN(), are based on alphabetical order, although this isn't always the case, especially when numbers and punctuation appear in strings. The next Try It Out uses the MAX() and MIN() functions to gather birth dates for the film club's chairperson.

Try It Out   **Selecting Data with MAX() and MIN()**

1. The film club chairperson wants to know the dates of birth of the youngest and oldest members in each state. Use the following SQL:

```
SELECT State, MAX(DateOfBirth), MIN(DateOfBirth)
FROM MemberDetails
WHERE State IS NOT NULL
GROUP BY State;
```

How It Works

This query is a little easier than the other examples because all the data comes from the same table; there is no need for joins. The SELECT statement lists the columns and expressions that form the final results:

```
SELECT State, MAX(DateOfBirth), MIN(DateOfBirth)
```

The FROM part is easy: everything comes from the MemberDetails table. However, some values in the State and DateOfBirth columns are NULL, so you use an IS NOT NULL operator in the WHERE clause to exclude them:

```
FROM MemberDetails
WHERE State IS NOT NULL
```

Finally, you want results grouped based on the State column, so you add a GROUP BY clause:

```
GROUP BY State
```

Although it's true that all columns listed in the SELECT statement must also appear in the GROUP BY clause, it's not true of aggregate functions like MAX() and MIN(), so they don't appear in the GROUP BY clause. Executing the entire statement produces the following results set:

State	MAX(DateOfBirth)	MIN(DateOfBirth)
Golden State	1997-05-28	1956-08-07
Mega State	1994-05-28	1937-01-20
New State	1992-07-17	1952-10-05

So far, you've learned how to group and summarize results with aggregation functions. The next section explains how to use the HAVING clause to limit which groups are displayed and how to use the HAVING clause with the aggregation functions.

Using the HAVING Clause with GROUP BY Statements

The HAVING clause enables you to specify conditions that filter which group results appear in the final results. In some ways, the HAVING clause resembles a WHERE clause for groups, in that you place it immediately after the GROUP BY statement. For example, the following SQL creates a list of cities that have three or more members in them:

```
SELECT City
FROM MemberDetails
GROUP BY City
HAVING COUNT(MemberId) >= 3;
```

The HAVING clause applies on a per-group basis, filtering out those groups that don't match the condition, whereas the WHERE clause applies on a per-record basis, filtering out records. The results for the preceding SQL are shown in the following table:

City
Orange Town

If you take away the HAVING clause and add details of the COUNT(MemberId), your SQL is as follows:

```
SELECT City, COUNT(MemberId)
FROM MemberDetails
GROUP BY City;
```

You can see how the database gets its results:

City	COUNT(MemberId)
NULL	1
Big City	2
Dover	1
New Town	1
Orange Town	4
Townsville	2
Windy Village	2

You can see from the list that only Big City and New Town have three or more members. It's important to note that the WHERE clause restricts the record set that the GROUP BY clause works with. However, the HAVING clause affects only the displayed final results. Now that you're acquainted with the HAVING clause's functions, the following Try It Out shows you how to use it in SQL statements.

Try It Out   Working with the HAVING Clause

1.   In an earlier example, the film club's chairperson wanted to know how many members listed each film category as their favorite. The chairperson also wanted the list ordered from the most popular to the least popular category. However, now the chairperson wants the list to include only those categories where four or more members listed that category as their favorite. Execute the following SQL to answer the chairperson's question:

```
SELECT Category, COUNT(FavCategory.CategoryId) AS Popularity
FROM FavCategory INNER JOIN Category
ON FavCategory.CategoryId = Category.CategoryId
GROUP BY Category.Category
HAVING COUNT(FavCategory.CategoryId) > 3
ORDER BY Popularity DESC;
```

If you're using MS Access, you need to change the ORDER BY clause as shown below:

```
ORDER BY COUNT(FavCategory.CategoryId) DESC;
```

How It Works

The best way to deal with queries that seem a bit tricky at first (recall the discussion of the COUNT() function) is to break them up into smaller stages.

You know that the FavCategory table contains data on each member's favorite film categories, so that is your starting point; this leads you to the following SQL:

```
SELECT FavCategory.CategoryId, COUNT(FavCategory.CategoryId) AS Popularity
FROM FavCategory
GROUP BY FavCategory.CategoryId;
```

While numbers are fine for a computer, humans prefer names. In order to make the answer more readable, you need to display the category name. To obtain the category name, you need to access the Category table, linking the results set so far with the data in the Category table via the CategoryId field. To do this, you need to join the tables with an inner join, resulting in the following SQL:

```
SELECT Category.Category, COUNT(FavCategory.CategoryId) AS Popularity
FROM FavCategory INNER JOIN Category
ON FavCategory.CategoryId = Category.CategoryId
GROUP BY Category.Category;
```

Next, to ensure that the results are ordered correctly (by popularity of category), add an ORDER BY clause:

```
SELECT Category.Category, COUNT(FavCategory.CategoryId) AS Popularity
FROM FavCategory INNER JOIN Category
ON FavCategory.CategoryId = Category.CategoryId
GROUP BY Category.Category
ORDER BY Popularity DESC;
```

Remember, though, that you want only groups where four or more members chose that category as their favorite, which is where a HAVING clause comes in. You can use a HAVING clause to restrict the final results to just those groups with four or more records inside them by adding HAVING COUNT(FavCategory.CategoryId) > 3:

```
SELECT Category, COUNT(FavCategory.CategoryId) AS Popularity
FROM FavCategory INNER JOIN Category
ON FavCategory.CategoryId = Category.CategoryId
GROUP BY Category.Category
HAVING COUNT(FavCategory.CategoryId) > 3
ORDER BY Popularity DESC;
```

Executing the final SQL provides the final results, shown in the following table:

Category	Popularity
War	4

Notice also that the ORDER BY clause must come last in the SELECT statement, otherwise an error occurs.

Summary

This chapter was all about summarizing and aggregating data, rather than getting results based on individual records. Central to this concept was the GROUP BY statement, which does the following:

❑ Enables results to be based on groups of common data

❑ Allows the aggregation and summary of those groups when used in conjunction with SQL's aggregate functions such as COUNT(), SUM(), AVG(), MAX(), and MIN()

The chapter examined thoroughly each of the aggregation functions, including the following:

❑ COUNT(), which counts the number of record in the results set.

❑ SUM(), which adds together the value of the specified column or expression for each record in the results set. SUM() works only with numerical data types.

❑ AVG(), which finds the average value for a particular column for each record in a results set. Like SUM(), AVG() works only with numerical data types.

❑ MAX() and MIN(), which find the lowest or highest value for a column in a results set. MAX() and MIN() work with date, time, character, and numerical data types.

Finally, this chapter explored the HAVING clause, which filters out the result of groups using various conditions, much like a WHERE clause does for a FROM statement. Whereas the WHERE clause filters records, the HAVING clause filters groups found by the GROUP BY clause.

The next chapter returns to joining tables, looks at subqueries, and shows you how to create complex queries.

Exercises

1. The film club's chairperson decides that she'd like a list showing all the film costs broken down by film category and detailing how many films the club would have to buy in each category. She also wants you to factor in a 10% sales tax into the cost of each DVD. Change the results to list only those categories where one DVD is listed.

2. Write a SQL query that finds out the highest and lowest ratings for each film category.

Selecting Data from Different Tables

In Chapter 3, you learned how to use inner joins to create results sets formed from more than one table. In this chapter, to use the words of Chef Elzar from Futurama, you take it up a notch and look at how you can deal with more complex problems using more sophisticated inner joins, and you also something you've not yet encountered: outer joins. Ultimately, this chapter is all about finding a way to get the data you need to answer a question, and you can expect to see lots of practical examples in this chapter.

Joins Revisited

In Chapter 3, you learned about inner joins and how they enable you to retrieve related data from different tables and display that data in one results set.

Remember, an inner join consists of the INNER JOIN keyword, which specifies which two tables are to be joined. After the INNER JOIN keyword, you specify an ON clause, which identifies the condition that must be true for a row from each table to be included in the final joined results. The basic syntax of an inner join is as follows:

```
name_of_table_on_left INNER JOIN name_of_table_on_right
ON condition
```

For example, the Attendance table doesn't contain the name and address of each person attending a meeting; rather, it contains only the MemberId. However, the MemberDetails table contains matching MemberIds as well as members' full details. So if you want to produce results that contain a meeting date and the name of the member attending, you'd have to create a SELECT statement (similar to the following) that produces a results set joining the two tables together:

```
SELECT MeetingDate, FirstName, LastName
FROM Attendance INNER JOIN MemberDetails
ON Attendance.MemberId = MemberDetails.MemberId;
```

The INNER JOIN links the Attendance and MemberDetails tables together in the results. Remember that the link is only for the results produced here; it doesn't change the database structure in any way. The glue that binds them, as it were, is the MemberId columns contained in each table. Strictly speaking, the column names don't have to be the same; it's just the way the database has been designed. In the Film Club database, they are linked so that a MemberId in the Attendance table must have a matching value in the MemberId column in the MemberDetails table.

Executing the statement provides the results you want:

MeetingDate	FirstName	LastName
2004-01-01	Katie	Smith
2004-01-01	John	Jones
2004-01-01	Jenny	Jones
2004-03-01	Katie	Smith
2004-03-01	Steve	Gee

This is an inner join, which requires each result in one table to match a result in the other table. For example, in the preceding table, Katie Smith's record has been matched by a record in the Attendance table, based on Katie's MemberId having an equal MemberId in the Attendance table, a condition that was specified in the ON clause. Shortly, this chapter examines outer joins, which don't require a matching record in every table involved in the join. However, before moving on to outer joins, you need to take a more in-depth look at inner joins.

Inner Joins: An In-Depth Look

Although Chapter 3 covered inner joins, it detailed only fairly simple ones. In fact, the fairly simple ones are also the most common. Occasions arise, though, when you can't obtain the necessary results with a basic inner join. This section refreshes your memory about inner joins but also covers more complex inner joins such as cross joins and self-joins. The section begins by looking at equijoins and non-equijoins.

Equijoins and Non-equijoins

An equijoin is simply the correct terminology for an inner join where the ON clause's condition contains an equals (=) operator. Although you haven't encountered the terminology *equijoin* before, Chapter 3 demonstrated them, and almost all of the joins in the book so far have been equijoins; they are far and away the most common and useful of all joins. An equijoin is simply an inner join where the join clause's condition specifies that a field in one table must equal a field in the other table. Consider this basic syntax:

```
one_table INNER JOIN another_table
ON one_table.some_field = another_table.another_field
```

A non-equijoin is, as you've probably already guessed, a join where the condition is not equal, which means that the condition uses operators such as less than (<), greater than (>), less than or equal to (<=), and greater than or equal to (>=). In theory, you can use most operators, even ones such as LIKE, which would be a bit unusual but perfectly legal. The syntax of a non-equijoin is identical to that of the equijoin, which you've been using throughout the book.

You could use a non-equijoin if, for example, you want a list of films released on or after the year of birth of each member living in Golden State. The SQL required for this example is as follows (note that the example won't work on Oracle, as Oracle doesn't support the YEAR() function):

```
SELECT FilmName, FirstName, LastName, State, YearReleased, YEAR(DateOfBirth) AS
YearOfBirth
FROM MemberDetails INNER JOIN Films
ON Films.YearReleased >= YEAR(MemberDetails.DateOfBirth)
WHERE State = 'Golden State'
ORDER BY LastName, FirstName;
```

The ON statement joins the two tables by the YearReleased column of the Films table and the result of the YEAR() function when passed to the DateOfBirth field in the MemberDetails table. (To refresh your memory about the YEAR() function, see Chapter 5.) The statement extracts the year as part of a date from a date expression. Non-equijoins often produce a lot of results — in this case, 31 records:

FilmName	FirstName	LastName	State	YearReleased	YearOfBirth
The Life of Bob	Seymour	Botts	Golden State	1984	1956
The Dirty Half Dozen	Seymour	Botts	Golden State	1987	1956
The Good, the Bad, and the Facially Challenged	Seymour	Botts	Golden State	1989	1956
The Lion, the Witch, and the Chest of Drawers	Seymour	Botts	Golden State	1977	1956
Soylent Yellow	Seymour	Botts	Golden State	1967	1956
Planet of the Japes	Seymour	Botts	Golden State	1967	1956
Raging Bullocks	Seymour	Botts	Golden State	1980	1956
Sense and Insensitivity	Seymour	Botts	Golden State	2001	1956
Gone with the Window Cleaner	Seymour	Botts	Golden State	1988	1956
The Wide-Brimmed Hat	Seymour	Botts	Golden State	2005	1956
On Golden Puddle	Seymour	Botts	Golden State	1967	1956
15th Late Afternoon	Seymour	Botts	Golden State	1989	1956
Nightmare on Oak Street, Part 23	Seymour	Botts	Golden State	1997	1956
One Flew over the Crow's Nest	Seymour	Botts	Golden State	1975	1956
15th Late Afternoon	Stuart	Dales	Golden State	1989	1956
Nightmare on Oak Street, Part 23	Stuart	Dales	Golden State	1997	1956

Table continued on following page

209

FilmName	FirstName	LastName	State	YearReleased	YearOfBirth
One Flew over the Crow's Nest	Stuart	Dales	Golden State	1975	1956
The Life of Bob	Stuart	Dales	Golden State	1984	1956
The Dirty Half Dozen	Stuart	Dales	Golden State	1987	1956
The Good, the Bad, and the Facially Challenged	Stuart	Dales	Golden State	1989	1956
The Lion, the Witch, and the Chest of Drawers	Stuart	Dales	Golden State	1977	1956
Soylent Yellow	Stuart	Dales	Golden State	1967	1956
Planet of the Japes	Stuart	Dales	Golden State	1967	1956
Raging Bullocks	Stuart	Dales	Golden State	1980	1956
Sense and Insensitivity	Stuart	Dales	Golden State	2001	1956
Gone with the Window Cleaner	Stuart	Dales	Golden State	1988	1956
The Wide-Brimmed Hat	Stuart	Dales	Golden State	2005	1956
On Golden Puddle	Stuart	Dales	Golden State	1967	1956
Sense and Insensitivity	Doris	Night	Golden State	2001	1997
The Wide-Brimmed Hat	Doris	Night	Golden State	2005	1997
Nightmare on Oak Street, Part 23	Doris	Night	Golden State	1997	1997

Originally, this example didn't include the WHERE clause, but that generated a whopping 130 results! The Film Club database actually has very few records, but if your database contains a large amount of records, be aware that you could end up with unmanageable numbers of results unless you use a WHERE clause in your non-equijoins.

Multiple Joins and Multiple Conditions

To reiterate a point from Chapter 3, you can have more than one join in a query, which is essential when you need to join more than two tables at a time. For example, if you want a list of members' names and the names of their favorite film categories, you need to join the MemberDetails, Category, and FavCategory tables with the following query:

```
SELECT FirstName, LastName, Category.Category
FROM MemberDetails INNER JOIN FavCategory
  ON MemberDetails.MemberId = FavCategory.MemberId
  INNER JOIN Category
  ON FavCategory.CategoryId = Category.CategoryId
ORDER BY LastName, FirstName;
```

Note that MS Access insists that you place brackets around joins where there are multiple joins, so you need to rewrite the preceding SQL as follows:

```
SELECT FirstName, LastName, Category.Category
FROM (MemberDetails INNER JOIN FavCategory
  ON MemberDetails.MemberId = FavCategory.MemberId)
  INNER JOIN Category
  ON FavCategory.CategoryId = Category.CategoryId
ORDER BY LastName, FirstName;
```

Notice the inner join on the MemberDetails and FavCategory tables. The results of that inner join are then joined with the Category table. This query produces the following results:

FirstName	LastName	Category
Stuart	Dales	Thriller
Stuart	Dales	War
Stuart	Dales	Historical
Stuart	Dales	Comedy
William	Doors	Sci-fi
William	Doors	Horror
Steve	Gee	Sci-fi
Steve	Gee	Comedy
Jamie	Hills	War
Jamie	Hills	Sci-fi
Jamie	Hills	Horror
Jenny	Jones	War
Jenny	Jones	Comedy
John	Jones	Thriller
Doris	Night	Romance
Doris	Night	Historical
Susie	Simons	Historical
Susie	Simons	Horror
Susie	Simons	Thriller
Katie	Smith	Romance
Katie	Smith	War

As mentioned, that works just fine for MS SQL Server 2000, IBM DB2, MySQL, and Oracle, but MS Access can't handle it. In order for this query to work in MS Access, you have two options. You saw the first in Chapter 3: using brackets to isolate the inner joins. Consider the following statement:

```
SELECT FirstName, LastName, Category.Category
FROM Category INNER JOIN
        (MemberDetails INNER JOIN FavCategory
        ON MemberDetails.MemberId = FavCategory.MemberId)
    ON FavCategory.CategoryId = Category.CategoryId
ORDER BY LastName, FirstName;
```

This is called nesting a query. The results are the same and it seems to keep MS Access happy!

The second option is to rewrite the query in a different syntax, with the explicit INNER JOIN statements removed, and instead join the tables with a WHERE clause, as shown in the following statement:

```
SELECT FirstName, LastName, Category.Category
FROM Category, MemberDetails, FavCategory
WHERE  MemberDetails.MemberId = FavCategory.MemberId
AND FavCategory.CategoryId = Category.CategoryId
ORDER BY LastName, FirstName;
```

Executing this statement produces the same results; they're simply written differently (based on pre-ANSI 92 syntax). It's preferable, however, to use the INNER JOIN keywords, because they make explicit what's happening and make the SQL easier to read and understand. As soon as you see the INNER JOIN keywords, you know that more than one table is involved in the query and that the tables are joined in some way.

Although there is no strict limit to the number of inner joins allowed in a query, you'll find that, depending on the circumstances, more than a dozen or so start to significantly slow down data retrieval.

Before moving on to cross joins, it's worth mentioning that the ON statement is not limited to just one condition; it can contain two or more. For example, the following SQL has two conditions in the ON clause, which join on the State and City fields in the Location and MemberDetails tables:

```
SELECT MemberDetails.City, MemberDetails.State
FROM Location INNER JOIN MemberDetails
ON Location.State = MemberDetails.State AND Location.City = MemberDetails.City;
```

The query provides the following results:

City	State
Orange Town	New State
Orange Town	New State
Orange Town	New State
Big City	Mega State
Windy Village	Golden State

City	State
Orange Town	New State
Windy Village	Golden State
Big City	Mega State

It may be easier to think of the ON clause as a WHERE clause that joins tables. The preceding SQL uses an AND operator to join the two conditions, but you can use any of the logical operators.

Cross Joins

A cross join is the most basic join, as there's no ON clause to join the tables. Instead, all the rows from all the tables listed in the join are included in the results set. Only the usual filtering clauses associated with SELECT statements, such as a WHERE clause, limit the results set. You can define a cross join in two ways. The first way of creating a cross join uses the CROSS JOIN statement, as shown in the following code, where the Category and Location tables are cross-joined:

```
SELECT Category, Street
FROM Category CROSS JOIN Location
ORDER BY Street;
```

The preceding syntax is supported by Oracle, MySQL, and SQL Server, but not by IBM's DB2 or MS Access. An alternative syntax for a cross join is simply to list all the tables to be cross-joined in the FROM clause, as shown here:

```
SELECT Category, Street
FROM Category, Location
ORDER BY Street;
```

Virtually all databases support the second way of cross joining, so it's likely the best way to perform a cross join. Both of the preceding queries do the same thing and produce the same results, which are shown here:

Category	Street
Thriller	Main Street
Romance	Main Street
Horror	Main Street
War	Main Street
Sci-fi	Main Street
Historical	Main Street
Comedy	Main Street
Thriller	Tiny Terrace

Table continued on following page

213

Category	Street
Romance	Tiny Terrace
Horror	Tiny Terrace
War	Tiny Terrace
Sci-fi	Tiny Terrace
Historical	Tiny Terrace
Comedy	Tiny Terrace
Thriller	Winding Road
Romance	Winding Road
Horror	Winding Road
War	Winding Road
Sci-fi	Winding Road
Historical	Winding Road
Comedy	Winding Road

As you can see, the queries produce a lot of results given that the Location table has only three records and the Category table has only seven records. Why so many results? The results set is the *Cartesian* product of the two tables, which in plain English means all the rows from one table combined with all the rows from the other. This means that every single combination of the two tables appears in the results set. If you look at the results in the preceding table, you'll see Main Street combined with Thriller, Main Street combined with Romance—indeed, Main Street combined with every record in the Category table. The number of records in a results set will always be the number of records in one table multiplied by the number of records in the other table, In this case, three records in the Location table multiplied by seven records in the Category table equals 21 total records.

Generally speaking, cross joins are not that useful. Inner joins are much more common when joining two or more tables.

Self-Joins

A *self-join* occurs when a table is joined to itself rather than to another table. Okay, the idea of joining a table to itself might sound a bit crazy, but there are uses for it. The main use is for finding matching pairs of records in a database. However, self-joins are also very useful in conjunction with subqueries, which are covered later in Chapter 8.

How to use a self-join becomes clearer shortly when you see an example. First, though, is the syntax necessary for a self-join. As a self-join is like any other join, the syntax is identical but with just one difference: When joining a table to itself, you must give the table an alias. (Aliases are discussed in Chapter 3.) To recap, to give a table or column an alias, you simply put the keyword AS after the table or column name and specify what you want the table to be known as. It doesn't change the table name in the database, only its name when the database system is generating the results set. For example, in the following SQL, the Films table receives the alias FM1:

```
SELECT FM1.FilmName
FROM Films AS FM1;
```

Self-joins require an alias because the same table is being used twice, so you need some way to distinguish between the same table that is included twice. An alias is also sometimes referred to as the *correlation name*. Note that while Oracle supports aliases, it does not use the AS keyword. Instead, simply put the alias after the table name but without the AS keyword, as shown here:

```
SELECT FM1.FilmName
FROM Films FM1;
```

To demonstrate how a self-join works, imagine that the film club's chairperson has asked you to provide a list of all members who are living in the same house as another member. For the purposes of this example, you can assume that the house is the same if the street and zip code are the same. Strictly speaking, you need the street address, but in the example database this is not recorded.

Is there any way you could do this example without resorting to a self-join? In short, the answer is no. In order to find out if the Street and ZipCode fields in one record are the same, you need to compare them. If you try this without a self-join, then all you're doing is comparing the Street and ZipCode fields for the same record, and obviously they'll be the same, as you can see from the following SQL:

```
SELECT FirstName, LastName
FROM MemberDetails
WHERE Street = Street AND ZipCode = ZipCode;
```

For example, taking just one row, if Street is Main Road and ZipCode is 123456, then the preceding SQL reads as follows:

```
SELECT FirstName, LastName
FROM MemberDetails
WHERE 'Main Road' = 'Main Road' AND '123456' = '123456';
```

This statement always evaluated to true, as the same column from the same row always equals itself! So you just end up with all the records in the table, just as if there were no WHERE clause.

If you need to compare the same fields but different records, you need a self-join. The following SQL is a first attempt at doing a self-join, but it doesn't produce the results you need. Remember to remove the AS keywords if you're using Oracle:

```
SELECT MD1.FirstName, MD1.LastName, MD2.FirstName, MD2.LastName,
MD1.ZipCode,MD2.ZipCode, MD1.Street,MD2.Street
FROM MemberDetails AS MD1 INNER JOIN MemberDetails AS MD2
ON MD1.Street = MD2.Street AND MD1.ZipCode = MD2.ZipCode;
```

There's nothing wrong with the syntax; it's a perfectly valid self-join. In the inner join, you have joined the MemberDetails table (giving it an alias of MD1) with the MemberDetails table, giving the second occurrence of MemberDetails the alias MD2. You can choose any alias name so long as it contains valid characters. The MD1 and MD2 tables are joined on the Street and ZipCode fields. However, while it's a valid query, you can see that it has gone wrong somewhere when you execute it to get the results:

MD1.First Name	MD1.Last Name	MD2.First Name	MD2.Last Name	MD1.Zip Code	MD2.Zip Code	MD1. Street	MD2. Street
Katie	Smith	Katie	Smith	123456	123456	Main Road	Main Road
Katie	Smith	Susie	Simons	123456	123456	Main Road	Main Road
Steve	Gee	Steve	Gee	99112	99112	45 Upper Road	45 Upper Road
John	Jones	John	Jones	88776	88776	Newish Lane	Newish Lane
John	Jones	Jenny	Jones	88776	88776	Newish Lane	Newish Lane
John	Jones	Jamie	Hills	88776	88776	Newish Lane	Newish Lane
Jenny	Jones	John	Jones	88776	88776	Newish Lane	Newish Lane
Jenny	Jones	Jenny	Jones	88776	88776	Newish Lane	Newish Lane
Jenny	Jones	Jamie	Hills	88776	88776	Newish Lane	Newish Lane
John	Jackson	John	Jackson	88992	88992	Long Lane	Long Lane
Jack	Johnson	Jack	Johnson	34566	34566	Main Street	Main Street
Seymour	Botts	Seymour	Botts	65422	65422	Long Lane	Long Lane
Seymour	Botts	Stuart	Dales	65422	65422	Long Lane	Long Lane
Susie	Simons	Katie	Smith	123456	123456	Main Road	Main Road
Susie	Simons	Susie	Simons	123456	123456	Main Road	Main Road
Jamie	Hills	John	Jones	88776	88776	Newish Lane	Newish Lane
Jamie	Hills	Jenny	Jones	88776	88776	Newish Lane	Newish Lane
Jamie	Hills	Jamie	Hills	88776	88776	Newish Lane	Newish Lane
Stuart	Dales	Seymour	Botts	65422	65422	Long Lane	Long Lane
Stuart	Dales	Stuart	Dales	65422	65422	Long Lane	Long Lane
William	Doors	William	Doors	34512	34512	Winding Road	Winding Road
Doris	Night	Doris	Night	68122	68122	White Cliff Street	White Cliff Street

Just looking at the first line, you can see that Katie Smith lives with Katie Smith! If you look at the ZipCode and Street fields, you can see why this record appears. The ON clause specifies that the Street and ZipCode fields should be the same and, of course, they are for the same person. What you're looking for is the same Street and ZipCode for two different people, so you need to add this to your query:

```
SELECT MD1.FirstName, MD1.LastName, MD2.FirstName, MD2.LastName,
MD1.ZipCode,MD2.ZipCode, MD1.Street,MD2.Street
FROM MemberDetails AS MD1 INNER JOIN MemberDetails AS MD2
ON  MD1.Street = MD2.Street AND
        MD1.ZipCode = MD2.ZipCode AND
        MD1.MemberId <> MD2.MemberId;
```

This statement adds the necessary condition to the ON clause, though you could add a WHERE clause and add it there; it's the same thing, just a different syntax. The new condition at the end of the ON clause checks to see that MD1 table's MemberId column doesn't equal MD2 table's MemberId column; you want to make sure you're getting a different member and not including the same member twice. Now when you execute the query, you almost get the results you want:

MD1.First Name	MD1.Last Name	MD2.First Name	MD2.Last Name	MD1.Zip Code	MD2.Zip Code	MD1. Street	MD2. Street
Katie	Smith	Susie	Simons	123456	123456	Main Road	Main Road
John	Jones	Jenny	Jones	88776	88776	Newish Lane	Newish Lane
John	Jones	Jamie	Hills	88776	88776	Newish Lane	Newish Lane
Jenny	Jones	John	Jones	88776	88776	Newish Lane	Newish Lane
Jenny	Jones	Jamie	Hills	88776	88776	Newish Lane	Newish Lane
Seymour	Botts	Stuart	Dales	65422	65422	Long Lane	Long Lane
Susie	Simons	Katie	Smith	123456	123456	Main Road	Main Road
Jamie	Hills	John	Jones	88776	88776	Newish Lane	Newish Lane
Jamie	Hills	Jenny	Jones	88776	88776	Newish Lane	Newish Lane
Stuart	Dales	Seymour	Botts	65422	65422	Long Lane	Long Lane

But if you look closely, you'll notice that there are still doubled-up rows. For example, the top row and the second from the bottom row contain the same data. First, Katie Smith's record from MD1 is matched to Susie Simons's in MD2, and then Susie Simons's record in MD1 is matched to Katie Smith's in MD2. You want only the one result, so you need to determine how to prevent both results from appearing in the results set. The easiest way to prevent both records from appearing is to include only the row where the MemberId field in MD1 is less than the MemberId field in MD2. Remember that the MemberId field is unique, so they can never be the same value, which means that one must be smaller than the other:

```
SELECT MD1.MemberId, MD1.FirstName, MD1.LastName, MD2.FirstName, MD2.LastName,
MD1.ZipCode,MD2.ZipCode, MD1.Street,MD2.Street
FROM MemberDetails AS MD1 INNER JOIN MemberDetails AS MD2
ON MD1.Street = MD2.Street AND
    MD1.ZipCode = MD2.ZipCode AND
    MD1.MemberId < MD2.MemberId;
```

The only change made from the previous version of the query is the last part of the ON clause. It had been the following:

```
MD1.MemberId <> MD2.MemberId
```

This ON clause applies only where the MemberId fields in both tables must be different. A row is included from MD1 or MD2 as long as the MemberId fields are different. It led to doubling up, though, as you saw.

However, the ON clause has been changed to the following:

```
MD1.MemberId < MD2.MemberId
```

Now a row from MD1 table appears in the results only if MemberId is less than MemberId from a row in MD2 table. This ensures that a member only ever appears once in the final results, and finally you get the results you want and only the results you want:

MD1.First Name	MD1.Last Name	MD2.First Name	MD2.Last Name	MD1.Zip Code	MD2.Zip Code	MD1. Street	MD2. Street
1	Katie	Smith	Susie	Simons	123456	123456	Main Road
5	John	Jones	Jenny	Jones	88776	88776	Newish Lane
5	John	Jones	Jamie	Hills	88776	88776	Newish Lane
6	Jenny	Jones	Jamie	Hills	88776	88776	Newish Lane
9	Seymour	Botts	Stuart	Dales	65422	65422	Long Lane

If you didn't have that unique ID column, you would have needed to do the same comparison after choosing another unique column or a set of columns that in combination are unique.

As you can see from this section, inner joins can be complicated, but they can also aid you in retrieving exactly the results you want to retrieve. The next section deals with creating outer joins, which are another useful SQL tool.

Outer Joins

So far, this book has discussed only inner joins. As you certainly recall, an inner join requires that both tables involved in the join must include matching records; indeed, the ON clause must evaluate to true.

An outer join, however, doesn't require a match on both sides. You can specify which table always returns results regardless of the conditions in the ON clause, although the results are still subject to the filtering effects of any WHERE clause. There are three types of outer join: right outer join, left outer join, and full outer join. The syntax for outer joins is identical to that for inner joins. The only elements that change are the OUTER JOIN keyword and the difference in results produced.

> *A word of warning: When using outer joins, MS Access requires that each column name be prefixed with the name of the table. For example, you would write* MemberDetails.Street *and not just* Street. *Other database systems require the table name only if two or more tables have a column or columns with the same name, as in the preceding example where* Street *is a field in both Location and MemberDetails. While this is true of* GROUP BY *and* WHERE *clauses, it's not strictly necessary in the column selection part of the* SELECT *statement unless it's not clear which table the column is from, such as when two or more tables have columns with the same name.*

The discussion begins with the left outer join.

Left Outer Join

In a *left outer join*, all the records from the table named on the left of the OUTER JOIN statement are returned, regardless of whether there is a matching record in the table on the right of the OUTER JOIN statement. The syntax for the left outer join is as follows:

```
SELECT column_list
FROM left_table LEFT OUTER JOIN right_table
ON condition
```

The following SQL is a left outer join that returns records from the Location and MemberDetails tables:

```
SELECT Location.Street, MemberDetails.Street
FROM Location LEFT OUTER JOIN MemberDetails
ON Location.Street = MemberDetails.Street;
```

Executing this query returns three results:

Location.Street	MemberDetails.Street
Main Street	NULL
Winding Road	Winding Road
Tiny Terrace	NULL

There are only three records in the Location table (the table on the left), and all of them are included in the results even when there's no match in the condition in the ON clause. When there's no match in the table on the right of the outer join, NULL is returned, though in your database system you might just see a blank space; either way, the value returned is NULL.

In another example, imagine that the film club chairperson asks for a list of all the film categories and all the films, if any, under each category. Because she wants all the film categories regardless of whether there are matching films, you need to use an outer join. Since this is the section on left outer joins, why don't you try a left outer join! Consider the following statement:

```
SELECT Category, FilmName
FROM Category LEFT OUTER JOIN Films
ON Category.CategoryId = Films.CategoryId;
```

It's a left outer join, so all records in the table on the left of the join statement are included in the results, even if the condition in the ON statement is false:

Category	FilmName
Thriller	The Maltese Poodle
Thriller	Raging Bullocks
Thriller	The Life of Bob
Romance	On Golden Puddle
Horror	The Lion, the Witch, and the Chest of Drawers
Horror	Nightmare on Oak Street, Part 23
Horror	One Flew over the Crow's Nest
War	The Dirty Half Dozen
War	Planet of the Japes
Sci-fi	The Wide-Brimmed Hat
Sci-fi	Soylent Yellow
Historical	Sense and Insensitivity
Historical	Gone with the Window Cleaner
Historical	The Good, the Bad, and the Facially Challenged
Historical	15th Late Afternoon
Comedy	NULL

The results include every row from the Category table, and if there's more than one film of that category, then the category name is included for each film. The Comedy category includes no matching films, so NULL is returned for the FilmName, though it might simply be displayed as an empty cell in your database system.

Don't forget that while a left outer join includes all records from the table on the left of the join, it provides just the initial results set. The database system then applies WHERE and GROUP BY clauses. Change the previous query and add a WHERE clause that includes only records from the Films table where the film is available on DVD:

```
SELECT Category, FilmName
FROM Category LEFT OUTER JOIN Films
ON Category.CategoryId = Films.CategoryId
WHERE AvailableOnDVD = 'Y';
```

Now re-execute the query. You get a much smaller results set due to the filtering effect of the WHERE clause:

Category	FilmName
Romance	On Golden Puddle
Horror	Nightmare on Oak Street, Part 23
Historical	Sense and Insensitivity
War	Planet of the Japes
Thriller	The Maltese Poodle
Horror	One Flew over the Crow's Nest
Thriller	The Life of Bob
Historical	Gone with the Window Cleaner
Historical	The Good, the Bad, and the Facially Challenged
Sci-fi	Soylent Yellow

Notice that there is no Comedy category in this results set. Although the left outer join returns all the records in the Category table, the WHERE clause filters these records and returns only the results where the Films table's AvailableOnDVD field equals Y. Because no films match the Comedy category, no results are returned.

Right Outer Join

A right outer join is simply the reverse of a left outer join, in that instead of all the records in the left table being returned regardless of a successful match in the ON clause, now records from the table on the right of the join are returned. The following is the basic syntax for a right outer join:

```
SELECT column_list
FROM left_table RIGHT OUTER JOIN right_table
ON condition
```

If you modify the earlier query joining the Location and MemberDetails tables from a left outer join to a right outer join, you can see the effects, where every row in the table on the right — MemberDetails — is included even where there is no matching row in the Location table:

```
SELECT Location.Street, MemberDetails.Street
FROM Location RIGHT OUTER JOIN MemberDetails
ON Location.Street = MemberDetails.Street;
```

Execute the query and you can see that this time every record from the MemberDetails table is returned, regardless of whether the ON clause is true and the Location table contains a matching record:

Location.Street	MemberDetails.Street
NULL	Main Road
NULL	45 Upper Road
NULL	Newish Lane
NULL	Newish Lane
NULL	Long Lane
NULL	Main Street
NULL	Long Lane
NULL	Main Road
NULL	Newish Lane
NULL	Long Lane
Winding Road	Winding Road
NULL	White Cliff Street
NULL	NULL

Because only one street name matches in the Location table, all the rows except one return NULL for Location.Street.

Given that you could simply change the table names so that Location is on the right and MemberDetails is on the left, is there really any need or advantage to using a left outer join compared to a right outer join? Not really. Just use whatever makes sense to you at the time — whichever outer join is easiest to read. Performance differences often occur between inner and outer joins, but between left and right outer joins, it's just a matter of personal preference.

The discussion continues with another demonstration of a right outer join, except this time it also uses a second left outer join in the query as well. Imagine that the chairperson wants a list of all the film categories and the members who like films in each category. She wants all the categories listed, even if no member has selected the category as one of their favorites.

Before starting, however, add a new category that no member has listed as his or her favorite, just to demonstrate that the query works and shows all categories even if no member has selected them as a favorite:

```
INSERT INTO Category (CategoryId, Category) VALUES (9,'Film Noir');
```

The Category table contains a list of all the categories, so this is the table from which you want all the rows to be returned, regardless of whether there are matches in any other tables to which you might join it. Clearly, this is going to be the outer join table.

The FavCategory table contains data on who likes which film categories, and each member's details come from the MemberDetails table. You need to outer-join Category and FavCategory together to get the category list and a list of which members like each category. To get details of the members' names, you need to join the results of the first join to the MemberDetails table, but again, you want the results from the previous join even if the MemberDetails table contains no match.

Start simple and create a query that returns all the categories and a list of IDs of members who chose that category as a favorite:

```
SELECT Category.Category, FavCategory.MemberId
FROM FavCategory
RIGHT OUTER JOIN Category ON FavCategory.CategoryId = Category.CategoryId
ORDER BY Category;
```

The Category table is on the right of the join, and as it's the table whose rows you want regardless of a match in FavCategory, the Category table requires a RIGHT OUTER JOIN. Executing the query so far produces the following results:

Category	MemberId
Comedy	4
Comedy	6
Comedy	12
Film Noir	NULL
Historical	10
Historical	12
Historical	14
Horror	10
Horror	11
Horror	13
Romance	1
Romance	14
Sci-fi	4
Sci-fi	11
Sci-fi	13
Thriller	5
Thriller	10
Thriller	12
War	1
War	6

Table continued on following page

Category	MemberId
War	11
War	12
Comedy	6
Comedy	12
Film Noir	NULL

The results include the Film Noir category despite no one having selected it as their favorite, which is why its MemberId value is NULL.

Finally, you need to display each member's name and not just his or her ID. To do this, you need to join to the MemberDetails table. Remember, you want the first outer join to produce the previous results, regardless of whether there is a match in the MemberDetails table. Add the new join after the existing join, but make it a left outer join so that the results to the left of the join are preserved even if no matching records are found in the MemberDetails table, which is the table on the right:

```
SELECT Category.Category, FirstName, LastName
FROM FavCategory
RIGHT OUTER JOIN Category ON FavCategory.CategoryId = Category.CategoryId
LEFT OUTER JOIN MemberDetails ON FavCategory.MemberId = MemberDetails.MemberId
ORDER BY Category;
```

Note that this query won't work on MS Access databases unless you add brackets around the results from the first join. In some instances, using brackets can help us humans see the different results sets and how they all link — and it appears Access needs that help, too.

The results of the query are as follows:

Category	FirstName	LastName
Comedy	Steve	Gee
Comedy	Jenny	Jones
Comedy	Stuart	Dales
Film Noir	NULL	NULL
Historical	Susie	Simons
Historical	Stuart	Dales
Historical	Doris	Night
Horror	Susie	Simons
Horror	Jamie	Hills

Category	FirstName	LastName
Horror	William	Doors
Romance	Katie	Smith
Romance	Doris	Night
Sci-fi	Steve	Gee
Sci-fi	Jamie	Hills
Sci-fi	William	Doors
Thriller	John	Jones
Thriller	Susie	Simons
Thriller	Stuart	Dales
War	Katie	Smith
War	Jenny	Jones
War	Jamie	Hills
War	Stuart	Dales

You've covered all the joins now apart from one — the full outer join — which is the topic of the next section.

Full Outer Join

The final join examined in this chapter is the full outer join. Of all the joins, this is the least well supported by database systems, and indeed, neither MS Access nor MySQL supports it. To be honest, it's not a huge loss, and you rarely need to use a full outer join. A full outer join is essentially a combination of left and right outer joins in that records from the table on the left are included even if there are no matching records on the right, and records from the table on the right are included even if there are no matching records on the left. Aside from the FULL OUTER JOIN keywords, the full outer join syntax is identical to that of the other joins:

```
SELECT column_list
FROM left_table FULL OUTER JOIN right_table
ON condition
```

Go back to the original example, which obtains records from the Location and MemberDetails tables, and modify it so that it's a full outer join:

```
SELECT Location.Street, MemberDetails.Street
FROM Location FULL OUTER JOIN MemberDetails
ON Location.Street = MemberDetails.Street;
```

Look at the results that this query gives when executed:

Location.Street	MemberDetails.Street
NULL	Main Road
NULL	45 Upper Road
NULL	Newish Lane
NULL	Newish Lane
NULL	Long Lane
NULL	Main Street
NULL	Long Lane
NULL	Main Road
NULL	Newish Lane
NULL	Long Lane
Winding Road	Winding Road
NULL	White Cliff Street
NULL	NULL
Main Street	NULL
Tiny Terrace	NULL

If you look back at the examples of a left outer join and a right outer join, notice that a full outer join is a combination of the two. These results display all the records from the Location table and all the results from the MemberDetails table. Where there isn't a matching record in the other table, a NULL value is returned.

That completes the look at all the joins supported by SQL. The most useful is the inner join, but left outer and right outer joins have their uses as well. The next section looks at how to combine two totally separate results sets using the UNION operator. Whereas joins link the different results from each table, a UNION operator simply combines them with no particular link.

Combining Results Sets with the UNION Operator

At times, you might want to combine the results of two quite distinct queries. There may be no link between the results of each query; you just want to display them all in one results set.

You can join the results from two or more SELECT queries into one results set by using the UNION operator. There are, however, a few ground rules. For starters, each query must produce the same number of columns. For example, the following statement is allowed:

```
SELECT myColumn, myOtherColumn, someColumn FROM MyTable
UNION
SELECT anotherColumn, yetAnotherColumn, MoreColumn FROM MyOtherTable;
```

Both queries have three columns in their results. The UNION operator is placed between the two queries to indicate to the database system that you want the results from each query to be presented as one results set.

However, this statement doesn't work because one query returns one column and the other returns three:

```
SELECT myColumn FROM MyTable
UNION
SELECT anotherColumn, yetAnotherColumn, MoreColumn FROM MyOtherTable;
```

Another ground rule is that the columns' data types must be the same, or at least the database system must be able to convert the data types to be the same. The data type for each column was determined when you created the table. If you're not sure what data type a column has, you can find out by looking at the database. For example, the following union works because both SELECT queries return columns with matching data types; in this case, FilmId and MemberId are integer data types, and FilmName and LastName are both varchar data types:

```
SELECT FilmName, FilmId FROM Films
UNION
SELECT LastName, MemberId FROM MemberDetails;
```

Smith	1
The Dirty Half Dozen	1
On Golden Puddle	2
The Lion, the Witch, and the Chest of Drawers	3
Gee	4
Nightmare on Oak Street, Part 23	4
Jones	5
The Wide-Brimmed Hat	5
Jones	6
Sense and Insensitivity	6
Jackson	7
Planet of the Japes	7
Johnson	8

Table continued on following page

227

The Maltese Poodle	8
Botts	9
One Flew over the Crow's Nest	9
Raging Bullocks	10
Simons	10
Hills	11
The Life of Bob	11
Dales	12
Gone with the Window Cleaner	12
Doors	13
The Good, the Bad, and the Facially Challenged	13
15th Late Afternoon	14
Night	14
Hawthorn	15
Soylent Yellow	15

The results have returned a combination of the results based on the parameters set forth in the SELECT statements joined by the UNION operator. The results comprise a list of film names and IDs, as well as member last names and IDs. The order is based on the MemberId and FilmId columns, as these are both primary key columns and therefore are ordered.

Remember, though, that the data types and order of the columns must match. For example, the following query doesn't work:

```
SELECT FilmName, FilmId FROM Films
UNION
SELECT MemberId, LastName FROM MemberDetails;
```

The query doesn't work because the first column in the results set is a varchar data type in the first SELECT statement and an integer data type in the second. You can't tell this just by looking at the query; the data type is set during the design of the database.

Try the following query:

```
SELECT FilmId FROM Films
UNION
SELECT MemberId FROM MemberDetails;
```

The preceding query is identical to the first example, except that it returns only the MemberId and FilmId columns in the results set. So the results, shown in the following table, should include all the MemberIds and FilmIds. However, when executed, the results are as follows:

1
2
3
4
5
6
7
8
9
10
11
12
13
14
15

But how can that be? When you ran the query earlier it returned 29 rows, and many of the FilmId and MemberId values were the same, and yet there's no duplication of MemberId and FilmId in this results set. These results are different from the previous results because, by default, the UNION operator merges the two queries but includes only rows that are unique. If you want all rows returned in the results set, regardless of whether they are unique, you need to use the ALL statement, as illustrated in the following SQL:

```
SELECT FilmId FROM Films
UNION ALL
SELECT MemberId FROM MemberDetails;
```

When you execute this query, you get all the rows even if some are identical:

1
2
3
4
5
6
7
8

Table continued on following page

9
10
11
12
13
14
15
1
10
14
6
5
8
7
11
15
4
13
12
1

You can also order the results by adding an ORDER BY clause. However, only one ORDER BY clause is allowed, and it must be after the last SELECT statement. In addition, you can use only column names from the first SELECT statement in your ORDER BY clause, although the clause orders all the rows in all the SELECT statements. The following query obtains the union of three queries and orders them by the FilmName column. Note that this query won't work in Oracle because Oracle doesn't support the YEAR() function and has a different ORDER BY syntax:

```
SELECT FilmName, YearReleased FROM Films
UNION ALL
SELECT LastName, YEAR(DateOfBirth) FROM MemberDetails
UNION ALL
SELECT City, NULL FROM Location
ORDER BY FilmName;
```

There are a few things to note about this query. First, even though the YearReleased and DateOfBirth columns have a different data type, the value returned by the YEAR() function is an integer data type, so this will match the YearReleased column, which is also an integer data type. Remove the YEAR()

function and the query still works, except you might find that YearReleased is converted from an `integer` into a `date` data type with some quite odd results. The `YEAR()` function is covered in Chapter 5, as is a discussion of data type conversion. Although normally `CAST()` can be used to convert data types, it's not necessary here because `YEAR()` returns the correct data type for the results.

Also notice that the `ORDER BY` clause comes at the end of the `UNION` statements and refers to the first `SELECT` query. Again, this doesn't work on IBM's DB2, which allows the `ORDER BY` statement to come last only if the name of the column being ordered appears in all the queries. Likewise, the `ORDER BY` syntax when using `UNION` is different in Oracle. Rather than specifying the name of the column to be ordered, you specify the position in which the column appears in the `SELECT` list. If you want to order by FilmName, which is the first column, the `ORDER BY` clause would look like the following:

```
ORDER BY 1;
```

If you want to order by the second column, change the 1 to a 2. If you want to order by the third column, then change the 1 to a 3, and so on.

Also note that the query includes only the City column from the Location table and that `NULL` is substituted for the second column. This works on many database platforms but not IBM DB2. Change the value from `NULL` to an integer value that makes it clear that the value is not a genuine piece of data (-1, for example).

Executing the query provides the following results:

15th Late Afternoon	1989
Big City	NULL
Botts	1956
Dales	1956
Doors	1994
Gee	1967
Gone with the Window Cleaner	1988
Hawthorn	NULL
Hills	1992
Jackson	1974
Johnson	1945
Jones	1952
Jones	1953
Night	1997
Nightmare on Oak Street, Part 23	1997

Table continued on following page

On Golden Puddle	1967
One Flew over the Crow's Nest	1975
Orange Town	NULL
Planet of the Japes	1967
Raging Bullocks	1980
Sense and Insensitivity	2001
Simons	1937
Smith	1977
Soylent Yellow	1967
The Dirty Half Dozen	1987
The Good, the Bad, and the Facially Challenged	1989
The Life of Bob	1984
The Lion, the Witch, and the Chest of Drawers	1977
The Maltese Poodle	1947
The Wide-Brimmed Hat	2005
Windy Village	NULL

The results are a combination of the three individual SELECT statements. The first statement is as follows:

```
SELECT FilmName, YearReleased FROM Films
```

It produces a list of film names and years of release. The second SELECT statement is shown here:

```
SELECT LastName, YEAR(DateOfBirth) FROM MemberDetails
```

This statement produces a list of members' last names and years of birth. The third and final statement is as follows:

```
SELECT City, NULL FROM Location
```

This particular statement produces a list of city names, and in the second column, it simply produces the value NULL.

That completes the look at the UNION operator, and you should know how to produce one single set of results based on the results of more than one query. While the UNION operator is in some ways similar to joins, the biggest difference is that each query is totally separate; there's no link between them.

Summary

This chapter advanced your knowledge of joins far beyond the simple inner joins covered in Chapter 3. You can now answer questions that were impossible to answer with a basic inner join. The chapter started off by revisiting inner joins. It looked at how to achieve multiple joins with multiple conditions. Additionally, this chapter covered the difference between equijoins, which use the equals operator, and non-equijoins, which use comparison operators such as greater than or less than.

The chapter then turned to outer joins. Whereas inner joins require the ON condition to return true, outer joins don't. The chapter covered the following types of outer joins:

- ❏ Left outer joins, which return rows from the table on the left of the join, whether the ON clause is true or not
- ❏. Right outer joins, which return rows from the table on the right, regardless of the ON clause
- ❏ Full outer joins, which return rows from the tables on both sides, even if the ON clause is false

In the final part of the chapter, you learned about how you can use the UNION statement to combine the results from two or more SELECT queries into just one set of results.

The next chapter introduces the topic of subqueries and shows you how you can include another query inside a query.

Exercises

1. List pairs of people who share the same favorite film category. The results set must include the category name and the first and last names of the people who like that category.

2. List all the categories of film that no one has chosen as their favorite.

Queries within Queries

This chapter examines how you can nest one query inside another. SQL allows queries within queries, or *subqueries*, which are SELECT statements inside SELECT statements. This might sound a bit odd, but subqueries can actually be very useful. The downside, however, is that they can consume a lot of processing, disk, and memory resources.

A subquery's syntax is just the same as a normal SELECT query's syntax. As with a normal SELECT statement, a subquery can contain joins, WHERE clauses, HAVING clauses, and GROUP BY clauses. Specifically, this chapter shows you how to use subqueries with SELECT statements, either returning results inside a column list or helping filter results when used inside a WHERE or HAVING clause; to update and delete data by using subqueries with UPDATE and DELETE statements; and with operators such as EXISTS, ANY, SOME, and ALL, which are introduced later in this chapter.

Subqueries are particularly powerful when coupled with SQL operators such as IN, ANY, SOME, and ALL, which are covered shortly. However, the chapter begins with a few easy examples of subqueries. Before starting, you should note that versions of MySQL prior to version 4.1 do not fully support subqueries and many of the examples in this chapter won't work on early versions of MySQL.

Subquery Terminology

Throughout this chapter, you'll notice references to the outer and inner subqueries. The *outer* query is the main SELECT statement, and you could say that so far all of your SELECT statements have been outer queries. Shown below is a standard query:

```
SELECT MemberId FROM Members;
```

Using the standard query, you can nest — that is, place inside the outer query — a subquery, which is termed the *inner* query:

```
SELECT MemberId FROM MemberDetails
WHERE MemberId = (SELECT MAX(FilmId) FROM Films);
```

A WHERE clause is added to the outer query, and it specifies that MemberId must equal the value returned by the nested inner query, which is contained within brackets in the preceding example. It's also possible to nest a subquery inside the inner query. Consider the following example:

```
SELECT MemberId FROM MemberDetails
WHERE MemberId = (SELECT MAX(FilmId) FROM Films
                    WHERE FilmId IN (SELECT LocationId FROM Location));
```

In the preceding example, a subquery is added to the WHERE clause of the inner query.

In this chapter, a subquery inside a subquery is referred to as the *innermost* query. Topics are explained more clearly as the chapter progresses, but you will start by looking at subqueries inside SELECT column lists.

Subqueries in a SELECT List

You can include a subquery as one of the expressions returning a value in a SELECT query, just as you can include a single column. However, the subquery must return just one record in one expression, in what is known as a *scalar subquery*. The subquery must also be enclosed in brackets. An example makes things a bit clearer:

```
SELECT Category,
    (SELECT MAX(DVDPrice) FROM Films WHERE Films.CategoryId = Category.CategoryId),
    CategoryId
    FROM Category;
```

The SELECT query starts off by selecting the Category column, much as you've already seen a hundred times before in the book. However, the next item in the list is not another column but rather a subquery. This query inside the main query returns the maximum price of a DVD. An aggregate function returns only one value, complying with the need for a subquery in a SELECT statement to be a scalar subquery. The subquery is also linked to the outer SELECT query using a WHERE clause. Because of this link, MAX(DVDPrice) returns the maximum price for each category in the Category table.

If you execute the whole query, you get the following results:

Category	DVDPrice	Category.CategoryId
Thriller	12.99	1
Romance	12.99	2
Horror	9.99	3
War	12.99	4
Sci-fi	12.99	5
Historical	15.99	6
Comedy	NULL	7
Film Noir	NULL	9

There are no films with a value in the DVDPrice columns for the Comedy or Film Noir categories, so NULL is returned.

Conceptually speaking, it's worth taking a little time to go over how the results were formed. Each DBMS has its own way of creating the results, but the underlying concept is the same.

Starting with the first row in the results, the Category is Thriller and the CategoryId is 1. The subquery is joined to the outer query by the CategoryId column present in both the Films and Category tables. For the first row, the CategoryId is 1, so the subquery finds the maximum DVDPrice for all films in the Films table where the CategoryId is 1. Moving to the next row in the outer query, the Category is Romance and the CategoryId is 2. This time, the subquery finds the maximum DVDPrice for all records where the CategoryId is 2. The process continues for every row in the Category table.

Without the WHERE clause in the subquery linking the subquery to the outer query, the result would simply be the maximum value of all rows returned by the subquery. If you change the SQL and remove the WHERE clause in the subquery, you get the following statement:

```
SELECT Category,
    (SELECT MAX(DVDPrice) FROM Films),
    CategoryId
    FROM Category;
```

Executing this query provides the following results:

Category	MAX(DVDPrice)	Category.CategoryId
Thriller	15.99	1
Romance	15.99	2
Horror	15.99	3
War	15.99	4
Sci-fi	15.99	5
Historical	15.99	6
Comedy	15.99	7
Film Noir	15.99	9

MAX(DVDPrice) is now simply the maximum DVDPrice for all records in the Films table and is not specifically related to any category.

Although aggregate functions such as MAX, MIN, AVG, and so on are ideal for subqueries because they return just one value, any expression or column is suitable as long as the results set consists of just one row. For example, the following subquery works because it returns only one row:

```
SELECT FilmName, PlotSummary, (SELECT Email FROM MemberDetails WHERE MemberId = 1)
    FROM Films;
```

MemberId is unique in the MemberDetails table, and therefore WHERE MemberId = 1 returns only one row, and the query works:

FilmName	PlotSummary	Email
The Dirty Half Dozen	Six men go to war wearing unwashed uniforms. The horror!	katie@mail.com
On Golden Puddle	A couple finds love while wading through a puddle.	katie@mail.com
The Lion, the Witch, and the Chest of Drawers	A fun film for all those interested in zoo/magic/furniture drama.	katie@mail.com
Nightmare on Oak Street, Part 23	The murderous Terry stalks Oak Street.	katie@mail.com
The Wide-Brimmed Hat	Fascinating life story of a wide-brimmed hat	katie@mail.com
Sense and Insensitivity	She longs for a new life with Mr. Arcy; he longs for a small cottage in the Hamptons.	katie@mail.com
Planet of the Japes	Earth has been destroyed, to be taken over by a species of comedians.	katie@mail.com
The Maltese Poodle	A mysterious bite mark, a guilty-looking poodle. First-class thriller.	katie@mail.com
One Flew over the Crow's Nest	Life and times of a scary crow.	katie@mail.com
Raging Bullocks	A pair of bulls get cross with each other.	katie@mail.com
The Life of Bob	A seven-hour drama about Bob's life. What fun!	katie@mail.com
Gone with the Window Cleaner	Historical documentary on window cleaners. Thrilling.	katie@mail.com
The Good, the Bad, and the Facially Challenged	Joe seeks plastic surgery in this spaghetti Western.	katie@mail.com
15th Late Afternoon	One of Shakespeare's lesser-known plays	katie@mail.com
Soylent Yellow	Detective Billy Brambles discovers that Soylent Yellow is made of soya bean. Ewwww!	katie@mail.com

The preceding results are a combination of FilmName and PlotSummary from the Films table and the results of the subquery, which is the email address of the member with an ID of 1.

If, however, you change the MemberDetails table to the Attendance table, where MemberId appears more than once, you get the following query:

```
SELECT FilmName, PlotSummary,
       (SELECT MeetingDate FROM Attendance WHERE MemberId = 1)
FROM Films;
```

Executing this query results in an error message similar to the following:

```
"Subquery returned more than 1 value. This is not permitted when the subquery
follows =, !=, <, <= , >, >= or when the subquery is used as an expression."
```

The error wording depends on the database system you're using, but the overall message is the same: More than one value—can't do that with a subquery!

An alternative to using a literal value would be to link the inner query to the outer query, so long as the result of the inner query produces only one row. For example, the following query shows the CategoryId from the FavCategory table, and in the subquery, it shows FirstName from the MemberDetails table. The MemberId in the subquery is linked to the FavCategory table's MemberId for each row in the outer query—thereby ensuring that the subquery returns only one row, as MemberIds are unique in the MemberDetails table:

```
SELECT CategoryId,
(SELECT FirstName FROM MemberDetails WHERE MemberId = FavCategory.MemberId)
FROM FavCategory;
```

The results of executing this query are as follows:

CategoryId	FirstName
1	John
1	Susie
1	Stuart
2	Katie
2	Doris
3	Susie
3	Jamie
3	William
4	Katie
4	Jenny
4	Jamie
4	Stuart
5	Steve
5	Jamie
5	William
6	Susie
6	Stuart
6	Doris
7	Steve
7	Jenny
7	Stuart

If you think that your join would work just as well as and more efficiently than a subquery, then you're right; it would make more sense to use a join, but unfortunately, doing so wouldn't demonstrate how to use a subquery!

Hopefully you have a good feel for how subqueries work. So far, this chapter has examined only subqueries inside a SELECT statement's column selection. In the next section, you look at subqueries used in conjunction with a WHERE clause, which is actually the more common use for subqueries. After that, you learn about some useful operators that you can use with subqueries.

Subqueries in the WHERE Clause

As far as subqueries are concerned, the WHERE clause is where it's at! Terrible pun, but it is true that subqueries are at their most useful in WHERE clauses. The syntax and form that subqueries take in WHERE clauses are identical to how they are used in SELECT statements, with one difference: now subqueries are used in comparisons. It's a little clearer with an example. Imagine that you need to find out the name or names, if there are two or more of identical value, of the cheapest DVDs for each category. You want the results to display the category name, the name of the DVD, and its price.

The data you need comes from the Category and Films tables. Extracting film and category data is easy enough; the problem is how to choose only the cheapest DVD from each category. You could use a GROUP BY clause, as shown in the following query:

```
SELECT Category, MIN(DVDPrice)
FROM Category INNER JOIN Films
ON Category.CategoryId = Films.CategoryId
GROUP BY Category;
```

The query's results, however, don't supply the name of the film, just the category name and the price of the cheapest DVD:

Category	MIN(DVDPrice)
Historical	8.95
Horror	8.95
Romance	12.99
Sci-fi	12.99
Thriller	2.99
War	12.99

The results are correct, but they don't contain a film name. Add FilmName to the list of columns in the SELECT statement, as shown in the following query:

```
SELECT Category, FilmName, MIN(DVDPrice)
FROM Category INNER JOIN Films
ON Category.CategoryId = Films.CategoryId
GROUP BY Category;
```

Now execute the query. You receive an error message because both Category and FilmName must appear in the GROUP BY clause:

```
SELECT Category, FilmName, MIN(DVDPrice)
FROM Category INNER JOIN Films
ON Category.CategoryId = Films.CategoryId
GROUP BY Category, FilmName;
```

Execute the preceding query and you get the wrong results:

Category	FilmName	MIN(DVDPrice)
Historical	15th Late Afternoon	NULL
Historical	Gone with the Window Cleaner	9.99
Horror	Nightmare on Oak Street, Part 23	9.99
Romance	On Golden Puddle	12.99
Horror	One Flew over the Crow's Nest	8.95
War	Planet of the Japes	12.99
Thriller	Raging Bullocks	NULL
Historical	Sense and Insensitivity	15.99
Sci-fi	Soylent Yellow	12.99
War	The Dirty Half Dozen	NULL
Historical	The Good, the Bad, and the Facially Challenged	8.95
Thriller	The Life of Bob	12.99
Horror	The Lion, the Witch, and the Chest of Drawers	NULL
Thriller	The Maltese Poodle	2.99
Sci-fi	The Wide-Brimmed Hat	NULL

The results are wrong because they're grouped by Category and FilmName, so the MIN(DVDPrice) value is not the minimum price for a particular category but rather the minimum price for a particular film in a particular category!

Clearly what you need is a list of all the lowest prices for a DVD per category, and this is where a subquery comes in. In the SQL query, you need to compare the price of a DVD with the minimum price for a DVD in that category, and you want the query to return a record only if they match:

```
SELECT Category, FilmName, DVDPrice
FROM Category INNER JOIN Films
ON Category.CategoryId = Films.CategoryId
WHERE Films.DVDPrice =
    (SELECT MIN(DVDPrice) FROM Films WHERE Films.CategoryId = Category.CategoryId);
```

In the query, the Category and Films tables are joined with an inner join based on CategoryId. The query then restricts which films form the results by use of a subquery in the WHERE clause. The subquery returns the lowest-priced DVD for a particular category. The category returned by the subquery is linked to the CategoryId of the Category table in the outer query. Note that `Films.CategoryId` inside the subquery refers to the Films table in that subquery, not to the Films table outside the subquery. Then in the WHERE clause of the outer query, `Films.DVDPrice` is compared with the minimum price for that category, which is returned by the subquery. If there's a match, then clearly the film's price matches the value of the minimum price.

The results are as follows:

Category	FilmName	DVDPrice
Thriller	The Maltese Poodle	2.99
Romance	On Golden Puddle	12.99
Horror	One Flew over the Crow's Nest	8.95
War	Planet of the Japes	12.99
Sci-fi	Soylent Yellow	12.99
Historical	The Good, the Bad, and the Facially Challenged	8.95

Now that you have a good handle on how subqueries function and how you can include them in SELECT lists and WHERE clauses, you can move on to more complex subqueries that employ various operators, including IN, ANY, SOME, and ALL.

Operators in Subqueries

So far, all the subqueries you've seen have been scalar subqueries — that is, queries that only return only one row. If more than one row is returned, you end up with an error. In this and the following sections, you learn about operators that allow you to make comparisons against a multirecord results set.

Revisiting the IN Operator

You first learned about the IN operator in Chapter 3. Just to recap, the IN operator allows you to specify that you want to match one item from any of those in a list of items. For example, the following SQL finds all the members who were born in 1967, 1992, or 1937:

```
SELECT FirstName, LastName, YEAR(DateOfBirth)
FROM MemberDetails
WHERE YEAR(DateOfBirth) IN (1967, 1992, 1937);
```

Note that this code, and any code that contains the YEAR() function, won't work in Oracle because it doesn't support the YEAR() function.

The query provides the following results:

FirstName	LastName	YEAR(DateOfBirth)
Steve	Gee	1967
Susie	Simons	1937
Jamie	Hills	1992

What you didn't learn in Chapter 3, however, is that you can also use the IN operator with subqueries. Instead of providing a list of literal values, a SELECT query provides the list of values. For example, if you want to know which members were born in the same year that a film in the Films table was released, you'd use the following SQL query. Again, these examples won't work in Oracle because it doesn't support the YEAR() function:

```
SELECT FirstName, LastName, YEAR(DateOfBirth)
FROM MemberDetails
WHERE YEAR(DateOfBirth) IN (SELECT YearReleased FROM Films);
```

Executing this query gives the following results:

FirstName	LastName	YEAR(DateOfBirth)
Katie	Smith	1977
Steve	Gee	1967
Doris	Night	1997

The subquery (SELECT YearReleased FROM Films) returns a list of years from the Films table. If a member's year of birth matches one of the items in that list, then the WHERE clause is true and the record is included in the final results.

You may have spotted that this is not the only way to get the result. You could have used an INNER JOIN coupled with a GROUP BY statement instead, as shown in the following SQL:

```
SELECT FirstName, LastName, YEAR(DateOfBirth)
FROM MemberDetails JOIN Films ON YEAR(DateOfBirth) = YearReleased
GROUP BY FirstName, LastName, YEAR(DateOfBirth);
```

Running this query gives the same results as the previous query. So which is best? Unfortunately, there's no definitive answer; very much depends on the circumstances, the data involved, and the database system involved. A lot of SQL coders prefer a join to a subquery and believe that to be the most efficient. However, if you compare the speed of the two using MS SQL Server 2000, in this case, on that system, the subquery is faster by roughly 15 percent. Given how few rows there are in the database, the difference was negligible in this example, but it might be significant with a lot of records. Which way should you go? You should go with the way that you find easiest, and fine-tune your SQL code only if problems occur during testing. If you find on a test system with a million records that your SQL runs like an arthritic snail with heavy shopping, then you should go back and see whether you can improve your query.

There is one area in which subqueries are pretty much essential: when you want to find something is not in a list, something very hard to do with joins. For example, if you want a list of all members who were not born in the same year that any of the films in the Films table were released, you'd simply change your previous subquery example from an IN operator to a NOT IN operator:

```
SELECT FirstName, LastName, YEAR(DateOfBirth)
FROM MemberDetails
WHERE YEAR(DateOfBirth) NOT IN (SELECT YearReleased FROM Films);
```

The new query gives the following results:

FirstName	LastName	YEAR(DateOfBirth)
John	Jones	1952
Jenny	Jones	1953
John	Jackson	1974
Jack	Johnson	1945
Seymour	Botts	1956
Susie	Simons	1937
Jamie	Hills	1992
Stuart	Dales	1956
William	Doors	1994

Now a match occurs only if YEAR(DateOfBirth) is not found in the list produced by the subquery SELECT YearReleased FROM Films. However, getting the same results using a join involves using an OUTER JOIN, as shown in the following SQL:

```
SELECT FirstName, LastName, YEAR(DateOfBirth)
    FROM MemberDetails
    LEFT OUTER JOIN Films
    ON Films.YearReleased = Year(MemberDetails.DateOfBirth)
    WHERE YearReleased IS NULL;
```

The query produces almost identical results, except in the case of Catherine Hawthorn, whose date of birth is NULL. The way the query works is that the left outer join returns all rows from MemberDetails, regardless of whether YearReleased from the Films table finds a match in the MemberDetails table. From the discussion of outer joins in Chapter 7, you know that NULL is returned when a match isn't found. NULLs indicate that YEAR(DateOfBirth) isn't found in the Films table, so by adding a WHERE clause that returns rows only when there's a NULL value in YearReleased, you make sure that the query will find all the rows in MemberDetails where there's no matching year of birth in the Films table's YearReleased column. The following query modifies the SQL to remove the WHERE clause and show the YearReleased column:

```
SELECT FirstName, LastName, YearReleased
    FROM MemberDetails
    LEFT OUTER JOIN Films
    ON Films.YearReleased = Year(MemberDetails.DateOfBirth)
ORDER BY YearReleased;
```

If you execute this query, you can see how the results came about:

FirstName	LastName	YearReleased
John	Jones	NULL
Jenny	Jones	NULL
John	Jackson	NULL
Jack	Johnson	NULL
Seymour	Botts	NULL
Susie	Simons	NULL
Jamie	Hills	NULL
Stuart	Dales	NULL
William	Doors	NULL
Catherine	Hawthorn	NULL
Steve	Gee	1967
Steve	Gee	1967
Steve	Gee	1967
Katie	Smith	1977
Doris	Night	1997

The advantage of using an outer join in this situation is that it's quite often more efficient, which can make a big difference when there are a lot of records involved. The other advantage if you're using MySQL before version 4.1 is that subqueries are not supported, so an outer join is the only option. The advantage of using subqueries is that they are easier to write and easier to read.

Using the ANY, SOME, and ALL Operators

The IN operator allows a simple comparison to see whether a value matches one in a list of values returned by a subquery. The ANY, SOME, and ALL operators not only allow an equality match but also allow any comparison operator to be used. In this section, I'll detail each of the ANY, SOME, and ALL operators, starting with ANY and SOME.

ANY and SOME Operators

First off, ANY and SOME are identical; they do the same thing but have a different name. The text and examples refer to the ANY operator, but you can use the SOME operator without it making one iota of difference. For ANY to return true to a match, the value being compared needs to match any one of the values returned by the subquery. You must place the comparison operator before the ANY keyword. For example, the following SQL uses the equality (=) operator to find out whether any members have the same birth year as the release date of a film in the Films table:

```
SELECT FirstName, LastName, YEAR(DateOfBirth)
FROM MemberDetails
WHERE YEAR(DateOfBirth) = ANY (SELECT YearReleased FROM Films);
```

The WHERE clause specifies that YEAR(DateOfBirth) must equal any one of the values returned by the subquery (SELECT YearReleased FROM Films). This subquery returns the following values, which you may remember from an earlier example:

YearReleased
1987
1967
1977
1997
2005
2001
1967
1947
1975
1980
1984
1988
1989
1989
1967

If YEAR(DateOfBirth) equals any one of these values, then the condition returns true and the WHERE clause allows the record into the final results. The final results of the query are as follows:

FirstName	LastName	YEAR(DateOfBirth)
Katie	Smith	1977
Steve	Gee	1967
Doris	Night	1997

Seem familiar? Yup, that's right, the results from = ANY are the same as using the IN operator:

```
SELECT FirstName, LastName, YEAR(DateOfBirth)
FROM MemberDetails
WHERE YEAR(DateOfBirth) IN (SELECT YearReleased FROM Films);
```

To obtain the same results as you would with the NOT IN operator, simply use the not equal (<>) operator, as shown in the following code:

```
SELECT FirstName, LastName, YEAR(DateOfBirth)
FROM MemberDetails
WHERE YEAR(DateOfBirth) <> ANY (SELECT YearReleased FROM Films);
```

Before you write off the ANY operator as just another way of using the IN operator, remember that you can use ANY with operators other than equal (=) and not equal (<>). The following example query finds a list of members who, while they were members, had the opportunity to attend a meeting:

```
SELECT FirstName, LastName
FROM MemberDetails
WHERE DateOfJoining < ANY (SELECT MeetingDate FROM Attendance);
```

The query checks to see whether the member joined before any one of the meeting dates. This query uses the less than (<) operator with ANY, and the condition evaluates to true if a member's DateOfJoining is less than any of the values returned by the subquery (SELECT MeetingDate FROM Attendance).

The results are shown in the following table:

FirstName	LastName
Katie	Smith
Steve	Gee

ALL Operator

The ALL operator requires that every item in the list (all the results of a subquery) comply with the condition set by the comparison operator used with ALL. For example, if a subquery returns 3, 9, and 15, then the following WHERE clause would evaluate to true because 2 is less than all the numbers in the list:

```
WHERE 2 < ALL (3,9,15)
```

However, the following WHERE clause would evaluate to false because 7 is not less than all of the numbers in the list:

```
WHERE 7 < ALL (3,9,15)
```

This is just an example, though, and you can't use ALL with literal numbers, only with a subquery.

Put the ALL operator into an example where you select MemberIds that are less than all the values returned by the subquery (SELECT FilmId FROM Films WHERE FilmId > 5):

```
SELECT MemberId
FROM MemberDetails
WHERE MemberId < ALL (SELECT FilmId FROM Films WHERE FilmId > 5);
```

The subquery (SELECT FilmId FROM Films WHERE FilmId > 5) returns the following values:

FilmId
6
7
8
9
10
11
12
13
14
15

Essentially, this means that the WHERE clause is as follows:

```
MemberId < ALL (6,7,8,9,10,11,12,13,14,15);
```

MemberId must be less than all of the listed values if the condition is to evaluate to true. The full results for the example query are displayed in the following table:

MemberId
1
4
5

There is something to be aware of when using ALL: the situation when the subquery returns no results at all. In this case, ALL will be true, which may seem a little weird, but it's based on fundamental principles of logic. So, if you change the subquery so that it returns no values and update the previous example, you end up with the following code:

```
SELECT MemberId
FROM MemberDetails
WHERE MemberId < ALL (SELECT FilmId FROM Films WHERE FilmId > 99);
```

You know for a fact that there are no FilmIds with a value higher than 99, so the subquery returns an empty set. However, the results set for the example is shown in the following table:

MemberId
1
10
14
6
5
8
7
11
15
4
13
12
9

The table represents every single row in the MemberDetails table; indeed, `MemberId < ALL (SELECT FilmId FROM Films WHERE FilmId > 99)` has evaluated to `true` every time due to an empty results set returned by the subquery.

That completes the look at the related operators `ANY`, `SOME`, and `ALL`. The next section continues the discussion of using operators with subqueries by examining the `EXISTS` operator.

Using the EXISTS Operator

The `EXISTS` operator is unusual in that it checks for rows and does not compare columns. So far you've seen lots of clauses that compare one column to another. On the other hand, `EXISTS` simply checks to see whether a subquery has returned one or more rows. If it has, then the clause returns `true`; if not, then it returns `false`.

This is best demonstrated with three very simple examples:

```
SELECT City
FROM Location
WHERE EXISTS (SELECT * FROM MemberDetails WHERE MemberId < 5);

SELECT City
FROM Location
WHERE EXISTS (SELECT * FROM MemberDetails WHERE MemberId > 99);

SELECT City
FROM Location
WHERE EXISTS (SELECT * FROM MemberDetails WHERE MemberId = 15);
```

Notice the use of the asterisk (*), which returns all columns, in the inner subqueries. EXISTS is row-based, not column-based, so it doesn't matter which columns are returned.

The first example uses the following SELECT query as its inner subquery:

```
(SELECT * FROM MemberDetails WHERE MemberId < 5);
```

This subquery provides a results set with three rows. Therefore, EXISTS evaluates to true, and you get the following results:

City
Orange Town
Windy Village
Big City

The second example uses the following inner subquery:

```
SELECT * FROM MemberDetails WHERE MemberId > 99
```

This returns no results because no records in MemberDetails have a MemberId greater than 99. Therefore, EXISTS returns false, and the outer SELECT statement returns no results.

Finally, the third example uses the following query as its inner subquery:

```
SELECT * FROM MemberDetails WHERE MemberId = 15
```

This query returns just one row, and even though some of the columns contain NULL values, it's still a valid row, and EXISTS returns true. In fact, even if the whole row contained NULLs, EXISTS would still return true. Remember, NULL doesn't mean no value; it means an unknown value. So, the results for the full query in the example are as follows:

City
Orange Town
Windy Village
Big City

You can reverse the logic of EXISTS by using the NOT operator, essentially checking to see whether no results are returned by the subquery. Modify the second example described previously, where the sub-query returns no results, adding a NOT operator to the EXISTS keyword:

```
SELECT City
FROM Location
WHERE NOT EXISTS (SELECT * FROM MemberDetails WHERE MemberId > 99);
```

Now NOT EXISTS returns true, and as a result the WHERE clause is also true. The final results are shown in the following table:

City
Orange Town
Windy Village
Big City

These examples are very simple and, to be honest, not that realistic in terms of how EXISTS is used. One issue with the examples is that the subqueries don't link in any way with the outer SELECT query, whereas normally you'd expect them to do so. The following Try It Out example is a lot more realistic. The task is to find out which categories have been chosen by three or more members as their favorite category of film, but these favorite categories must contain at least one film with a rating higher than 3.

Try It Out   Using the EXISTS Operator

Build the necessary query by following these steps:

1. First of all, formulate a SELECT statement that returns the values you want. In this case, you just want the Category from the Category table:

```
SELECT Category
FROM Category
```

2. Now you need to add a WHERE clause to ensure that you get only categories that have films rated 4 or higher and that have also been selected as a favorite by three or more members.

```
SELECT Category
FROM Category
WHERE EXISTS (SELECT * FROM Films
            WHERE Category.CategoryId =  Films.CategoryId
            AND Rating > 3
            )
```

3. Finally, you just want categories that three or more members have chosen as their favorite.

```
SELECT Category
FROM Category
WHERE EXISTS (SELECT * FROM Films
            WHERE Category.CategoryId =  Films.CategoryId
            AND Rating > 3
            AND (SELECT COUNT(CategoryId)
                FROM FavCategory
                WHERE FavCategory.CategoryId = Category.CategoryId)
                    >= 3
            );
```

4. You should receive the following results:

Category
Thriller
War
Sci-fi
Historical

How It Works

In the first step, you simply selected all the category names from the Category table — the main table from which the data is extracted. The subqueries come in Step 2 to filter the results.

In Step 2, begin with the rating first. Information about films' ratings is contained in the Films table, but all you want to know is whether there are films in a particular category that have a rating higher than 3. You're not interested in knowing the names of the films, so you used an EXISTS operator with a sub-query that returns a list of films rated higher than 3.

Next, you linked the outer and inner queries using the CategoryId column in the Category and Films tables. Now, if for a particular category there are films rated higher than 3, the subquery returns rows and EXISTS evaluates to true.

Finally, you used another subquery, nested inside the other subquery. This innermost subquery counts how many members like a particular category; then in the WHERE clause of the outer subquery, you check to see whether that value is 3 or more.

Using the HAVING Clause with Subqueries

Chapter 5 first introduced the HAVING clause, which is used to filter the groups displayed in a results set when a GROUP BY clause has been used. For example, to get a list of cities where the average year of birth of members in each city is greater than 1990, you could use the HAVING clause like this:

```
SELECT City
FROM MemberDetails
GROUP BY City
HAVING AVG(YEAR(DateOfBirth)) > 1990;
```

The preceding query compares against an actual value, 1990. A subquery is useful where you want to compare against a value extracted from the database itself rather than a predetermined value. For example, you might be asked to create a list of cities where the average year of birth is later than the average for the membership as a whole. To do this, you could use a HAVING clause plus a subquery that finds out the average year of birth of members:

```
SELECT City
FROM MemberDetails
GROUP BY City
HAVING AVG(YEAR(DateOfBirth)) >
       (SELECT AVG(YEAR(DateOfBirth)) FROM MemberDetails);
```

This is the same as the query just mentioned, except 1990 is replaced with a subquery that returns the average year of birth of all members, which happens to be 1965. The final results table is as follows:

City
Big City
Dover
New Town
Orange Town

Sometimes it's necessary to refer to the outer query, or even a query nested inside a subquery. To do this, you must give aliases to the tables involved, which is the topic of the next section on correlated subqueries.

Correlated Subquery

A *correlated subquery* is a subquery that references the outer query. A *correlation variable* is an alias given to tables and used to reference those tables in the subquery. In Chapter 3 you learned how to give tables a correlation, or alias name.

The following example demonstrates a correlated subquery. This example isn't necessarily the only way to get the result, but it does demonstrate a nested subquery. The query obtains from each category the cheapest possible DVD with the highest rating:

```
SELECT FilmName, Rating, DVDPrice, Category
FROM Films AS FM1 INNER JOIN Category AS C1 ON C1.CategoryId = FM1.CategoryId
WHERE FM1.DVDPrice =
    (SELECT MIN(DVDPrice)
     FROM Films AS FM2
     WHERE FM2.DVDPrice IS NOT NULL
       AND FM1.CategoryId = FM2.CategoryId
       AND FM2.Rating =
              (SELECT MAX(FM3.Rating)
               FROM Films AS FM3
               WHERE FM3.DVDPrice IS NOT NULL
                 AND FM2.CategoryId = FM3.CategoryId
               GROUP BY FM3.CategoryId)
     GROUP BY FM2.CategoryId)
ORDER BY FM1.CategoryId;
```

If you're using Oracle, remove the AS *keywords because Oracle doesn't require or support them when creating an alias.*

This is a big query, but when broken down it's actually fairly simple. There are three queries involved: the outer query and two inner subqueries. Begin with the most nested inner query:

```
(SELECT MAX(FM3.Rating)
            FROM Films AS FM3
            WHERE FM3.DVDPrice IS NOT NULL
              AND FM2.CategoryId = FM3.CategoryId
            GROUP BY FM3.CategoryId)
```

This inner query returns the highest-rated film within each category. Films that have no price (where DVDPrice is NULL, for example) are excluded, because you don't want them forming part of the final results. The Films table is given the alias FM3. The query also refers to the FM2 table, which is the alias given to the subquery in which this query is nested. The CategoryId columns of FM2 and FM3 are inner-joined to ensure that the MAX rating and MIN price are both from the same category. If you expand the SQL and now include the innermost query just described, and also the nested subquery that it was inside, you arrive at the following SQL:

```
(SELECT MIN(DVDPrice)
 FROM Films AS FM2
 WHERE FM2.DVDPrice IS NOT NULL
    AND FM1.CategoryId = FM2.CategoryId
    AND FM2.Rating =
            (SELECT MAX(FM3.Rating)
             FROM Films AS FM3
             WHERE FM3.DVDPrice IS NOT NULL
                AND FM2.CategoryId = FM3.CategoryId
             GROUP BY FM3.CategoryId)
 GROUP BY FM2.CategoryId)
```

The outer query here returns the minimum DVD price for the highest-rated film in each category. Remember that the innermost subquery returns the rating of the highest-rated DVD. The outer query's WHERE clause is set to specify that the film should also have a rating equal to the one returned by the subquery—thereby ensuring that it has a rating equal to the highest in the same category. Note that although an inner query can refer to any alias of a table outside the query, an outer query can't reference any tables in a query nested inside it. For example, this SQL won't work:

```
(SELECT MIN(DVDPrice)
    FROM Films AS FM2
    WHERE FM2.CategoryId = FM3.CategoryId
...
...
...
```

The table with alias FM3 is referenced, but that table is a nested subquery inside, and therefore it can't be referenced.

Finally, the entire query, with the outermost SELECT statement, is as follows:

```
SELECT FilmName, Rating, DVDPrice, Category
FROM Films AS FM1 INNER JOIN Category AS C1 ON C1.CategoryId = FM1.CategoryId
WHERE FM1.DVDPrice =
    (SELECT MIN(DVDPrice)
...
...
...
ORDER BY FM1.CategoryId;
```

The outermost query is a join between the Films table with an alias of FM1 and the Category table with an alias of C1. A WHERE clause specifies that FM1.DVDPrice must be equal to the DVD price returned by the subquery, the lowest price of a DVD in that category. This inner query, as you've seen, has a WHERE clause specifying that the film's rating must be equal to the highest-rated film for that category, as returned by the innermost subquery. So, three queries later, you have the lowest-priced, highest-rated film for each category. The results are displayed in the following table:

FilmName	Rating	DVDPrice	Category
The Maltese Poodle	1	2.99	Thriller
On Golden Puddle	4	12.99	Romance
One Flew over the Crow's Nest	2	8.95	Horror
Planet of the Japes	5	12.99	War
Soylent Yellow	5	12.99	Sci-fi
The Good, the Bad, and the Facially Challenged	5	8.95	Historical

That completes this chapter's coverage of subqueries used with SELECT statements. The next section looks at other SQL statements with which you can use subqueries.

Subqueries Used with Other Statements

So far, all the attention as far as subqueries go has been lavished on the SELECT statement. However, you can also use subqueries with statements inserting new data, updating data, or deleting data. The principles are the same, so what you've learned so far about subqueries pretty much applies the same to INSERT, DELETE, and UPDATE statements.

Using Subqueries with the INSERT Statement

Chapter 5 covered using SELECT and INSERT INTO statements. You no longer have to insert literal values, like this

```
INSERT INTO FavCategory (CategoryId, MemberId) VALUES (7,15)
```

Instead, you can use data from the database:

```
INSERT INTO FavCategory (CategoryId, MemberId) SELECT 7, MemberId FROM
   MemberDetails WHERE LastName = 'Hawthorn' AND FirstName = 'Catherine';
```

You can take this one step further and use subqueries to provide the data to be inserted. The film club chairperson has discovered that no one has selected the Film Noir category as their favorite. She's decided that people who like thrillers might also like film noir, so she wants all members who put the Thriller category down as a favorite to also now have Film Noir added as one of their favorite categories.

Film Noir has a CategoryId of 9; Thriller has a CategoryId of 1. You could use SQL to extract these values, but to keep the SQL slightly shorter and clearer for an example, use the CategoryId values without looking them up.

It's quite important not to make a mistake when using INSERT INTO with SELECT queries, or else a whole load of incorrect data might get inserted. Unless your query is very simple, it's preferable to create the SELECT part of the SQL first, double-check that it is giving the correct results, and then add the INSERT INTO bit, which is very simple anyway.

For the SELECT part of the query, you need to extract a MemberId from the MemberDetails table, where that member has selected the Thriller category, that is, where CategoryId equals 1. To prevent errors, you need to make sure that the member hasn't already selected the Film Noir category, a CategoryId of 9. It's playing safe, as currently no one has selected the Film Noir category, but just in case someone updates the database in the meantime, you should check that a member hasn't selected CategoryId 9 as a favorite before trying to make CategoryId 9 one of their favorites.

Try It Out   Nesting a Subquery within an INSERT Statement

In order to create the necessary statement, follow these steps:

1. Begin by building the outer part of the SELECT query:

```
SELECT 9, MemberId FROM MemberDetails AS MD1;
```

This portion of the query returns all the rows from the MemberDetails table. Oracle doesn't support the AS keyword as a way of defining an alias — it just needs the alias name — so remove the AS after MemberDetails if you're using Oracle.

2. Now add the first part of your WHERE clause that checks to see whether the member has selected Thriller as one of their favorite categories:

```
SELECT 9, MemberId FROM MemberDetails AS MD1
WHERE EXISTS
            (SELECT * from FavCategory FC1
              WHERE FC1.CategoryId = 1 AND FC1.MemberId = MD1.MemberId);
```

3. Now modify the subquery so that it returns rows only if the member hasn't already selected CategoryId 9 as one of their favorites:

```
SELECT 9, MemberId FROM MemberDetails AS MD1
WHERE EXISTS
        (SELECT * from FavCategory FC1
          WHERE FC1.CategoryId = 1 AND FC1.MemberId = MD1.MemberId
                   AND NOT EXISTS
                               (SELECT * FROM FavCategory AS FC2
                                 WHERE FC2.MemberId = FC1.MemberId AND
                                 FC2.CategoryId = 9));
```

Notice the nested subquery inside the other subquery that checks that there are no rows returned (that they do not exist), where the current MemberId has selected a favorite CategoryId of 9. Execute this query and you get the following results:

Literal Value of 9	MemberId
9	5
9	10
9	12

4. Next, quickly double-check a few of the results to see whether they really are correct. Having confirmed that they are, you can add the INSERT INTO bit:

```
INSERT INTO FavCategory (CategoryId, MemberId)
SELECT 9, MemberId FROM MemberDetails AS MD1
WHERE EXISTS
     (SELECT * from FavCategory FC1
      WHERE FC1.CategoryId = 1 AND FC1.MemberId = MD1.MemberId
                 AND NOT EXISTS
                           (SELECT * FROM FavCategory AS FC2
                            WHERE FC2.MemberId = FC1.MemberId AND
                            FC2.CategoryId = 9));
```

The INSERT INTO inserts the literal value 9 (representing the Film Noir's CategoryId) and MemberId into the FavCategory table. When you execute the SQL, you should find that four rows are added. Execute it a second, a third, or however many times, and no more rows will be added as the query checks for duplication, a good safeguard.

How It Works

In the first step, you selected 9, or the CategoryId of the Thriller category, and also MemberId from the MemberDetails table.

In the next step, you added a WHERE clause that uses a subquery. Using the EXISTS operator, it checks to see whether there are any rows when selecting records from the FavCategory table where the MemberId is the same as that in the MemberDetails table and where CategoryId is equal to 1 (the Thriller ID). Using FC1.MemberId = MD1.MemberId joins MemberDetails and FavCategory, making sure that the current rows in the MemberDetails and FavCategory tables are the same; otherwise the subquery would just return rows where any member had selected a CategoryId of 1. You also gave an alias to the FavCategory table of the inner query. The alias is then used in the inner query's WHERE clause and in the third step when another query is nested inside the inner query from Step 2.

Step 3 sees an inner, inner query added to the previous subquery's WHERE clause. Its role is to look for members who already have category 9 as one of their favorites. It does this by checking that the inner-most query doesn't return rows where the CategoryId is 9. The inner subquery, with its FavCategory table with an alias of FC1, is linked to the innermost query where the FavCategory table has been given the alias FC2. They are linked by MemberId, because you want to make sure when checking for a member's current favorites that it's the same member. The second condition in the innermost query's WHERE clause checks to see whether the favorite category is one with an ID of 9.

In the final step, the outer query is used to provide the data for an INSERT INTO statement that adds favorite category 9 as a member's favorite.

Using Subqueries with the UPDATE Statement

As with INSERT INTO, you can use subqueries to supply values for updating or to determine the WHERE clause condition in the same way that subqueries can be used with regular queries' WHERE clauses. An example makes this clear. Imagine that the film club chairperson has decided to boost profits by selling DVDs. To maximize profits, she wants films that are rated higher than 3 and that appear in four or more members' favorite categories to have their prices hiked up to that of the highest price in the database.

To tackle this query, you need to break it down. First, the new DVDPrice is to be the maximum price of any film in the Films table. For this, you need a subquery that returns the maximum DVDPrice using the MAX() function. Note that neither MS Access nor MySQL support updating a column using a subquery:

```
SELECT MAX(DVDPrice) FROM Films;
```

This query is used as a subquery in the UPDATE statement's SET statement, but before executing this statement, you need to add the WHERE clause:

```
UPDATE Films
SET DVDPrice = (SELECT MAX(DVDPrice) FROM Films);
```

You should create and test the WHERE clause inside a SELECT query before adding the WHERE clause to the UPDATE statement. A mistake risks changing, and potentially losing, a lot of DVDPrice data that shouldn't be changed.

Now create the WHERE clause. It needs to limit rows to those where the film's rating is higher than 3 and where the film is in a category selected as a favorite by three or more members. You also need to check whether the film is available on DVD — no point updating prices of films not for sale! The rating and availability parts are easy enough. You simply need to specify that the AvailableOnDVD column be set to Y and that the Films.Rating column be greater than 3:

```
SELECT CategoryId, FilmName FROM Films
WHERE AvailableOnDVD = 'Y' AND Films.Rating > 3;
```

Now for the harder part: selecting films that are in a category chosen as a favorite by three or more members. For this, use a subquery that counts how many members have chosen a particular category as their favorite:

```
SELECT CategoryId, FilmName FROM Films
WHERE (SELECT COUNT(*) FROM FavCategory
                WHERE FavCategory.CategoryId = Films.CategoryId) >= 3
      AND AvailableOnDVD = 'Y' AND Films.Rating > 3;
```

The COUNT(*) function counts the number of rows returned by the subquery; it counts how many members have chosen each category as their favorite. The WHERE clause of the subquery makes sure that the Films table in the outer query is linked to the FavCategory table of the inner query.

Execute this query and you should get the following results:

CategoryId	FilmName
4	Planet of the Japes
6	The Good, the Bad, and the Facially Challenged
5	Soylent Yellow

Now that you've confirmed that the statement works and double-checked the results, all that's left to do is to add the WHERE part of the query to the UPDATE statement you created earlier:

```
UPDATE Films SET DVDPrice = (SELECT MAX(DVDPrice) FROM Films)
WHERE (SELECT COUNT(*) FROM FavCategory WHERE FavCategory.CategoryId =
Films.CategoryId) >= 3
    AND AvailableOnDVD = 'Y' AND Films.Rating > 3;
```

Execute the final SQL and you should find that three rows are updated with DVDPrice being set to 15.99. This SQL won't work on MySQL or MS Access, as they don't support using subqueries to update a column, so you'll need to change the query to the following if you want the results displayed to match those shown later in the book:

```
UPDATE Films SET DVDPrice = 15.99
WHERE (SELECT COUNT(*) FROM FavCategory WHERE FavCategory.CategoryId =
Films.CategoryId) >= 3
    AND AvailableOnDVD = 'Y' AND Films.Rating > 3;
```

Using Subqueries with the DELETE FROM Statement

The only place for a subquery to go in a DELETE statement is in the WHERE clause. Everything you've learned so far about subqueries in a WHERE clause applies to its use with a DELETE statement, so you can launch straight into an example. In this example, you want to delete all locations where one or fewer members live and where a meeting has never been held.

As before, create the SELECT queries first to double-check your results, and then use the WHERE clauses with a DELETE statement. First, you need a query that returns the number of members living in each city:

```
SELECT COUNT(*), City
FROM MemberDetails
GROUP BY City, State;
```

This query is used as a subquery to check whether one or fewer members live in a particular city. It provides the following results:

COUNT(*)	City
1	NULL
1	Dover
2	Windy Village
2	Big City
2	Townsville
1	New Town
4	Orange Town

Now you need to find a list of cities in which a meeting has never been held:

```
SELECT LocationId, City
FROM Location
WHERE LocationId NOT IN (SELECT LocationId FROM Attendance);
```

The subquery is used to find all LocationIds from the Location table that are not in the Attendance table. This subquery provides the following results:

LocationId	City
3	Big City

Now you need to combine the WHERE clauses and add them to a DELETE statement. Doing so combines the WHERE clause of the preceding query, which included the following condition:

```
LocationId NOT IN (SELECT LocationId FROM Attendance);
```

Likewise, it combines the SELECT statement of the first example as a subquery:

```
SELECT COUNT(*), City
FROM MemberDetails
GROUP BY City, State;
```

The condition and the subquery are merged into the WHERE clause of the DELETE statement:

```
DELETE FROM Location
WHERE (SELECT COUNT(*) FROM MemberDetails
       WHERE Location.City = MemberDetails.City
       AND
       Location.State = MemberDetails.State
       GROUP BY City, State) <= 1
  AND
LocationId NOT IN (SELECT LocationId FROM Attendance);
```

In the first subquery, you count how many members live in a particular location from the Location table. If it's one or less, then that part of the WHERE clause evaluates to true. Note that the Location table of the DELETE statement and the MemberDetails tables of the subquery have been joined on the State and City fields:

```
Location.State = MemberDetails.State
```

This is absolutely vital, otherwise the subquery returns more than one result.

The second condition in the WHERE clause specifies that LocationId must not be in the Attendance table. Because an AND clause joins the two conditions in the WHERE clause, both conditions must be true.

If you execute the query, you find that no records match both conditions, and therefore no records are deleted from the Location table.

Summary

This chapter covered the nesting of a query inside another query, a powerful tool that you can use when faced with tricky data extraction questions. Specifically, this chapter covered the following topics:

❑ A subquery is just like a normal query, with SELECT clauses, WHERE statements, and GROUP BY and HAVING clauses.

❑ Subqueries can be included in a SELECT statement's column listing, or they can be used inside a WHERE statement to enable results to be filtered.

❑ Aggregate functions are commonly used with subqueries because a subquery must normally return just one record for each record in the main query.

❑ A subquery can return multiple rows when used with an IN, ANY, ALL, or EXISTS operator. These operators function as follows:

❑ The IN operator is used to find out whether a value is in one of the values returned by a subquery.

❑ The ANY operator allows a comparison between a value and any of the values returned by a subquery. Comparisons are not limited to just equals (=); rather, you can use any comparison operator, such as greater than (>), less than (<), and so on.

❑ The ALL operator requires that every item in the list, or all the results of a subquery, comply with the condition set by the comparison operator used with ALL.

❑ Whereas the other operators work on a column basis, EXISTS simply checks that a subquery returns one or more rows. It doesn't make any comparison of column values.

❑ Although queries are the main place where subqueries are used, you can also use them with INSERT INTO, UPDATE, and DELETE statements, either to filter what's changed or deleted or to provide the data to be inserted or changed.

That concludes this chapter's coverage of writing queries. This book has covered many of the things you'll encounter in your everyday SQL programming. The next chapter tackles all the theory and practice learned so far and puts it to use with some tricky query writing. That chapter also shows you how to tackle those mind-boggling queries and come out sane!

Exercises

1. The film club chairperson decides that she'd like a list of the total cost of all films for each category and the number of members who have chosen each category as their favorite.

2. List all towns that have two or more members but are not currently listed in the Location table.

Advanced Queries

In database programming, you'll find that roughly 95 percent of queries are fairly straightforward and are just a matter of working out what columns are required and including a simple WHERE clause to filter out the unwanted results. This chapter is all about how to tackle the other 5 percent, which are difficult and complex queries. This chapter also presents a number of questions and examines how to write the SQL to answer them. Specifically, this chapter covers the following:

❑ Tackling complex queries

❑ Formulating precise SELECT column lists and FROM clauses

❑ Writing ruthlessly efficient queries

Before getting into the specifics of the chapter, you need to begin by making some additions to the Film Club database.

Updating the Database

In order to give more scope for tricky queries and avoid repeating examples from previous chapters, this chapter extends the Film Club database and adds some new tables and data. Imagine that the film club chairperson wants to sell DVDs to members; the film club will employ salespeople to contact members and sell them DVDs. Therefore, you want to store details of the salespeople, details of orders taken, and details of what each order contains. In order to do this, you need to create three new tables (Orders, OrderItems, and SalesPerson), as shown in Figure 9-1:

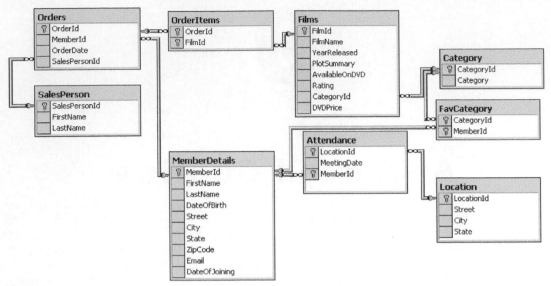

Figure 9-1

The SQL needed to create the new tables is shown subsequently. Note, however, that MS SQL Server doesn't support the `date` data type but instead uses the `datetime` data type. Therefore, you need to change the data type for the OrderDate column in the Orders table from `date` to `datetime`.

```
CREATE TABLE SalesPerson
(
  SalesPersonId integer NOT NULL PRIMARY KEY,
  FirstName varchar(50) NOT NULL,
  LastName varchar(50) NOT NULL
);

CREATE TABLE Orders
(
  OrderId integer NOT NULL Primary Key,
  MemberId integer,
  SalesPersonId integer,
  OrderDate date,
  CONSTRAINT SalesPerOrders_FK
  FOREIGN KEY (SalesPersonId)
  REFERENCES SalesPerson(SalesPersonId),
  CONSTRAINT MemberDetOrders_FK
  FOREIGN KEY (MemberId)
  REFERENCES MemberDetails(MemberId)
);

CREATE TABLE OrderItems
(
  OrderId INTEGER NOT NULL,
  FilmId INTEGER NOT NULL,
  CONSTRAINT Orders_FK
```

```
     FOREIGN KEY (OrderId)
     REFERENCES Orders(OrderId),
     CONSTRAINT Films_FK
     FOREIGN KEY (FilmId)
     REFERENCES Films(FilmId),
     CONSTRAINT OrderItems_PK PRIMARY KEY (OrderId, FilmId)
);
```

You need to execute this SQL against the database before continuing with the chapter. As well as creating the tables, also notice that primary keys and foreign keys are specified where appropriate. For example, MemberId in the Orders table is actually taken from the MemberId in the MemberDetails table — it's a foreign key. Therefore, a foreign key relationship is specified between MemberId in the Orders and MemberDetails tables to ensure that no invalid data is entered.

You also need to add some salesperson data to the SalesPerson table:

```
INSERT INTO SalesPerson(SalesPersonId, FirstName, LastName)
VALUES (1,'Sandra','Hugson');

INSERT INTO SalesPerson(SalesPersonId, FirstName, LastName)
VALUES (2,'Frasier','Crane');

INSERT INTO SalesPerson(SalesPersonId, FirstName, LastName)
VALUES (3,'Daphne','Moon');
```

Likewise, you need to add some Orders and OrderItems. Again, you can save a whole lot of typing by downloading the following code from www.wrox.com. Remember, if you're using Oracle, you need to change the date format for the OrderDate column to day-month_name-year

```
INSERT INTO Orders(OrderId, MemberId, SalesPersonId, OrderDate)
VALUES (10,7,1,'2006-07-30');

INSERT INTO OrderItems(OrderId,FilmId) Values (10,4);
INSERT INTO OrderItems(OrderId,FilmId) Values (10,8);

INSERT INTO Orders(OrderId, MemberId, SalesPersonId, OrderDate)
VALUES (11,4,1,'2006-08-06');

INSERT INTO OrderItems(OrderId,FilmId) Values (11,13);


INSERT INTO Orders(OrderId, MemberId, SalesPersonId, OrderDate)
VALUES (12,6,1, '2006-08-18');

INSERT INTO OrderItems(OrderId,FilmId) Values (12,9);
INSERT INTO OrderItems(OrderId,FilmId) Values (12,8);


INSERT INTO Orders(OrderId, MemberId, SalesPersonId, OrderDate)
VALUES (13,4,1,'2006-09-29');

INSERT INTO OrderItems(OrderId,FilmId) Values (13,12);
```

```
INSERT INTO OrderItems(OrderId,FilmId) Values (13,9);

INSERT INTO Orders(OrderId, MemberId, SalesPersonId, OrderDate)
VALUES (14,11,1,'2006-09-30');

INSERT INTO OrderItems(OrderId,FilmId) Values (14,8);



INSERT INTO Orders(OrderId, MemberId, SalesPersonId, OrderDate)
VALUES (15,15,1, '2006-10-01');

INSERT INTO OrderItems(OrderId,FilmId) Values (15,11);


INSERT INTO Orders(OrderId, MemberId, SalesPersonId, OrderDate)
VALUES (16,14,1,'2006-10-01');

INSERT INTO OrderItems(OrderId,FilmId) Values (16,2);
INSERT INTO OrderItems(OrderId,FilmId) Values (16,8);
INSERT INTO OrderItems(OrderId,FilmId) Values (16,15);

INSERT INTO Orders(OrderId, MemberId, SalesPersonId, OrderDate)
VALUES (17,9, 1,'2006-11-23');

INSERT INTO OrderItems(OrderId,FilmId) Values (17,4);



INSERT INTO Orders(OrderId, MemberId, SalesPersonId, OrderDate)
VALUES (18,6,1, '2006-11-27');

INSERT INTO OrderItems(OrderId,FilmId) Values (18,9);
INSERT INTO OrderItems(OrderId,FilmId) Values (18,8);

INSERT INTO Orders(OrderId, MemberId, SalesPersonId, OrderDate)
VALUES (19,9,1,'2006-11-29');

INSERT INTO OrderItems(OrderId,FilmId) Values (19,13);


INSERT INTO Orders(OrderId, MemberId, SalesPersonId, OrderDate)
VALUES (20,4,1,'2006-12-02');

INSERT INTO OrderItems(OrderId,FilmId) Values (20,12);
INSERT INTO OrderItems(OrderId,FilmId) Values (20,2);
INSERT INTO OrderItems(OrderId,FilmId) Values (20,13);
INSERT INTO OrderItems(OrderId,FilmId) Values (20,15);



INSERT INTO Orders(OrderId, MemberId, SalesPersonId, OrderDate)
VALUES (21,9,1, '2006-12-12');

INSERT INTO OrderItems(OrderId,FilmId) Values (21,11);
```

```
INSERT INTO Orders(OrderId, MemberId, SalesPersonId, OrderDate)
VALUES (22,8,1,'2006-12-19');

INSERT INTO OrderItems(OrderId,FilmId) Values (22,9);
INSERT INTO OrderItems(OrderId,FilmId) Values (22,15);


INSERT INTO Orders(OrderId, MemberId, SalesPersonId, OrderDate)
VALUES (23,9,1,'2007-01-01');

INSERT INTO OrderItems(OrderId,FilmId) Values (23,2);


INSERT INTO Orders(OrderId, MemberId, SalesPersonId, OrderDate)
VALUES (24,6,1, '2007-01-09');

INSERT INTO OrderItems(OrderId,FilmId) Values (24,15);


INSERT INTO Orders(OrderId, MemberId, SalesPersonId, OrderDate)
VALUES (25,7, 1,'2007-01-13');

INSERT INTO OrderItems(OrderId,FilmId) Values (25,8);

--


INSERT INTO Orders(OrderId, MemberId, SalesPersonId, OrderDate)
VALUES (1,7,2,'2006-10-23');

INSERT INTO OrderItems(OrderId,FilmId) Values (1,12);
INSERT INTO OrderItems(OrderId,FilmId) Values (1,15);


INSERT INTO Orders(OrderId, MemberId, SalesPersonId, OrderDate)
VALUES (2,4,2,'2006-10-30');

INSERT INTO OrderItems(OrderId,FilmId) Values (2,4);
INSERT INTO OrderItems(OrderId,FilmId) Values (2,12);
INSERT INTO OrderItems(OrderId,FilmId) Values (2,13);

INSERT INTO Orders(OrderId, MemberId, SalesPersonId, OrderDate)
VALUES (3,9,2, '2006-10-11');

INSERT INTO OrderItems(OrderId,FilmId) Values (3,8);


INSERT INTO Orders(OrderId, MemberId, SalesPersonId, OrderDate)
VALUES (4,7,2,'2006-11-12');

INSERT INTO OrderItems(OrderId,FilmId) Values (4,11);


INSERT INTO Orders(OrderId, MemberId, SalesPersonId, OrderDate)
```

```
VALUES (5,7, 2,'2006-12-02');

INSERT INTO OrderItems(OrderId,FilmId) Values (5,9);
INSERT INTO OrderItems(OrderId,FilmId) Values (5,8);
INSERT INTO OrderItems(OrderId,FilmId) Values (5,12);
INSERT INTO OrderItems(OrderId,FilmId) Values (5,11);
INSERT INTO OrderItems(OrderId,FilmId) Values (5,2);


INSERT INTO Orders(OrderId, MemberId, SalesPersonId, OrderDate)
VALUES (6,10,2, '2006-12-11');

INSERT INTO OrderItems(OrderId,FilmId) Values (6,8);


INSERT INTO Orders(OrderId, MemberId, SalesPersonId, OrderDate)
VALUES (7,4,2,'2006-10-23');

INSERT INTO OrderItems(OrderId,FilmId) Values (7,6);


INSERT INTO Orders(OrderId, MemberId, SalesPersonId, OrderDate)
VALUES (8,4,2,'2006-10-30');

INSERT INTO OrderItems(OrderId,FilmId) Values (8,13);
INSERT INTO OrderItems(OrderId,FilmId) Values (8,6);

INSERT INTO Orders(OrderId, MemberId, SalesPersonId, OrderDate)
VALUES (9,10,2, '2006-10-11');

INSERT INTO OrderItems(OrderId,FilmId) Values (9,13);
INSERT INTO OrderItems(OrderId,FilmId) Values (9,2);
INSERT INTO OrderItems(OrderId,FilmId) Values (9,4);


--



INSERT INTO Orders(OrderId, MemberId, SalesPersonId, OrderDate)
VALUES (26,11,3, '2006-11-09');

INSERT INTO OrderItems(OrderId,FilmId) Values (26,6);
INSERT INTO OrderItems(OrderId,FilmId) Values (26,15);
INSERT INTO OrderItems(OrderId,FilmId) Values (26,11);
INSERT INTO OrderItems(OrderId,FilmId) Values (26,4);

INSERT INTO Orders(OrderId, MemberId, SalesPersonId, OrderDate)
VALUES (27,13,3,'2006-11-19');

INSERT INTO OrderItems(OrderId,FilmId) Values (27,6);
INSERT INTO OrderItems(OrderId,FilmId) Values (27,15);
INSERT INTO OrderItems(OrderId,FilmId) Values (27,11);
INSERT INTO OrderItems(OrderId,FilmId) Values (27,4);
INSERT INTO OrderItems(OrderId,FilmId) Values (27,9);
```

```sql
INSERT INTO OrderItems(OrderId,FilmId) Values (27,2);
INSERT INTO OrderItems(OrderId,FilmId) Values (27,12);


INSERT INTO Orders(OrderId, MemberId, SalesPersonId, OrderDate)
VALUES (28,4,3,'2006-12-12');


INSERT INTO OrderItems(OrderId,FilmId) Values (28,12);
INSERT INTO OrderItems(OrderId,FilmId) Values (28,4);
INSERT INTO OrderItems(OrderId,FilmId) Values (28,15);
INSERT INTO OrderItems(OrderId,FilmId) Values (28,2);
INSERT INTO OrderItems(OrderId,FilmId) Values (28,11);
INSERT INTO OrderItems(OrderId,FilmId) Values (28,13);


INSERT INTO Orders(OrderId, MemberId, SalesPersonId, OrderDate)
VALUES (29,9,3, '2006-12-20');

INSERT INTO OrderItems(OrderId,FilmId) Values (29,13);
INSERT INTO OrderItems(OrderId,FilmId) Values (29,9);
INSERT INTO OrderItems(OrderId,FilmId) Values (29,11);


INSERT INTO Orders(OrderId, MemberId, SalesPersonId, OrderDate)
VALUES (30,12,3,'2006-12-21');


INSERT INTO OrderItems(OrderId,FilmId) Values (30,2);
INSERT INTO OrderItems(OrderId,FilmId) Values (30,4);
INSERT INTO OrderItems(OrderId,FilmId) Values (30,6);
INSERT INTO OrderItems(OrderId,FilmId) Values (30,8);
INSERT INTO OrderItems(OrderId,FilmId) Values (30,9);
INSERT INTO OrderItems(OrderId,FilmId) Values (30,11);
INSERT INTO OrderItems(OrderId,FilmId) Values (30,12);
INSERT INTO OrderItems(OrderId,FilmId) Values (30,13);


INSERT INTO OrderItems(OrderId,FilmId) Values (30,15);


INSERT INTO Orders(OrderId, MemberId, SalesPersonId, OrderDate)
VALUES (31,1,3,'2007-01-14');

INSERT INTO OrderItems(OrderId,FilmId) Values (31,2);
INSERT INTO OrderItems(OrderId,FilmId) Values (31,15);
INSERT INTO OrderItems(OrderId,FilmId) Values (31,11);
INSERT INTO OrderItems(OrderId,FilmId) Values (31,4);

INSERT INTO Orders(OrderId, MemberId, SalesPersonId, OrderDate)
VALUES (32,5,3, '2007-01-21');

INSERT INTO OrderItems(OrderId,FilmId) Values (32,6);
INSERT INTO OrderItems(OrderId,FilmId) Values (32,2);
```

Now that you've added the necessary data to the Film Club database, you can start writing and executing complex, difficult queries.

Tackling Difficult Queries

In this section, you learn some tips and techniques for writing difficult queries. Unfortunately, there's no quick fix, but hopefully by the time you've finished this section you'll be ready and raring to go solve some mind-bending queries.

The following list details the basic principles you should follow when creating a complex query:

❑   Decide what data you want. You might find that it helps to actually write a small portion of data on paper. That way, you know what results you're expecting and roughly how to get them.

❑   Create the SELECT clause and populate its column list. When you know what columns you're after, writing queries becomes much easier.

❑   Work out which tables to get your data from and create the FROM clause of the SELECT statement.

❑   Work through the FROM clause a bit at a time. Don't try to create all the table selections and joins all at once. Start simple and test the code at each stage to see if it works and gives the results that you expect. Then work out the FROM clause using a database diagram, and determine where you need to get your next column's data from and where the next join links to.

❑   Query elements that don't affect the final results (such as the ORDER BY clause) can wait until the end.

Considering the preceding list, the first tip might seem strange, but it's this: Ask yourself whether you really need to write a complex query? While it's quite satisfying to spend a day writing a query so complex that it confounds even the most gifted database guru, doing so might not always suit your needs. If you're in a project under tight deadlines, it might be a whole lot easier to write a few simple queries and do the data manipulation from a high-level language such as Visual Basic, C++, Java, or whatever language you use for application development. Writing multiple simple queries is sometimes quicker and the code is easier to understand.

Work Out What You Want, What You Really, Really Want

Leaping right into the middle of writing a query can be tempting, but in fact the first step is working out what the query's requirements are. You need to sit down and analyze what's been asked for and what the end results should be. A simple example might be if you're asked to delete a member from the MemberDetails table. On the face of it, this is just a simple DELETE FROM MemberDetails and a WHERE clause ensuring that only the member you want deleted is deleted. However, it has a ripple effect, as references to the member are also contained in the FavCategory table, in the Attendance table, and the Orders table. If the database is set up correctly, as the Film Club one is, then trying to delete a member but not deleting references to them in other tables will throw up an error. That's because constraints were set up to stop this from happening. However, if restraints don't exist, then it's all too easy to end up with orphaned data — for example, references to a member's favorite category for a member who doesn't exist!

A more complex question could be, "Who's the most successful salesperson?" Sounds easy enough — surely the most successful is the person who obtained the most orders. Or is it the person who sold the most number of DVDs? Or is it the salesperson who sold the most DVDs per order? Perhaps the most successful salesperson got the highest number of repeat customers?

The possibilities are endless, but hopefully you can see that deciding what data you're actually obtaining from the database is vital. The following example uses the total value of orders for each salesperson for each month. Having decided what you want, you need to look at where you're going to get the data.

Choosing the SELECT Column List

Now that you know the question, it's time to work out what data supplies the answer and where that data comes from. In order to answer the question, "What is the total value of orders for each salesperson for each month," you first need to work out what data is to be returned and populate the SELECT column list. The question asks for each salesperson's total value of orders for each month, so you need to know which salesperson, which month and year, and the total cost of orders placed. Your SELECT list should include the following:

```
SELECT FirstName, LastName, MONTH(OrderDate),  Year(OrderDate), SUM(DVDPrice)
```

FirstName and LastName are those of the salesperson. You use the MONTH() and YEAR() functions to extract the month and year from the OrderDate table. Finally, you add together all the DVDPrice values using the SUM() function. The next task is to work out where the data is going to come from and create the FROM clause.

Creating the FROM Clause

You know what you want, so now you need to work out which tables supply the data. For the salesperson's first and last names, this is easy — the data comes from the SalesPerson table. Start by including these details in the SELECT column list and then add the FROM clause:

```
SELECT FirstName, LastName
FROM SalesPerson
```

That's easy enough. Now you need details of when the orders were placed. This data can be found in the Orders table. However, you also need to link each order in the Orders table to the appropriate salesperson, whose details are found in the SalesPerson table. Use an inner join to link the SalesPersonId in the SalesPerson table with the SalesPersonId in the Orders table, as shown in the following statement:

```
SELECT FirstName, LastName,MONTH(OrderDate)AS Month, YEAR(OrderDate) As Year
FROM Orders INNER JOIN SalesPerson
    ON Orders.SalesPersonId = SalesPerson.SalesPersonId;
```

Note that this example won't work in Oracle because it does not support the YEAR() *function.*

If you run this SQL, you end up with details of every order placed:

FirstName	LastName	Month	Year
Frasier	Crane	10	2006
Frasier	Crane	10	2006
Frasier	Crane	10	2006
Frasier	Crane	11	2006
Frasier	Crane	12	2006
Frasier	Crane	12	2006
Frasier	Crane	10	2006
Frasier	Crane	10	2006
Frasier	Crane	10	2006
Sandra	Hugson	7	2006
Sandra	Hugson	8	2006
Sandra	Hugson	8	2006
Sandra	Hugson	9	2006
Sandra	Hugson	9	2006
Sandra	Hugson	10	2006
Sandra	Hugson	10	2006
Sandra	Hugson	11	2006
Sandra	Hugson	11	2006
Sandra	Hugson	11	2006
Sandra	Hugson	12	2006
Sandra	Hugson	12	2006
Sandra	Hugson	12	2006
Sandra	Hugson	1	2007
Sandra	Hugson	1	2007
Sandra	Hugson	1	2007
Daphne	Moon	11	2006
Daphne	Moon	11	2006
Daphne	Moon	12	2006
Daphne	Moon	12	2006
Daphne	Moon	12	2006
Daphne	Moon	1	2007
Daphne	Moon	1	2007

What you really want, however, is to group the orders according to the month and year in which they were placed, necessitating a GROUP BY clause:

```
SELECT FirstName, LastName,MONTH(OrderDate)AS Month, YEAR(OrderDate) As Year
FROM Orders INNER JOIN SalesPerson
    ON Orders.SalesPersonId = SalesPerson.SalesPersonId
GROUP BY FirstName,LastName,MONTH(OrderDate), YEAR(OrderDate);
```

Executing the preceding query groups the results by salesperson, month, and year, as shown in the following table:

FirstName	LastName	Month	Year
Daphne	Moon	1	2007
Daphne	Moon	11	2006
Daphne	Moon	12	2006
Frasier	Crane	10	2006
Frasier	Crane	11	2006
Frasier	Crane	12	2006
Sandra	Hugson	1	2007
Sandra	Hugson	7	2006
Sandra	Hugson	8	2006
Sandra	Hugson	9	2006
Sandra	Hugson	10	2006
Sandra	Hugson	11	2006
Sandra	Hugson	12	2006

So far, you have a list of salespeople as well as month and year values. There's no link to the items contained in each order. Your next task is to link the current tables, SalesPerson and Orders, to items in each order. This data is contained in the OrderItems table, which is the next table to which you must create a link. The value that links the current tables and OrderItems is the OrderId present in the Orders and OrderItems tables. Join OrderItems to the current tables using an inner join, as illustrated in the following statement:

```
SELECT FirstName, LastName,MONTH(OrderDate)AS Month, YEAR(OrderDate) AS Year
FROM (Orders INNER JOIN SalesPerson ON Orders.SalesPersonId =
SalesPerson.SalesPersonId)
INNER JOIN OrderItems ON OrderItems.OrderId = Orders.OrderId
GROUP BY FirstName,LastName,MONTH(OrderDate), YEAR(OrderDate);
```

If you run this query, you won't see any difference between these results and the previous results. Also, what you're really after is the total cost of all orders placed in each month by each salesperson, which is represented by the SUM(DVDPrice) data in the original SELECT list described previously. However, the

DVDPrice column is in the Films table, so you need to find a link between the currently included tables in the FROM clause, which are the SalesPerson, Orders, OrderItems, and Films tables. That link is provided by the OrderItems table, which has the FilmId of the film purchased. Begin by adding the Films table and linking it with the current tables using an inner join:

```
SELECT FirstName, LastName, MONTH(OrderDate)AS Month, YEAR(OrderDate) AS Year
FROM (((Orders INNER JOIN SalesPerson ON Orders.SalesPersonId =
SalesPerson.SalesPersonId)
INNER JOIN OrderItems ON OrderItems.OrderId = Orders.OrderId))
INNER JOIN Films ON Films.FilmId = OrderItems.FilmId
GROUP BY FirstName,LastName,MONTH(OrderDate), YEAR(OrderDate);
```

Finally, you can add the total sales per month to the SELECT clause:

```
SELECT FirstName, LastName, MONTH(OrderDate)AS Month, YEAR(OrderDate) AS Year,
SUM(DVDPrice) AS Total
FROM ((Orders INNER JOIN SalesPerson ON Orders.SalesPersonId =
SalesPerson.SalesPersonId)
INNER JOIN OrderItems ON OrderItems.OrderId = Orders.OrderId)
INNER JOIN Films ON Films.FilmId = OrderItems.FilmId
GROUP BY FirstName,LastName,MONTH(OrderDate), YEAR(OrderDate);
```

Remember that the SQL groups orders placed by salesperson and by month, so the SUM(DVDPrice) is the sum of all the DVDs sold by salesperson and by month. The results are as follows:

FirstName	LastName	Month	Year	Total
Daphne	Moon	1	2007	80.94
Daphne	Moon	11	2006	141.85
Daphne	Moon	12	2006	221.74
Frasier	Crane	10	2006	151.88
Frasier	Crane	11	2006	12.99
Frasier	Crane	12	2006	50.90
Sandra	Hugson	1	2007	31.97
Sandra	Hugson	7	2006	12.98
Sandra	Hugson	8	2006	27.93
Sandra	Hugson	9	2006	21.93
Sandra	Hugson	10	2006	44.96
Sandra	Hugson	11	2006	37.92
Sandra	Hugson	12	2006	92.89

The query is nearly complete, save two things. First, what if two or more salespeople have the same name? This would mean that all their results would be lumped together because you've grouped by

FirstName and LastName. You need to add SalesPersonId, which is unique to each salesperson, to the GROUP BY clause, as well as display it in the final results:

```
SELECT SalesPerson.SalesPersonId, FirstName, LastName, MONTH(OrderDate)AS Month,
YEAR(OrderDate) AS Year, SUM(DVDPrice) AS Total
FROM ((Orders INNER JOIN SalesPerson ON Orders.SalesPersonId =
SalesPerson.SalesPersonId)
INNER JOIN OrderItems ON OrderItems.OrderId = Orders.OrderId)
INNER JOIN Films ON Films.FilmId = OrderItems.FilmId
GROUP BY SalesPerson.SalesPersonId, FirstName,LastName,MONTH(OrderDate),
YEAR(OrderDate);
```

Executing the query provides the following results:

SalesPersonId	FirstName	LastName	Month	Year	Total
1	Sandra	Hugson	1	2007	31.97
1	Sandra	Hugson	7	2006	12.98
1	Sandra	Hugson	8	2006	27.93
1	Sandra	Hugson	9	2006	21.93
1	Sandra	Hugson	10	2006	44.96
1	Sandra	Hugson	11	2006	37.92
1	Sandra	Hugson	12	2006	92.89
2	Frasier	Crane	10	2006	151.88
2	Frasier	Crane	11	2006	12.99
2	Frasier	Crane	12	2006	50.90
3	Daphne	Moon	1	2007	80.94
3	Daphne	Moon	11	2006	141.85
3	Daphne	Moon	12	2006	221.74

The second slight issue is the order of the results. They would be easier to read if they were ordered by salesperson and then by month and year, as shown in the ORDER BY clause of the following statement:

```
SELECT SalesPerson.SalesPersonId, FirstName, LastName, MONTH(OrderDate)AS Month,
YEAR(OrderDate) AS Year, SUM(DVDPrice) AS Total
FROM ((Orders INNER JOIN SalesPerson ON Orders.SalesPersonId =
SalesPerson.SalesPersonId)
INNER JOIN OrderItems ON OrderItems.OrderId = Orders.OrderId)
INNER JOIN Films ON Films.FilmId = OrderItems.FilmId
GROUP BY SalesPerson.SalesPersonId, FirstName,LastName,MONTH(OrderDate),
YEAR(OrderDate)
ORDER BY LastName, FirstName, YEAR(OrderDate), MONTH(OrderDate);
```

The final results are as follows:

SalesPersonId	FirstName	LastName	Month	Year	Total
2	Frasier	Crane	10	2006	160.83
2	Frasier	Crane	10	2006	151.88
2	Frasier	Crane	11	2006	12.99
2	Frasier	Crane	12	2006	50.90
1	Sandra	Hugson	7	2006	12.98
1	Sandra	Hugson	8	2006	27.93
1	Sandra	Hugson	9	2006	21.93
1	Sandra	Hugson	10	2006	44.96
1	Sandra	Hugson	11	2006	37.92
1	Sandra	Hugson	12	2006	92.89
1	Sandra	Hugson	1	2007	31.97
3	Daphne	Moon	11	2006	141.85
3	Daphne	Moon	12	2006	221.74

Hopefully this example has given you an idea of how to tackle slightly more complex queries. The following Try It Out puts your knowledge to the test, asking you to write a complex query that identifies how many repeat customers each salesperson has had.

Try It Out   Identifying Repeat Customers

1. Although total sales is a good indicator of a salesperson's success, the film club chairperson is interested to know how many people have ordered again from the same salesperson. First, the chairperson wants to know details of orders where the customer had ordered more than once from the same salesperson. The SQL to do this is as follows:

```
SELECT SalesPerson.SalesPersonId,
       SalesPerson.FirstName,
       SalesPerson.LastName,
       MemberDetails.MemberId,
       MemberDetails.FirstName,
       MemberDetails.LastName
FROM (Orders INNER JOIN MemberDetails
ON Orders.MemberId = MemberDetails.MemberId)
INNER JOIN SalesPerson
ON Orders.SalesPersonId = SalesPerson.SalesPersonId
GROUP BY SalesPerson.SalesPersonId,
       SalesPerson.FirstName,
       SalesPerson.LastName,
       MemberDetails.MemberId,
       MemberDetails.FirstName,
       MemberDetails.LastName
HAVING COUNT(Orders.MemberId) > 1
ORDER BY SalesPerson.SalesPersonId;
```

2. The film club chairperson also wants to know how many repeat orders each customer placed with the salesperson. The SQL to do this is shown below:

```
SELECT SalesPerson.SalesPersonId,
       SalesPerson.FirstName,
       SalesPerson.LastName,
       MemberDetails.MemberId,
       MemberDetails.FirstName,
       MemberDetails.LastName,
       COUNT(*) - 1
FROM (Orders INNER JOIN MemberDetails
ON Orders.MemberId = MemberDetails.MemberId)
INNER JOIN SalesPerson
ON Orders.SalesPersonId = SalesPerson.SalesPersonId
GROUP BY SalesPerson.SalesPersonId,
       SalesPerson.FirstName,
       SalesPerson.LastName,
       MemberDetails.MemberId,
       MemberDetails.FirstName,
       MemberDetails.LastName
HAVING COUNT(Orders.MemberId) > 1
ORDER BY SalesPerson.SalesPersonId;
```

How It Works

First, you need to think about what the question involves. Basically, it involves counting how many times a customer has ordered from the same salesperson. If the customer makes repeat orders from the same salesperson, then display that record in the results.

Now you need to work out where the data to answer the question comes from. Details about orders are found in the Orders table. Start simple and create a SELECT list that obtains the SalesPersonId and MemberId — the customer who placed the order:

```
SELECT SalesPersonId, MemberId
FROM Orders;
```

This basic query gives the following results:

SalesPersonId	MemberId
2	7
2	4
2	9
2	7
2	7
2	10
2	4
2	4

Table continued on following page

SalesPersonId	MemberId
2	10
1	7
1	4
1	6
1	4
1	11
1	15
1	14
1	9
1	6
1	9
1	4
1	9
1	8
1	9
1	6
1	7
3	11
3	13
3	4
3	9
3	12
3	1
3	5

Using this table, how would you manually work out the answer? You would group the data into each salesperson and customers who ordered from them and then count how many identical customers each salesperson had. To do this in SQL, you need to add a GROUP BY clause grouping salespeople and customers:

```
SELECT SalesPersonId, MemberId
FROM Orders
GROUP BY SalesPersonId, MemberId
ORDER BY SalesPersonId
```

Executing the preceding query provides these results:

SalesPersonId	MemberId
1	4
1	6
1	7
1	8
1	9
1	11
1	14
1	15
2	4
2	7
2	9
2	10
3	1
3	4
3	5
3	9
3	11
3	12
3	13

Identical SalesPersonId and MemberId records are now grouped, but the results still include members who placed only one order with a salesperson. You want only those customers who ordered more than once, so you need to count the number of customers in each group who ordered from a specific salesperson. If the MemberId appears more than once, that particular customer has ordered more than once from that salesperson:

```
SELECT SalesPersonId, MemberId
FROM Orders
GROUP BY SalesPersonId, MemberId
HAVING COUNT(MemberId) > 1
ORDER BY SalesPersonId
```

Each group contains all the rows with the same salesperson and customer. The COUNT(MemberId) function counts the number of rows in each group, and the HAVING clause restricts the display of groups to only those where the count is more than 1 — that is, more than one order by the same customer with the same salesperson. This query provides the following results:

SalesPersonId	MemberId
1	4
1	6
1	7
1	9
2	4
2	7
2	10

Although you now have the answer to the question, it would be a whole lot nicer to see the names rather than SalesPersonId and MemberId. To display the names, create a join between the SalesPerson and MemberDetails tables:

```
SELECT SalesPerson.SalesPersonId,
       SalesPerson.FirstName,
       SalesPerson.LastName,
       MemberDetails.MemberId,
       MemberDetails.FirstName,
       MemberDetails.LastName
FROM (Orders INNER JOIN MemberDetails
ON Orders.MemberId = MemberDetails.MemberId)
INNER JOIN SalesPerson
ON Orders.SalesPersonId = SalesPerson.SalesPersonId
GROUP BY SalesPerson.SalesPersonId,
       SalesPerson.FirstName,
       SalesPerson.LastName,
       MemberDetails.MemberId,
       MemberDetails.FirstName,
       MemberDetails.LastName
HAVING COUNT(Orders.MemberId) > 1
ORDER BY SalesPerson.SalesPersonId
```

Although you added a lot of new code, it's just a result of joining two new tables, MemberDetails and SalesPerson. The various names and IDs of the salespeople and members have been added to the SELECT column list, as shown in the following:

```
SELECT SalesPerson.SalesPersonId,
       SalesPerson.FirstName,
       SalesPerson.LastName,
       MemberDetails.MemberId,
       MemberDetails.FirstName,
       MemberDetails.LastName
```

The column names appear in more than one of the tables, so each has to be prefixed by the name of the table the column comes from. The GROUP BY clause requires that columns in the SELECT column list also appear in the GROUP BY list, so you added them there also:

```
GROUP BY SalesPerson.SalesPersonId,
         SalesPerson.FirstName,
         SalesPerson.LastName,
         MemberDetails.MemberId,
         MemberDetails.FirstName,
         MemberDetails.LastName
```

The FROM clause has two INNER JOIN statements added to it, joining the MemberDetails and SalesPerson tables:

```
FROM (Orders INNER JOIN MemberDetails
ON Orders.MemberId = MemberDetails.MemberId)
INNER JOIN SalesPerson
ON Orders.SalesPersonId = SalesPerson.SalesPersonId
```

Finally, you updated the ORDER BY clause so that it orders by the SalesPerson table's SalesPersonId column, because this column appears in the GROUP BY clause, and only columns in GROUP BY can be ordered.

```
ORDER BY SalesPerson.SalesPersonId
```

The final results are shown in the following table:

SalesPersonId	FirstName	LastName	MemberId	FirstName	LastName
1	Sandra	Hugson	4	Steve	Gee
1	Sandra	Hugson	6	Jenny	Jones
1	Sandra	Hugson	7	John	Jackson
1	Sandra	Hugson	9	Seymour	Botts
2	Frasier	Crane	4	Steve	Gee
2	Frasier	Crane	7	John	Jackson
2	Frasier	Crane	10	Susie	Simons

That completes the first part of the Try It Out — on to the second part.

The second step asked you to find out how many repeat orders each customer placed with each salesperson.

It's fairly easy to modify the SQL from the first step so that in addition to the current results it also shows the number of total repeat orders in each group. Remember that each group consists of a SalesPerson and the orders by the same Customer. However, the question asks for the number of repeat orders each customer made, not the total number of orders. The first order made doesn't count, so you need to add COUNT(*) but then deduct 1 from it:

```
SELECT SalesPerson.SalesPersonId,
       SalesPerson.FirstName,
       SalesPerson.LastName,
       MemberDetails.MemberId,
```

```
        MemberDetails.FirstName,
        MemberDetails.LastName,
        COUNT(*) - 1
FROM (Orders INNER JOIN MemberDetails
ON Orders.MemberId = MemberDetails.MemberId)
INNER JOIN SalesPerson
ON Orders.SalesPersonId = SalesPerson.SalesPersonId
GROUP BY SalesPerson.SalesPersonId,
         SalesPerson.FirstName,
         SalesPerson.LastName,
         MemberDetails.MemberId,
         MemberDetails.FirstName,
         MemberDetails.LastName
HAVING COUNT(Orders.MemberId) > 1
ORDER BY SalesPerson.SalesPersonId
```

There's very often more than one way to write a query. This section shows you one alternative way of writing the same query you wrote in the previous Try It Out, though there may be even more ways. This alternative way uses a self-join, with the Orders table joined to itself. Consider the following statement:

```
SELECT SalesPerson.SalesPersonId,
       SalesPerson.FirstName,
       SalesPerson.LastName,
       MemberDetails.MemberId,
       MemberDetails.FirstName,
       MemberDetails.LastName,
 COUNT(*) AS "Repeat Orders"
FROM ((Orders O1 INNER JOIN Orders O2
ON O1.MemberId = O2.MemberId AND O1.SalesPersonId = O2.SalesPersonId
AND O1.OrderId > O2.OrderId)
INNER JOIN MemberDetails
ON O1.MemberId = MemberDetails.MemberId)
INNER JOIN SalesPerson
ON O1.SalesPersonId = SalesPerson.SalesPersonId
GROUP BY SalesPerson.SalesPersonId,
         SalesPerson.FirstName,
         SalesPerson.LastName,
         MemberDetails.MemberId,
         MemberDetails.FirstName,
         MemberDetails.LastName
ORDER BY SalesPerson.SalesPersonId;
```

The SELECT column list is virtually identical, except that repeat order values are now obtained using COUNT(*), whereas before they were obtained with COUNT(*) - 1. The reason for this change is that this query, you see shortly, returns only the repeat orders and not the first order placed by a member. Also, because of this change, you don't need a HAVING clause that limits records where each group has more than one member.

The difference between this query and the query you previously wrote is in the FROM clause and its use of a self-join. The Orders table is joined to itself, the first table being given an alias of O1 and the second an alias of O2. The MemberId and SalesPersonId columns are joined on the basis of being the same, and the OrderDate column is joined on the basis of O1's OrderDate being after O2's, which ensures that only the repeat orders are included. If there's only one order, then clearly O1.OrderDate can never be higher than O2.OrderDate, as the order in O2 is the same record with identical values.

Executing the preceding SQL creates the following results set:

SalesPersonId	FirstName	LastName	MemberId	FirstName	LastName	Repeat Orders
1	Sandra	Hugson	4	Steve	Gee	3
1	Sandra	Hugson	6	Jenny	Jones	3
1	Sandra	Hugson	7	John	Jackson	1
1	Sandra	Hugson	9	Seymour	Botts	6
2	Frasier	Crane	4	Steve	Gee	3
2	Frasier	Crane	7	John	Jackson	3
2	Frasier	Crane	10	Susie	Simons	1

As you would expect, these results are identical to the previous SQL's results. So which query is best? First, it depends on which query you find easiest to use. Programmer time is often more expensive than computer time, so if one way of writing a query is easier for you, then stick with it unless there's a good reason to do it another way.

The other side of things is efficiency — which query runs faster? In the two different ways shown, the first is slightly more efficient. It has one less join than the second way, because the second way has to have an INNER JOIN of the Orders table to itself. The first way gets the same results but filters out nonduplicate orders using a HAVING clause.

You may even be able to think of a third or fourth (or fifth or sixth) way of writing the same query, one that might be even faster. In the real world, however, most programmers don't have the time to write the same code in five different ways in a bid to save fractions of a second. Unless, of course, efficiency is absolutely paramount — for example, where there are millions and millions of records and your initial SQL runs with all the speed of a tortoise through molasses.

To help you speed up your queries, the next section covers some tips on writing efficient queries.

Top Tips for Efficient Queries

❑ **When using AND, put the condition least likely to be true first.** The database system evaluates conditions from left to right, subject to operator precedence. If you have two or more AND operators in a condition, the one to the left is evaluated first, and if and only if it's true is the next condition evaluated. Finally, if that condition is true, then the third condition is evaluated. You can save the database system work, and hence increase speed, by putting the least likely condition first. For example, if you were looking for all members living in New State and born before January 1, 1940, you could write the following query:

```
SELECT FirstName, LastName
FROM MemberDetails
WHERE State = 'New State' AND DateOfBirth < '1940-01-01';
```

The query would work fine; however, the number of members born before that date is very small, whereas plenty of people live in New State. This means that State = New State will occur a number of times and the database system will go on to check the second condition, DateOfBirth < '1940-01-01'. If you swap the conditions around, the least likely condition (DateOfBirth < '1940-01-01') is evaluated first:

```
SELECT FirstName, LastName
FROM MemberDetails
WHERE DateOfBirth < '1940-01-01' AND State = 'New State';
```

Because the condition is mostly going to be false, the second condition will rarely be executed, which saves time. It's not a big deal when there are few records, but it is when there are a lot of them.

❑ **When using OR, put the condition most likely to be true first.** Whereas AND needs both sides to be true for the overall condition to be true, OR needs only one side to be true. If the left-hand side is true, there's no need for OR to check the other condition, so you can save time by putting the most likely condition first. Consider the following statement:

```
SELECT FirstName, LastName
FROM MemberDetails
WHERE State = 'New State' OR DateOfBirth < '1940-01-01';
```

If New State is true, and it is true more often than DateOfBirth < '1940-01-01' is true, then there's no need for the database system to evaluate the other condition, thus saving time.

❑ **DISTINCT can be faster than GROUP BY.** DISTINCT and GROUP BY often do the same thing: limit results to unique rows. However, DISTINCT is often faster with some database systems than GROUP BY. For example, examine the following GROUP BY:

```
SELECT MemberId
FROM Orders
GROUP BY MemberId;
```

The GROUP BY could be rewritten using the DISTINCT keyword:

```
SELECT DISTINCT MemberId
FROM Orders;
```

❑ **Restrict join results.** The less information the database has to pull out, the better. This is particularly true with joins, which are very expensive time-wise. Put the restrictive condition on the outer table of the join. The outer table is the table on the right of the INNER JOIN keyword. For example, in the following code, the table with the restriction — a condition in the WHERE clause restricting results — is the MemberDetails table, which is the outer table in the join:

```
SELECT MemberDetails.MemberId, FirstName, LastName
FROM Orders INNER JOIN MemberDetails
ON Orders.MemberId = MemberDetails.MemberId
WHERE MemberDetails.DateOfBirth BETWEEN '1900-01-01' AND '1970-12-31';
```

❏ **Use IN with your subqueries.** When you write a query similar to the following, the database system has to get all the results from the subquery to make sure that it returns only one value:

```
SELECT FirstName, LastName
FROM MemberDetails
WHERE MemberId = (SELECT MemberId FROM Orders WHERE OrderId = 2);
```

If you rewrite the query using the IN operator, the database system only needs to get results until there's a match with the values returned by the subquery; it doesn't necessarily have to get all the values:

```
SELECT FirstName, LastName
FROM MemberDetails
WHERE MemberId IN (SELECT MemberId FROM Orders WHERE OrderId = 2);
```

❏ **Avoid using SELECT * FROM.** Specifying which columns you need has a few advantages, not all of them about efficiency. First, it makes clear which columns you're actually using. If you use SELECT * and actually use only two out of seven of the columns, it's hard to guess from the SQL alone which ones you're using. If you say SELECT FirstName, LastName...then it's quite obvious which columns you're using. From an efficiency standpoint, specifying columns reduces the amount of data that has to pass between the database and the application connecting to the database. This is especially important where the database is connected over a network.

❏ **Search on integer columns.** If you have a choice, and often you don't, search on integer columns. For example, if you are looking for the member whose name is William Doors and whose MemberId is 13, then it makes sense to search via the MemberId because it's much faster. In the Film Club database, it's also the primary key column, so there's even more of a speed boost.

Summary

This chapter looked at how to tackle difficult query writing. You examined some fairly involved queries and learned how to break them down into manageable chunks, and then you saw a few tips on how to increase the efficiency of your queries. Specifically, this chapter covered the following topics:

❏ Working out what the question is and what it actually involves

❏ How to create complex queries by following a basic process:

   ❏ Creating the SELECT list first

   ❏ Looking at the FROM clause and how you need to obtain your data

❏ Tackling difficult queries

❏ Using tips to write more efficient queries

By now, you should be familiar enough with SQL to design databases; populate tables and columns in those databases; add, insert, retrieve, and delete data from your databases; and write complex queries that obtain exactly the information you want. The chapters that follow cover topics more tangentially related to SQL, such as views, transactions, security, and methods for tuning your database so that it performs optimally. The next chapter covers views and discusses how to use them to pull specific data for specific users and create coherent data sets that are of interest to a particular user or application.

Exercises

Assume that a new table called FilmStars has been added to the Film Club database and that it has been populated with the following values:

```
CREATE TABLE FilmStars
(
 StarId integer,
 StarName varchar(100),
 StarAge integer
);

INSERT INTO FilmStars(StarId, StarName, StarAge)
VALUES (1,'Boris Carlot',102);

INSERT INTO FilmStars(StarId, StarName, StarAge)
VALUES (1,'Scarlet O''Hairpin',89);

INSERT INTO FilmStars(StarId, StarName, StarAge)
VALUES (3,'Boris Carlot',102);

INSERT INTO FilmStars(StarId, StarName, StarAge)
VALUES (4,'Michael Hourglass',56);

INSERT INTO FilmStars(StarId, StarName, StarAge)
VALUES (5,'Dusty Hoffperson',48);

INSERT INTO FilmStars(StarId, StarName, StarAge)
VALUES (6,'Boris Carlot',102);

INSERT INTO FilmStars(StarId, StarName, StarAge)
VALUES (7,'Dusty Hoffperson',48);
```

You can either type the code in yourself or download this file from the book's Web site, found at www.wrox.com.

1. As you can see, there are quite a few duplicate entries. Write the SQL to remove the unneeded duplicate rows, leaving just the one row.

Views

Views, as the name implies, are queries used to provide users with a specific view of the data in the database. In doing so, views serve a variety of purposes. They may tie related tables together and then pull selected fields out that specific users need, or they may pull selected interesting rows of data from a table that contains other rows of no interest to specific users. They may summarize large data sets, returning averages, counts, and the like. Relational databases are sets of data in tables, which, taken alone, are rarely of any use to anyone. Views allow the database administrator (DBA) to pull fields of interest from tables of interest and return a coherent data set useful to some specific user or application.

In this chapter, you learn how to build and save views for reuse, how to use views to tie related data back together, how to use views to narrow or limit the data that users are allowed to see, and how views may be used for security purposes.

Introducing Views

A normalized database is created by designing tables for each object or event being modeled, with the fields of each table representing an attribute of the object or event. Once the developer creates the normalized structure, it becomes necessary to allow users to view specific pieces of data. The users rarely understand the structure, so the DBA is often tasked with building the views that various users require. A *view* is nothing more than a SQL statement that is stored in the database with an associated name. Views allow the DBA to do the following:

❑ Structure data in a way that users or classes of users find natural or intuitive

❑ Restrict access to the data such that a user can see and (sometimes) modify exactly what they need and no more

❑ Simplify the DBA's job by building base data structures that the DBA can use to build other views in a natural progression

❑ Summarize data for reports

Now that you know what views allow the DBA to do, the following list shows you how views can be enormously useful and provide a variety of benefits to the DBA.

❑ Views are often used to provide security, limiting results sets to exactly the fields and records needed by a particular user. This security allows the DBA to set up results sets for users that prevent them from seeing data intended for other users or that allow them to see sensitive data that other users are not allowed to see.

❑ Views can provide the basis for other views or queries. Once a results set is defined, you can manipulate that base data set using column functions such as `Sum()`, `Avg()`, `Count()`, `Max()`, and `Min()`. You can also sort or filter base data in another query or view. Views can thus be built up, layer after layer, each layer performing some specific function to transform the base data in some way.

❑ Views can provide personalization of data, turning a bewildering array of normalized tables into one or more views of the data familiar to a user.

❑ Views can rename fields so that users with different backgrounds can view data in familiar terms.

❑ Because a view is just a saved query, they can often be used interchangeably with queries.

Although they provide a variety of benefits, views also impose some limitations on what you can do with the data sets they create, and they may create performance problems.

❑ Views are nothing more than queries saved with a query name. As such, if you base your query on a view, the view name must be looked up and the SQL statement retrieved and then executed. Creating views based on views based on views can eventually cause performance problems.

❑ Each view can cause its own restrictions in updating data. As you build up views based on views, the results may not allow you to update the data. It may not matter for a given purpose, but you must keep this in mind when your intent is to create views that allow updates, and you should always test extensively.

❑ Used improperly, views may allow users to add or delete records that are not part of the view, causing data integrity and security issues.

Creating Views

A view is often called a *virtual* table because the view has the appearance of a table, but the data set is not physically stored in the database but rather pulled from the underlying tables on demand. The view's data set doesn't exist anywhere until the moment that the view is used. When the view is executed, the DBMS pulls the data and performs any operations or calculations required by the SQL statement, and then it presents that data to the user.

To the user, the view looks exactly like a table, with columns and rows of data, but usually the data is not persisted. A view can be as simple as a handful of fields from a single table or as complex as a system of joined tables pulling fields from any or all tables in a database.

The following Try It Out shows you how to create a simple view.

Try It Out   Building a View

1. The process of building a view begins with building a syntactically correct SQL statement.

```
SELECT LastName, FirstName, Email, DateOfJoining
FROM MemberDetails;
```

2. Once you have the SQL statement, you can save the view in some database systems by adding the following SQL as the top line of the statement:

```
CREATE VIEW MyViewName AS
```

3. Executing the following statement causes the database to save the view:

```
CREATE VIEW MemberNameEmail AS
SELECT LastName, FirstName, Email, DateOfJoining
FROM MemberDetails;
```

Notice that the CREATE VIEW statement does not pull data from the tables and display it, but rather causes the database to store the SELECT statement as a view named MemberNameEmail.

How It Works

As you become fluent in SQL, you do not need to do things in this manner, but when you are learning to create views, it is useful to create the SQL statement that actually pulls the data that you are interested in as demonstrated in the first step of the preceding Try It Out. This process is often iterative — tweak, run, view results, tweak, run, view results, and so forth — until you have the results you need. Of course, not every view you create needs to be saved; sometimes you just need to look at data, print it, and move on. The second step is used to save a view permanently in the database so that it can be reused at a later date.

Having created the view, you can now use it in a SELECT statement:

```
SELECT *
FROM MemberNameEmail
```

Executing the statement gives you results similar to what appears in Figure 10-1.

	LastName	FirstName	Email	DateOfJoining
1	Smith	Katie	katie@mail.com	2004-02-23 00:00:00.000
2	Robson	Bob	rob@mail.com	2004-03-13 00:00:00.000
3	Jakes	Sandra	sandra@her_mail.com	2004-04-13 00:00:00.000
4	Gee	Steve	steve@gee.com	2004-02-22 00:00:00.000
5	Jones	John	jj@jonesmail.org	2005-01-02 00:00:00.000
6	Jones	Jenny	jj@jonesmail.org	2005-01-02 00:00:00.000

Figure 10-1

Note that the CREATE VIEW works in only some databases. Microsoft Access, for example, does not recognize the keywords but has other methods for creating stored queries. This brings up an important point: SQL syntax is very platform-specific even when the platform supposedly conforms to a given standard. Be aware that differences exist and be prepared to read up on the platform of your choice.

Types of Views

Given that most SQL statements can be coerced into a view, you can build up many different types of views to fit your needs. But first, for the purposes of simplifying your life, build a base view that pulls all of the fields you need from a set of tables. Later in the chapter, you build other views based on that original view.

Suppose that you need to analyze meeting attendance. The first, or base, view pulls data from MemberDetails, Attendance, and Location. The user is generally not interested in the table's primary and foreign keys, so you just pull all the data fields from each table. You are not going to perform any filtering or ordering on the base data; you will just pull the required data. This may not be efficient for large tables or results sets. This strategy is not recommended in general, but it makes your results sets more interesting for your limited data.

Table Join Views

Table join views are views that join related tables back together in order to pull specific fields out of the related tables and display a view across more than one table. Getting all of the tables joined, with lookup tables, outer joins where needed, and all the other little things required to gather data from a half dozen or more tables, can take a while to get correct. Once correct, there may be little need to do it over and over again. Queries that join multiple tables are called *base queries* because they form the base of other queries that simply need to use all this data. A single base query may serve to gather data for dozens of other queries.

Base View

The SQL for a base view might look like the following (in SQL Server):

```
SELECT dbo.MemberDetails.LastName, dbo.MemberDetails.FirstName,
dbo.MemberDetails.DateOfBirth, dbo.MemberDetails.Street, dbo.MemberDetails.City,
dbo.MemberDetails.State, dbo.MemberDetails.ZipCode, dbo.MemberDetails.Email,
dbo.MemberDetails.DateOfJoining, dbo.Attendance.MeetingDate,
dbo.Attendance.MemberAttended, dbo.Location.Street AS [Meeting Street],
dbo.Location.City AS [Meeting City], dbo.Location.State AS [Meeting State]
FROM dbo.MemberDetails
INNER JOIN dbo.Attendance
ON dbo.MemberDetails.MemberId = dbo.Attendance.MemberId
INNER JOIN dbo.Location
ON dbo.Attendance.LocationId = dbo.Location.LocationId
```

Notice that SQL Server places a ton of qualifier data in the SQL statement, the `dbo.MemberDetails` part. In some instances, the table qualifiers are a necessity, specifically when you pull identical field names from different tables, such as City from MemberDetails and from Location. In any event, SQL statements like this can be a little tough to wade through.

Once you have the SQL statement working, however, you can now add the `CREATE VIEW` statement and use this SQL to build a named view.

```
CREATE VIEW dbo.MemberAttendance AS
SELECT dbo.MemberDetails.LastName, dbo.MemberDetails.FirstName,
dbo.MemberDetails.DateOfBirth, dbo.MemberDetails.Street, dbo.MemberDetails.City,
dbo.MemberDetails.State, dbo.MemberDetails.ZipCode, dbo.MemberDetails.Email,
dbo.MemberDetails.DateOfJoining, dbo.Attendance.MeetingDate,
dbo.Attendance.MemberAttended, dbo.Location.Street AS [Meeting Street],
dbo.Location.City AS [Meeting City], dbo.Location.State AS [Meeting State]
```

```
FROM dbo.MemberDetails
INNER JOIN dbo.Attendance
ON dbo.MemberDetails.MemberId = dbo.Attendance.MemberId
INNER JOIN dbo.Location
ON dbo.Attendance.LocationId = dbo.Location.LocationId
```

Having run this SQL statement, you now have a view named MemberAttendance. If you build a query selecting all the fields from that view, you end up with a much more readable statement:

```
SELECT LastName, FirstName, DateOfBirth, Street, City, State, ZipCode, Email,
DateOfJoining, MeetingDate, MemberAttended, [Meeting Street], [Meeting City],
[Meeting State]
FROM MemberAttendance
```

Executing this statement provides the following results shown in Figure 10-2.

LastName	FirstName	DateOfBirth	Street	City	State	ZipCode	Email	DateOfJoining	MeetingDate	MemberAttended	Meeting Street	Mee
Gee	Steve	10/5/1967	3 The Road	Windy Village	Golden State	65424	steve@gee.com	2/22/2004	3/1/2004	Y	2 Main Steet	Big
Jakes	Sandra	1/1/1900	23 The Avenue	Windy Village	Golden State	65423	sandra@her_mail.com	4/13/2004	1/1/2004	Y	77 Winding Roa	Win
Jakes	Sandra	1/1/1900	23 The Avenue	Windy Village	Golden State	65423	sandra@her_mail.com	4/13/2004	3/1/2004	Y	2 Main Steet	Big
Jones	Jenny	8/25/1953	7 New Lane	Big Apple City	New State	88776	jj@jonesmail.org	1/2/2005	1/1/2004	Y	77 Winding Roa	Win
Jones	John	10/5/1952	7 New Lane	Big Apple City	New State	88776	jj@jonesmail.org	1/2/2005	1/1/2004	Y	77 Winding Roa	Win
Smith	Katie	1/1/1900	Main Road	Townsville	Stateside	123456	katie@mail.com	2/23/2004	1/1/2004	Y	77 Winding Roa	Win
Smith	Katie	1/1/1900	Main Road	Townsville	Stateside	123456	katie@mail.com	2/23/2004	3/1/2004	Y	2 Main Steet	Big

Figure 10-2

More important, you now have a base upon which you can build the various queries you might want.

The name of the base view, MemberAttendance, is used in the subsequent query just as if it were a real table, and the field names from that view are used just as if they were real field names in a real table. In appearance, MemberAttendance is a table. As you have just seen, however, it is not, but rather a query pulling specific fields from specific tables. Because the view definition is saved in the database, the DBMS can perform all the necessary work required to translate the SQL statement into a data set, which is then presented to the new query to use as if it really were a table.

Row Views

Using a WHERE clause to filter down a results set is often useful when pulling all of the fields for a given set of records. Row views are views that select a subset of all the rows in the larger dataset. Perhaps you want to pull the records for all the members who attended any meetings.

```
SELECT      MemberAttendance.*
FROM        MemberAttendance
WHERE       (MemberAttended = 'Y')
ORDER BY LastName, FirstName, MeetingDate
```

Should you need to build other views of members who actively attend meetings, you could simply save this query as a view:

```
CREATE VIEW ActiveMemberAttendance AS
SELECT      MemberAttendance.*
FROM        MemberAttendance
WHERE       (MemberAttended = 'Y')
ORDER BY LastName, FirstName, MeetingDate
```

Perhaps you need to view attendance for all active members in Golden State.

```
SELECT      ActiveMemberAttendance.*
FROM        ActiveMemberAttendance
WHERE       (State = 'Golden State')
ORDER BY LastName, FirstName
```

The preceding results sets (illustrated in Figure 10-3) give you all of the fields from all three base tables, filtered by attendance and sorted by name and meeting attended. Because you are basing the results on one or more base queries, the SQL is easy to work with and easy to read. As you can see, you built a base query that joins all the required tables together. Once you did that, you could easily filter out only the active members or only the active members in Golden State.

Figure 10-3

Field Views

Another type of view is the *field view*, which selects all of the records but only some of the fields. For example, suppose you need to build a list of all members, meeting dates, and meeting addresses.

```
SELECT      LastName, FirstName, MeetingDate, MemberAttended, [Meeting Street],
[Meeting City], [Meeting State]
FROM        MemberAttendance
ORDER BY LastName, FirstName
```

This query provides exactly the fields you requested and does so for every row of the view, ordered by last name, as shown in Figure 10-4

Figure 10-4

Filtered Windowed Views

Windowed views display selected columns from selected rows. In other words, they limit the view of data in both the number of columns displayed as well as the number of rows displayed. The limitation on the number of columns is created by specifying only a subset of all the columns in the SELECT clause of the statement. The limitation on the number of rows is created by the WHERE clause, which specifies a subset of all the rows in the table. Thus, you create a rectangular window into the larger possible data set.

For example, you might want a list of all the members who did not attend a specific meeting, with their email addresses so that you could send an email outlining what you did at that meeting and inviting them to attend the next meeting.

```
SELECT     LastName, FirstName, Email, MeetingDate, MemberAttended
FROM       MemberAttendance
WHERE      (MemberAttended = 'N') AND (MeetingDate = CONVERT(DATETIME, '2004-01-01',
102))
```

Executing this SELECT statement provides the results shown in Figure 10-5.

	LastName	FirstName	Email	MeetingDate	MemberAttended
1	Robson	Bob	rob@mail.com	2004-01-01 00:00:00.000	N
2	Gee	Steve	steve@gee.com	2004-01-01 00:00:00.000	N

Figure 10-5

Or perhaps you need the names and birth dates of members who have attended any meeting so that you can invite active members to a birthday bash to thank them for their participation.

```
SELECT DISTINCT LastName, FirstName, Email
FROM       MemberAttendance
WHERE      (MemberAttended = 'Y')
```

Figure 10-6 displays the results of this query.

	LastName	FirstName	Email
1	Gee	Steve	steve@gee.com
2	Jakes	Sandra	sandra@her_mail.com
3	Jones	Jenny	jj@jonesmail.org
4	Jones	John	jj@jonesmail.org
5	Smith	Katie	katie@mail.com

Figure 10-6

As you can see, windowed queries are trivial to build when you have a good base view to work with.

Summary Views

Finally, you might wish to perform data analysis, perhaps determining the most (or least) active members.

```
SELECT     COUNT(MemberAttended) AS CntOfAttendance, FirstName, LastName
FROM       Attendance INNER JOIN
                MemberDetails ON Attendance.MemberId = MemberDetails.MemberId
WHERE      (MemberAttended = 'Y')
GROUP BY FirstName, LastName
```

Executing this statement gives you the results depicted in Figure 10-7.

	CntOfAttendance	FirstName	LastName
1	1	Steve	Gee
2	2	Sandra	Jakes
3	1	Jenny	Jones
4	1	John	Jones
5	2	Katie	Smith

Figure 10-7

Summary views actually perform various operations on entire sets of rows, returning a single row representing some operation on the set. These views are never updateable.

Notice that because MemberAttendance does all the grunt work of joining tables, such as aliasing field names, and so on, you can concentrate on the work you want to get done, filtering out a small set of fields from a small set of records. You no longer need to worry about what fields to join or look at ID field data (although the primary keys might be useful for joins further up the line).

Updating Views

If you need to update data through your views, as opposed to simply reporting data sets, things can get a little trickier. A variety of things can cause a view to become non-updateable. Begin with what can be updated.

Suppose you need to update member addresses from a sign-up list passed around during a meeting. The following view simply pulls records from the MemberDetails table.

```
CREATE VIEW MemberUpdate
AS
SELECT     FirstName, LastName, DateOfBirth, Street, State, City, ZipCode, Email,
DateOfJoining
FROM       MemberDetails
```

The preceding CREATE VIEW statement provides the results shown in Figure 10-8.

FirstName	LastName	DateOfBirth	Street	State	City	ZipCode	Email	DateOfJoining
Katie	Smith	1/9/1977	Main Road	Stateside	Townsville	123456	katie@mail.com	2/23/2004
Bob	Robson	1/9/1987	Little Street	Small State	Big City	34565	rob@mail.com	3/13/2004
Sandra	Jakes	5/15/1957	23 The Avenue	Golden State	Windy Village	65423	sandra@her_mail.c	4/13/2004
Steve	Gee	10/5/1967	3 The Road	Golden State	Windy Village	65424	steve@gee.com	2/22/2004
John	Jones	10/5/1952	7 New Lane	New State	Big Apple City	88776	jj@jonesmail.org	1/2/2005
Jenny	Jones	8/25/1953	7 New Lane	New State	Big Apple City	88776	jj@jonesmail.org	1/2/2005

Figure 10-8

You can expect to edit the records, add new records, or delete existing records because it is straightforward for the DBMS to translate this request and figure out where the data came from and which table and fields need to be updated.

In general, you can expect to be able to update most views against a single table, whether the entire row or just a few fields. These views can always be traced back to specific rows or columns in real tables, and there will almost never be a problem with these updates. The view may not be possible, however, if the view contains calculated fields. Many DBMSs allow this operation as long as you do not attempt an update to the calculated field itself.

However, if you take the case of MemberAttendance, where you pulled fields from three different tables, an attempt to edit that view gives errors in SQL Server. In general, views containing multiple joined tables probably will not be updateable. Remember that one database may be able to handle some things that others can't. In any event, by joining three tables together, you ended up with a view that was not updateable in at least one major DBMS.

Another type of view that is just never updateable is the summary query. Obviously, these queries pull data from many rows and summarize them in some manner. Calculations occur over entire data sets, and it simply doesn't make sense to try to update a calculated field, an OrderBy field, and so on.

Update Restrictions

The ANSI standard defines restrictions (see the following list) that may cause an update to fail. Again, remember that each major DBMS may be able to work around some of the restrictions, but there are others that are simply hard-and-fast rules — no summary functions, for example.

- ❏ The SELECT clause may not contain the keyword DISTINCT.
- ❏ The SELECT clause may not contain summary functions.
- ❏ The SELECT clause may not contain set functions.
- ❏ The SELECT clause may not contain set operators.
- ❏ The SELECT clause may not contain an ORDER BY clause.
- ❏ The FROM clause may not contain multiple tables.
- ❏ The WHERE clause may not contain subqueries.
- ❏ The query may not contain GROUP BY or HAVING.
- ❏ Calculated columns may not be updated.
- ❏ All NOT NULL columns from the base table must be included in the view in order for the INSERT query to function.

Obviously, a view that breaks any of these rules is not updateable.

Check Option

A view containing a WHERE clause retrieves only data meeting the search conditions. Many rows in the table may not be visible through the view. Because one of the functions of a view is to assist in securing data, it is necessary to ensure that updates and additions cannot occur through a view that would impact records not included in the view. For example, suppose you build a view to display all members with a birth date before January 1, 1970.

```
CREATE VIEW MemberBirthdayFiltered AS
SELECT     MemberId, FirstName, LastName, DateOfBirth
FROM       dbo.MemberDetails
WHERE      (DateOfBirth >= CONVERT(DATETIME, '1970-01-01', 102))
```

Having created the view, you can now execute a SELECT * statement:

```
SELECT *
FROM MemberBirthdayFiltered
```

This statement gives you the following results shown in Figure 10-9.

	MemberID	FirstName	LastName	DateOfBirth
1	1	Katie	Smith	1977-01-09 00:00:00.000
2	2	Bob	Robson	1987-01-09 00:00:00.000

Figure 10-9

Suppose you then edit a member's birth date such that the date is before January 1, 1970:

```
UPDATE     MemberBirthdayFiltered
SET            DateOfBirth = 1 / 1 / 1969
WHERE      MemberId = 1
```

The UPDATE query modifies the birthday to a date in 1969, but MemberBirthdayFiltered pulls only records for members with birthdays after January 1, 1970. Therefore, the record no longer matches the criteria and disappears from the records pulled in the view, and the record would disappear from the view.

```
SELECT *
FROM MemberBirthdayFiltered
```

	MemberID	FirstName	LastName	DateOfBirth
1	2	Bob	Robson	1987-01-09 00:00:00.000

Figure 10-10

While it would still be in the table, the result would be disconcerting to the user, to say the least.

Another problem associated with views is that you could potentially insert or delete records that you are not supposed to edit. Assume that the membership is divided by state with different people assigned to maintenance of member records according to state. Build a view for birthdays in Golden State:

```
CREATE VIEW MemberBirthdaysGoldenState
AS
SELECT     MemberId, FirstName, LastName, DateOfBirth, Street, City, State,
ZipCode, Email, DateOfJoining
FROM        MemberDetails
WHERE     (State = 'Golden State')
```

Having created the view, you can now execute the following SELECT * statement:

```
SELECT *
FROM MemberBirthdaysGoldenState
```

Executing the statement provides the results shown in Figure 10-11.

	MemberId	FirstName	LastName	DateOfBirth	Street	City	State	ZipCode
1	3	Sandra	Jakes	1957-05-15 00:00:00.000	23 The Avenue	Windy Village	Golden State	65423
2	4	Steve	Gee	1967-10-05 00:00:00.000	3 The Road	Windy Village	Golden State	65424

Figure 10-11

However, someone writes a query that mistakenly inserts a member in another state:

```
INSERT INTO MemberBirthdaysGoldenState
                    (MemberId, LastName, FirstName, DateOfBirth, Street, City,
State, ZipCode, Email, DateOfJoining)
VALUES     (7, 'Smith', 'Marty', '3/23/1974', '123 North Rd', 'Idlewild', 'New
State', 65421, 'msmith@SmithSonJonSon.com', '3/01/2004')
```

This is a perfectly valid SQL statement, however, and the query inserts a new record into the MemberDetails table in a state that is not visible in the view, and which does not belong to the user doing the update. This user cannot see the new record and thinks that the DBMS ignored his request, and some other user now finds a record in his state for a member he didn't add.

In order to prevent this kind of problem, you might want to disallow these updates from occurring through the view. The DBMS can do this for you using the CHECK OPTION keyword in the CREATE VIEW statement, as shown below in the new version of the view:

```
CREATE VIEW MemberBirthdaysGoldenStateCheckOption AS
SELECT     MemberId, FirstName, LastName, DateOfBirth, Street, City, State,
ZipCode, Email, DateOfJoining
FROM       dbo.MemberDetails
WHERE      (State = 'Golden State')
WITH CHECK OPTION
```

When you specify the CHECK OPTION keyword in a CREATE VIEW statement, the DBMS stores the CHECK OPTION with the view. Whenever a user performs an UPDATE, INSERT, or DELETE on the view, the DBMS checks each operation to ensure that it meets the WHERE criteria. Any operations failing to meet the WHERE criteria are not performed. For example, an attempt to execute the following statement would fail:

```
INSERT INTO MemberBirthdaysGoldenStateCheckOption
        (MemberId, LastName, FirstName, DateOfBirth, Street, City, State, ZipCode,
Email, DateOfJoining)
VALUES
        (7, 'Smith', 'Marty', '3/23/1974', '123 North Rd', 'Idlewild', 'New State',
65421,
            'msmith@SmithSonJonSon.com', '3/01/2004')
```

You would see results similar to Figure 10-12.

```
Server: Msg 550, Level 16, State 1, Line 1
The attempted insert or update failed because the target view either specifies WITH CHECK OPTION or spans a vi
The statement has been terminated.
```

Figure 10-12

As you might imagine, CHECK OPTION can add significant overhead to an action query. Each record being updated has to be checked for conformance with the view. Additionally, you can build views based on other views, and each may have a CHECK OPTION. Each level must be checked to ensure that the requested operation passes its check.

The CHECK OPTION plays an important role in security and data integrity. You certainly don't want to allow updates on data that the user is not supposed to see or modify. Furthermore, if the update is valid, it should usually not occur through that view. Thus, whenever you create a view to use for updates, it is a good idea to seriously consider whether to use CHECK OPTION.

Dropping Views

Obviously, where you have a view, you need a way to drop the view if it is no longer needed. The syntax is simple enough:

```
DROP VIEW MYVIEWNAME
```

Dropping a view can be a bit hazardous, however, because other views might be based on the view being dropped. Suppose that you have a view of all members in Golden State:

```
CREATE VIEW MembersFromGoldenState AS
SELECT       *
FROM         MemberDetails
WHERE     (State = 'Golden State')
```

You then build a view based on that view:

```
CREATE VIEW MembersFromGoldenStateBirthdays AS
SELECT      FirstName, LastName, DateOfBirth
FROM        MembersFromGoldenState
```

What happens now if you attempt to drop MembersFromGoldenState?

```
DROP VIEW MembersFromGoldenState
```

In order to explicitly specify what to do, there are two additional keywords: CASCADE and RESTRICT.

```
DROP VIEW MembersFromGoldenState CASCADE
```

The CASCADE keyword tells the DBMS that if you attempt to drop a view and other views depend on that view, it should delete the dependent views as well. The DBMS searches through all other views, looking for references to the view being dropped. If it finds any, then the DBMS drops that view as well. Because you can build layered views, using the CASCADE keyword can result in entire chains of views being dropped because views depend on views being dropped.

The RESTRICT keyword, on the other hand, tells the DBMS that the drop should fail if any other views depend on the view being dropped.

```
DROP VIEW MembersFromGoldenState RESTRICT
```

The DROP command (shown above) should fail with an error.

A DROP VIEW statement with no qualifiers may be valid syntax because early versions of SQL did not support RESTRICT and CASCADE, so for backward compatibility some DBMSs may accept the statements. Specifying exactly what you want to happen when you drop a view, however, is highly advisable.

Summary

As you learned, views are little more than specific SQL statements stored in a database that is associated with a particular data set. You can use views to provide security, to build other views, or to personalize data. In this chapter, you learned the following:

❑ A view is a virtual table allowing users to view and sometimes update specific pieces of data. The database stores the view definition, but the data that the view displays is created at the moment the view is executed.

❑ Views can be built on other views to build up queries that might be tough to construct or extremely confusing to work with if attempted in a single view.

❑ Typically a view supplies data in a format familiar to the user and restricts access to data that the user should not see or update. A view can be a simple row or set of columns, pulled from a single table, or it can contain data from literally dozens of tables, joined behind the scenes in other views, with calculated fields, groupings, and summations.

❑ Updates may be possible through views but often cannot be performed due to restrictions in how updates are performed. If views are used for updates, checks must be performed to ensure that the updates do not compromise the security that may very well be the purpose of the view.

The next chapter covers transactions, another aspect of data security, which are used to ensure that multiple related changes to the database are correctly written as a group or backed out as a group if something prevents the write.

Exercises

1. Build a saved field view named vFirstLastDOB to display the first name, last name, and birth date for all members in the MemberDetails table.

2. Build a saved row view named vGoldenStateMembers displaying all the fields from the MemberDetails table for all members in Golden State.

3. Build a windowed view named vGoldenStateMembersFirstLastDOB building on vGoldenStateMembers, pulling only the first name, last name, and birth date fields.

4. Drop all the views just created.

Transactions

When you move out of the realm of single-user databases, ensuring the validity of the data from the time you start to make modifications to the time you finally finish making modifications becomes critical. Modern databases may host hundreds or even thousands of users and even host programs running autonomously and automatically without human input or intervention. If each of these users and programs can independently make changes to data throughout the database, the probability of collisions between users updating the data becomes almost a certainty.

Even in so-called small databases, it isn't uncommon for the majority of users to all be using a small segment of the data, typically the most recent data. In many cases, older data is used for historical purposes only, examined only for reports about past performance. In many databases, the data entered in the last month or even the last few days is far more likely to be updated and examined than data from a year ago. An insurance company has thousands or even millions of claim records but is actively working on only a few hundred or thousand right now. A manufacturing company may have hundreds of thousands of orders over the last 10 years but only a few hundred that are currently being processed. A hospital has thousands of patient records in their database but only a couple hundred people currently in the hospital and a few hundred more being seen on a daily or weekly basis.

Most users need to see only these *active* records. Users add new records, other users immediately use these new records to cause related processes to occur, other records in other tables are updated, or new records are created, all causing a big ripple effect caused by some triggering event such as an accident claim, a product order, or a patient admission. Everybody needs concurrent access to this small set of new data, and then as the claim is processed, the product is manufactured, the order is shipped, or the patient is treated and released, these records tend to go dormant with little or no activity for long periods of time. Perhaps a few reports are run to show how many claims were processed or a warranty claim is processed by the manufacturer, but this is often a tiny percentage of the total processing volume and tends to occur on a more random data set.

Now think about most of the database users all trying to update records, add new records, delete records, and report on the last month's (or even week's) data at once, and you can see that a small handful of records is often used many times by many users at any given time. Which records are being used changes as the data ages and new claims or orders are processed, but the fact remains that with all of this emphasis on a small percentage of the data, collisions are virtually inevitable. It is critical, therefore, that the DBMS be capable of ensuring that such collisions are handled so that data loss does not occur. For exactly this reason, you use *transactions*.

The information that follows comes with a huge caveat: Virtually everything that follows varies depending on your specific implementation. Transaction and locking implementation is very specific to a particular vendor's product and the details vary, sometimes immensely. The best you can expect from this book is to get a feeling for what is possible, and then you should read the documentation for the DBMS you are working with for the exact details of how that product works.

Introducing Transactions

In SQL, a transaction is a group of SQL statements taken together as a logical unit of work. Oftentimes, the process of entering data requires adding data into several different tables and perhaps modifying data in a couple of tables. If any of those operations fail, then the entire set of operations must be undone. In order to ensure that you perform all of the operations or none of the operations, you use transactions.

In order for a group of statements to be considered a transaction, it must pass the ACID test. ACID is an acronym that stands for the following:

❑ **Atomic:** This property refers to the all-or-none behavior of the group of statements. If any of the statements fail, then the entire group of statements must be undone or rolled back. Only when all of the statements execute without error are the results of the entire group of statements saved to the database. When a patient checks in to the hospital, a new patient record may need to be created or an existing record updated. A check-in record needs to be created. A bed needs to be assigned to that patient. It would not be good to get the patient all the way checked in but not assign a bed to the patient. Losing patients is considered very bad practice.

❑ **Consistent:** The database must be in a consistent state at the end of the transaction. The SQL statements must be applied without error, and all database structures must be correct and saved. A consistent state really means that as the DBMS makes decisions on available data, updates to data do not overwrite previous updates, and records are not added or deleted based on data that is not a real, permanent part of the database.

❑ **Isolated:** Data that transactions change must not be visible to other users before or during the changes being applied. Other database users must see the data as it would exist at the end of the transaction so that they do not make decisions or errors based on data that is no longer valid. If a product order is rolled back because the customer decides at the last minute to order a different part, another order should not be back-ordered because the first order was momentarily visible and there appeared to be insufficient stock to fill the next order.

❑ **Durable:** At the end of the transaction, the database must save the data correctly. Power outages, equipment failures, or other problems should not cause partial saves or incomplete data changes. Most DBMSs manage this requirement through the use of transaction logs kept on an entirely different drive from the main database.

In order to use transactions in a meaningful way, you need to build some data not included in the original database. In the next section, you build tables with inventory to implement a very simple rental database. You examine how these tables are created and how data is inserted, and you start to think about which pieces should use transactions. Later on, after you have learned a great deal more about transactions, you learn how to wrap some of these operations in transactions and why you would do so.

Example Data

This section creates example code to demonstrate the concepts you are about to learn. This section introduces some SQL statements that modify the database structure itself by adding tables. Further, you add initial data to some of the tables and then use that data and existing data from other tables to add entirely new data to the new tables. The following discussion shows you the importance of using transactions when they are useful but likewise how it is necessary to avoid using transactions when there is no reason to do so. Transactions have costs, primarily in locks and processing time, and you need to avoid these costs where they simply don't add any value to your process. The database changes are introduced here so that you can think about them as this chapter discusses the issues that come with the use of transactions. Later sections, after you know how and why things work, reexamine these database changes and discuss which should use transactions, which should not, and why.

On to the example. The film club has started renting movies to its members as a way to earn money. To do this, several new tables have to be added to the database structure; when in use, several different tables have to be updated as a unit, or the database could be left in an inconsistent state.

In order to track rentals, you need to add a few new tables to the database.

Use the following SQL to add the Movie Format table:

```
CREATE TABLE [Format] (
  [FormatId] [int] IDENTITY (1, 1) NOT NULL,
  [Format] [char] (10))
```

This SQL adds the Inventory table:

```
CREATE TABLE [Inventory] (
  [InventoryId] [int] IDENTITY (1, 1) NOT NULL ,
  [FilmId] [int] NOT NULL ,
  [FormatId] [int] NOT NULL ,
  [CheckedOut] [char] (1))
```

Finally, the following SQL adds the Rentals table:

```
CREATE TABLE [Rentals] (
  [RentalId] [int] IDENTITY (1, 1) NOT NULL ,
  [InventoryId] [int] NOT NULL ,
  [MemberId] [int] NOT NULL ,
  [DateOut] [datetime] NOT NULL ,
  [DateIn] [datetime] NULL ,
  [Charge] [money] NULL
) ON [PRIMARY]
```

Once you add the tables to the database, you need to add initial data to the Movie Format and Inventory tables. Each of these processes involves SQL statements, and they depend on the previous operation succeeding or the next operation is not valid. For example, you need to build the Movie Format table and place two records in that table. The three formats are DVD, VHS, and Beta. If the statement that builds the table fails, obviously the process of placing the three records in the format table fails as well. Next, you need to build the Inventory table and then place several inventory records in the table, which tell you what movies are available for rental and in what format. Then you can start renting movies.

This SQL adds formats (data) to the format table:

```
INSERT INTO [Format]([Format])
VALUES('VHS')
INSERT INTO [Format]([Format])
VALUES('Beta')
INSERT INTO [Format]([Format])
VALUES('DVD')
```

The primary key of this table is an identity, which means it automatically creates a number for the key (1, 2, and 3). Thus, 1, 2, and 3 are used as the foreign key in the next table.

This SQL adds data to the Inventory table:

```
INSERT INTO Inventory(FilmId, FormatId, CheckedOut)
VALUES(1,1,'N')
INSERT INTO Inventory(FilmId, FormatId, CheckedOut)
VALUES(1,2,'N')
INSERT INTO Inventory(FilmId, FormatId, CheckedOut)
VALUES(2,1,'N')
INSERT INTO Inventory(FilmId, FormatId, CheckedOut)
VALUES(2,2,'N')
INSERT INTO Inventory(FilmId, FormatId, CheckedOut)
VALUES(2,3,'N')
INSERT INTO Inventory(FilmId, FormatId, CheckedOut)
VALUES(3,2,'N')
INSERT INTO Inventory(FilmId, FormatId, CheckedOut)
VALUES(4,2,'N')
INSERT INTO Inventory(FilmId, FormatId, CheckedOut)
VALUES(4,3,'N')
INSERT INTO Inventory(FilmId, FormatId, CheckedOut)
VALUES(5,2,'N')
INSERT INTO Inventory(FilmId, FormatId, CheckedOut)
VALUES(5,3,'N')
```

The process of renting movies consists of running a query to find out what is available, selecting a specific inventory item and marking it as rented, and building a new record in the Rentals table with the member ID, the inventory ID, and the date rented.

Try It Out   Renting Movies without Transactions

1.   Select all available inventory records so that you can pick a movie:

```
SELECT Inventory.InventoryId, Films.FilmName, Films.PlotSummary, Format.Format
FROM (Inventory
INNER JOIN Films ON Inventory.FilmId = Films.FilmId)
INNER JOIN Format ON Inventory.FormatId = Format.FormatId
WHERE (((Inventory.CheckedOut)= 'N'));
```

2.   Select a specific movie and mark it as rented:

```
UPDATE Inventory
SET Inventory.CheckedOut = 'Y'
WHERE (((Inventory.InventoryId)=7));
```

3. Build a record in the Rentals table:

```
INSERT INTO Rentals ( InventoryId, MemberId, DateOut )
SELECT 7 AS InventoryId, 3 AS MemberId, '3/21/2004' AS dateout;
```

4. When the movie is returned, the rental record has to be updated with the date returned:

```
UPDATE Rentals
SET Rentals.DateIn = '3/23/2004', Rentals.Charge = 5
WHERE (((Rentals.InventoryId)=7) AND ((Rentals.MemberId)=3));
```

5. Also update the record with the amount paid, and update the inventory record to indicate that the movie is back in stock:

```
UPDATE Inventory SET Inventory.CheckedOut = 'n'
WHERE (((Inventory.InventoryId)=7));
```

How It Works

Some of these operations are examples of transactions that should be completed only if all the operations succeed. A rental consists of finding an available inventory item, marking that item as rented, and creating the rental record. If any of these operations fail, they should all fail, and the entire set should be performed again. If the inventory item was marked as rented, but the rental record was not created, then that unit would never be updated as available later and would "disappear" from the list of available movies. Likewise, upon returning the movie to inventory, the rental record is marked with the date returned and the amount paid, and then the inventory record is updated to indicate that the unit is back in stock. Furthermore, what would happen if two database users tried to rent the same movie at the same time? As you can see, doing things as you did previously with no transactions could quickly lead to chaos, with the database left in an indeterminate state.

On the other hand, creating a new table and initializing that table with new records may not require a transaction. If the table has never existed before, and the processes are not in place to use that data, then no other users would attempt to add, delete, or modify the records in or the structure of the table, so why perform all the overhead associated with a transaction?

As you soon discover, it is critical to learn when to use transactions and when not to. Transactions have overhead associated with them and can cause serious performance issues if not used judiciously.

ANSI Model

The ANSI SQL standard defines a specific *transaction model*, the COMMIT and ROLLBACK statements, and their roles in ensuring data integrity. Many commercial DBMS products use this model, while other products add enhancements or refinements to the model that allow better control over the processing of transactions. This is one area where finding out what your DBMS provides is beneficial. Enhancements almost always provide additional flexibility and make using transactions easier or more powerful in some way.

The idea behind transactions is to bracket sets of SQL statements with transaction keywords such that all the statements between the keywords are processed as a unit. Either they all succeed or they all fail. Furthermore, they can be used to prevent or allow other users to see changes that you are making in certain circumstances. In the ANSI model, only COMMIT and ROLLBACK are specifically defined. The BEGIN

TRANSACTION statement is not defined but is implied to be executed as the first SQL statement and the first statement following every COMMIT statement. In Transact-SQL, BEGIN TRANSACTION is a defined keyword and there is no such implied first BEGIN TRANSACTION statement.

One problem with an implied BEGIN TRANSACTION as the first SQL statement, and as the first statement after every COMMIT statement, is that it is not possible to have SQL statements that are not part of a transaction. Transactions have costs, and not to be able to turn them on or off is an inconvenience.

COMMIT

The COMMIT statement tells the DBMS that all the statements executed since the last COMMIT statement have completed successfully and that the database is consistent. At this point, the data modifications caused by the previous SQL statements are actually written to disk. After the COMMIT statement, you cannot undo the changes made to the data without running more SQL statements to perform the undo. Figure 11-1 shows you a series of SQL statements, which taken together constitute a transaction. At any point up to the COMMIT, a ROLLBACK can be performed, which undoes all the changes to the database caused by the SQL statements. Once the COMMIT occurs, the changes are written to the disk and you can no longer undo the previous statements.

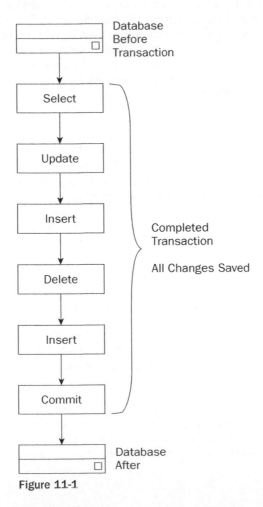

Figure 11-1

The other statement that the ANSI SQL standard defines is the ROLLBACK statement.

ROLLBACK

If for any reason you need to undo the transaction as a whole, execute the ROLLBACK statement. ROLLBACK tells the DBMS that all changes to data caused by all SQL statements since the last COMMIT statement must be undone. It is very important to understand where the transaction begins. Many interactive applications perform a COMMIT after each statement the user enters, which essentially means that ROLLBACK is unavailable. On the other hand, many of these same DBMSs when used programmatically start a transaction with the first SQL statement executed by the program and never perform a COMMIT until explicitly told to do so. Thus, a ROLLBACK statement undoes every statement since the program began or back to the first statement after the last COMMIT. Figure 11-2 shows a set of three SQL statements occurring and then a ROLLBACK statement. The ROLLBACK causes the previous three statements to be undone. After the ROLLBACK, the database is left in the same state as if the first three SQL statements had never even been performed.

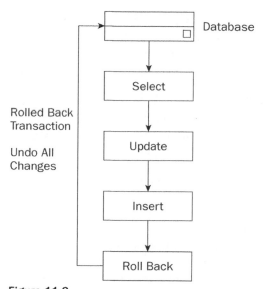

Figure 11-2

COMMIT and ROLLBACK are executable SQL statements, which for this discussion are called *transaction statements* or *keywords*. In the ANSI model, either of these transaction statements is valid after at least one nontransaction statement such as SELECT, INSERT, DELETE, and so on.

In fact, many DBMSs perform a COMMIT after every statement entered directly into the user interface. This is known as *autocommit* and can be turned on or off in some products. In other words, you receive a COMMIT immediately after each SQL statement typed in, and a ROLLBACK is not valid in that environment.

Additionally, if a DBMS is used programmatically and does not COMMIT until told to do so, it is critical that your program perform this explicit COMMIT as often as is reasonable. If you fail to do so, all the records you update (or in some instances even look at) become locked and other transactions cannot update (or in some instances even look at) any data used inside your transaction. In these environments, the rule of thumb is COMMIT early and COMMIT often.

The ANSI model does not provide an explicitly defined keyword for beginning a transaction. A BEGIN TRANSACTION statement is assumed as the first statement and as the first statement following each COMMIT. This is a bit confusing and additionally does not allow the programmer to create statements that are not part of a transaction. As you see in a moment, all transactions have costs, and there are cases where transactions simply aren't necessary. For these and other reasons, many DBMSs have added extensions to the SQL language to allow explicit BEGIN TRANSACTION statements and other enhancements. These extensions are generally known as Transact-SQL.

Transact-SQL

Transact-SQL is an extension to the SQL syntax that some DBMSs use to allow a finer degree of control over processing transactions. In essence, whereas the ANSI standard assumes a BEGIN TRANSACTION before the first SQL statement and immediately after a COMMIT or ROLLBACK, Transact-SQL requires a BEGIN TRANSACTION statement to initiate a transaction.

BEGIN TRANSACTION

The BEGIN TRANSACTION statement tells the DBMS that the SQL statements that follow form a transaction group and must be processed as an *atomic unit*, either all processed or none processed. Unlike the ANSI transaction model, which assumes an automatic BEGIN TRANSACTION and must receive a COMMIT or a ROLLBACK statement at some point, Transact-SQL acts as if a COMMIT is performed after every SQL statement unless a BEGIN TRANSACTION is processed. This is a very different model with very different results from the SQL model.

COMMIT TRANSACTION

The COMMIT TRANSACTION statement is identical in function to COMMIT from the ANSI model. It causes all SQL statements since the opening BEGIN TRANSACTION to be written to the database as an atomic unit. Unlike the ANSI model, Transact-SQL does not automatically assume a new BEGIN TRANSACTION. Any SQL statements between the COMMIT TRANSACTION and the next BEGIN TRANSACTION are committed individually as they occur. Figure 11-3 shows a series of SQL statements where the first two statements are outside of any transaction. These statements are committed immediately with no opportunity to undo or roll them back. Then a BEGIN TRANSACTION is explicitly executed telling the DBMS that everything that follows should be considered part of a transaction until either a ROLLBACK or a COMMIT is encountered. In this figure, a COMMIT is executed, and at that point, the INSERT and UPDATE statements are actually saved to the disk.

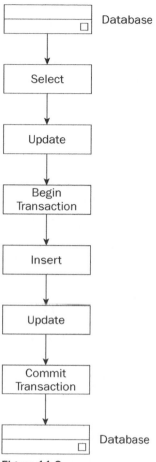

Figure 11-3

SAVE TRANSACTION

The SAVE TRANSACTION statement allows you to create named *Savepoints* that mark points inside of a large transaction. This allows the ROLLBACK TRANSACTION to perform partial rollbacks by providing a Savepoint name to the ROLLBACK statement. The SAVE TRANSACTION statement does not perform a save (that is the function of the COMMIT TRANSACTION statement); rather it simply sets up markers within the transaction. Figure 11-4 shows a series of SQL statements with SAVE TRANSACTION statements inserted along the way. In this case, a COMMIT is eventually performed, but if required, a ROLLBACK could be performed back to either of these two named Savepoints.

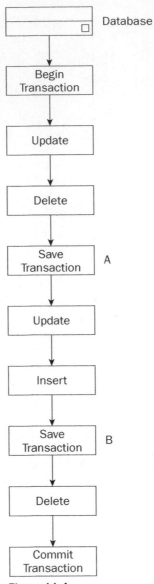

Figure 11-4

ROLLBACK TRANSACTION

The ROLLBACK TRANSACTION statement causes the DBMS to *roll back*, or undo, some or all of the changes made to the database. If any SAVE TRANSACTION statements have been executed, then the ROLLBACK TRANSACTION can be performed back to one of these Savepoints, or all the way back to the BEGIN TRANSACTION. In Figure 11-5 you see a partial rollback as the second-to-last statement. This ROLLBACK causes a rollback to the Savepoint named B, and then the COMMIT that follows causes all the SQL statements up to that named Savepoint to be stored to disk.

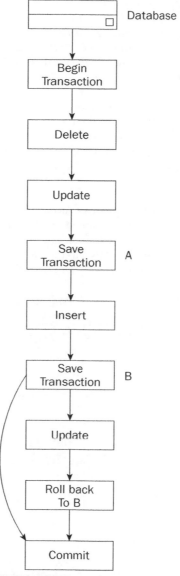

Figure 11-5

The next section discusses the log file, the key to being able to perform a rollback. A transaction log is generally a text file that is written outside of the database, usually on a completely different physical drive. All potential changes to the database are written to the log file, and then that file is used to actually write the data changes back into the database when a COMMIT is encountered. Should a catastrophic failure occur, such as an abrupt shutdown caused by power loss, the log file holds all changes to that point in time.

Transaction Logs

How does a DBMS perform this magic of making changes to many different records in different tables, guaranteeing that all or none of these operations occur, when hundreds or even thousands of other users are doing the same kinds of things at the same time? The answer lies in *locks*, which are will be discussed in a moment, and something called a *transaction log*.

Conceptually, a transaction log is basically a record of what the data looks like before the operation and what the data looks like after the operation, all written to a separate file. As you execute each SQL statement, the original data is copied to the log, and then the modified data is also copied to the log. As you execute each SQL statement, its resulting pre- and post-state information is copied to the transaction log. Because you know what the data looked like before the modification, you can undo the modification if necessary.

Figure 11-6 shows a conceptualization of the process. As each SQL statement is executed, the DBMS writes the state of the data before the change is applied and then the state after it is applied. The UPDATE causes a before/after state, the DELETE causes a before/after state, and so on. When the COMMIT statement is finally encountered, the after data is written to the disk. Should a ROLLBACK be encountered, the before data is used to undo any changes and restore the unmodified state to the database.

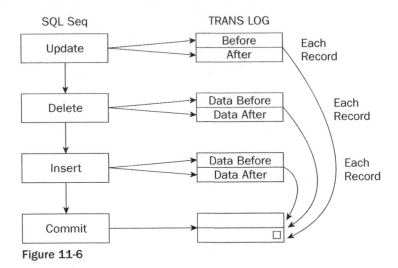

Figure 11-6

Logs should also generally be saved on a different physical drive from the main database so that if the database drive fails, the logs are available to bring the database current from the last backup point.

As you might imagine, transaction logs have a huge impact on performance since all modifications are written to the log, with pre- and post-modification data states, as well as to the actual database records. These logs generally just accumulate forever, getting larger and larger. The DBMS usually allows you to specify things such as maximum size, percentage of database, and so on. You also usually have tools for backing up the logs and then truncating them to save on disk space.

In spite of all of these performance issues, there are very real and powerful benefits that result from having a transaction log. Usually a machine failure, power outage, or other catastrophe has little or no effect on the database since the transaction logs record modifications. If you need to roll back changes, everything required to perform this function is available in the transaction log. Oftentimes the DBMS automatically recognizes a failure and looks at the transaction logs to figure out what needs to be done to restore the database to a consistent state. Sometimes you must use a special recovery utility to perform this function.

Remember that this discussion is just conceptual. The exact implementation details will vary dramatically from DBMS to DBMS, and in fact you do not need to be concerned with these details. Turning on and off transaction logs, tuning their size, and so forth are the domain of the database administrator (DBA). If you have such a person, you are not normally allowed to even touch these database properties yourself, and you need to go through the DBA if you need them changed for some reason. What you should take away from this discussion is the concept of automatically recording every change in the transaction log and then using these log files to roll back a transaction when required.

And finally, realize that the smaller database products, such as Microsoft Access, do not use transaction logs, even though they do implement transactions. If you have a catastrophic failure in the middle of a transaction, you have nothing to fall back on to help you out.

Locks

Locks are the key to implementing transactions in all DBMSs, and as such, the following sections spend considerable time discussing locks, how they function, how they can help ensure consistency, and especially how they can affect performance. The term *lock* means much the same thing in a database that it does in life, to make some thing unavailable to some people at some times. In the case of a database, it specifically means to make some data or data structure unavailable to other valid users of that data or structure for some period of time. Perhaps you need to make the entire MemberDetails table unavailable to every other user because you need to add or drop a field. Or perhaps you need to lock the data in the Inventory table so that you can select and update specific records without other users seeing inconsistent data as you do so.

Locks have nothing to do with user-level security, specifically, preventing a specific user or group of users from accessing data. Their function is simply to prevent other users from momentarily accessing data while an update or other critical usage of data is under way. Furthermore, in general you don't apply locks yourself; the DBMS applies the locks as it sees fit, although there is a LOCK TABLE syntax for acquiring a lock of an entire table. Even though you don't generally apply locks yourself, you still need an understanding of how they operate so that you can understand how transactions impact system performance because of the locks the system applies.

Locking Granularity

The term *granularity* refers to the level or size of the structure to which a lock is applied. Most DBMSs have the ability to apply locks at many different levels within the database, and it is useful to understand what these levels are. Every lock has the potential to inconvenience other users, so you really want to apply locks to the smallest unit possible so that you minimize the inconvenience. The following sections examine granularity from the largest data unit (the entire database) down to the smallest common unit (the record).

Database

There are perfectly valid reasons for locking the entire database. Perhaps a process requires making changes to most of the tables in the database, perhaps even the structure of a large number of tables. Getting locks to each table to be modified, in the correct order, can take a long time. It might make sense in this instance just to lock the entire database, but of course you should do this as seldom as possible. Do so at times when you have the fewest users trying to access data, and make your updates as quickly as possible.

Table

The next level of locking is an entire table. Say a manufacturer wants to update the price on every item they sell by 5 percent. Rather than locking each record, locking the table that contains the record, running an UPDATE query on every record in a single SQL statement, and then releasing the lock would be far faster.

Page

DBMSs tend to work with the physical medium that they are stored on to help them manage the data. The DBMS may break its table data down into chunks that fit in a sector on the disk. These chunks are called *pages*, and of course the page size often corresponds to the sector size of the hard disk. Thus, if the disk has a sector size of 16K, the DBMS applies locks to an entire page since this maps easily to lock requests sent to the operating system. For this reason, disks used for storing databases may be most efficient if formatted with the smallest sector size available (within reason). Obviously, a 2K sector locks fewer data rows than an 8K or a 32K sector. In the end, a record in a given table usually holds a specific number of bytes. If a record has five fields that hold 400 bytes, then a 2K sector locks roughly five or six such records (assuming page locks are used), but an 8K sector locks 20 records, and a 32K sector locks 80 records. As you can see, large sector sizes lock very large chunks of a table even if you need to lock only a small part of the table.

Row

Many modern databases allow locking to the *row*, or *record*, level. This means that other users without interactions may use adjacent records in the database. Of course, this is good, but remember that each lock requires manipulation by the DBMS. If 40 percent of all the records in a table need to be updated by a mass update, and the table contains a million records, it makes much more sense to just lock the table rather than apply for 400,000 record-level locks. On the other hand, if only 100 of those million records need updating, asking for 100 record locks minimizes the inconvenience to other users who still need to use the table.

Column

Although it is theoretically possible to lock data at the column level, few if any DBMSs do so. The overhead to track the locks at this granularity is simply too high and the benefit too small.

Locking Levels

In addition to the granularity or size of the data unit being locked, locks also have a property known as the *level*. The level determines how rigidly the lock is applied and whether any other user can use the data in any manner. The first locking level is the shared lock.

Shared

A *shared* lock essentially means that no one can modify the data, but other users may look at and use the data for any purpose not requiring an update. A user may need to run a report that asks different questions about a set of records. If any of those records were to be updated by another user, then the questions would not provide consistent answers since the data provided at the end would not be the same as the data at the beginning. On the other hand, it is perfectly valid for other users to ask questions about that same set of data. It is not necessary to lock the data such that no one else can see it.

Exclusive

An exclusive lock means that other users should not be allowed to see the data because the data is about to be changed. If one user is updating the price of every inventory item by 5 percent and another user is running a report about the value of all the items in the inventory, the report would return a different answer depending on when the report started running and how many items had already been updated.

Deadlocks

If you think about users locking different records in different tables, it becomes obvious that the database could get in a situation where user 1 is waiting for data locked by user 2, and user 2 is waiting for data locked by user 1. Each user needs the data locked by the other user before they can finish their process and release their locks. This situation is known as a *deadlock*. Deadlocks inevitably occur, and the DBMS must have a means to identify a deadlock and then must have a strategy for breaking the deadlock and allowing one of the users to gain control of the data they need in order to release the locks they applied. Unless the DBMS intervenes, both user requests wait forever for the other to unlock the necessary data. This is a simple two-way deadlock, but of course deadlocks can occur between many different users at once. Figure 11-7 shows a situation where two different transactions have locks applied, and each is waiting for the data locked by the other transaction in order to continue. Transaction A has locked record 2 in the Products table, and Transaction B is waiting to use record 2 in the Products table. Transaction B has locked record 79 in the Orders table, and Transaction A is waiting for record 79 in the Orders table. Neither transaction can continue until it gains control of the record locked by the other transaction.

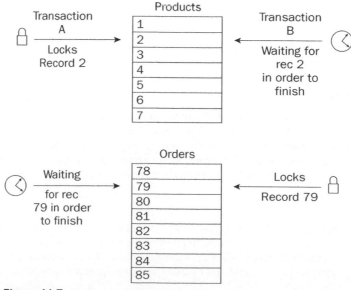

Figure 11-7

In order to find and fix such situations, most DBMSs periodically scan for deadlocks by checking all the locks held by the active transactions. If it detects a deadlock, the DBMS simply picks one transaction at random and rolls it back, thereby releasing the locks it applied. That transaction is considered the "loser" of the deadlock since the work already applied for that transaction is undone and must be rerun. The other user can now gain control of the data they need to finish their transaction and release their locks. The losing transaction receives an error message informing it of the deadlock loss and the ensuing roll-back. Of course, this is a highly simplified scenario. It is not only possible but also likely that a DBMS sees deadlocks involving several different users, necessitating multiple rollbacks so that a single transaction can proceed and release its locks.

This method of breaking deadlocks means that any transaction could potentially be rolled back even if all of its SQL statements are perfectly valid and would otherwise process without error. Any statement, even a simple SELECT statement, could be a deadlock loser and be rolled back. The statement is rolled back not because of any fault of its own, but simply because it is involved in a deadlock and loses the coin toss for which transaction gets rolled back. This is a small price to pay given the alternatives: a deadlock or a database corruption.

If the deadlock loser is an actual person in an interactive program, the user can simply reenter the SQL statements. In any program using SQL, the program must be prepared to handle the error codes that the DBMS returns informing the code of the deadlock loss and consequent rollback. Typically, just as would happen with a live user, the program simply resubmits the transaction.

In addition to lock levels, the next section discusses how you can also set parameters to your locks.

Setting Lock Parameters

Over time, the DBMSs from various vendors have evolved capabilities not necessarily provided in the original SQL specifications. These capabilities may or may not be present in a given platform, and even if present, they may act differently. Locks affect many different operations, and efficient locking is an area that every vendor takes seriously. The vendors have provided the DBMS administrator various parameters to use in adjusting the database, which are covered here.

Lock Size

As discussed earlier, most modern databases can lock data at various levels of granularity; thus a DBMS may offer database-, table-, page-, and row-level locking.

Number of Locks

The DBMS typically has a lock pool with a finite number of locks available to all the transactions concurrently processing. Thus, the total number of locks is distributed to and recovered from transactions as the transactions begin and end. The administrator may need to adjust the total number of locks to allow for very complex transactions or very large numbers of transactions. Likewise, limiting the number of locks can force the DBMS to escalate locking earlier, increasing the efficiency of the database.

Escalation

The process of requesting locks, checking the locks against requests for data by other users, and other such overhead can be very time-consuming. In an effort to minimize the overhead, the database may escalate a set of locks. Escalation refers to the database's ability to consolidate many locks at one level of granularity into a single lock at a higher granularity. For example, if a transaction applies for hundreds of record locks, the DBMS may decide that it is more efficient to simply lock pages of the database instead, or even the entire table. If a transaction locks records in dozens of tables, it may make sense to attempt to lock the entire database. In Figure 11-8, you see a situation where an extreme percentage of the records in a table are locked individually. In a situation like this, the DBMS may promote the many individual locks into a single lock on the entire table.

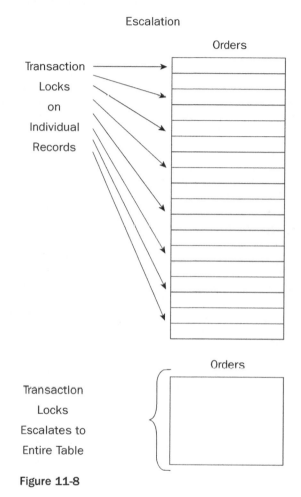

Figure 11-8

Escalation is simply an automatic process by the DBMS to attempt to consolidate many locks into a smaller number of locks. Even though it is an automatic process, the administrator may have some control over the process.

Timeout

As the number and complexity of transactions climb, the time required to obtain the locks necessary for any given transaction to proceed can mount, and any given transaction may have to wait a very long time to process. Most DBMSs have parameters that the administrator can set that cause a transaction to time out and return an error if the locks cannot be obtained in a reasonable time.

When discussing locking, the phrases *optimistic* and *pessimistic* inevitably come up. *Optimistic* locking generally presumes that transactions do not interfere with each other and thus prefer less restrictive locking strategies. *Pessimistic* locking assumes that transactions definitely interfere with each other and thus presumes more restrictive locking strategies. In general, locks work very well as long as the locks are of short duration, usually milliseconds or seconds. If locks last hours or days, they can tie a database up in knots, which is where versioning (discussed shortly) comes into play.

Isolation Levels

With some DBMSs, you can set the *isolation level*, which simply means the level of isolation between users of the database and their transactions and how much they are allowed to interfere with each other. To this point, this chapter has discussed transactions as if they were absolutely isolated from each other, but this may not be necessary or even desirable. Remember that transactions and locks have costs associated with them, and to force absolute isolation at all times would cause maximum cost. However, insufficient isolation between transactions can cause serious problems, displaying inconsistent views of the data and even causing data corruption. It is important to understand the issues that insufficient isolation can cause, as well as issues that unnecessary isolation causes.

SET TRANSACTION

The SQL2 standard provides an actual SET TRANSACTION statement that tells the DBMS which isolation level the transaction that follows uses. You can use this statement only as the first statement of a transaction, and thus you cannot change it in the middle of a transaction. It is possible to change levels at the beginning of any transaction, allowing different processes the freedom to select the isolation level necessary for the transaction that follows. Each level has its uses and should be used where applicable. After all, the lower the isolation level, the lower the impact on the database, on other users and processes, and on the hardware and software that implement the database platform.

Isolation levels are set using SQL code as shown below. Only one of the isolation levels can be set at any given time, and it remains in effect until explicitly changed. Generally, if no SET TRANSACTION statement is issued, the SERIALIZABLE level is in effect.

```
SET TRANSACTION ISOLATION LEVEL ISOLATION LEVEL
BEGIN TRANSACTION
```

The four isolation levels are discussed in the following sections.

SERIALIZABLE

A SERIALIZABLE isolation is essentially the maximum isolation possible. At this level, the DBMS guarantees that concurrently processing transactions operate as if they occurred in sequence (serially). SERIALIZABLE isolation is the default level in the ANSI standard, and this is how most database users expect transactions to perform. If a transaction sequence needs to be able to read a specific set of data twice during the transaction and return exactly the same set of data, SERIALIZABLE is the level that you need to use. It is implemented by using the following statement:

```
SET TRANSACTION ISOLATION LEVEL SERIALIZABLE
BEGIN TRANSACTION
```

No updates, additions, or deletions to the record set by other transactions are allowed while your transaction is processing. SERIALIZABLE transactions are absolutely required where multiple transactions occur on the same table, with updates and deletes that could cause data corruption if not handled properly. This scenario is covered in greater detail in the lost update and uncommitted data examples later in this chapter.

REPEATABLE READ

REPEATABLE READ is the second most rigorous level of isolation and essentially states that updates by other transactions to the existing records involved in your transaction must not be seen. However, insertions are allowed. In other words, existing data rows that your transaction reads may not be modified or deleted, but additional rows may be added. You set REPEATABLE READ by using the following statement:

```
SET TRANSACTION ISOLATION LEVEL REPEATABLE READ
BEGIN TRANSACTION
```

A multirow query run by your transaction at the beginning of your transaction may return additional records late — the phantom insert problem discussed a little bit later.

READ COMMITTED

READ COMMITTED is the third isolation level. READ COMMITTED guarantees that your transaction cannot see uncommitted updates from other transactions. This prevents the lost updates and uncommitted data problems discussed later. Use the following statement to specify the READ COMMITTED isolation level:

```
SET TRANSACTION ISOLATION LEVEL READ COMMITTED
BEGIN TRANSACTION
```

However, any transactions committed between reads of a data set may be seen. A process reading a row of data twice could see changed data in the second read since another process could commit a change to that data which would be seen the second time the data is read. If your process attempts to write updates to data updated by another process, your update is automatically rolled back to prevent the lost update problem, which is discussed later.

READ UNCOMMITTED

READ UNCOMMITTED is the last isolation level specified by the ANSI standard. In READ UNCOMMITTED, any updates performed by other transactions affect your transaction, either committed or uncommitted. This allows the uncommitted data, inconsistent data, and phantom data problems, which are all discussed in detail later in this chapter. However, the DBMS prevents the lost update problem (also discussed later) by causing a rollback of your changes if it would cause lost updates. The following statement shows you how to set the isolation level to READ UNCOMMITTED:

```
SET TRANSACTION ISOLATION LEVEL READ UNCOMMITTED
BEGIN TRANSACTION
```

The SET TRANSACTION statement also allows you to specify READ ONLY, which means that the transaction only reads data. You can also specify READ WRITE, in which case, the transaction expects to update, add, or delete records. Specifying READ WRITE allows the DBMS to optimize the transaction since it knows in advance how the transaction may impact other processes and transactions.

Usually, the default isolation level is SERIALIZABLE. If you specify READ UNCOMMITTED, then the DBMS assumes READ ONLY, and you cannot specify READ WRITE. If not otherwise specified, the DBMS assumes READ WRITE. The purpose of these assumptions is twofold: to allow the DBMS to optimize its operation and to protect inexperienced programmers from suffering the problems associated with transactions, which are detailed in the next section.

Versioning

Versioning is a method of working around the issue of locks. The idea is that as modifications to records are performed, *versions* of the data are made available to other users. Instead of just locking a user out, the DBMS decides whether the other users need to see the modified or the unmodified version of the data. There may in fact be several different versions of the data. The DBMS tracks the isolation levels of the various transactions and makes decisions as to which version of the data any given transaction should be allowed to see based on its isolation level. As far as I know, of all the major DBMSs, only Oracle uses versioning.

Locks are inherently restrictive in nature and limit concurrent operations on data. If one transaction has a write lock on data and another transaction has a SERIALIZABLE isolation level set, that transaction cannot even see the locked data. Thus that transaction simply halts processing until the data it needs to see is finally written. In a versioning system, as soon as the first transaction makes its modifications to the data, the second transaction may be allowed to see the modified or unmodified data, depending on what the DBMS decides is applicable to the operations the transaction is doing and its isolation level. Thus the second transaction can keep right on processing.

Versioning databases can, under the right circumstances, increase the number of concurrent transactions executing in parallel. Because the transactions do not wait for locks to release, they can continue whatever they are doing as if each process had exclusive access to the data. Unfortunately, there is significant overhead in tracking whether the various processes did in fact interfere with each other, and in those cases, the system must undo the damage and start over from the point where the interference occurred.

Problem Examples

In order to understand some of the problems that transactions help to prevent and that isolation levels address, it is useful to discuss a well-known set of problems. These problems are so well known, in fact, that they have been given names and are routinely discussed when learning transactions. The following text identifies these problems, provides you with a scenario in which you might encounter each one, and classifies the isolation level you should set in order to prevent them from occurring. Following the discussion of the problems is a table that summarizes the problems and how the various isolation levels affect the problem.

The Lost Update

The lost update problem illustrates what can occur when two programs read the same data from a table, use that data in calculations, and then try to update that data. A SERIALIZABLE isolation level helps you to prevent the lost update. The following situation gives you an idea of how the lost update can pop up in the real world.

International Board Manufacturer has a data entry system that the company uses for entering orders into its database. Sue takes a call for 100 vt-50 video cards from her client. Checking the Inventory table, she finds 175 vt-50 cards in stock. Meanwhile, John receives a call from his client who wants to order 130 of the vt-50 cards. John also checks the stock level and, finding 175 vt-50 cards in stock, assures his client that there is no problem filling the order. John enters his order for 130 cards in the Order table, and his order entry program deducts 130 from the 175 shown in the Inventory table, leaving 45 in stock. A few seconds later, Sue creates a new record in the Order table for 100 vt-50 cards and then updates the Inventory table, subtracting 100 from the 175 that her copy showed in the table, leaving 75 vt-50 video cards in stock.

The improper use of transactions leaves the database in an inconsistent state. John's update to the Inventory table for 130 vt-50 video cards was lost when Sue's update overwrote the previous update. Both Sue and John assured their clients that they would receive the product ordered, when in fact there were not enough video cards in stock to fill both orders. There are orders in the Order table for 230 vt-50 boards, but there are only 175 boards available to fill the two orders. Even worse, the Inventory table shows 75 boards still in stock after filling these orders!

The Uncommitted Data

Later that same day, John receives an order for 80 vt-100 video cards. Checking stock, John discovers that there are 95 cards in stock. He enters the order and updates the Inventory table to reflect the order, leaving 15 cards in inventory. As John was entering the order, his customer starts asking about the latest and greatest vt-150.

Meanwhile, Sue gets a call for 75 of that same vt-100 video card. Looking in the Inventory table, she sees that there are only 15 cards in stock, so she tells her customer that she will back-order the part and ship the whole order when the parts are in stock.

John's client finally makes up his mind and decides to order 45 of the vt-150. John rolls back his order for the vt-100, leaving the original 95 cards in stock.

In this case, because Sue was able to view uncommitted data from John's transaction, she has mistakenly told her client that there was insufficient inventory to fill their order, and she has placed a back order for even more stock. Had Sue decided to ship the 15 cards, the situation would have been even worse because John's subsequent rollback would have set the Inventory record back to 95, when in fact 15 of those cards had actually been ordered.

The Inconsistent Data

John receives an order for 100 vt-150 video cards and starts entering the order. Sue's customer calls and asks how many of the vt-150 can be sent to him overnight. Sue executes a query and discovers 135 cards in stock. Sue's customer asks about a couple of different cards, keeping Sue busy checking inventory about different products. John finishes his order for 100 of the cards and commits the order transaction, leaving 35 cards in stock. Sue's customer finally decides to just take the available vt-150s. Sue queries the Inventory table again, only to discover that the quantity in stock has changed from 135 to 35.

In this case, the database is left in a consistent state; no problem was created in the data itself. Sue saw the actual quantity left; there really are only 35 cards in stock because the rest of the stock was ordered in a transaction that managed to correctly save its data. She did not place an order for inventory that didn't exist, and she didn't overwrite John's data.

From Sue's perspective, however, the data appeared inconsistent. Two reads of the same record a few moments apart returned different results. Even though this did not cause an issue, in this case it might very well have. Suppose that Mary had been running reports that showed sales by office and then sales by salesperson. The two reports would not return usable data for John's office because his office would show sales figures without the sale he just made, whereas the Salesperson report would show that sale. If Sue's manager were to see such a report, his faith in the database would no doubt be diminished, and with good reason. Furthermore, explaining the differences would be extremely difficult.

The Phantom Insert

The sales manager for John's office is running a transaction that scans the Order table and generates a long series of reports showing sales by region, sales by salesperson, and so forth. The report by region is finished, but several more reports are still running. While this transaction is running, John receives an order for $20,000, which he finishes entering just as the queries begin running for sales by salesperson. Because the transaction is allowed to see the new order, the data by salesperson is $20,000 higher than the sales by region would indicate possible.

As in the previous example, the problem is that the data is inconsistent between views of the data. The database itself is in a consistent state at any given instant, but the data in the database is changing over the time that the reports are being generated. Reads of two supposedly identical sets of records return a different number of rows. In the previous example, an update to a record between reads caused the problem. In this case, the insertion of a new record between reads caused the problem. Both of these problems cause the same symptom: data that appears to be (and in fact is) different between points in time.

Now that you understand isolation levels and the most common problems associated with them, the following table gives you a snapshot of how each isolation level helps you deal with each specific problem.

Isolation Level	Lost Update	Uncommitted Data	Inconsistent Data	Phantom Data
SERIALIZABLE	Prevented	Prevented	Prevented	Prevented
REPEATABLE READ	Prevented	Prevented	Prevented	Possible
READ COMMITTED	Prevented	Prevented	Possible	Possible
READ UNCOMMITTED	Prevented	Possible	Possible	Possible

Revisiting the Example Code

Remember that it is important to use transactions when they are required and to avoid them or set the isolation level correctly when the highest level of isolation is not required. In the majority of common DBMSs, locks enforce transactions, and locks inevitably cause performance issues. Using your admittedly simple example, this section discusses which code you might want to wrap in transactions and which you probably wouldn't.

The first process you need to do is to create a handful of new tables. Using a transaction at all when creating an entirely new table is probably not necessary. No other users know about the new tables, and since they simply don't even exist until the CREATE TABLE is executed, there is no chance of lock or data contention. You could wrap your new tables in a transaction, but that would only tie up valuable locks for a process that really doesn't need locking at all. Therefore, you do not wrap the statements that create the tables in transaction statements. Once the tables are added to the database, you need to add initial data to the Movie Format table and the Inventory table. Each of these processes entails writing SQL statements, and they depend on the previous operation succeeding or the next operation is not valid. For example, you need to build the Movie Format table and place two records in that table. The three formats are DVD, VHS, and Beta. If the statement that builds the table fails, obviously the process of placing the three records in the format table also fails. Again, transactions are not necessary, and you receive errors if the previous CREATE TABLE statements fail.

Next, you need to build the Inventory table and then place several inventory records in the table, which tells you what movies are available to be rented and in what format. Then you can start renting movies.

The process of renting movies consists of running a query to find out what is available, selecting a specific inventory item and marking it as rented, and building a new record in the Rentals table with the member ID, the inventory ID, and the date rented.

Try It Out   Renting Movies with Transactions

Select all available inventory records so that you can pick a movie. To do this, you really should wrap the stuff that follows in a transaction. You are filling an order and don't want the items you are modifying to also be modified by other users.

1.   Remember that in ANSI SQL you have to specifically end the previous transaction in order to begin another transaction, so the first thing you do is run a COMMIT statement:

```
COMMIT
```

In Transact-SQL (SQL Server for example) this would not be required since you never explicitly started a transaction.

In addition, for Transact-SQL you would need to explicitly start a transaction:

```
BEGIN TRANSACTION
```

2.   For non-Transact-SQL you do not need to run a BEGIN TRANSACTION statement because it is implicit.

```
SELECT Inventory.InventoryId, Films.FilmName, Films.PlotSummary, Format.Format
FROM (Inventory
INNER JOIN Films ON Inventory.FilmId = Films.FilmId)
INNER JOIN Format ON Inventory.FormatId = Format.FormatId
WHERE (((Inventory.CheckedOut)= 'n'));
```

3.   Select a specific movie and mark it as rented:

```
UPDATE Inventory
SET Inventory.CheckedOut = 'Y'
WHERE (((Inventory.InventoryId)=7));
```

4.   Build a record in the Rentals table:

```
INSERT INTO Rentals ( InventoryId, MemberId, DateOut )
SELECT 7 AS InventoryId, 3 AS MemberId, '3/21/2004' AS dateout;
```

5. At this point, you need to run a COMMIT statement to cause your modifications to be committed or written to the database. In SQL Server (Transact-SQL) the TRANSACTION keyword is optional and thus can be dropped.

```
COMMIT
```

How It Works

Transactions always have a BEGIN, whether it be implicit, as in the ANSI standard, or an explicit BEGIN TRANSACTION, as in the Transact-SQL extension. If you are not using Transact-SQL, then you need to perform a COMMIT to explicitly end one transaction and begin the next. Using Transact-SQL, you explicitly executed a BEGIN TRANSACTION.

Having told the DBMS that a transaction is desired, you then executed the statements that need to be executed as a unit. View and select a record, mark it as rented, and then create a rental record. Once all of these statements are finished, a COMMIT statement causes the entire sequence to be written to disk and the transaction is finished.

Likewise, the statements checking the movie back in to inventory should probably be a transaction. Again, use a simple COMMIT statement for users on ANSI SQL:

```
COMMIT
```

Users of Transact-SQL should use an explicit BEGIN TRANSACTION statement:

```
BEGIN TRANSACTION
```

When the movie is returned, the rental record has to be updated with the date returned and the amount paid, and the inventory record must be updated to indicate that the movie is back in stock:

```
UPDATE Rentals
SET Rentals.DateIn = '3/23/2004', Rentals.Charge = 5
WHERE (((Rentals.InventoryId)=7) AND ((Rentals.MemberId)=3));
UPDATE Inventory SET Inventory.CheckedOut = 'n'
WHERE (((Inventory.InventoryId)=7));
```

At this point, you need to run a COMMIT statement to cause your modifications to be committed or written to the database.

```
COMMIT
```

In SQL Server (Transact-SQL) the TRANSACTION keyword is optional and thus can be dropped if desired.

Using transactions in this manner prevents potential problems such as another database user trying to rent the same movie at the same time or a movie being marked as returned in the Rentals table but never being marked as available to be rented in the Inventory table.

Summary

Transactions ensure that users who need to modify data don't see data that is about to be modified or in the process of being modified. Transactions lock data sets so that you can perform modifications to records without overwriting other users' changes or allowing other users to overwrite your changes.

In this chapter, you learned the following:

❏   That in order to be considered a transaction, the set of statements must pass the ACID test: Atomic, Consistent, Isolated, and Durable.

❏   That the original ANSI standard used only COMMIT and ROLLBACK statements, but the various database vendors have extended the standards, in particular adding the BEGIN TRANSACTION and SAVE TRANSACTION statements to add flexibility to the process of starting a transaction and allowing partial rollbacks.

❏   How transaction logs allow the DBMS to record the transaction and how the statements in the transaction affect the data to protect against catastrophic failures that could corrupt the database.

❏   How to use locks to control access to different levels of objects in the database, starting at the database level and working down to the individual record in a specific table. You learned that locks have an associated significant overhead, and that hundreds or thousands of users trying to get locks can cause database slowdown and general efficiency issues.

❏   How locking levels can allow you to reduce the impact of locks by allowing users to see or not see locked records only when appropriate.

❏   How to prevent or minimize the four common problems with concurrent data access through a good understanding of the issues involved, through an understanding of how transactions and locks work, and by the careful use of isolation levels.

This has been a very technical chapter, one that is difficult to demonstrate in the typical tutorial method because of that fact that transactions and their implementation are so very vendor- and product-specific. At the same time, transactions are a key concept to correctly handling concurrency in a multiple-user database. Failure to understand the issues can lead to huge consistency problems.

The next chapter covers SQL security, how users are created, and once created, how users are restricted from using or are allowed to use objects of the database. Security allows you to determine who gets to see what, as well as who is allowed to modify data in the tables that make up the database.

Exercises

1.   Rewrite the update to the Inventory and insert data into the Rentals table using a READ COMMITTED isolation level.

2.   Write a SELECT statement to view all titles in the Films table using the READ UNCOMMITTED isolation level.

3.   Write an UPDATE query to update all inventory to CheckedOut (= 'Y') using the SERIALIZABLE isolation level.

SQL Security

In today's world, the security of the data in your database is a primary concern. Privacy concerns and laws often make exposure of corporate data a catastrophic problem. Exposure of personal information such as social security numbers or medical information can bring costly lawsuits or even government fines and litigation. In the Internet age, the theft or exposure of such information can be performed from half a world away. No longer can you just lock the door to the server and remove the floppy disks from the workstations and consider yourself secure. The security issues that you must deal with in the database world involve who can see what when, and they break down into a handful of basic situations:

❑ The data in a specific table should be accessible to some users but not others.

❑ Some users should be able to modify particular tables, but other users should not.

❑ In some instances, access to tables should be broken down into columns of the tables. One set of users should be able to see columns a, b, and d, while another set of users should be able to access only columns c, e, and f.

❑ In other instances, the access to tables should be limited by rows. Perhaps department managers should be able to see data about their department but not data about other departments.

This chapter describes the methods that SQL provides to implement this security.

Security Concepts

Implementing the security system and enforcing the required restrictions are the responsibility of the DBMS. The SQL language implements a security framework and provides a rather basic syntax used to specify security restrictions. SQL *grants* access to objects by users; it does not *restrict* access. In other words, a user cannot perform any action without first being granted the power to do so.

SQL security is centered around three concepts or ideas:

❑ **Users:** Users, or more correctly user IDs, represent people or programs performing actions on objects in the database. Whenever the DBMS creates a new table, inserts or deletes records in that table, or modifies the records in that table, it does so on behalf of a user ID. The DBMS grants user IDs privileges to perform specific actions on specific tables.

❑ **Objects:** The SQL standards define specific objects in the database that users can manipulate. Originally the only objects were tables and views, but the standard has been expanded to include specific columns in tables as well as domains and character sets, and the individual DBMS often adds its own objects that it allows users to manipulate.

❑ **Privileges:** The third leg of SQL security comprises privileges that allow users to manipulate objects. These privileges start with SELECT, INSERT, DELETE, and UPDATE for tables and views but have been expanded to include privileges appropriate to non-data objects.

Setting up security on a database involves creating objects such as tables and views, creating users, and finally granting authority to perform specific actions on specific objects to specific users. Previous chapters have described the SQL syntax that creates the tables and fields; this chapter focuses on the process of creating users and granting authority.

In Figure 12-1, Mary has been granted full privileges on the Personnel table, but Sue has been granted only SELECT, UPDATE, and INSERT privileges on specific columns. Likewise, an Order Entry group has been created and full access given to this group on the Orders table, while a Shipping group was created and granted only UPDATE privileges and only on some columns.

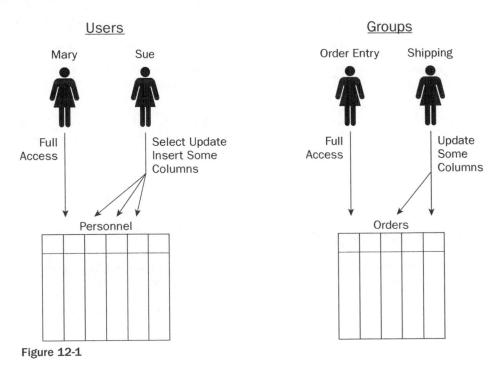

Figure 12-1

Setting up security begins with creating user IDs and passwords. How this is done varies enormously from DBMS to DBMS. In fact, some DBMSs can have the operating system itself perform all user/password validations for it and simply use the operating system username in the DBMS. For the purposes of this chapter, you can assume that user IDs and passwords are created in the DBMS. You may need to do a little digging to determine specifically how it is done in your OS and DBMS.

User IDs

Users IDs are the foundation of SQL security. At least one user ID is created by the database, known variously as the database owner (DBO), system administrator (SA), or something similar. This user is a *superuser* who starts the ball rolling, typically creating the first tables and creating the user IDs of all the other users allowed in the table.

In simple databases, it is quite common for all users to log in as the system administrator, which means that every user has all privileges to all objects. Anyone can do anything to any database object. In a small office where there is no one capable of understanding and maintaining database security, this may be an appropriate model, but for large corporations this is a recipe for disaster.

In a secure DBMS, a *user ID* is a name/password pair that allows some entity to perform actions in the database. The entity may be a person, a program, or a program directly manipulated by a person, but the end result is that the entity has to *log in* to the database, providing a valid username and password. The DBMS looks up the username and password, performs validation to ensure that that pair is legal in the system, and then determines what the user is allowed to do in the database.

In a database where security is implemented, a user is typically assigned a user ID and the user ID is assigned a password. The user ID then becomes the central character in the security system. Every SQL statement is executed on behalf of a user ID, and the privileges assigned to a user ID determine which statements can legally be performed by that user ID. User IDs are not necessarily used by people, however; machines quite often add, delete, and update records in databases with no input from any specific person. Machines in factories log production or assembly of objects, airplanes log sensor inputs from throughout the aircraft, and so forth.

In Figure 12-2, Mary, Sue, and John from the Personnel department are all given a common user ID and password. In some respects, this emulates the creation of a group with users assigned to the group. Betty, the personnel manager, has been given a unique user ID and password. Likewise, Cyndi has been given her own user ID and password.

> *Technically, the user ID is the object internal to the database, and the user is someone or something in the real world using a user ID to manipulate data. For ease of discussion, user is equated to user ID, but understand that they are not the same thing.*

DBMSs vary widely in how a user is validated. For example, the user may be required to log in to the DBMS directly, providing a username and password. On the other hand, the DBMS may accept user validation performed by the operating system: The user logs in to Windows, and the DBMS then accepts the username and password from Windows and looks up that username to determine whether to allow privileges.

However, before a user can do anything in the DBMS, the system administrator must create the user and define which privileges he or she has.

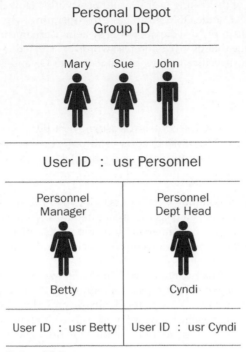

Figure 12-2

Creating User IDs

The system administrator (SA) sets up users and defines the privileges those users have. In many cases, this is done through a program interface to the DBMS, where the SA simply opens a form and starts creating users, typing their initial password and telling the DBMS whether the user can change their password, whether they must change their password the first time they log on, and so forth. In fact, some DBMSs can allow all of the user/password validation to be performed by the OS, which means no user IDs or passwords are required inside of the database itself.

Some DBMSs have SQL statements, extensions to the SQL standard specific to that DBMS, to allow creating users. For example, in Oracle the statement looks like this:

```
CREATE USER username
IDENTIFIED {BY password | EXTERNALLY | GLOBALLY AS external_name}
Options
```

After creating users and determining privileges for those users, the SA can then alter users and privileges.

Alter User

The SA can always modify the user by changing the password and, in some systems, by making a user inactive or setting times of day or days of the week that the user can log in to the database. Some DBMSs provide SQL statements for these functions. For example, in Oracle, the statement may look like the following:

```
ALTER USER username options
ALTER USER username,... {GRANT|REVOKE} proxy_options
```

In other cases, the DBMS provides other methods of doing this, oftentimes using a dedicated form or stored procedures.

Drop User

And finally, what the SA can do, the SA can always undo, in this case completely deleting a user if required. Again, in Oracle, the following statement drops a user from the database:

```
DROP USER username [CASCADE]
```

In SQL Server, all of these functions and more are performed using *stored procedures*, which in this case are pre-existing functions provided by the system, such as the following:

❑ **sp_addlogin:** Creates a new login that allows users to connect to SQL Server using SQL Server authentication

❑ **sp_grantlogin:** Allows a Windows NT/2000 user account or group to connect to SQL Server using Windows authentication

❑ **sp_droplogin:** Drops an SQL Server login

❑ **sp_revokelogin:** Drops a Windows NT/2000 login/group from SQL Server

❑ **sp_denylogin:** Prevents a Windows NT/2000 login/group from connecting to SQL Server

❑ **sp_password:** Adds or changes the password for an SQL Server login

❑ **sp_helplogins:** Provides information about logins and their associated users in each database

❑ **sp_defaultdb:** Changes the default database for a login

❑ **sp_grantdbaccess:** Adds an associated user account in the current database for a SQL Server login or Windows NT/2000 login

❑ **sp_revokedbaccess:** Drops a user account from the current database

❑ **sp_helpuser:** Reports information about the Microsoft users and roles in the current database

Security is an area where implementation is completely dependent on a variety of factors such as the operating system itself, as well as the DBMS system you are using. In fact, this is the job of the database administrator, and in a large show, you will never be allowed to perform these tasks. For these reasons, it is impossible to provide a generalized operation for setting up a user that works for everyone. In the following section, you learn how users are set up in SQL Server so that you can see how it is done on one of the major OSs as well as one of the major DBMSs. After that, you need to read up on your specific platform and try it there. For example, the information in the following Try It Out can be found in Books Online for SQL Server.

Try It Out   Implementing Security in SQL Server

Follow these steps to implement security in Microsoft SQL Server:

1.   If SQL Server manager is not started, open it and start the service.

2.   Open Query Analyzer.

3. In the SQL window, type in this command:

```
USE FilmClub
```

This tells SQL Server that the commands to follow are to be used in the Film Club database. This syntax is useful only for users of SQL Server, and the details of the syntax can be found in Books Online.

4. The `sp_addlogin` stored procedure creates a new Microsoft SQL Server login that allows a user to connect to an instance of SQL Server using SQL Server authentication. It does not give permissions for that user to do anything.

```
sp_addlogin [ @loginame = ] 'login'
    [ , [ @passwd = ] 'password' ]
    [ , [ @defdb = ] 'database' ]
    [ , [ @deflanguage = ] 'language' ]
    [ , [ @sid = ] sid ]
    [ , [ @encryptopt = ] 'encryption_option' ]
```

5. In the SQL window, type the following:

```
EXECUTE sp_addlogin @loginame =   'John', @passwd = 'ASDFG'
EXECUTE sp_addlogin @loginame =   'Joe', @passwd = 'qwerty'
EXECUTE sp_addlogin @loginame =   'Lynn', @passwd = 'zxcvbn'
EXECUTE sp_addlogin @loginame =   'Fred', @passwd = 'mnbvc'
EXECUTE sp_addlogin @loginame =   'Amy', @passwd = 'lkjhg'
EXECUTE sp_addlogin @loginame =   'Beth', @passwd = 'poiuy'
```

```
EXECUTE sp_adduser 'John', 'John'
EXECUTE sp_adduser 'Joe', 'Joe'
EXECUTE sp_adduser 'Lynn', 'Lynn'
EXECUTE sp_adduser 'Fred', 'Fred'
EXECUTE sp_adduser 'Amy', 'Amy'
EXECUTE sp_adduser 'Beth', 'Beth'
```

How It Works

The `sp_addlogin` stored procedure simply adds a new user to the SQL Server login system, allowing a user to log in to SQL Server using a specific username and password. After executing these two statements, a user can log in using the name John and the password ASDFG or the name Joe and the password qwerty.

Group IDs (Roles)

Given a large database with hundreds or thousands of users, administration of user privileges becomes extremely complex and unwieldy. If every user has to be assigned every privilege they need, the process soon becomes unmanageable. In order to deal with this problem, the concept of *groups* or *roles* has evolved.

Groups or roles build on the idea of users, when more than one user needs the same privileges to the same objects. Users in Accounting need access to salary information for all employees, while users in Manufacturing need access to inventory data. In order to provide this logical grouping, group IDs are created and privileges are then granted to the group. A group can access tables and columns of tables, add records, and so forth. Once the group is defined and the privileges assigned, users are added to the group.

In Figure 12-3, three different groups are created, and privileges are assigned to the groups. The Personnel group is given SELECT, INSERT, and UPDATE privileges on tblPersonnel. The Order Entry group is given SELECT, INSERT, UPDATE, and DELETE privileges on tblOrders, whereas the Shipping group is given only UPDATE privileges on tblOrders. Once groups are created, user IDs are added to and deleted from the groups as required. Users belonging to groups inherit the privileges of the group to which they belong.

Unfortunately, SQL does not directly support groups. Under ANSI/ISO SQL security, you have two options for handling such needs:

❑   You can assign the same user ID to all the users in the logical group as shown in Figure 12-1. This simplifies database administration because you can specify privileges once for a large number of people, but there is no way to determine who is logged in to the database. Furthermore, you have problems with security when people leave and should no longer have access to the database. Using this scheme, the only way to handle this is to issue a new password to all the users of the ID.

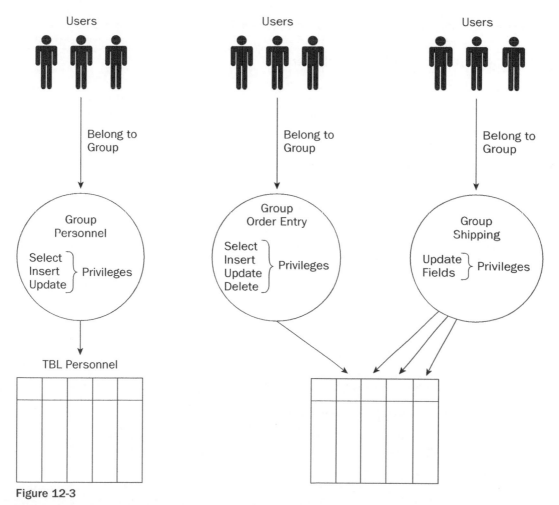

Figure 12-3

❑ You can assign a different user ID for each user in the group. This distinguishes the users in the database, allows you to assign different privileges as needed later, and allows locking that user out when the user leaves or is no longer allowed access to the database. Unfortunately, this option causes large headaches in administration when many users need access to the database.

Many modern DBMSs address this problem by implementing the group or role concept. Privileges can be granted to individual users if needed, but privileges can also be granted to groups, and then users can be added to the groups. Users of the groups inherit the privileges of the group. Users can then perform activities allowed by their individual user ID or by the group or groups to which they belong. Because the SQL standard does not support group IDs, using them leads to non-portability between DBMS systems.

IBM DB2 takes a different approach to the problem. A user ID can be associated with other user IDs. When a user logs in to a specific ID, the DBMS looks up all the associated IDs and builds a merged set of privileges based on the sum of all privileges of all these associated IDs. This neatly sidesteps the portability issue since there is no group ID per se, only user IDs with privileges that any other user ID can associate with.

The following Try It Out walks you through the process of adding a new role to your database.

Try It Out   Adding Roles in SQL Server

In order to add a new role, follow these steps:

1. The sp_addrole stored process creates a new Microsoft SQL Server role in the current database. It does not grant privileges to any objects in the database. This syntax is useful only for users of SQL Server, and the details of the syntax can be found in Books Online.

```
sp_addrole [ @rolename = ] 'role'
    [ , [ @ownername = ] 'owner' ]
```

2. In the SQL window, type the following:

```
EXECUTE sp_addrole @rolename =  'DataEntry'
EXECUTE sp_addrole @rolename =  'Management'
EXECUTE sp_addrole @rolename =  'Supervisor'
```

Once the role has been created, members are added to the role. This step allows members to inherit privileges for the roles that they play in the database.

3. The sp_addrolemember stored process adds a security account as a member of an existing Microsoft SQL Server database role in the current database. This syntax is useful only for users of SQL Server, and the details of the syntax can be found in Books Online.

```
sp_addrolemember [ @rolename = ] 'role' ,
    [ @membername = ] 'security_account'
```

4. In the SQL window, type the following:

```
EXECUTE sp_addrolemember @rolename =  'DataEntry', @membername = 'John'
EXECUTE sp_addrolemember @rolename =  'Management', @membername = 'Lynn'
```

How It Works

After you run this statement, you will see a role in the database called `DataEntry` that can be used to assign privileges allowing users to add data to tables. The role `Management` can be used to run reports to view data entered by `DataEntry`. Once the roles are created, you then add one or more members to each role. All that's left is to assign privileges to roles (and members if desired).

Objects

The SQL standard defines security in terms of objects on which actions can be performed. In the SQL1 standard, the only objects that security applied to were tables and views. Thus, privileges were assigned to a user ID to perform an action on a table or a view. If a user is not granted a privilege to an object, then that user can't access that object. SQL2 extended the security syntax and added new objects such as user-defined character sets and domains.

Figure 12-4 shows that user ID Fred is granted `SELECT` privileges on `tblPersonnel`, whereas user ID John is granted `SELECT` privileges on `tblPersonnel` as well as `UPDATE` privileges on `tblOrders`.

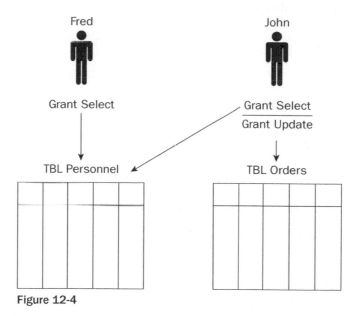

Figure 12-4

Modern DBMSs have added additional objects to the security syntax to cover objects such as stored procedures in SQL Server. Stored procedures are programming functions that can be created by users and that can perform all sorts of tasks. The ability to create and drop these functions can be controlled by the security system, with certain user IDs granted permission to create or drop stored procedures, while others are not. In some cases, the physical tablespaces where tables are created and stored are treated as security objects, with user IDs granted permission to create tables in a given tablespace. In essence, the modern DBMS has simply extended the SQL syntax to allow granting of privileges to objects not considered by the SQL standard. These extensions vary from DBMS to DBMS, and because the extensions are specific to the DBMS, the methods used to grant these privileges vary considerably.

Privileges

Privileges are the ability to perform some action on some object. The SQL1 standard defines only privileges on tables and views and thus defines only four basic privileges that work on these objects:

❑ The SELECT privilege allows the user to create data sets of columns and rows from tables or views. With this privilege, the user can specify a view or table name in the FROM clause of a SELECT query. The SELECT privilege means that the user is allowed to view or use data from the table or view on which the SELECT privilege is granted.

❑ The INSERT privilege allows the user to insert new rows into the table or view on which the INSERT privilege is granted; thus they can use that table or view name in the INTO clause of an INSERT statement.

❑ The DELETE privilege allows the user to delete rows from the table or view on which the DELETE privilege is granted; thus they can use the name of that table or view in the FROM clause of a DELETE statement.

❑ The UPDATE privilege allows the user to update rows from the table or view on which the DELETE privilege is granted; thus they can use the name of that table or view in the UPDATE statement.

These four privileges are all that the SQL1 standard allowed, and these privileges are implemented in all commercial SQL-compliant DBMSs.

Extended Privileges

SQL2 expanded on the concepts of SQL1 in several ways. First, it added the ability to the INSERT and UPDATE statements to operate on specific columns instead of on the entire table. Suppose that a new vice president is hired. The Personnel department is tasked with setting up all new personnel records, entering the name, address, personnel ID, and so forth. The salary and compensation information is not their department, however, and they should not have access to this information. Only the personnel manager is allowed to edit these fields. In SQL1, in order to get this capability, you had to implement views that retrieved the columns of interest and then use those views in an INSERT or UPDATE statement. Although this works, it leads to dozens of views whose sole purpose is to enforce security and makes administering security unnecessarily complex. In SQL2, however, you can directly create INSERT statements that insert only specific columns of the new record and then UPDATE statements that allow other users to update the columns for which they are responsible.

Unfortunately, the SQL2 standard does not allow the SELECT statement to specify only selected columns, so for these statements you are back to creating views that pull specific columns and use them instead of a SELECT statement on the table directly. Many of the major DBMSs allow applying privileges to columns as an extension to the SQL2 syntax, using the same syntax as is used in the INSERT and UPDATE statements.

In addition to the new column-specific privileges, the SQL2 standard adds the REFERENCES privilege, which addresses some rather subtle issues dealing with using foreign keys and check constraints. The issue here is that by including valid foreign keys in a SQL statement, a user can determine whether the key is valid or not, even if they are not supposed to have any access to the table from which the foreign key comes. An INSERT statement can be constructed that successfully inserts a record. Then the foreign key is added as a column to the statement. If a statement succeeds, the key is valid; if the statement fails, then the key is not valid. Suppose that the foreign key was the social security number (SSN) of an employee. The user would now be able to determine whether an employee existed with that SSN even though they are not supposed to be able to see the SSNs of the Employee table. Likewise, check constraints can be used in a similar manner. Because check constraints do not expose data to viewing, update, and deletion, they are often treated differently by the DBMS when it comes to security. Thus, a user could include tables and fields in a check constraint to which he otherwise wouldn't have access. This opens up a similar security hole in that a user could try different values in a check constraint to discover the values of a field that he isn't supposed to be able to see.

To eliminate this hole in security, the REFERENCES keyword was added. The REFERENCES privilege is assigned to specific rows of tables. Unless assigned a REFERENCES privilege, a user cannot reference that column in that table in any manner.

The USAGE Privilege

The USAGE privilege is used to control access to domains, or the sets of legal values in a given column, as well as user-defined character sets, translations, and collating sequences. USAGE is a simple true/false property that says a user has access to one of these objects for individual user ID. This privilege is aimed at the corporate developer more than the individual database user.

Ownership

When you create a table in SQL using the CREATE TABLE statement, you become the owner of that table and control security on that table. You have full privileges for SELECT, INSERT, DELETE, and UPDATE for that table. You also are able to grant privileges to that table to other user IDs. In fact, other users have no privileges on that table until you specifically grant those privileges to those users.

The situation for views is a little different, however. In order to create a view, you must have specific privileges on the table or tables from which you pull data. You must at least have SELECT privileges to the underlying tables. Thus, the DBMS automatically gives you SELECT privileges to the resulting view. The other privileges (INSERT, DELETE, and UPDATE) depend on your privileges in the underlying tables for the view, and you must have each privilege for *every* table in the view before you are granted that privilege in the resulting view. Furthermore, you can grant privileges to other user IDs for the view only if you have been granted the privilege to grant those privileges. You learn about granting privileges in a later section of this chapter, but first you learn more about the relationship between views and security.

Views and Security

Views are often used to enforce security on *viewing* data. By creating views that display specific columns from specific tables, a user can be granted SELECT privileges for that view but not for the underlying table. Using this strategy makes it possible to determine exactly what information a specific user is allowed to view.

Vertical and Horizontal Views

Vertical views represent select columns of one or more tables such that the user can see only portions of a table or tables. This allows you to hide sensitive data columns from certain users while allowing access to those columns to other users.

For example, suppose you had a business rule that states that employees in the Personnel department should be able to see the names and addresses of all employees, but not the SSN or salary. You might implement this view with a SQL statement similar to the following:

```
CREATE VIEW vEmployeeNonSensitive AS
SELECT Name, Address, City, State, ZIP, Phone FROM tblEmployees
```

You could then give SELECT privileges to the usrPrsnl user ID. That user can now view any of the non-sensitive fields from tblEmployees, as shown in Figure 12-5.

In order to give Payroll access to the SSN and Salary fields, you might implement a view with a SQL statement similar to the following:

```
CREATE VIEW vEmployeeSensitive AS
SELECT Name, SSN, Salary FROM tblEmployees
```

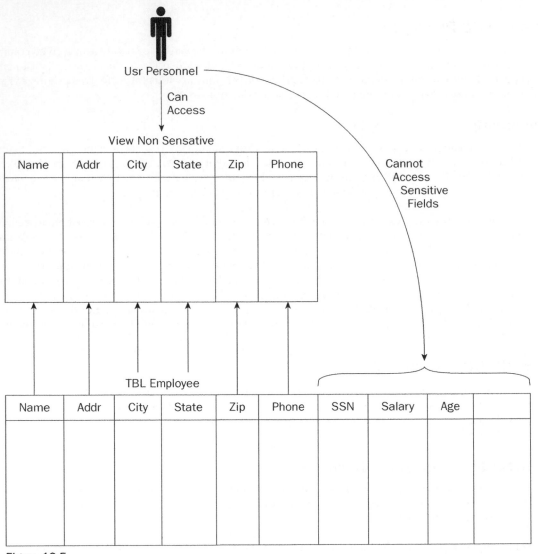

Figure 12-5

You could then give SELECT privileges to vEmployeeSensitive to the usrPayroll user ID. Figure 12-6 illustrates that the user usrPayroll can now view only the person's name, SSN, and salary fields while hiding address and phone numbers.

Horizontal views, on the other hand, allow the user to view all the fields in the table but only for selected sets of records.

For example, suppose you had a business rule that states that a department manager should be able to view all personnel information for only the employees in their department.

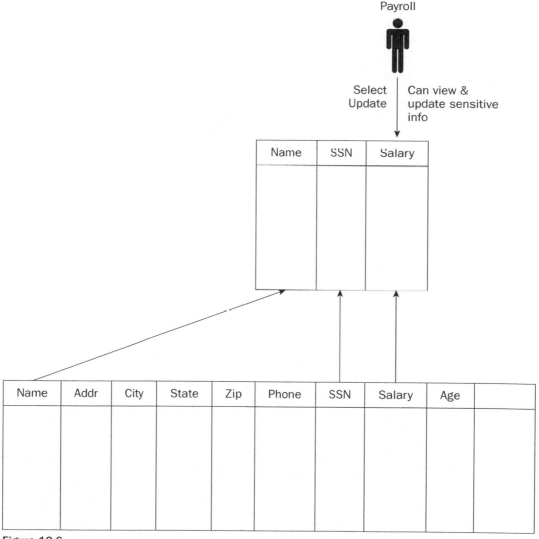

Figure 12-6

You might implement this view with the following SQL statement:

```
CREATE VIEW vEngineeringEmployee AS
SELECT * FROM tblEmployees
WHERE Department = 'Engineering'
```

This view creates a horizontal view of all the fields in the Personnel table for any employee in the Engineering department, thus restricting the user to only data about the employees in that department. You can now give SELECT privileges to this view to the EngMgr user ID.

Grouped Views

Grouped views refer to summary data where totals and counts are rolled up into a query that summarizes large quantities of data in a small set of records. These views represent a many-to-one relationship to the source table and allow managers to get an overview of performance for some business unit, sales for sales areas, production for a manufacturing facility by month, and so forth. SELECT privileges on these views can be granted to only those in management that need access to the data.

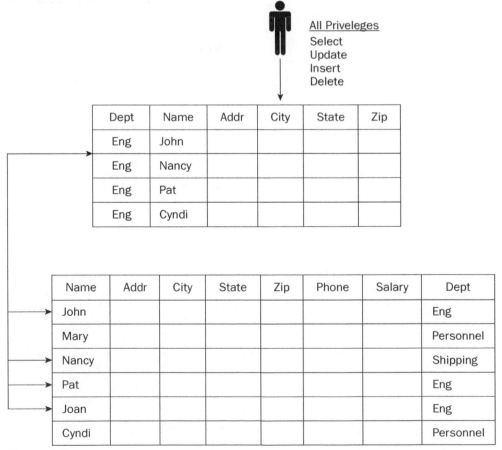

Figure 12-7

Limitations on Views

Views are by their nature SELECT statements and thus are read-only in most security schemes. If the user needs to be able to modify, insert, or delete the data in the view, the user must be granted those privileges to the underlying tables. If more than a single table is used in the view, it may not be possible to perform updates on the view even with privileges, depending on the complexity of the view and the specific implementation of the DBMS that you are using.

Remember also that views have a negative impact on the performance of the database since the view has to be translated into queries on the underlying tables.

Granting Privileges

The basic GRANT statement is used to grant security privileges on database objects to specific users or, in some DBMS implementations, to groups. For SQL2 compatibility, the GRANT statement works only for user IDs; groups don't exist. When you create a table, you are the owner of that table and you can use the GRANT statement to grant privileges to any user you want. With views, you can use the GRANT ALL statement to grant all privileges on the view. However, if you don't own the underlying tables, the GRANT you give is only as good as the privileges you hold on the underlying tables; furthermore, you have to hold a WITH GRANT OPTION on the privileges you are granting, as explained later in this section.

Tables and Views

In SQL1, GRANT dealt only with tables. Users are granted privileges on the entire table. The GRANT statement looks similar to the following:

```
GRANT SELECT, INSERT, DELETE, UPDATE
ON tblPersonnel
TO usrPersonnel
```

This statement gives all privileges on tblPersonnel to the user ID usrPersonnel.

The statements to allow an order entry clerk to add orders but to allow only shipping to view the orders might look like this:

```
GRANT SELECT, INSERT
ON tblOrders
TO usrOrderEntry

GRANT SELECT
ON tblOrders
TO usrShipping
```

Instead of specifically listing SELECT, INSERT, DELETE, and UPDATE for an object (as illustrated in the preceding code), the GRANT syntax also has a shortcut used to grant ALL PRIVILEGES to a specific user or group:

```
GRANT ALL PRIVILEGES
ON tblPersonnel
TO usrPersonnel
```

Another shortcut, using the PUBLIC keyword, grants privileges to all users:

```
GRANT SELECT
ON tblHolidays
TO PUBLIC
```

Using the PUBLIC keyword has the advantage of not having to explicitly grant privileges to users, since any current or even future authorized users are automatically in the listed privilege.

Try It Out   Using the GRANT Statement

The GRANT statement creates an entry in the security system that allows a user in the current database to work with data in the current database or execute specific Transact-SQL statements.

In the SQL window, type the following statement:

```
GRANT SELECT, INSERT, UPDATE
ON Attendance
TO DataEntry
GO
GRANT SELECT
ON Attendance
TO Management
GO
```

How It Works

Once the role is created, members are added to the role. This step allows members to inherit privileges for the roles that they play in the database. By running a GRANT statement on a given table or object, you assign specific privileges to that group (role in SQL Server) or user for that specific object. In this case, you have granted SELECT, INSERT, and UPDATE privileges to the DataEntry group, and you have granted only SELECT privileges to the Management group.

Columns

The SQL1 standard allowed GRANT UPDATE privilege on individual columns of a table or view, while the SQL2 standard expanded that to include INSERT and REFERENCES privileges. The syntax lists the columns after the PRIVILEGE keyword, and they must be between parentheses and comma-delimited (separated by commas) if there are more than one. As an example, to give shipping personnel privileges to specific columns in the order item table, you could write a GRANT statement similar to the following:

```
GRANT UPDATE (ShipDate, Quantity)
ON tblOrderItem
TO usrShipping
```

As you have already seen, the SQL standard does not permit a column list for a SELECT privilege. The SELECT privilege must apply to all columns of the table or view. The normal method of handling this restriction is simply to create a view of the desired columns and then grant a SELECT privilege on the view. Of course, this forces you to design views that wouldn't be necessary if a column list were allowed. For this reason, many of the DBMSs provide extensions to the standard to allow column lists in the SELECT grant statements. These extensions allow you to write statements like this:

```
GRANT SELECT (NAME, SSN, SALARY)
ON tblPersonnel
TO usrPayroll
```

This eliminates the requirement for the view described in Figure 12-6, and the availability of SELECT column lists eliminates the need for many views used to restrict access to column data. Unfortunately the extension is not in the SQL standard, so it may or may not be available on the DBMS you use.

The GRANT OPTION Clause

When you create a table, you own all privileges to that table, and it is your responsibility to grant privileges to any other users that require access to the data. When you grant privileges to these other users, they can access the data as specified in the GRANT statement you create, but in general they cannot pass on these privileges to other users. This provides tight control to the owner of the table over who can access the data and how they can access it. However, it is occasionally useful to allow other users to pass on privileges to others. Suppose, for example, that you create a view of Production with the following SQL:

```
CREATE VIEW vProductionEastCoast AS
SELECT * FROM tblProduction
WHERE Region = 'EAST'
```

You want to allow the East Coast production manager to be able to view the data, so you create a GRANT statement to allow her to use the view:

```
GRANT SELECT
ON vProductionEastCoast
TO usrMary
```

Suppose, however, that Mary needs to allow her office staff to use the view. The GRANT statement as written does not allow transferring privileges to other users. In order to accomplish this, you need to add the WITH GRANT OPTION clause, as shown in the following:

```
GRANT SELECT
ON vProductionEastCoast
TO usrMary
WITH GRANT OPTION
```

Because of the WITH GRANT OPTION clause, Mary now has the right to assign the privilege she was given to anyone she chooses. Thus, she could create a GRANT statement similar to the following:

```
GRANT SELECT
ON vProductionEastCoast
TO usrBob, usrSharon
```

Because she used no WITH GRANT OPTION clause in that statement, usrBob and usrSharon do not have the authority to pass on the GRANT to anyone else. However, if Mary adds WITH GRANT OPTION to the statement (as shown below), Bob and Sharon can also pass the privileges along:

```
GRANT SELECT
ON vProductionEastCoast
TO usrBob, usrSharon
WITH GRANT OPTION
```

As you can imagine, giving GRANT OPTION privileges to other users allows them unlimited ability to pass on the privileges to other users, which can be very dangerous in some circumstances, particularly for the UPDATE and DELETE privileges. You should use GRANT OPTION with discretion.

Revoking Privileges

If you've granted privileges that you need to revoke, you do so using the REVOKE statement. Revoking privileges can yield unexpected results depending on the implementation used by your DBMS, whether more than one user granted privileges on an object, and the time sequence of the grants. You see that in a little while, but first you need to learn the REVOKE statement's basic syntax.

The REVOKE Statement

The REVOKE syntax looks very similar to the GRANT syntax. The REVOKE statement can take away some or all of the privileges assigned in a GRANT statement, to some or all of the user IDs. For example, suppose you granted some privileges on the Personnel table:

```
GRANT SELECT, UPDATE, INSERT
ON tblPersonnel
TO usrTom, usrJim
```

You can then use the following statement to revoke various INSERT privileges from Tom:

```
REVOKE INSERT
ON tblPersonnel
FROM usrTom
```

You can likewise revoke SELECT and INSERT privileges from Jim using this statement:

```
REVOKE SELECT, INSERT
ON tblPersonnel
FROM usrJim
```

Revoking UPDATE privileges from Jim and Tom requires a statement similar to the following:

```
REVOKE UPDATE
ON tblPersonnel
FROM usrJim, usrTom
```

You can revoke only privileges that *you* granted. If the user was granted privileges on the same object by another user, only the privileges *you* granted are revoked. Thus, if the user you are revoking privileges for was granted privileges on the same object by another user, they are still able to access that object using any privileges that the other user gave them.

You grant Jim privileges on tblPersonnel with this statement:

```
GRANT SELECT, UPDATE, INSERT
ON tblPersonnel
TO usrJim
```

Betsey also grants privileges to Jim on `tblPersonnel` using this statement:

```
GRANT UPDATE, DELETE
ON tblPersonnel
TO usrJim
```

The first thing to notice is that `usrJim` now has all privileges on `tblPersonnel` and can select, update, insert, or delete records in `tblPersonnel`. You subsequently revoke some of the privileges that you granted to Jim with the following statement:

```
REVOKE UPDATE
ON tblPersonnel
FROM usrJim
```

Notice that even though you revoked the UPDATE privilege that you gave Jim, he still has full privileges on `tblPersonnel` because Betsey also gave him UPDATE privileges. You subsequently revoke the rest of the privileges you gave Jim:

```
REVOKE SELECT, INSERT
ON tblPersonnel
FROM usrJim
```

Jim still has all the privileges that Betsey granted him and can still perform updates and deletes on `tblPersonnel` using those privileges.

Another scenario, however, must be considered, which is how the GRANT chain is handled by the DBMS.

Revoking GRANT

Suppose that Jim issues a GRANT to Sue WITH GRANT OPTION:

```
GRANT SELECT
ON tblPersonnel
TO usrSue
WITH GRANT OPTION
```

Sue now has the ability to grant the SELECT privileges to another user and does so, issuing a GRANT to Frank:

```
GRANT SELECT
ON tblPersonnel
TO usrFrank
```

Jim now revokes the GRANT from Sue:

```
REVOKE SELECT
ON tblPersonnel
FROM usrSue
```

In this case, it can be clearly established that Frank received his privileges because Sue had GRANT OPTION privileges, and therefore when Sue loses her privileges on `tblPersonnel`, Frank also loses his privileges.

The situation gets a little sticky, though, when Sue has received GRANT OPTION on a table from two different sources and has issued a GRANT to Frank.

Jim issues a GRANT to Sue WITH GRANT OPTION:

```
GRANT SELECT
ON tblPersonnel
TO usrSue
WITH GRANT OPTION
```

Sue now issues a GRANT to Frank:

```
GRANT SELECT
ON tblPersonnel
TO usrFrank
```

Mary comes along and issues GRANT OPTION to Sue as well:

```
GRANT SELECT
ON tblPersonnel
TO usrSue
WITH GRANT OPTION
```

Jim now revokes the GRANT from Sue:

```
REVOKE SELECT
ON tblPersonnel
FROM usrSue
```

What happens to the privileges that Sue granted to Frank? In this case, some DBMSs would revoke Frank's privileges because it can be demonstrated that he was granted privileges derived from Jim because Mary had not yet granted GRANT OPTION privileges to Sue at the time Sue issued the GRANT privilege to Frank. On the other hand, Sue still has the right to issue privileges from the GRANT OPTION given her by Mary, so it is not a cut-and-dry case that Frank's privileges should be revoked, and some DBMSs leave Frank with his privileges.

As you can see, it is not always a simple case of who issued the WITH GRANT OPTION but may also be a matter of timing, and how this scenario is handled may vary from DBMS to DBMS.

In the SQL1 standard, the REVOKE statement is missing from the syntax. Access to tables and views is determined by GRANT statements at the time the database is set up, and there is no mechanism for changing the privileges once the database structure is defined. In spite of this, almost all commercial DBMSs provided the REVOKE statement. The next section covers a couple of syntax extensions that provide you more flexibility when using the REVOKE statement.

The CASCADE and RESTRICT Options

The SQL2 standard added the REVOKE statement and in fact added some extensions to give the REVOKE statement more flexibility. The CASCADE extensions gave the user the ability to determine how privileges are revoked when the privileges have been further granted down to other users. The other extension, RESTRICT, allows revoking the GRANT OPTION without revoking the privileges themselves.

The CASCADE option tells the DBMS that a REVOKE of the GRANT OPTION should cause a ripple down the chain and also revoke any privileges issued because of the GRANT OPTION.

Suppose Jim issues a GRANT to Sue WITH GRANT OPTION:

```
GRANT SELECT
ON tblPersonnel
TO usrSue
WITH GRANT OPTION
```

Sue now issues a GRANT to Frank:

```
GRANT SELECT
ON tblPersonnel
TO usrFrank
```

Jim now issues a REVOKE to Sue:

```
REVOKE SELECT
ON tblPersonnel
FROM usrSue CASCADE
```

In this case, both Sue and Frank lose their SELECT privilege on tblPersonnel because Jim placed the CASCADE option on the REVOKE statement.

Assume that Jim issued the same GRANT to Sue, and Sue issued the same GRANT to Frank. Jim later issues the following REVOKE:

```
REVOKE SELECT
ON tblPersonnel
FROM usrSue RESTRICT
```

In this case, the REVOKE fails and issues an error warning Jim that there are privileges cascading down from the GRANT that he issued, and that he may be revoking privileges that he doesn't intend to revoke. If Jim does decide to revoke Sue's privileges, he can simply issue the REVOKE again with the CASCADE option. The RESTRICT option is just a way to let a user know that the REVOKE will cause a cascade REVOKE.

In addition, the SQL2 syntax now includes the ability to specify the privilege in the REVOKE GRANT statement instead of just revoking all GRANT privileges. Consider the following statement:

```
REVOKE GRANT OPTION ON INSERT, DELETE
ON tblPersonnel
FROM usrSue CASCADE
```

This statement revokes the ability to GRANT OPTION on these privileges but does not take away the privileges themselves.

Summary

Database security is a subject that simply cannot be ignored. The SQL standard contains statements designed to enforce privileges to use objects in the database, primarily tables and views but also other objects. This chapter covered the following topics:

❑ SQL security centers around users (or user IDs) that can grant privileges on database objects such as tables and views.

❑ Data in specific tables and views, and even columns of specific tables and views, should be available to some users but not available to others.

❑ Views may be required to restrict access to specific columns in some DBMSs where an extension to the SELECT syntax is not available.

❑ The GRANT statement grants SELECT, UPDATE, INSERT, and DELETE privileges to specific users.

❑ The GRANT OPTION allows a user to extend the privileges she has been granted down the line to other users.

❑ The REVOKE statement is used to revoke privileges granted to a user as well as revoke the GRANT OPTION itself.

In the next chapter, you learn about optimizing your database and how to write efficient SQL queries to speed up data retrieval.

Exercises

1. Create DataEntry, Supervisor, and Management groups.
2. Create users John, Joe, Fred, Lynn, Amy, and Beth.
3. Add John, Joe, and Lynn to the DataEntry group, add Fred to the Supervisor group, and add Amy and Beth to the Management group.
4. Give the DataEntry group SELECT, INSERT, and UPDATE privileges on the Attendance table.
5. Give the Supervisor group SELECT and DELETE privileges on the Attendance table.
6. Give the Management group SELECT privileges on the Attendance table.

Database Tuning

SQL is a language that describes how you retrieve data from a database. Just as in any language, you can say things that make sense but that may not mean what you intend or that can be misinterpreted and cause results that are not what you expect. By now you should be pretty good at expressing yourself in SQL and you should be getting the results, or at least the data, that you intend. On the other hand, you might get exactly the data you expect but it takes a long time to get the data back. That is the subject that this chapter addresses. Specifically, this chapter addresses the following questions:

❑   Why does your query take so long to execute?

❑   Is this just normal, or is there something you can do to get the results faster?

❑   When does it matter?

In fact, tuning SQL is just one piece of the bigger puzzle, which is tuning the system itself. In-depth system tuning is outside the scope of this chapter, but an overview of the subject is useful since it is possible to get large improvements in speed at this level. You may find that the database is administered by professionals and that they have already done all that can be done at this level. On the other hand, you may find yourself playing system administrator and realize that you are the only one around who can look at whether some of these issues can be addressed. Or you may find that the database is being administered by a network administrator with no real experience as a database administrator and that a little friendly advice to him will get you a long way. For all these reasons, this chapter covers some subjects that you might not expect to find in a book on basic SQL.

Tuning Hardware

If you have any control over the subject, the first place to start tuning is at the hardware level. It is a common misconception that servers don't necessarily need to be extremely powerful machines, and so you may find that while the workstations are the latest and greatest multi-gigahertz machines with a half-gigabyte of RAM, the server is a five-year-old machine running at a few hundred megahertz with a few hundred megabytes of memory. Indeed, since servers tend to be robust, fault-tolerant machines that cost a lot of money when new, they end up being used well past their prime and tend to be overloaded running many different types of server applications such as Web servers, firewalls, database servers, Dynamic Host Configuration Protocol (DHCP) servers assigning Internet Protocol addresses, and so forth, all too often all on the same machine.

One of the problems is that depending on the type of server and the number of users, older machines may indeed be very useful as servers. Older and slower Web servers handling only a handful of simultaneous users can easily handle the load. After all, they are probably only translating requests for Web pages and transmitting out a small piece of text or a few graphics. System administrators with no database experience may simply believe that since all the other servers run just fine on this old machine, the database server should, too.

Unfortunately, databases are not one of the applications where old and slow works very well. Database servers, particularly client servers, have to be able to handle tremendous processing loads to find the requested data and then transmit large quantities of data back to the client machine. Database servers probably need to be as fast as the organization can afford and have copious amounts of memory for reasons discussed in a moment.

By no means is this chapter arguing that tuning the application (and SQL) itself should not be done; it simply looks at this from a cost-benefit basis. If you pay a consultant $100 per hour for 50 hours to tune a database application, you have just spent $5000 and all you have for your money is a single tuned database application. If you spend that same $5000 for more memory, more or faster hard disks, or a faster processor or machine, you have purchased faster execution of every application that runs on that machine. Back in the day when the machine cost one million dollars and memory was a quarter million dollars per megabyte, tuning made much more sense than buying faster hardware. The situation is very much reversed now. Highly skilled labor is more expensive than ever and hardware is many orders of magnitude cheaper.

In terms of hardware specific to databases, the following sections discuss subjects that you should have at least a basic understanding of in case you need to argue for the upgrade of the hardware. You may not have the expertise to determine exactly what is needed, but at least you can be aware of what is possible and some of the issues involved. The objective is to start with the obvious (and cheap) changes that can mean real speed increases in many cases.

Workstations

If the users of old, slow machines have to multitask, keeping a lot of different applications open all the time — the database, Word, Excel, a browser — it may pay big dividends to just upgrade memory in their machines. Adding a 256M memory module to an old 128M workstation costs almost nothing but can make the machine useable again until new systems can be budgeted.

Depending on the application, specific users may benefit from workstation upgrades. With low-end but very powerful computers available for $500 or even less sans monitor, it may make sense to target specific users with new machines. Suppose that one of your clients has the vast majority of their workstations running 450MHz processors and Windows 98. They target one specific area of the company that has a high call load with new machines, replacing all of those workstations with new 2.8GHz machines and Windows XP. Ten new machines would cost them around $4000–$5000, and the productivity increase just from new hardware would be pretty impressive. Even after making tuning modifications to the application, it still runs radically faster on those machines than for the rest of the users.

Perhaps this doesn't sound remotely like application tuning, but the application runs on machines. If the machines don't support the application, you are never going to tune it enough to make a difference!

Database Files

Client server DBMSs (as opposed to file server DBMSs such as Microsoft Access) often allow you to distribute the database across many different hard disks. The objective is to split the database into files, with each disk holding a single file containing one or a set of tables, or even sets of indexes. By splitting the database up like this, you can get the physical input/output (I/O) distributed across many electronic channels, you get the disks accessing their pieces of the data in parallel so that the data from one disk can be read while the other disks are looking for data being requested, and finally you get cache on each hard drive holding a piece of the database.

DBMSs like SQL Server and Oracle have tools that allow you to set up complex, time-consuming queries and then watch the physical IO (disk access) to see if you are saturating the data channel(s), in other words transferring the maximum amount of data that the disk is capable of putting out. If this happens, then you have discovered a bottleneck and should consider splitting the database down into more files, one file per hard disk, which means adding hard disks to the system. Correctly implemented, adding hard disks to the system raises the amount of data that can be read out of the database. When the point is reached where the hard disks can feed data faster than the processor can handle it, you have eliminated one bottleneck and can look elsewhere for the next bottleneck.

Processors

DBMSs are one of the applications that are specifically written to utilize multiprocessor systems. *Multiprocessing* simply means having more than a single central processing unit (CPU) in the server box. While they are not cheap, adding processors to a database server can in certain circumstances make the database significantly faster. The reason is that queries can be broken down into pieces, and those pieces assigned to different processors. The individual processors handle pulling the indexes for their individual piece of the puzzle, narrowing down the data and finally returning a small data set to a processor that puts all the pieces back together into the original query. Just like breaking the database itself down into files on different hard disks, the net effect is to get parallel processing happening so that the whole process is executed faster.

Unfortunately you usually can't simply pop in an additional processor to upgrade your server. The motherboard has to be designed to hold multiple CPUs before you can do this. Even if you can add a new processor (there is an empty CPU socket), if the machine is old, adding the new processor may be difficult or impossible. Getting your hands on the processor for a five-year-old machine may be difficult, and even if you manage to do so, the slow speed of the processor may make the performance boost less than you might hope for compared to buying a new multi-gigahertz machine. On the other hand, if you can find a processor to pop into your multiprocessor machine, doing so almost certainly would provide some performance increase and would almost assuredly be better than no upgrade at all.

If your current database server system has a clock speed of less than 1GHz, and certainly if it is a single-processor system with a clock speed of less than 1GHz, moving up to a modern machine (possibly with multiprocessors) would almost assuredly provide large efficiency gains over what you have now. It isn't cheap, but if the budget allows it, this may go a long way toward speeding up almost any slow database application.

Gigahertz Networks or Compartmentalized Networks

Another area where you can sometimes get large speed increases is by analyzing how your network is holding up to the load. Companies tend to grow haphazardly, adding employees all over the building and plopping down new workstations with little thought to what is happening to network traffic. In the Internet age, employees may be logging in to their workstations or the server using remote access, which can cause significant network overhead. Internet music and video downloads also cause massive congestion. It is not uncommon to end up with overloaded networks that can no longer keep up with the traffic being encountered.

Oftentimes, new workstations can be purchased with gigahertz network cards. If the network is approaching saturation, moving up to gigahertz networks can open up the bandwidth enough to allow the applications to breathe again. Another thing that you can do is to compartmentalize the network such that different sections of the company come in to the server on separate routers, switches, or network interface cards (NICs). This is another area where there are tools to allow you to accurately measure whether the network is a bottleneck. Networks require expert assistance if you need to modify them, but if they are a bottleneck, then making those modifications can pay huge dividends.

Caches

A *cache* is a place where data is stored for fast access after it is retrieved from a location that takes significantly longer to access. This definition is flexible enough to work for all the various caches that you find on your computer, and there are many of them. The reason that you need to have at least a basic understanding of caches is that your queries are filling the caches with data, and your queries are also flushing the data out of the caches and replacing the old data with newer data. You might optimize a query and discover that it becomes lightning fast. The reason it becomes fast, however, may have less to do with your prowess as a SQL optimizer than because what you did allowed the data being worked on to remain in one of the caches. If this is the case, then if the amount of data suddenly exceeds the size of the cache, your query slows right back down again as the data needed gets flushed from the cache and replaced with other necessary data.

Processor Cache

The processor has a cache for instructions and data. This is typically a small cache, often as little as 8K for instructions and 32K for data, but in modern processors that amount may be in the hundreds of kilobytes or even megabytes. The processor caches are the fastest caches in the system. Getting data from the processor cache into the processor happens typically in a matter of one to a few clock cycles. At current processor speeds of 3GHz, a clock cycle is 0.33 billionths of a second, or one-third of one-billionth of a second. If your data fits in the processor cache, you are golden, and you get your results in the smallest possible time.

Hard Disk Cache

The physical disk storage medium tends to require milliseconds (thousandths of a second) to access. Thus, getting data off the physical disk and into the disk cache (or into the system) takes as much as 10 milliseconds, or one-hundredth of a second — and that assumes that the disk is just sitting idle waiting for you to ask for data, a very rare occurrence. Thus, accessing data on the physical disk is more than 10 million times slower than accessing data in the processor cache. Remember that this is the time it takes to even start seeing the data.

When an application asks for data from the disk subsystem, the disk often reads a much larger block of data than asked for on the theory that the data around the data that was asked for is eventually requested as well. The hard disk or disks used to store data have a small cache that holds large blocks of data read off of the disk. This cache is typically 2M or 8M and physically resides on the circuit board inside of the hard disk. While this doesn't sound like a lot, remember that it is quite common for databases to be split up into files stored on different hard disks. Thus, if a database is physically split into four different files and each file is the only thing on its disk, the disk subsystem itself is caching anywhere from 8M to 32M of the database at any one time. Figure 13-1 illustrates the relationship between the cache and the hard disk.

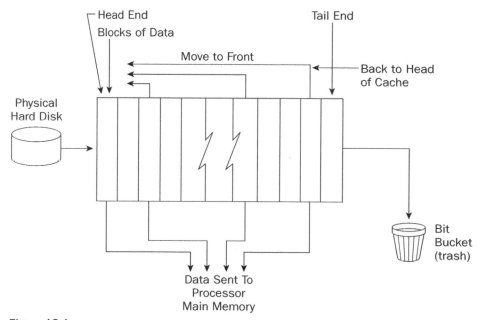

Figure 13-1

As data is read off the disk, it is placed into memory in blocks, typically of the sector size. If any block of memory is requested by the system, that block is logically moved to the head of the cache using pointers to indicate the location of the blocks in the cache. Thus, blocks of cache asked for frequently stay in the cache, whereas blocks asked for less frequently move toward the tail end of the cache. If any block gets to the tail end, it is dropped out of the cache. This happens when the latest data being read into the cache fills the data block and is placed at the front of the cache.

Once the data is in the hard disk cache, getting at it is still a lot slower than accessing the processor cache, but it is definitely much faster than physical disk access. The amount of time required to move data from the disk cache to memory depends on a slew of things, such as how the disks physically interface to the machine, but assuming a transfer rate of 50M per second, a good ballpark today is that you can get the entire contents of an 8M hard disk cache moved to memory in about one-sixth of a second. That doesn't tell the whole story, however, because you can start to access it instantly — instantly being defined as a few hundred millionths of a second. Thus, you can see that the hard disk cache plays a very important role in speeding up disk-intensive applications, and a database is about as disk-intensive as applications get. Even so, it takes thousands and perhaps tens of thousands of processor cycles to start getting data from the disk cache into the processor itself so that it can be used by your application.

Database Cache

In addition to the processor and disk caches, databases build their own cache that resides in system memory. The database cache (illustrated in Figure 13-2) is the only cache discussed so far that you have any direct control over, and you can in fact often tell the DBMS how much memory to request from the system to reserve for caches. In fact, it is often the other way around. With SQL Server, you must specify how much main memory *not* to use — to leave for the server and other applications running on the server. SQL Server takes all of the memory less this amount to use for its own purposes, and those purposes are mainly caching data.

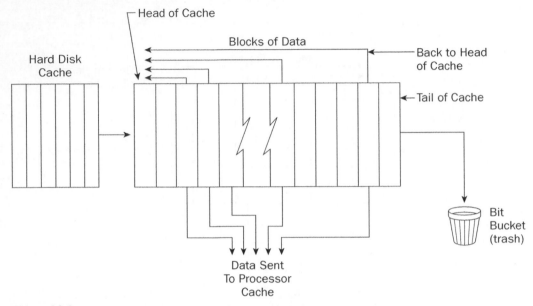

Figure 13-2

The database cache looks very similar to the hard disk cache. The biggest difference is the location of the cache. Whereas the hard disk cache physically resides on the hard disk and has to be read into main memory over the cables connecting the disk to the computer, the database cache resides in main memory. When data is read out of this database cache, it is on its way to the processor cache, and from there to the processor itself.

Caches in system memory are second only to the processor cache in terms of speed. In today's hardware, main system memory is approximately 25 to 100 times slower than processor cache; if the processor cache can move data into the processor in a single clock cycle, main memory takes 25 to 100 clock cycles to get the data into the processor. While this sounds a lot slower than processor cache (and it is), it is also the only cache that you have any direct control over, and so it is extremely useful to be aware of this level of caching. If your database is running on a machine with too little main memory, you can often get immense speed gains simply by throwing memory at the problem. At the price of memory today, it may very well cost less to double or quadruple the amount of main memory than for you to spend a week on query optimization. When it comes to databases, the more main memory, the better.

The point of all the discussion of cache is simply that you can tune your application to your heart's content, but if the hardware infrastructure doesn't support the application, all of your work yields minuscule improvements in the application speed and could cost a lot of money to get that minuscule improvement. It is critical to look at the big picture and understand exactly where the bottlenecks lie. Attack the bottlenecks in order of severity, quitting when the application runs at an acceptable speed.

Okay, so you have determined that application bottlenecks exist in the application itself, and your hardware is sufficient. What next?

Tuning SQL

There is an axiom in programming that says that 90 percent of the time is spent in 10 percent of the code. If you want to make your program run faster, you only need to optimize that 10 percent of the code. SQL is programming and thus can be viewed in the same manner, and it is very useful to do so. Very few databases have only a few queries. Databases often service entire applications, and those applications have pieces and parts that query the database. Often the applications have entire subprograms, each with their own sets of queries. You need to do a little investigative work and discover which specific piece is causing the slowdown.

You might be saying, "Yes, but that doesn't matter, just show me how to optimize a query," but that is very much putting the cart before the horse. Optimizing a query involves a set of techniques and uses a set of tools, which you get to shortly, but before you do, it is important to understand that you should not just take a shotgun approach to the subject of optimization. In the end, the intent is usually to make a process run faster, which in the end may mean making a query run faster, but which query? Since a process may be made up of dozens of subqueries, simply starting at the top and attempting to optimize every query in the process is an exercise in frustration, and perhaps in futility.

Given the nature of applications, it's impossible to tell you specifically where to look to discover what needs to be optimized, so you need to always keep the preceding advice in mind and your stopwatch in hand. As you get into production systems, you may find that you are trying to make a whole process run faster, and that involves breaking that process down into pieces and then timing the pieces. As you discover the high-cost pieces, you may very well be able to break those down into smaller pieces looking for high-cost pieces, and so forth, until you end up with one or a small number of queries that represent that 10 percent where the process is spending 90 percent of its time. Once you get there, what you learn next in this chapter becomes useful.

What Does SQL Tuning Mean?

Tuning an individual query means examining the structure of the query (and subqueries), the SQL syntax, to discover whether you have designed your tables to support fast data manipulation and written the query in an optimum manner, allowing your DBMS to manipulate the data efficiently. Queries do many things, from adding entirely new records to tables, to updating existing records, to pulling data out of multiple related tables for reporting purposes. It is this last part that many people think of when discussing optimizing queries, but in fact, a database must be viewed as a whole entity or you risk speeding up one piece while crippling another. As this chapter demonstrates, there are techniques (particularly when optimizing other people's queries) that are essentially free, while others (specifically creating new indexes) can be applied only at a price.

Again, the shotgun approach just as often causes problems as solves them. Adding indexes may very well speed up whatever it is you are trying to speed up, but it may cripple some other piece of the application. Deleting an index may speed up one part of the application but cripple another.

The intention here is not to cripple you with fear of doing anything because you may cause more problems than you fix, but simply to cause you to always think about the implications of your changes, beyond the area you are working on. Whenever you make a change, particularly on a large system, you need to keep your ears open to users complaining that the application seems slower lately. Where possible, record the changes that you make so that they can be backed out if necessary.

Why Do You Do It?

The answer to this question is always "because someone complains that a process is too slow." It is nevertheless useful to ask the question because thinking about the answer puts the problem squarely into perspective. There is never just one task to do in a system; as a developer, you are always juggling your time trying to get the most important things accomplished first, then moving down the list to less important things.

I once had the honor of redesigning a call center application. Since there is never enough time, I took some things that worked and just used them with as little modification as I could get away with and concentrated on getting other more important tasks accomplished. The application had a search screen that looked up a person on a variety of conditions — claim number, social security number, last name, and first name. Any of these were supposed to be searchable on just pieces — the first few characters of the last name plus the first few pieces of the first name, any number of characters of the SSN, and so on. Once the data search was entered, a set of matching records was pulled. The user would then select one of those records and pull the information about that person.

The original application had only a few thousand claim records to search through and the database was horribly normalized, so the application designer just pulled all of the records out into a record set that the form could display, left the form open, and then moved back and forth in that record set, keeping the form open and the data set loaded. Once a primary key of the record was found using the search algorithm, it was lightning fast to get to that record.

Having correctly normalized the database, the process of pulling all that data was a tad more complex and took a lot longer, and it also took a lot longer to move the form to the right record. It became much faster to just ask the database for and display a single record at a time. In the end, I used almost exactly the same query for the data entry form, but I placed a WHERE on the primary key that retrieved only a single record instead of all the records and then asked the form to move to the right record for each search.

The point is that, yes, I did optimize the query, but not in the way you might expect. I didn't add any indexes; I didn't modify any joins. I actually examined the process and discovered that a different way of performing the process was in order.

How Do You Do It?

And herein lies the heart of the matter: How do you optimize a query? As you discovered previously, optimizing the query may in fact be a matter of optimizing the application itself. There are, however, certain generally accepted methods for optimizing a query, and in the sections that follow, you start to examine these specific methods. Indexes are often touted as the be-all and end-all of optimization, knowing what to index and why. Before you examine these methods, though, it is helpful to get an overview of how indexes work and how they speed up (or slow down!) a database.

Indexes — What Are They?

The first thing to understand about indexes is that they are not necessary; they are a convenience used to speed up accessing data. They are simply a means of getting at a data item in a table without having to start at the beginning of the table and examine every item in the table. Indexes on static data tables are essentially free (other than storage costs), but indexes on frequently changing data have very high costs, as this section explains.

Database indexes are often compared to indexes in a book — a set of references in a table that tell where in the physical database to go to find a specific item. While it is true that indexes function in the same manner in databases as they do in books, they are implemented very differently. A book index takes a word or phrase and gives you a list of pages on which you can find the word.

In databases, however, indexes are usually implemented as a balanced-tree (b-tree) structure, so called because it looks like an upside-down tree, and the number of data items in each page is kept balanced by the b-tree engine (see Figure 13-3). In any b-tree, there is a root page that holds pointers to other pages (called leaves), which hold pointers to other pages, and so forth. Each page holds the data items from the column being indexed, plus a pointer to the data record holding that item out in the table. To search for data, the DBMS comes in to the top (root) page and looks for its data there. If it doesn't find the data, it looks up which leaf to go to that has data most similar to the data being searched for and then looks through that leaf page. If it doesn't find the data there, the DBMS looks for the next leaf down, and so on. Once the data item is found, the actual pointer to the data record is available to pull the entire record. By placing a few hundred data items in each page (with pointers to the actual data record for each item in that page), the total depth of the structure is usually very small. I have heard numbers thrown about indicating that each page points to as many as 300 other leaves, which means that finding a single record in a table with up to 27 million records requires searching through only three levels of leaves.

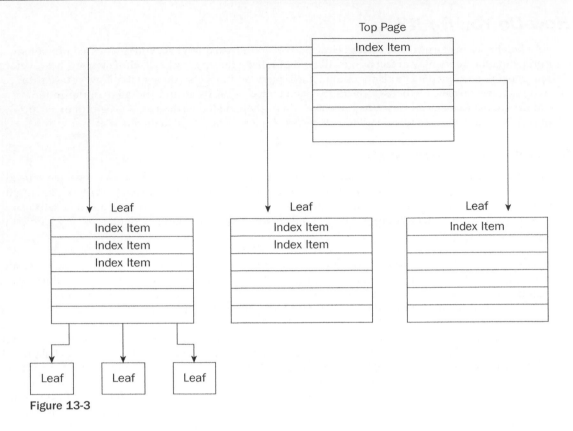

Figure 13-3

As mentioned, an index holds a copy of the data being searched for. This has a couple of implications that you need to be aware of. The first is that every index created increases the storage requirements of the database by the amount of data in the indexed column plus the pointers to the real data. The next is that, as mentioned, indexes cause issues with updating or deleting data.

Deleting a record causes its slot in the index page to be emptied. If there are a lot of deletes, you end up with lots of empty slots in the pages, which of course causes the DBMS to look through empty slots on its way to finding the requested data. As data is deleted, the DBMS tracks these empty slots, and if they pile up, eventually the DBMS has to do a compact or balance of the tree. Any maintenance of that nature requires locks on the index pages, which will slow down accesses to the indexes by the application while the balance is in progress.

Updating data causes a similar issue, perhaps even larger in terms of performance hit. As you can visualize from knowing the tree structure, if an indexed data item changes, the item has to be moved from one position in the tree to another. If the movement causes the item to move from one index page to another, then a hole is left in the old page, but even worse, the data has to be muscled into the new page where it now belongs. Even if there are "holes" in the destination page, the existing slots have to be relinked to insert the data in the correct place. If there are no holes in the destination page, a major rebalance has to be performed, which involves moving items out of the page to other pages to open up holes.

The slots are often implemented as a doubly linked list (illustrated in Figure 13-4). A doubly linked list is a structure where each container holding data has two pointers to other containers, one to the previous container and another to the next container. This structure allows very fast movement or sorting of data since the data itself is never physically moved; rather the two links are simply modified to point to different neighbors. Of course, the old neighbors' pointers also have to be modified since they no longer point to this data item, and the new neighbors' links have to be updated to point to this data item.

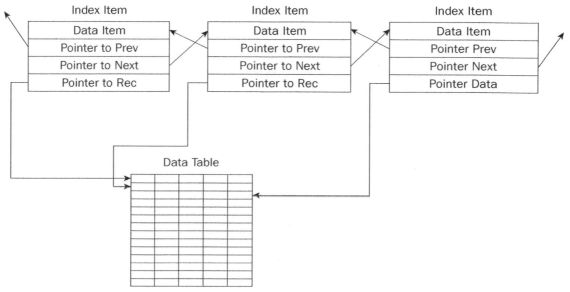

Figure 13-4

Implementing a doubly linked list means finding the two slots that the new data belongs between, adjusting the pointers of each of these neighbor slots to point to the new data item, and then adjusting the pointers of the empty slot into which the data was placed to point to the data slots on either side. All of this is just grunt work that the DBMS has to go through, and it isn't a reason not to build an index where one is needed, but just keep in mind that every index causes these data shuffles any time the data in that indexed column changes or is deleted.

Perhaps you've heard the advice, "It may be faster to drop an index and rebuild it after a bulk insert." This data shuffle is exactly the reason why that may be the case. If the number of records added, deleted, or modified is a very high percentage of the number of records already in the table, then moving the index items around may be slower than just deleting the index and rebuilding it from scratch. This is also the reason why you want to do large bulk imports during off hours (if any) so that the overhead of shuffling index items or rebuilding indexes does not impact the users.

If you are going to be doing large inserts or other modifications of data to indexed tables, it can be beneficial to drop the indexes before doing the insert and then rebuild the index after the data is inserted. Obviously, given the example database used in this book, you will not be able to really see the effects. However, in a production database with millions of records already in a table and deletes or inserts of large quantities of records, you may find dropping indexes *very* beneficial.

Follow these steps to drop an index and perform a bulk import:

1. The assumption here is that an index was created on the ZipCode field of the MemberDetails table using the following SQL syntax:

```
USE FILMCLUB
CREATE INDEX IND_ZIP
ON MemberDetails (ZipCode)
```

2. You are getting ready to merge thousands of new members from a membership drive that the club held last month. Before performing the bulk import, you want to remove the index on the table. Use the following SQL to remove the index:

```
USE FILMCLUB
DROP INDEX MemberDetails.IND_ZIP
```

3. Now you can perform the bulk import of the new members. Having done that, you now want to replace any indexes that you dropped. To do so, use this SQL:

```
USE FILMCLUB
CREATE INDEX IND_ZIP
ON MemberDetails (ZipCode)
```

How It Works

The DROP INDEX statement completely deletes all traces of the index mentioned in the statement. Having done that, any subsequent data changes to the column that previously had the index on it no longer cause the data shuffle slowdown issue, as that slowdown was caused by shuffling the data item pointers in the index that you deleted. Once all the massive data manipulations have been accomplished, the index is created from scratch using the CREATE INDEX statement.

If you are going to delete indexes, just be very sure that you re-create them all. If you are not the only developer in the database, the index you drop may be used by other developers' queries, and forgetting to re-create the indexes would wreak havoc with your associates.

Indexes — When They Help, Hurt, or Don't Matter

The generic advice on indexes is to index any column used in a table join or in any WHERE clause. Join columns probably should always be indexed. The WHERE clause advice is more iffy and plays back into the question of whether the good outweighs the bad.

Indexes are extremely useful when they are on a field containing data with relatively small data duplication. A social security number index is an example where an index returns a single row (hopefully), and it is the best return on investment you can get. In a database of 60 million U.S. addresses, a zip code index returns a few thousand records, which is a tiny percent of the total records in the database, again a great return on investment.

On the other hand, an index on a true/false field is not so useful, again depending on the data in the field. If the distribution is 50/50, then you return half of the records. If the distribution is 5% true and 95% false, and you are searching for true, then the index might help. The problem in a case like this is that the DBMS may incorrectly assume that the index is going to return so many records that it simply ignores the index when it performs the query optimize phase. If that happens, then you have a query that takes up space on the disk (and has to be updated on inserts or changes) but is never used.

I have read that in cases where the distribution is 50/50, it is better just to leave the column nonindexed and use a table scan to find the data. I find this difficult to believe, at least on large tables, since the disk I/O to search through an index and pull out all of the pointers to the records on the disk would seem to be much less than the disk I/O to search through every record. Remember that any index column has just the column data plus the pointer to the record, and therefore an index tends to be very compact relative to the table itself and thus can stay in the cache longer.

If you are using this index by itself and you are pulling a 50/50 mix, then that may very well be true since you have to perform the disk I/O anyway to retrieve all those records. However, if you are using the index in conjunction with other indexes to narrow down and pull only a small set of records off the disk, then having the index saves the work of actually looking in each data record to see whether it matches the search criteria.

Indexes in general tend to be used often, and thus they stay in the cache. In addition, the actual data pulled from using indexes tends to be cached better since only those rows actually used get pulled into the cache. Since you aren't pulling huge blocks of data, you aren't inadvertently flushing the cache of useful data. Indexed reads only examine the exact pieces of the bigger data block containing the data records, reducing the amount of CPU time spent examining the data. And finally, indexed reads can scale up as the table size grows, giving stable and consistent results for data retrieval, even when the table itself grows huge.

Table Scans — What Are They?

As the name implies, a *table scan* is where the DBMS has to physically retrieve every record in the table to examine one or more columns to see whether the data in that column matches a join or WHERE condition. A table scan is what happens when no index exists on a column that has to be compared to something else in a query. In the absence of an index, the DBMS scans the table, looking at the data item in that field in every record in the table.

Data is usually organized in sectors, with multiple grouped sectors called extents. In SQL Server, for example, it is common for the database to use 8K blocks (the maximum size of a data record) with eight of these blocks read or written at one time by the database, resulting in 64K of data being read or written at once. See Figure 13-5 for an illustration of a table scan.

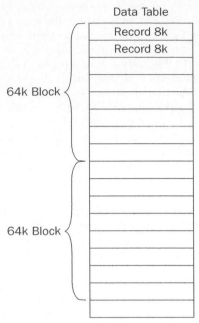

Figure 13-5

Table scans can cause absolutely huge performance hits or may not impact performance much at all. Imagine a table of 60 million records with dozens of fields, where the DBMS has to read every data record off the disk to examine the contents of a single field looking for matches. This operation could take hours or even days and of course trashes the various system caches. In another case, however, you may be scanning a table of just 100 records with only two or three columns. Again, the DBMS has to pull all the records, but the size of the task is so much smaller that the impact on the query may be negligible. In the first case, the probability of the data being in any of the various caches is negligible; in fact, it is simply impossible. In the second case, the data may very well be in a cache, and in fact if the table is scanned repeatedly, the data may very well stay in a cache permanently.

Another impact that sometimes is not considered is the impact of a large table scan on the various system caches. Because so much data is being read off the disk, it is possible to flush data that would otherwise have remained in the cache forever and replace it with data used only this one time. Obviously, all that other data is reread and placed back in the cache once the table scan is finished since the normally cached data is used so often.

When Table Scans Help, Hurt, or Don't Matter

Table scans can be useful when the table is small, and particularly when the table is used often enough to remain in the cache. Table scans tend to cause linear performance degradation as the table size grows. Thus, table scans might work perfectly well when a particular table is new with not much data, but they get slower and slower as new records are added to the table. Keep this in mind if you build queries with WHERE conditions or joins on nonindexed columns of active tables. Performance may be quite acceptable initially, but it may worsen over time. If the table is a static table, such as a state or country lookup table, the performance might be fine and never changes since new states are so rarely added to the table.

Tuning Tips

The following list contains some helpful database tuning tips:

❑ Reduce the amount of data pulled. Avoid using SELECT * queries; instead pull exactly and only the fields that you need. It is very easy to get lazy and use the asterisk (*), figuring that as new columns are needed they will already be there and the query will not have to be revisited. Although this is true, you are also forcing the DBMS to retrieve data that will never be used, flushing useful data out of caches, loading the network with data that will never be used, and burdening the workstation with unused data.

❑ Think carefully before creating new indexes, particularly indexes on columns other than primary keys or foreign keys. Indexes may negatively impact other areas of the application. Unfortunately, if you work in a large database with other developers, you cannot simply delete indexes, even if you created them, since you can never be sure that queries you didn't create don't use the index you did create to good effect.

❑ Watch for *filter redundancy*, conditions where a filter on one column guarantees values in a different column. This problem is not uncommon and often occurs where a single condition did not provide a narrow-enough match, so a second or even third condition was added to the filter.

❑ WHERE conditions such as NOT NULL may cause the optimizer to assume that the number of rows matched will be too large to be useful. Remember that optimizers try to look at the entire query and figure out how to minimize the work required to return the data. Particularly if you have a lot of filter conditions, the optimizer may simply ignore some of the conditions if the filter in that condition is too broad.

❑ Use pattern matching judiciously. LIKE COL% is a valid WHERE condition, reducing the returned set to only those records with data starting with the string COL. However, COL%Y does not further reduce the returned results set since %Y cannot be effectively evaluated; the effort to do the evaluation is too large to be considered. In this case, the COL% is used, but the %Y is thrown away. For the same reason, a leading wildcard %COL effectively prevents the entire filter from being used.

❑ Avoid number-to-character conversions with pattern matching, particularly with the < and > operator. Numbers and characters compare differently and can lead to odd behaviors.

❑ The "not equal" operators can cause the optimizer to throw out the WHERE condition since it may consider the range of values returned to be too broad to be useful.

❑ Be very careful of equality operators with real numbers and date/time values. Both of these can have small differences that are not obvious to the eye but that make an exact match impossible, thus preventing your queries from ever returning rows.

❑ Cartesian joins are actually a non-join — where two tables are selected, but no join is specified. The result of Cartesian joins is that a row is returned for the product of the two tables — one row for each row in the first table and one row for each row in the second table. If each table has 10 rows, 100 rows are returned. If each table has 100 rows, 10,000 rows are returned. Such queries are occasionally useful but are most often a simple mistake in syntax. Luckily, they are usually easy to spot since the results set has far more records than expected or processes very slowly. This assumes that the results set ever comes back, of course. If the two tables are large, the results set can be so huge that the query simply can't complete in a reasonable time. The DBMS may very well time out the query.

❏ Inner joins look like an equality on a pair of fields, and in fact if you are doing such an equality compare between fields in two tables, an inner join (with an index on each field) may be a more efficient method of expressing the query.

Summary

Performance tuning is not a simple matter of timing sections of code. You may find that the application isn't the problem at all; perhaps old, slow workstations are just inadequate for the job. Or perhaps you have other hardware issues, such as too little workstation memory, network saturation, or insufficient server horsepower. You may find that the database needs to be split into pieces so that more disks can shovel data at the processor, keeping it busy. If you have these issues, you may find that it is cheaper to throw money at hardware rather than throwing money at the developer. Money spent on hardware affects everything the user does rather than just making a single application faster.

On the other hand, if the hardware is adequate, then it is time to look at the application itself. In order to understand application tuning, it is useful to have at least a passing knowledge of the various caches that buffer the application, understand how they interact, and know what you can do to keep the cache filled with the most-used data.

It also helps to understand how indexes work so that you understand the trade-offs of indexing versus table scans. Be sure to remember the following points when deciding between indexes and table scans:

❏ Index pages with index items using doubly linked list algorithms have to be updated for any inserts, deletes, or updates.

❏ On static tables, there is virtually no downside to indexes, but on very active tables, the CPU time required to update these links between index items can cause major performance problems, particularly with large data inserts but also with large deletes or updates.

❏ Periodic index maintenance by the DBMS causes index locks, which affect database users. Try to schedule large block operations to take place during off hours to reduce the impact on users.

❏ Table scans can help prevent index locks since they do not use indexes, and table scans can work quite well on small tables, particularly when these tables are active, often-used tables and can fit entirely in one of the various caches.

❏ Large table scans, on the other hand, cause a variety of serious performance issues, starting with expensive physical disk I/O, and cause caches to flush often-used data to be replaced with the mass of data being read off the disks.

There is usually no single thing that you can do to tune an application. You must keep a variety of issues in mind and always ask, "Where's the bottleneck?" Be prepared to accept whatever answer comes up, whether hardware or software.

Exercises

1. Create an index on the LastName and FirstName columns in the MemberDetails table.

2. Create an index on the State column in the MemberDetails table.

3. Create a unique index on the MemberId column in the MemberDetails table.

4. Delete all the indexes on the MemberDetails table.

5. Rebuild all the indexes on the MemberDetails table.

Exercise Answers

Chapter 1

Exercise 1 Solution

A separate table, which you can call the Location table, with a primary key field of `integer` data type should hold the meeting location details. The table should look like the table shown below:

Field Name	Data Type	Notes
LocationId	integer	Primary key
Location	varchar(200)	

You need to alter the Attendance table so that instead of storing the whole address in the Location field for every record, the table stores the integer value from the Location table shown above. The new Attendance table looks like this:

Field Name	Data Type	Notes
MeetingDate	date	Change to `datetime` data type if using MS SQL Server
LocationId	integer	Foreign key
MemberAttended	char(1)	
MemberId	integer	Foreign key linking to MemberDetails table

Exercise 2 Solution

The Location field is no longer needed and needs to be deleted. First, drop the Location field and add a LocationId field to the Attendance table. The SQL to do so is as follows:

```
ALTER TABLE Attendance
  DROP COLUMN Location;

ALTER TABLE Attendance
  ADD LocationId integer;
```

IBM's DB2 doesn't support the dropping of individual columns. One way around this is to drop the whole table and then re-create it with the new LocationId column:

```
DROP TABLE Attendance;
CREATE TABLE Attendance
(
    MeetingDate date,
    LocationId integer,
    MemberAttended char(1),
    MemberId integer
);
```

Now you need to create the Location table. The fields that compose the table are as follows:

Field Name	Data Type	Notes
LocationId	integer	Primary key
Street	varchar(100)	
City	varchar(75)	
State	varchar(75)	

The SQL to create the Location table is as follows:

```
CREATE TABLE Location
(
    LocationId integer,
    Street varchar(100),
    City varchar(75),
    State varchar(75)
);
```

Using a separate Location table to store details of meeting locations that members have attended saves on storage space used by the database.

Chapter 2

Exercise 1 Solution

There are two different solutions to this exercise (both displayed subsequently) because of the way in which Oracle requires you to write dates.

Non-Oracle Solution

If you're using SQL Server, IBM DB2, MySQL, or MS Access, use the following solution:

```
INSERT INTO MemberDetails
(
  MemberId,
  FirstName,
  LastName,
  DateOfBirth,
  Street,
  City,
  State,
  ZipCode,
  Email,
  DateOfJoining
)
VALUES
(
  7,
  'John',
  'Jackson',
  '1974-05-27',
  'Long Lane',
  'Orange Town',
  'New State',
  '88992',
  'jjackson@mailme.net',
  '2005-11-21'
);


INSERT INTO MemberDetails
(
  MemberId,
  FirstName,
  LastName,
  DateOfBirth,
  Street,
  City,
  State,
  ZipCode,
  Email,
  DateOfJoining
)
VALUES
```

```
  (
  8,
  'Jack',
  'Johnson',
  '1945-06-09',
  'Main Street',
  'Big City',
  'Mega State',
  '34566',
  'jjohnson@me.com',
  '2005-06-02'
  );


INSERT INTO MemberDetails
(
  MemberId,
  FirstName,
  LastName,
  DateOfBirth,
  Street,
  City,
  State,
  ZipCode,
  Email,
  DateOfJoining
)
VALUES
  (
  9,
  'Seymour',
  'Botts',
  '1956-10-21',
  'Long Lane',
  'Windy Village',
  'Golden State',
  '65422',
  'Seymour@botts.org',
  '2005-07-17'
  );
```

Oracle Solution

If you're using Oracle, the date format needs to be different, so use the following solution:

```
INSERT INTO MemberDetails
(
  MemberId,
  FirstName,
  LastName,
  DateOfBirth,
  Street,
  City,
  State,
  ZipCode,
```

```
    Email,
    DateOfJoining
)
VALUES
 (
  7,
  'John',
  'Jackson',
  '27 May 1974',
  'Long Lane',
  'Orange Town',
  'New State',
  '88992',
  'jjackson@mailme.net',
  '21 Nov 2005'
 );


INSERT INTO MemberDetails
(
  MemberId,
  FirstName,
  LastName,
  DateOfBirth,
  Street,
  City,
  State,
  ZipCode,
  Email,
  DateOfJoining
)
VALUES
 (
  8,
  'Jack',
  'Johnson',
  '9 June 1945',
  'Main Street',
  'Big City',
  'Mega State',
  '34566',
  'jjohnson@me.com',
  '02 June 2005'
 );


INSERT INTO MemberDetails
(
  MemberId,
  FirstName,
  LastName,
  DateOfBirth,
  Street,
  City,
  State,
```

```
    ZipCode,
    Email,
    DateOfJoining
)
VALUES
  (
    9,
    'Seymour',
    'Botts',
    '21 Oct 1956',
    'Long Lane',
    'Windy Village',
    'Golden State',
    '65422',
    'Seymour@botts.org',
    '17 July 2005'
  );
```

Exercise 2 Solution

First, remove Bob Robson's details from the database. His member details are stored in the
MemberDetails table, and his favorite film categories are in the FavCategory table. Each record in the
FavCategory table contains only the MemberId and the CategoryId. Remember from Chapter 1 that the
MemberId field in this table is a foreign key; its value is referenced from the MemberDetails table, where
it's a primary key. Therefore, you must delete the records from the FavCategory and Attendance tables
first:

```
DELETE FROM FavCategory WHERE MemberId = 2;
DELETE FROM Attendance WHERE MemberId = 2;
```

Once you delete Bob from the FavCategory table, you can delete him from the MemberDetails table:

```
DELETE FROM MemberDetails WHERE MemberId = 2;
```

Exercise 3 Solution

Update the database to reflect the Orange Town boundary changes. You need to change the City field
from Orange Town to Big City where the street is Long Lane and the city is Orange Town.
Remember that there is also a Long Lane in Windy Village, so you can't just check the street name. You
need to update only if the street is in Orange Town:

```
UPDATE MemberDetails SET City = 'Big City'
WHERE Street = 'Long Lane' AND City = 'Orange Town';
```

Chapter 3

Exercise 1 Solution

First of all, you need to consider which columns and from what table or tables you need to get the answer. In this case, you get answers from the MemberDetails table and the Street, City, State, and ZipCode columns. Because you already know the MemberId (13), all you need to do is filter results by adding a WHERE clause that contains only rows where MemberId equals 13:

```
SELECT Street, City, State, ZipCode
FROM MemberDetails
WHERE MemberId = 13;
```

Executing this query provides the following results:

Street	City	State	ZipCode
Winding Road	Big City	Mega State	34512

Exercise 2 Solution

You need to find the names of the members, so the FirstName and LastName columns from the MemberDetails table need to be selected. Now you need to add a WHERE clause with a condition that checks for last names starting with J. The LIKE operator will do this:

```
SELECT FirstName, LastName
FROM MemberDetails
WHERE LastName LIKE 'J%';
```

The percent sign (%) means one or more of any character. Note that in MS Access you need to use an asterisk (*) instead of the percent sign (%).

Executing the final query provides the following results:

FirstName	LastName
John	Jackson
John	Jones
Jenny	Jones
Jack	Johnson

Exercise 3 Solution

First, decide which columns you want. In this case, you want the LastName and FirstName columns from the MemberDetails table:

```
SELECT LastName, FirstName
FROM MemberDetails
```

Now you need to ensure that only members whose date of joining was on or before December 31, 2004, are included in the results set. Use a WHERE clause and specify that the DateOfJoining column be before (or less than) that date:

```
SELECT LastName, FirstName
FROM MemberDetails
WHERE DateOfJoining <= '2004-12-31';
```

If you're using Oracle, don't forget that you might need to change the date format to day-month-year:

```
SELECT LastName, FirstName
FROM MemberDetails
WHERE DateOfJoining <= '31 Dec 2004';
```

If you're using MS Access, then you need to use the hash sign (#) to delimit the date:

```
SELECT LastName, FirstName
FROM MemberDetails
WHERE DateOfJoining <= #2004-12-31#;
```

Finally, to obtain results in the correct order, use an ORDER BY clause:

```
SELECT LastName, FirstName
FROM MemberDetails
WHERE DateOfJoining <= '2004-12-31'
ORDER BY LastName, FirstName;
```

The final results are as follows:

LastName	FirstName
Gee	Steve
Smith	Katie

Exercise 4 Solution

First, you need to identify which tables and which columns from those tables will form the results. The three tables supplying the data are Attendance, Location, and MemberDetails. These need to be joined using an INNER JOIN in order to join the three tables into one results set. The LocationId field links the Attendance and Location tables. The MemberId field links the Attendance and MemberDetails tables.

As well as joining the tables, you also need to restrict the results set to only the location Windy Village, Golden State. The member also must have attended the meeting, so MemberAttended must be Y. The WHERE clause filters the results as required:

```
SELECT FirstName, LastName
FROM Attendance INNER JOIN Location
ON Attendance.LocationId = Location.LocationId
INNER JOIN MemberDetails
ON Attendance.MemberId = MemberDetails.MemberId
WHERE Location.City = 'Windy Village' AND Location.State = 'Golden State'
AND Attendance.MemberAttended = 'Y';
```

Executing the query provides the following results:

FirstName	LastName
Katie	Smith
John	Jones
Jenny	Jones

If you're using MS Access, don't forget that you need to wrap the first inner join inside brackets:

```
SELECT FirstName, LastName
FROM (Attendance INNER JOIN Location
ON Attendance.LocationId = Location.LocationId)
INNER JOIN MemberDetails
ON Attendance.MemberId = MemberDetails.MemberId
WHERE Location.City = 'Windy Village' AND Location.State = 'Golden State'
AND Attendance.MemberAttended = 'Y';
```

Chapter 4

Exercise 1 Solution

Although the field definitions are fine, all the data is lumped into one table, which leads to a huge amount of data redundancy.

First normal form is partially complete. The data is defined, a table is set up, and columns are created. However, there are repeating groups, such as book authors. Also, you must create a primary key for the table. Figure A-1 creates two new tables: Author and WrittenBy. The Author table contains a list of authors and their details, and the WrittenBy table contains a list of books and their authors:

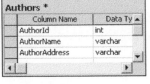

Figure A-1

ISBN is a unique reference that identifies books and makes up part of the primary key. BookSellerId uniquely identifies a bookseller and provides the second part of the primary key. Finally, PublisherCode is the third part of the primary key for Table1. For the WrittenBy table, the primary key is the ISBN and AuthorId. In Authors, the AuthorId is the primary key, a newly created column that Table1 references.

So far, the database is roughly in first normal form. Second normal form specifies that no partial dependencies can exist between any of the columns on the primary key. In Table1, BookTitle and YearPublished are dependent on ISBN but not dependent on BookSellerId or PublisherCode. BookSellerName and BookSellerTelNo are dependent only on the BookSellerId and not on any of the other parts of the primary key. Finally, PublisherCode determines PublisherName and PublisherAddress, but no dependency exists between any of the other parts of the primary key. Therefore, in order to make the table comply with second normal form, the three independent parts need to be split up into three tables, which you can call something like Books, BookSellers, and Publishers. Figure A-2 illustrates how this might look:

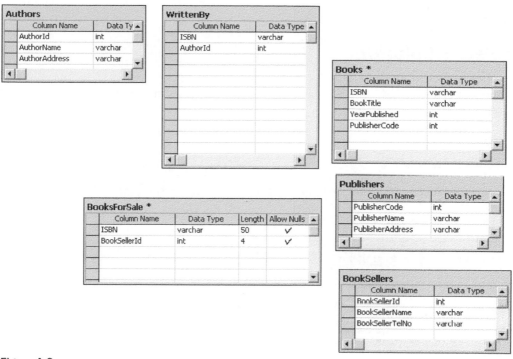

Figure A-2

Notice that Table1 is renamed BooksForSale and that all the columns except ISBN, PublisherCode, and BookSellerId are deleted. The database is now in second normal form.

Exercise 2 Solution

The FavCategory table links to two other tables: Category and MemberDetails. They are both the primary tables, the columns in FavCategory being foreign keys. Therefore, you must create two FOREIGN KEY constraints:

```
ALTER TABLE FavCategory
ADD CONSTRAINT favcat_cat_fk
FOREIGN KEY (CategoryId)
REFERENCES Category(CategoryId);

ALTER TABLE FavCategory
ADD CONSTRAINT favcat_member_fk
FOREIGN KEY (MemberId)
REFERENCES MemberDetails(MemberId);
```

Chapter 5

Exercise 1 Solution

To prevent NULLs from displaying, you need to use the COALESCE() function. The first argument is the column name; the second is the message to be displayed if the column for that record contains NULL values:

```
SELECT FirstName,
       LastName,
       COALESCE(Street, 'No address details available for this member.'),
       COALESCE(ZipCode,'')
FROM MemberDetails;
```

The results from this query are as follows:

FirstName	LastName	Street	ZipCode
Katie	Smith	Main Road	123456
Steve	Gee	45 Upper Road	99112
John	Jones	Newish Lane	88776
Jenny	Jones	Newish Lane	88776
John	Jackson	Long Lane	88992
Jack	Johnson	Main Street	34566
Seymour	Botts	Long Lane	65422
Susie	Simons	Main Road	123456
Jamie	Hills	Newish Lane	88776
Stuart	Dales	Long Lane	65422
William	Doors	Winding Road	34512
Doris	Night	White Cliff Street	68122
Catherine	Hawthorn	No address details available for this member	

Exercise 2 Solution

Write a query that cuts down the results into something manageable. Given that the exact spelling of the name is unknown, you have to find some alternative way of searching. The following SQL uses the DIF-FERENCE() function to match names that sound like *Jilly Johns*:

```
SELECT MemberId,
       FirstName,
       LastName
FROM MemberDetails
WHERE DIFFERENCE(LastName,'Johns') >= 3 AND DIFFERENCE(FirstName, 'Jilly') >= 3;
```

Executing the query provides the following results on SQL Server; you may get slightly different ones with DB2 or Oracle:

MemberId	FirstName	LastName
6	Jenny	Jones
5	John	Jones
8	Jack	Johnson
7	John	Jackson

Because the chairwoman knows she spoke to a woman, she could deduce that she's looking for Jenny Jones. Keeping track of gender in the MemberDetails table would make getting these results even easier.

How should you decide a good value for the results returned by the DIFFERENCE() function? It's a matter of guesswork based on how many results are returned and whether those results are likely to contain the one result you want. Any value 3 or higher has a strong possibility of being a close match, and you can usually rule out anything below that.

Chapter 6

Exercise 1 Solution

The first part of the question's answer is as follows:

```
SELECT Category, COUNT(DVDPrice), SUM(DVDPrice * 1.1)
FROM Films
INNER JOIN Category
ON Films.CategoryId = Category.CategoryId
WHERE AvailableOnDVD = 'Y'
GROUP BY Category;
```

The preceding SQL provides the following results:

Category	COUNT(DVDPrice),	SUM(DVDPrice * 1.1)
Historical	3	38.423
Horror	2	20.834
Romance	1	14.289
Sci-fi	1	14.289
Thriller	2	17.578
War	1	14.289

You might receive slightly different results after the decimal point due to rounding errors by database systems.

As with all of the more complex queries, start simple and build up. The first job is identifying which tables contain the data needed to answer the question. With this example, the Films table contains the price and film category information. However, you want to display the category name rather than just an ID, and name data comes from the Category table. Use a FROM statement to join the two tables, linked by the CategoryId, which is the primary key in the Category table and a foreign key in the Films table:

```
FROM Films
INNER JOIN Category
ON Films.CategoryId = Category.CategoryId
WHERE AvailableOnDVD = 'Y';
```

Add a WHERE clause that includes only records where the AvailableOnDVD field is Y, as there's no point counting films that are not available on DVD.

The question requires that the results be grouped into categories and that the results should return the category name, the number of DVDs in the category, and the total price for the DVDs in each category group. Therefore, you need to add a GROUP BY clause, grouping by Category:

```
FROM Films
INNER JOIN Category
ON Films.CategoryId = Category.CategoryId
WHERE AvailableOnDVD = 'Y'
GROUP BY Category;
```

Finally, add the columns and expressions that make up the final results: the Category column, the count of the number of DVDs per group, and the total price of the DVDs in that group including a 10% sales tax:

```
SELECT Category, COUNT(DVDPrice), SUM(DVDPrice * 1.1)
FROM Films
INNER JOIN Category
ON Films.CategoryId = Category.CategoryId
WHERE AvailableOnDVD = 'Y'
GROUP BY Category;
```

The second part of the question asks you to limit the results to just those groups where the number of DVDs is just one. To do this, add a HAVING clause with a condition that allows only groups with one record in them to be included in the final results:

```
SELECT Category, COUNT(DVDPrice), SUM(DVDPrice * 1.1)
FROM Films
INNER JOIN Category
ON Films.CategoryId = Category.CategoryId
WHERE AvailableOnDVD = 'Y'
GROUP BY Category
HAVING COUNT(DVDPrice) = 1;
```

The final SQL provides the results in the following table:

Category	COUNT(DVDPrice),	SUM(DVDPrice * 1.1)
Romance	1	14.289
Sci-fi	1	14.289
War	1	14.289

Exercise 2 Solution

The SQL required is as follows:

```
SELECT Category, MAX(Rating) AS "Highest Rated", MIN(Rating) AS "Lowest Rated"
FROM Films  INNER JOIN Category
ON Films.CategoryId = Category.CategoryId
GROUP BY Category;
```

Executing the query produces the results shown in the following table:

Category	Highest Rated	Lowest Rated
Historical	5	3
Horror	2	1
Romance	4	4
Sci-fi	5	1
Thriller	4	1
War	5	2

The necessary data comes from the Films and Category tables, which have been joined using an INNER JOIN on the CategoryId field. The results are grouped by the Category column, and the highest and lowest values for each group are obtained using the MAX() and MIN() functions.

Chapter 7

Exercise 1 Solution

The following is the SQL that answers the question:

```
SELECT C1.Category, MD1.FirstName, MD1.LastName, MD2.FirstName, MD2.LastName
FROM FavCategory FC1 INNER JOIN FavCategory FC2
ON FC1.CategoryId = FC2.CategoryId
INNER JOIN Category C1 ON C1.CategoryId = FC1.CategoryId
INNER JOIN MemberDetails MD1 ON  MD1.MemberId = FC1.MemberId
INNER JOIN MemberDetails MD2 ON MD2.MemberId = FC2.MemberId
WHERE FC1.MemberId < FC2.MemberId;
```

You should use the following SQL if you're using MS Access:

```
SELECT C1.Category, MD1.FirstName, MD1.LastName, MD2.FirstName, MD2.LastName
FROM (((FavCategory AS FC1 INNER JOIN FavCategory AS FC2
ON FC1.CategoryId = FC2.CategoryId)
INNER JOIN Category AS C1 ON C1.CategoryId = FC1.CategoryId)
INNER JOIN MemberDetails MD1 ON  MD1.MemberId = FC1.MemberId)
INNER JOIN MemberDetails MD2 ON MD2.MemberId = FC2.MemberId
WHERE FC1.MemberId < FC2.MemberId;
```

It might look horrendously long, but broken down into its parts it's not that bad. The very first step is to pair up people with the same favorite category. To get pairs of people in the same row, you need to use a self-join of the FavCategory table:

```
SELECT FC1.CategoryId, FC1.MemberId, FC2.MemberId
FROM FavCategory FC1 INNER JOIN FavCategory FC2
ON FC1.CategoryId = FC2.CategoryId
WHERE FC1.MemberId < FC2.MemberId;
```

The WHERE clause is there to prevent the same person from being listed as a pair of themselves on the same row. This gives you the CategoryId and MemberIds involved, but the question requires the category name and the first and last names of the people. First, get the category title from the Category table by joining it to the current results:

```
SELECT C1.Category, FC1.MemberId, FC2.MemberId
FROM FavCategory FC1 INNER JOIN FavCategory FC2
ON FC1.CategoryId = FC2.CategoryId
INNER JOIN Category C1 ON C1.CategoryId = FC1.CategoryId
WHERE FC1.MemberId < FC2.MemberId;
```

Now you need to get the first and last names. For this, you need to join the MemberDetails table to the current results. However, on the same row are two different MemberIds: for FC1 and for FC2. You can't just join MemberDetails once; you need two copies of the table joined. The first copy provides the first and last names for FC1's MemberId, and the second copy provides the lookup for the first and last names from FC2's MemberId:

```
SELECT C1.Category, MD1.FirstName, MD1.LastName, MD2.FirstName, MD2.LastName
FROM FavCategory FC1 INNER JOIN FavCategory FC2
ON FC1.CategoryId = FC2.CategoryId
INNER JOIN Category C1 ON C1.CategoryId = FC1.CategoryId
INNER JOIN MemberDetails MD1 ON  MD1.MemberId = FC1.MemberId
INNER JOIN MemberDetails MD2 ON MD2.MemberId = FC2.MemberId
WHERE FC1.MemberId < FC2.MemberId;
```

This is the final SQL and gives the following results:

C1.Category	MD1.FirstName	MD1.LastName	MD2.FirstName	MD2.LastName
Thriller	John	Jones	Susie	Simons
Thriller	John	Jones	Stuart	Dales
Thriller	Susie	Simons	Stuart	Dales
Romance	Katie	Smith	Doris	Night
Horror	Susie	Simons	Jamie	Hills
Horror	Susie	Simons	William	Doors
Horror	Jamie	Hills	William	Doors
War	Katie	Smith	Jenny	Jones
War	Katie	Smith	Jamie	Hills
War	Katie	Smith	Stuart	Dales
War	Jenny	Jones	Jamie	Hills
War	Jenny	Jones	Stuart	Dales
War	Jamie	Hills	Stuart	Dales
Sci-fi	Steve	Gee	Jamie	Hills
Sci-fi	Steve	Gee	William	Doors
Sci-fi	Jamie	Hills	William	Doors
Historical	Susie	Simons	Stuart	Dales
Historical	Susie	Simons	Doris	Night
Historical	Stuart	Dales	Doris	Night
Comedy	Steve	Gee	Jenny	Jones
Comedy	Steve	Gee	Stuart	Dales
Comedy	Jenny	Jones	Stuart	Dales

Exercise 2 Solution

The SQL that answers the question is as follows:

```
SELECT Category.Category
FROM FavCategory
RIGHT OUTER JOIN Category ON FavCategory.CategoryId = Category.CategoryId
WHERE FavCategory.CategoryId IS NULL;
```

Your answer may differ, as there's more than one way to answer this question, but that doesn't matter as long as the results are the same. The right outer join obtains all rows from the Category table, regardless of whether there is a matching CategoryId in the FavCategory table. If there is no matching CategoryId in the FavCategory table, then it means that no member has chosen that category as their favorite. When this happens, `FavCategory.CategoryId` has a NULL value, so all you need to do is add a WHERE clause that specifies that `FavCategory.CategoryId` must be NULL, and you ensure that only those categories not picked as a favorite are included in the results. The final results are as follows:

Category
Film Noir

Chapter 8

Exercise 1 Solution

Obtaining the CategoryId, name, and total cost of films in a particular category is fairly easy. The difficult part is obtaining the count of how many members put that category down as one of their favorites. For this, you should use a subquery in the SELECT statement's column listing.

```
SELECT Category.Category,
       SUM(DVDPrice) AS "Total Cost For Category",
       (SELECT COUNT(*) FROM FavCategory
       WHERE FavCategory.CategoryId =
               Category.CategoryId) AS "Members Favorite Category"
FROM Films INNER JOIN Category
ON Films.CategoryId = Category.CategoryId
WHERE Films.AvailableOnDVD = 'Y'
GROUP BY Category.CategoryId, Category.Category;
```

In the preceding query, the following subquery obtains the count of how many members listed that category as their favorite:

```
(SELECT COUNT(*) FROM FavCategory
WHERE FavCategory.CategoryId = Category.CategoryId)
```

The subquery is joined to the outer query on the CategoryId columns in the FavCategory and Category tables.

Notice that because the subquery references the CategoryId from the Category table in the main query, you must include it in the GROUP BY clause.

The results from the query are as follows:

Category	Total Cost For Category	Members Favorite Category
Thriller	15.98	3
Romance	12.99	2
Horror	18.94	3
War	15.99	4
Sci-fi	15.99	3
Historical	41.97	3

Exercise 2 Solution

All the hard work in creating this query is in the WHERE clause. There are two important conditions for the WHERE clause: that a town must have two or more members, and that the town must not currently be listed in the Location table. The WHERE clause is broken down into two subqueries, one nested inside the other. The outer subquery returns the number of members living in a particular city. The inner subquery returns all rows from the Location table that match the city name and state:

```
SELECT City, State FROM MemberDetails MD1
WHERE (SELECT COUNT(*) from MemberDetails MD2
WHERE NOT EXISTS (SELECT * FROM Location L1 WHERE L1.City = MD2.City AND L1.State =
MD2.State)
AND MD1.City = MD2.City AND MD1.State = MD2.State
GROUP BY City, State) >= 2
GROUP BY City, State;
```

The nested inner subquery is this:

```
(SELECT * FROM Location AS L1 WHERE L1.City = MD2.City AND L1.State = MD2.State)
```

If this returns rows, then it means that the city already exists in the Location table, but because you want only cities not already in that table, use a NOT EXISTS operator in the outer subquery to remove those cities from the results.

The outer subquery is as follows:

```
(SELECT COUNT(*) from MemberDetails MD2
WHERE NOT EXISTS (SELECT * FROM Location L1 WHERE L1.City = MD2.City AND L1.State =
MD2.State)
AND MD1.City = MD2.City AND MD1.State = MD2.State
GROUP BY City, State)
```

This SQL returns the number of members living in a city, where the city does not exist in the Location table. In the main query, you then check to see that this value is 2 or more:

```
WHERE (SELECT COUNT(*) from MemberDetails MD2
WHERE NOT EXISTS (SELECT * FROM Location L1 WHERE L1.City = MD2.City AND L1.State =
MD2.State)
AND MD1.City = MD2.City AND MD1.State = MD2.State
GROUP BY City, State) >= 2
```

The final query gives the following results:

City	State
Townsville	Mega State

Chapter 9

Exercise 1 Solution

The easiest and safest way to delete data is first to write a SELECT query that selects the data you want to delete and then to change the SELECT statement to a DELETE statement.

Begin with the SELECT column list and FROM clause:

```
SELECT StarId, StarName, StarAge FROM FilmStars S1;
```

This query simply returns all rows and columns from the table. The table has a primary key and the StarId column, and luckily enough, the values entered there are unique. However, the star's name should be unique, but it isn't. Therefore, you need to search for instances where there are duplicate names but where the StarId is different. To do this, you can use an IN operator and a subquery that simply returns all rows:

```
SELECT StarId, StarName, StarAge FROM FilmStars S1
WHERE StarName IN (SELECT StarName FROM FilmStars);
```

If you run this query, you get the following results:

StarId	StarName	StarAge
1	Boris Carlot	102
1	Scarlet O'Hairpin	89
3	Boris Carlot	102
4	Michael Hourglass	56
5	Dusty Hoffperson	48
6	Boris Carlot	102
7	Dusty Hoffperson	48

Clearly this query hasn't returned just the duplicates. That's because you need to add a link between the subquery and the outer query. Remember, you want only those rows where the name is the same but the StarId is different. You have the same names, but you need to add a link between the query and subquery that ensures that the StarIds are different:

```
SELECT StarId, StarName, StarAge FROM FilmStars S1
WHERE StarName IN (SELECT StarName FROM FilmStars S2
WHERE S2.StarId < S1.StarId)
ORDER BY StarName;
```

In the preceding code, a clause is added to the subquery that ensures that only rows where the StarIds are different between the subquery and outer query are returned. This is done by specifying that S2.StarId—the subquery's StarId column—should have a value that is less than the StarId column in S1 (the outer query's StarId table).

The ORDER BY clause is there only to make the results easier to read, and it isn't needed for the final DELETE query. When you run this query, you get the following results:

StarId	StarName	StarAge
3	Boris Carlot	102
6	Boris Carlot	102
7	Dusty Hoffperson	48

As you can see, the query has selected the unwanted duplicate data. Having confirmed that the query works, you can now convert it to a DELETE statement:

```
DELETE FROM FilmStars
WHERE StarName IN
    (SELECT StarName FROM FilmStars S2 WHERE S2.StarId < FilmStars.StarId);
```

All you have to do is change SELECT to DELETE. You can also remove the alias, as some database systems don't allow aliases with DELETE statements. In the subquery, S1 is changed to FilmStars, which references the outer FilmStars table mentioned in the DELETE FROM statement. Execute the query and you should find that three rows are deleted.

Chapter 10

Exercise 1 Solution

```
CREATE VIEW vFirstLastDOB AS
SELECT FirstName, LastName, DateOfBirth
FROM MemberDetails
```

Exercise 2 Solution

```
CREATE VIEW vGoldenStateMembers  AS
SELECT *
FROM MemberDetails
WHERE State = 'Golden State'
```

Exercise 3 Solution

```
CREATE VIEW vGoldenStateMembersFirstLastDOB AS
SELECT FirstName, LastName, DateOfBirth
FROM vGoldenStateMembers
```

Exercise 4 Solution

```
DROP VIEW vGoldenStateMembersFirstLastDOB
DROP VIEW vGoldenStateMembers
DROP VIEW vFirstLastDOB
```

Chapter 11

Exercise 1 Solution

```
USE FILMCLUB
SET TRANSACTION ISOLATION LEVEL READ COMMITTED
BEGIN TRANSACTION
UPDATE Inventory
SET Inventory.CheckedOut = 'Y'
WHERE (((Inventory.InventoryId)=7));
INSERT INTO Rentals ( InventoryId, MemberId, DateOut )
SELECT 7 AS InventoryId, 3 AS MemberId, '3/21/2004' AS DateOut;
COMMIT
```

Exercise 2 Solution

```
USE FILMCLUB
SET TRANSACTION ISOLATION LEVEL READ UNCOMMITTED
BEGIN TRANSACTION
SELECT * from Films
```

Exercise 3 Solution

```
USE FILMCLUB
SET TRANSACTION ISOLATION LEVEL SERIALIZABLE
BEGIN TRANSACTION
UPDATE Inventory
SET Inventory.CheckedOut = 'Y'
COMMIT
```

Chapter 12

Exercise 1 Solution

```
EXECUTE sp_addrole @rolename =  'DataEntry'
EXECUTE sp_addrole @rolename =  'Management'
EXECUTE sp_addrole @rolename =  'Supervisor'
```

Exercise 2 Solution

```
EXECUTE sp_addlogin @loginame =  'John', @passwd = 'ASDFG'
EXECUTE sp_addlogin @loginame =  'Joe', @passwd = 'qwerty'
EXECUTE sp_addlogin @loginame =  'Fred', @passwd = 'mnbvc'
EXECUTE sp_addlogin @loginame =  'Lynn', @passwd = 'zxcvbn'
EXECUTE sp_addlogin @loginame =  'Amy', @passwd = 'lkjhg'
EXECUTE sp_addlogin @loginame =  'Beth', @passwd = 'poiuy'


EXECUTE sp_adduser 'John', 'John'
EXECUTE sp_adduser 'Joe', 'Joe'
EXECUTE sp_adduser 'Fred', 'Fred'
EXECUTE sp_adduser 'Lynn', 'Lynn'
EXECUTE sp_adduser 'Amy', 'Amy'
EXECUTE sp_adduser 'Beth', 'Beth'
```

Exercise 3 Solution

```
EXECUTE sp_addrolemember @rolename =  'DataEntry', @membername = 'John', 'Joe',
'Lynn'
EXECUTE sp_addrolemember @rolename =  'Management', @membername = 'Amy', 'Beth'
```

Exercise 4 Solution

```
GRANT SELECT, INSERT, UPDATE
ON Attendance
TO DataEntry
```

Exercise 5 Solution

```
GRANT SELECT, DELETE
ON Attendance
TO Supervisor
```

Exercise 6 Solution

```
GRANT SELECT
ON Attendance
TO Management
```

Chapter 13

Exercise 1 Solution

```
USE FILMCLUB
CREATE INDEX IND_Name
ON MemberDetails (FirstName, LastName)
```

Exercise 2 Solution

```
USE FILMCLUB
CREATE INDEX IND_State
ON MemberDetails (State)
```

Exercise 3 Solution

```
USE FILMCLUB
CREATE UNIQUE INDEX IND_MemberId
ON MemberDetails (MemberId)
```

Exercise 4 Solution

```
USE FILMCLUB
DROP INDEX MemberDetails.IND_State
DROP INDEX MemberDetails.IND_Name
DROP Index MemberDetails.IND_MemberId
```

Exercise 5 Solution

```
USE FILMCLUB
CREATE INDEX IND_Name
ON MemberDetails (FirstName, LastName)

CREATE INDEX IND_State
ON MemberDetails (State)

CREATE UNIQUE INDEX IND_MemberId
ON MemberDetails (MemberId)
```

Setting Up and Using the Five Database Systems

This appendix covers how to install the five database systems supported by this book. It also covers enough detail on using each database system to enable you to create the example database used throughout the book. This appendix also shows you how each database system allows you to enter and run SQL queries. With the knowledge gained here, you'll be in a position to create the example database and try out all of the SQL examples in the book. The coverage of each database system is quite brief, and although it is sufficient for this book, each of the database systems comes with help files and tutorials that help you learn more.

Installing and Using MySQL Version 4.1

The first thing you need to do is download the MySQL database installation files from www.mysql.com. The direct link is http://dev.mysql.com/downloads/mysql/4.1.html.

At the time of writing, version 4.1 is the latest version for new developments. You often find beta versions of the MySQL software, but these are not 100 percent stable, and so they carry risks. The front-end interface for MySQL is fairly limited, but there are a number of add-on consoles you can install that make administering MySQL and writing queries much easier. In addition to the MySQL binaries, there are helpful tools such as MySQL Administration console and the MySQL Query Browser, all of which can be downloaded from http://dev.mysql.com/downloads/. Also available is MySQL Control Center. This tool is slightly older and no longer in development, but at the time of writing, it was more reliable than MySQL Query Browser. In addition, MySQL Control Center allows more than one query to be executed simultaneously. However, Query Browser gives more details when there are errors in your SQL, and as it's developed, Query Browser is likely to get more and more reliable. In fact, there's no harm in installing both if you wish, though this book uses MySQL Query Browser.

Begin by installing MySQL database, which is based on the Windows version and shows the Windows screenshots. Most of what's said here also applies to other operating systems.

Having downloaded the install files, click Start ➪ Run and browse to the MySQL database install file.

Click the database install file, usually called `mysql` and then its version number. For example, in my system, the install file is called `mysql-4.1.5-gamma-essential-win`. Then click the Open button, and the Run dialog box appears.

Click the OK button to start the MySQL installation, and the screen displayed in Figure B-1 appears:

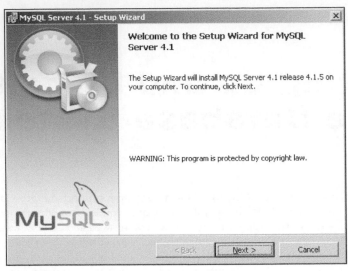

Figure B-1

Click the Next button to continue. The next screen displays the license agreement, and you need to click `I agree`. Click Next and you're taken to a screen containing notes about MySQL that you might want to read. Click Next once you've read them, and you are presented with the option of where to install the database system. Leave it at the default setting (shown in Figure B-2) if you have no particular preference:

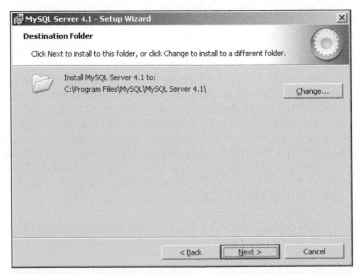

Figure B-2

Next, you come to a screen that gives you the choice of whether you want to customize the installation components of MySQL. See Figure B-3.

Figure B-3

For the purposes of this book, the default Typical option is fine. Ensure that Typical is selected and click Next to continue. You're presented with a summary screen (shown in Figure B-4).

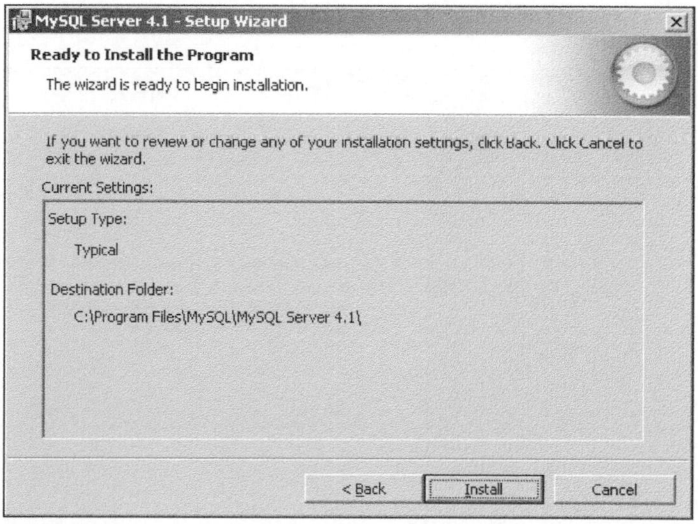

Figure B-4

Click Install to begin installation, which usually takes a few minutes, depending on how fast your PC is. When installation is finished, you're returned to a screen giving you the option to create a MySQL.com account or to log in with an existing account. This account is purely for the use of certain members-only features of the www.mysql.com Web site and isn't related to the installed database system. You can select the Skip Sign-Up option, as shown in Figure B-5.

Figure B-5

Click Next to proceed to the final screen of the installation, shown in Figure B-6.

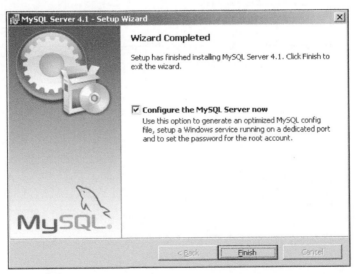

Figure B-6

Leave the check box for "Configure the MySQL Server now" checked, and then click Finish. The installation is over, but you're now taken to the first of the Configuration Wizard screens, illustrated in Figure B-7.

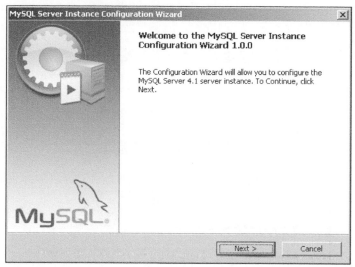

Figure B-7

Click Next to configure the new MySQL installation. You're now presented with a screen (shown in Figure B-8) allowing you to choose a detailed configuration or a standard configuration.

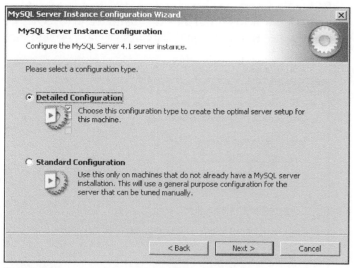

Figure B-8

Select the Detailed Configuration option and click Next. The screen displayed (shown in Figure B-9) now allows you to choose the role of your PC—that is, what you use it for. For this book, you're using it as a developer, and it's likely that you use your PC for other development work, and therefore you don't want MySQL hogging all the memory and CPU resources. If that sounds like your situation, go for the first option, Developer Machine.

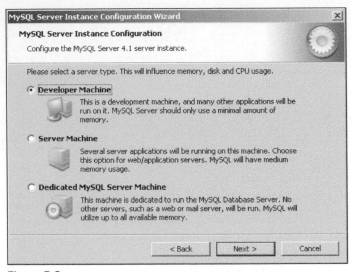

Figure B-9

The other options dedicate increasing amounts of system resources to MySQL, which means less memory for other programs to run, which is fine if the PC is dedicated to MySQL usage. Click Next and you're presented with the screen shown in Figure B-10, which allows you to choose how you plan to use your database.

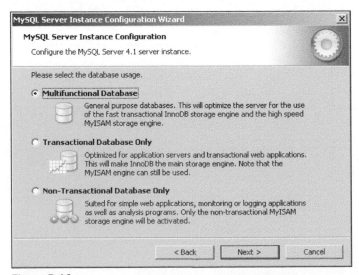

Figure B-10

For this book, the default option of Multifunctional Database is fine, so ensure that this option is selected, and then click Next, whereupon you're taken to a screen (see Figure B-11) allowing you to specify a drive for the `InnoDB` tablespace.

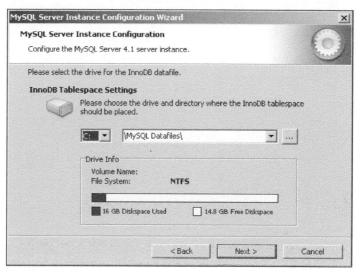

Figure B-11

Leave it at the default option and click Next to continue. You're taken to the screen shown in Figure B-12, which allows you to set the number of concurrent connections to your server.

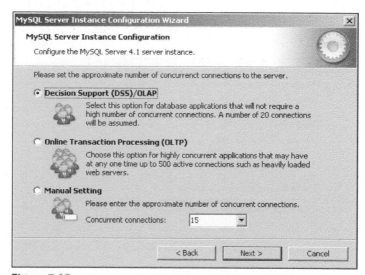

Figure B-12

Leave it at the default Decision Support option and click Next for the following screen (see Figure B-13), which allows you to set networking options.

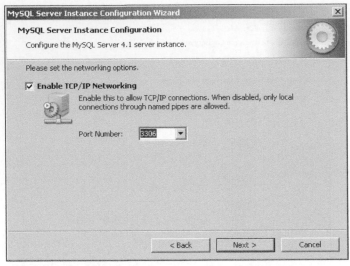

Figure B-13

Again, leave it at the default settings, shown in Figure B-13. Click Next to continue. Now you're asked which character set you want to use for storing text-based data. The standard character set is fine in many circumstances, but it doesn't support characters from languages such as Chinese. If you're planning to use the database for Web-based applications, then you could have people from all over the world accessing and possibly inputting data. In the screen shown in Figure B-14, choose the Best Support For Multilingualism option.

Figure B-14

Now click Next to continue. In the next screen (see Figure B-15), you're asked whether you want MySQL to run as a Windows service:

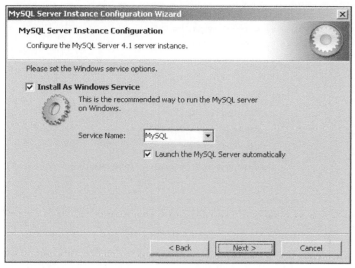

Figure B-15

Leave it at the default setting, as shown in Figure B-15, and click Next. Now you come to the user password screen (shown in Figure B-16), where you must enter a password of your choice in the password box and confirm the password in the second box:

Figure B-16

Having entered your new password, click the Next button. This takes you to the final screen, depicted in Figure B-17. If you're happy with the settings you've set so far, click Execute:

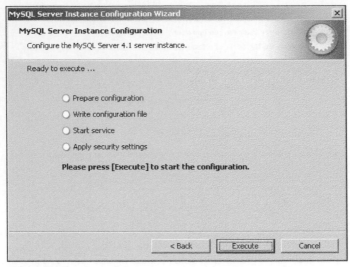

Figure B-17

Once MySQL has finished configuring the database system, you should get a success confirmation message, shown in Figure B-18:

Figure B-18

Click Finish, and congratulate yourself—the database install is now complete!

Click Start ⇨ Programs, and browse to the new folder containing the MySQL programs. As evident in Figure B-19, there's a command line interface, the default way of managing and accessing MySQL, and there is also the configuration wizard, the wizard you just ran. You may also see an option for the MySQL Manual.

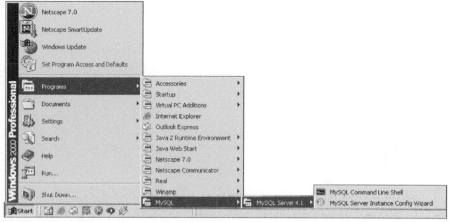

Figure B-19

Although using only the command line interface to access MySQL is fine, you may prefer nice, easy-to-use consoles and user interfaces. The next section shows you how to install very useful tools for managing the MySQL system.

Installing the MySQL Tools

As mentioned previously, the MySQL Administration console and the MySQL Query Browser are available to download and provide excellent user interfaces for managing MySQL. Both the Administration console and the Query Browser can be downloaded from http://dev.mysql.com/downloads/.

The Administration console is very handy but not essential for this book, and discussing its use could easily fill another book. However, once you've completed this book, you might want to go back and install the console because it does make life a lot easier than does the default command line interface.

To start installing the Query Browser interface, which is extremely useful for this book, click Start ⇨ Run and browse to where you downloaded the Query Browser installation file.

If you download the Windows installer version, then you need to make sure to select All Files from the Files of Type drop-down box, or else you won't see the installation file listed. Click Open, and then Click OK to start the installation. You should see the initial installation screen depicted in Figure B-20:

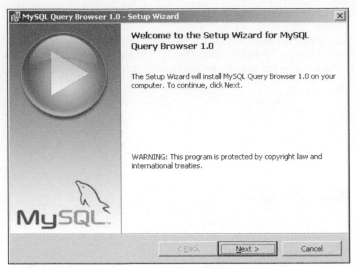

Figure B-20

The installation is very simple. All the default options are fine, so installation is just a matter of clicking Next, apart from the license agreement screen where you must ensure that you agree to the license for installation to continue. On the final screen, click Finish, and the installation takes place.

Once it is installed you should find a MySQL Query Browser icon on your desktop. Double-click the icon to launch the program.

The first time you run the program, simply fill in the username, password, and hostname boxes as shown in Figure B-21:

Figure B-21

Click OK, and you get a box (see Figure B-22) warning you that you didn't enter a schema name:

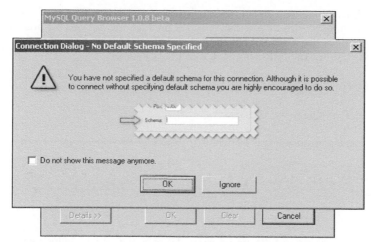

Figure B-22

Click Ignore to continue. You're now into the main program and should see a screen like that shown in Figure B-23:

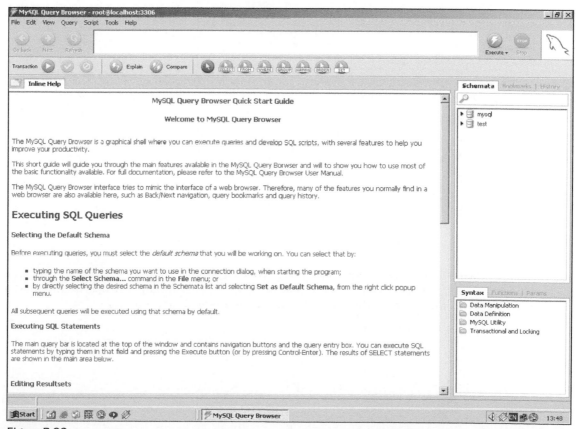

Figure B-23

At the very top of the program screen is a large textbox, which is where you enter your SQL. Once it's entered and you're happy with it, you need to click the Execute button (the button with a flash through it directly to the right of the textbox). This then runs or executes the SQL. The first task is to create the Film Club database. Enter the following SQL into the SQL box:

```
CREATE DATABASE FILMCLUB;
```

Figure B-24 shows the SQL in the SQL box:

Figure B-24

This is not a query returning information; rather, it is SQL that changes the database system, in this case, adding a new database. Therefore, you don't see any results as such, but if you right-click in the Schemata box (on the right-hand side of the window) and select Refresh Schemata List, you see that the database, or what MySQL calls a schema, called `filmclub` now appears (see Figure B-25):

Figure B-25

Now close down Query Browser and reopen it. The same login-type screen appears, but this time you need to create a connection to the Film Club database. Click the button with three dots inside it next to the Connection drop-down box. The screen shown in Figure B-26 should appear:

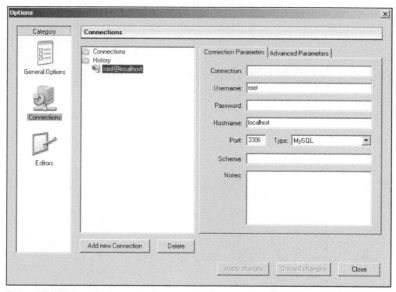

Figure B-26

Click the Add New Connection button to add a new connection and fill in the Connection, Password, Port, Type, Schema, and Notes boxes as shown in Figure B-27:

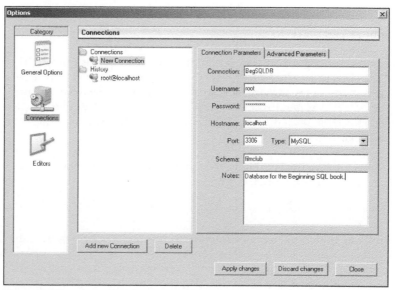

Figure B-27

Having done that, make sure that you click the Apply Changes button, and then click Close to close the window. You're returned to the Query Browser's default login screen, and the details for connection BegSQLDB are already entered, as shown in Figure B-28:

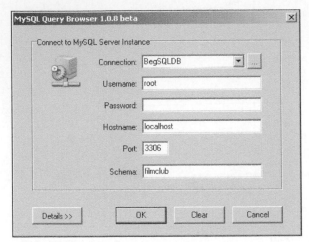

Figure B-28

Every time you start up, you can select the login details by simply selecting the connection name from the Connections drop-down box. It saves filling in the details every time because you only need to enter the password.

Click OK to continue and open Query Browser.

Because you selected the BegSQLDB connection, any queries or SQL is run against the Film Club database. Also note that unlike MySQL Control Center, only one SQL statement can be executed at one time. Chapter 1 contains all the SQL for adding tables to the example database, and Chapter 2 covers how to insert data. So this appendix simply demonstrates how to create one new table, add two rows to it, and then delete the table from the database. Don't worry if the SQL itself doesn't make sense; it will once you've read Chapters 1 through 3.

Type the following SQL into the SQL box at the top of Query Browser, the same box in which you previously entered CREATE DATABASE FilmClub:

```
CREATE TABLE MyTable (MyColumn int)
```

Now click the Execute button to create the table. Now refresh the schemata by right-clicking the Schemata box and choosing the Refresh Menu option. A small triangle now appears next to the film-club database name in the schemata. Click the triangle and you can see that it lists the addition of MyTable, as shown in Figure B-29:

Figure B-29

Click the triangle next to MyTable to see the column named MyColumn listed under MyTable.

Now you need to insert some data. There are two records to be inserted. If you enter the statements in the query box, then each INSERT statement must be entered and executed separately, so first type the following into the SQL entry box:

```
INSERT INTO MyTable(MyColumn) VALUES(123);
```

Then click the Execute button, and the data is entered into MyTable. Now clear the SQL entry box and type the following command, and click Execute:

```
INSERT INTO MyTable(MyColumn) VALUES(888);
```

However, an easier alternative when you have to write more than one SQL statement is to write the code in the script box. Choose New Script Table from the File menu. Now type both lines into the script box, which is the large lower textbox that has now been created. Make sure that you end each statement with a semicolon, as shown in the preceding code. Once you've entered both lines, click the Execute button on the toolbar just above the script textbox.

To see what data is in MyTable, clear the SQL entry box and execute the following SELECT statement:

```
SELECT * FROM MyTable
```

You should see the screen that appears in Figure B-30:

Figure B-30

MyTable isn't needed again in this book, so delete it by entering the following statement into the SQL entry box and clicking Execute:

```
DROP TABLE MyTable
```

Refresh the schemata view, and you can see that MyTable is no longer listed under the Film Club database.

If you decide to download the SQL text files for this book, you can open them by selecting File ⇨ Open Script. By default, SQL files have the .sql extension, so make sure that All Files is selected from the Files of Type drop-down box when you're loading plaintext files.

One final thing to note is the very handy SQL reference guide in the bottom-right corner of Query Browser; there you can find a wealth of useful information specific to MySQL's implementation of SQL. The reference guide contains details pertaining to all the SQL statements and operators used in MySQL. For example, click on Syntax, then on Data Manipulation, and then on the SELECT statement, and you have a whole lot of information on the SELECT statement and all the possible usage variations. The reference may look like gibberish until you've read the first few chapters of this book, but it's invaluable for your later SQL adventures.

Installing and Using IBM DB2

A free trial version of IBM DB2 for development purposes can be downloaded from the IBM Web site. The good news is that it's free to download; the bad news is that it's a huge, huge download even if you have a broadband connection. The current URL for the download page is `www14.software.ibm.com/webapp/download/product.jsp?id=TDUN-49EVGU&q=%20DB2+Personal+Developer`.

Download the DB2 Personal Developer's Edition suitable for your operating system.

Having downloaded the installation, you'll almost certainly find that it's a single compressed file that needs to be uncompressed before installation can take place. Simply run the downloaded file and select where you want to extract it. Anywhere on your hard drive is fine; just make sure you have plenty of space because it's a big file.

This appendix guides you through the Windows installation, but the principles are the same for whichever operating system you're using. To start the installation you need to run the setup program. Click Start ➪ Run and browse to where you extracted the setup files.

Double-click `setup.exe`, and then click OK in the Run dialog box to start the installation.

It might take a little while depending on how fast your computer is, but eventually the first screen (see Figure B-31) of the installation appears:

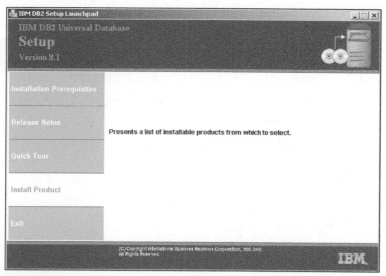

Figure B-31

You may wish to double-check that your PC has the required prerequisites; once you've done that, click on the Install Product link. A screen (shown in Figure B-32) allowing you to choose which product to install appears, though usually it's an option of one!

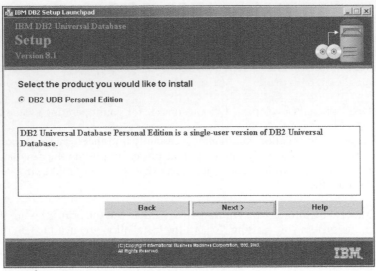

Figure B-32

Click Next to continue. Again, it might take a little while, but eventually the next install screen, shown in Figure B-33, opens:

Figure B-33

Click Next to continue to the ubiquitous license agreement where selecting "I accept" is the only option if you want to continue.

Select "I accept," and click Next to continue to the screen that allows you to choose which components you want to install, as shown in Figure B-34:

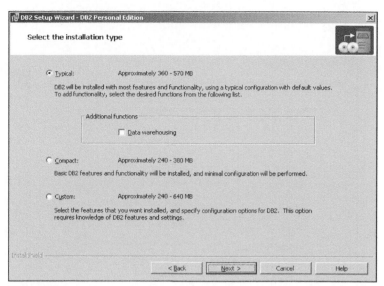

Figure B-34

The default option of Typical is fine. Click Next and you get to choose where you want the database system to be installed (see Figure B-35):

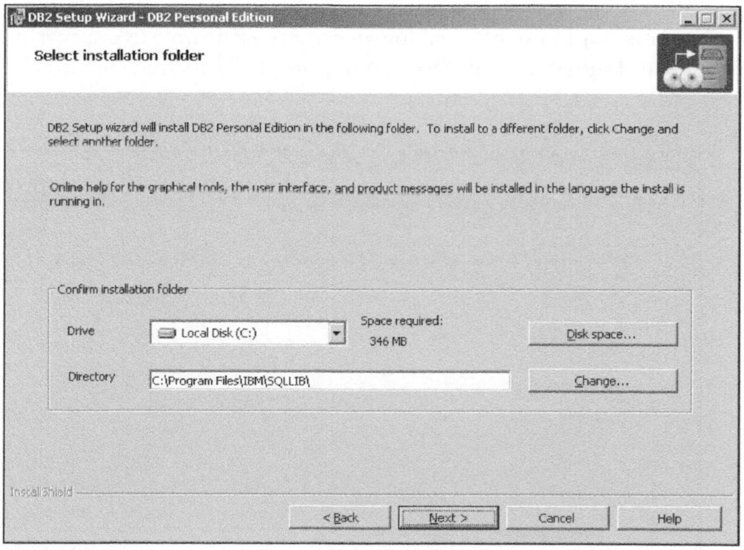

Figure B-35

If the default location is fine, go for that; otherwise just choose somewhere with lots of free disk space!

Click Next to continue. The next screen (shown in Figure B-36) allows you to choose the user who administers the database:

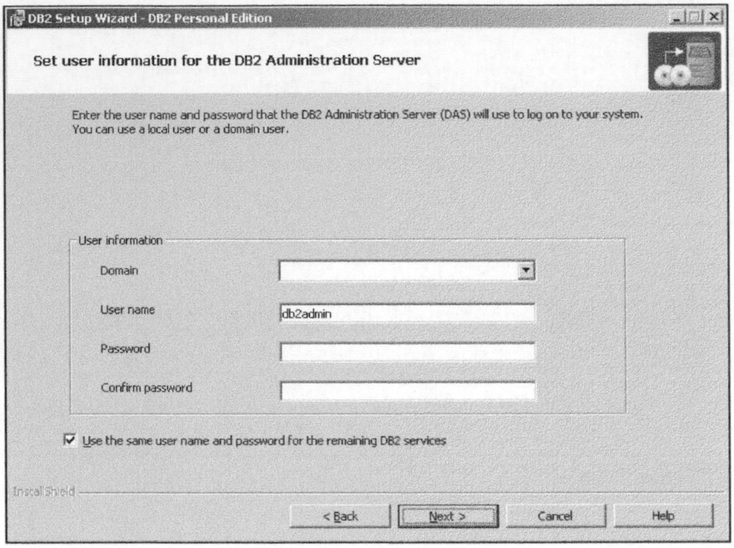

Figure B-36

For the purposes of this book, you should enter the username and password of the local user with which you normally log in. This might not be ideal for security reasons on a live server, but it's fine in a test environment. Enter your login details as shown in Figure B-37, making sure to select details appropriate to your PC:

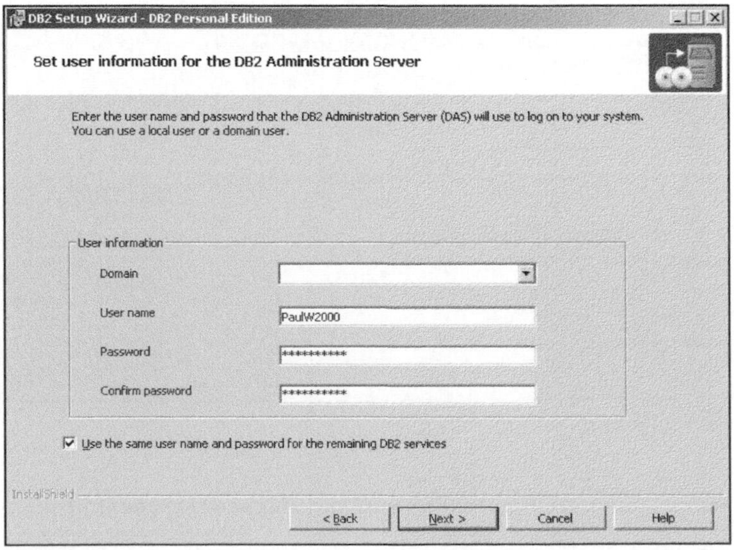

Figure B-37

Click Next to continue to the contact details screen, which is depicted in Figure B-38:

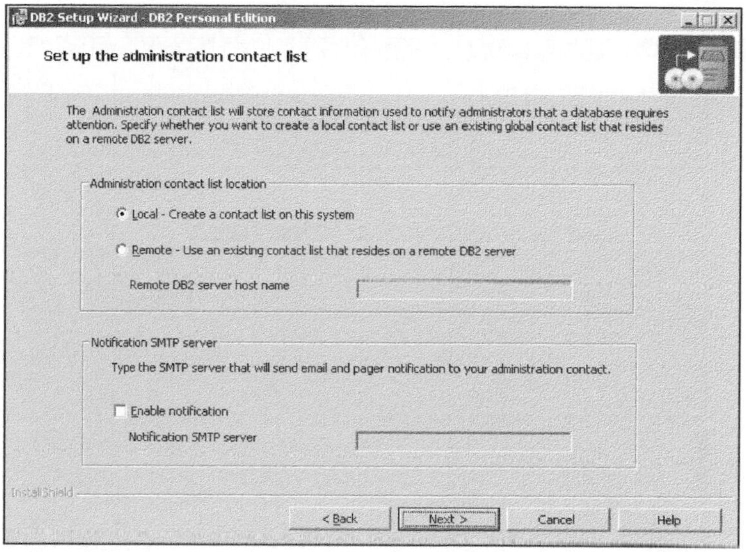

Figure B-38

Leave it at the default settings shown in Figure B-38 and click Next. You receive a message (shown in Figure B-39) warning you that the Notification SMTP service isn't specified, but that's something for administrators of live servers to worry about:

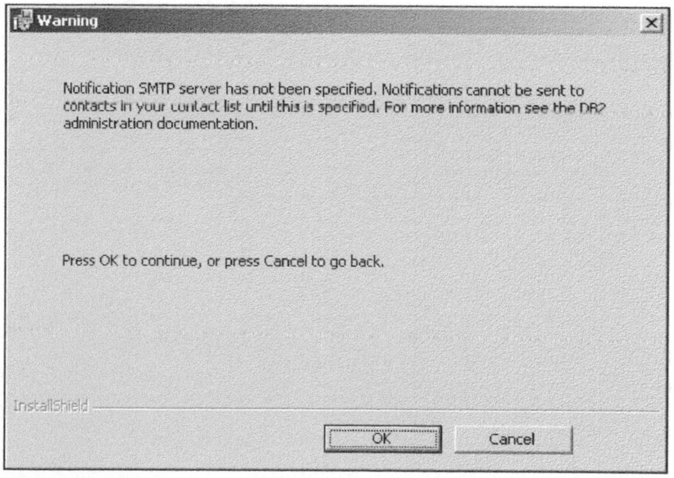

Figure B-39

Click OK to clear the message and continue. The next screen, displayed in Figure B-40, allows you to configure protocol details:

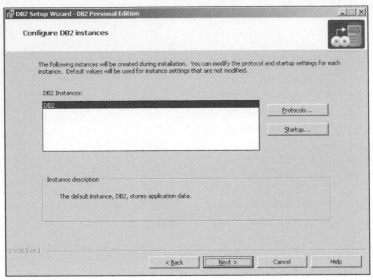

Figure B-40

The default values are fine for the purposes of this book, so just click Next to continue. The next screen allows you to set up DB2's task scheduler, but because you don't need it for this book, just accept the default shown in Figure B-41 and click Next:

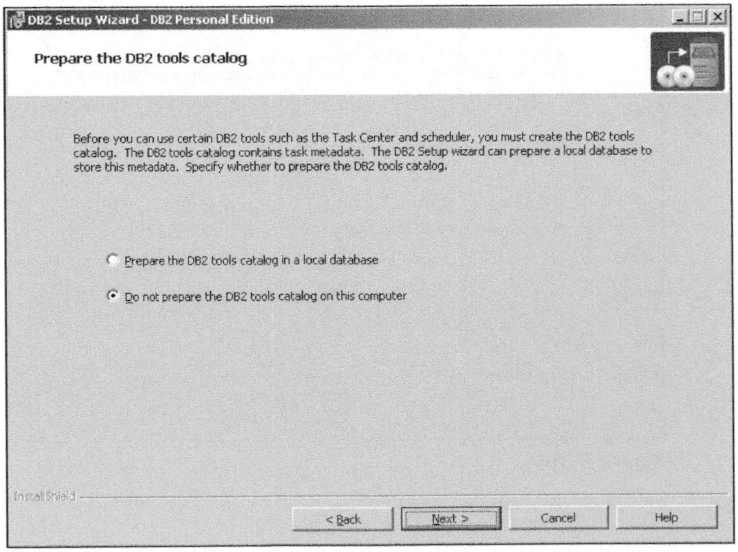

Figure B-41

The screen in Figure B-42 allows you to enter contact details for DB2's database system health monitor. Select the "Defer the task..." option:

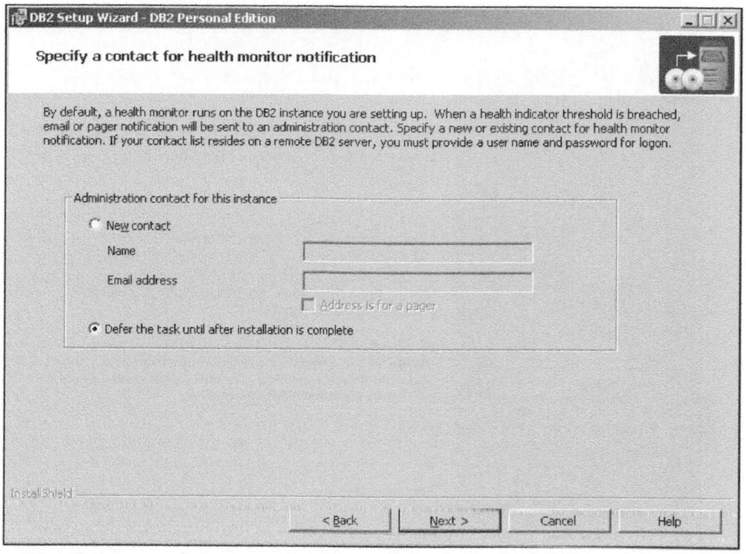

Figure B-42

Click Next to continue, and finally you're on the installation summary (shown in Figure B-43), just one button press from installing DB2:

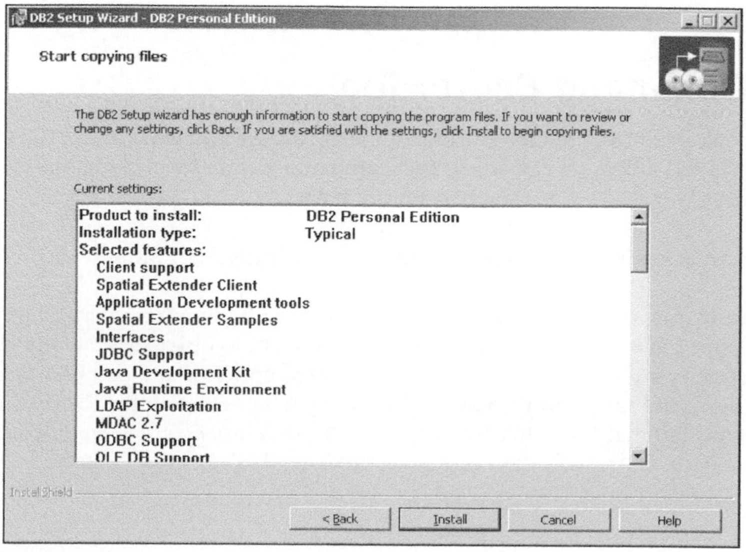

Figure B-43

If you're ready and happy with the options chosen, pull up a comfy seat, grab a magazine, click the Install button, and wait while DB2 installs. If everything goes fine, you should see the screen depicted in Figure B-44:

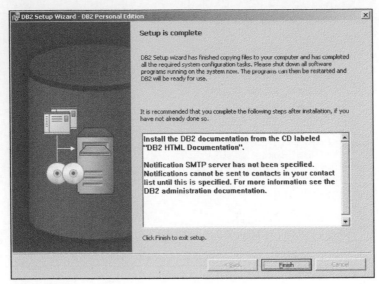

Figure B-44

Click Finish, and installation is now complete and the IBM First Steps screen appears with helpful tutorials and sample databases. The next section introduces the Command Center tool and creates the Film Club database.

Using the Command Center Tool

To create this book's example database and run the examples, you need to use the Command Center tool. Having installed DB2, you can access the Command Center by clicking Start ⇨ Programs ⇨ IBM DB2 ⇨ Command Line Tools, as shown in Figure B-45:

Once the program is loaded, you should see the screen depicted in Figure B-46:

There are 4 tabs near the middle of the screen, and by default the program loads up with the Script tab selected. The Script tab allows more than one SQL statement to be executed at once. Each statement must be separated by a semicolon at the end of the statement. You can load files of SQL statements into the Script textbox, edit them, and then execute them by either clicking the Execute icon in the toolbar (the icon on the far left that looks like two cogs next to each other) or choosing Execute from the Script menu.

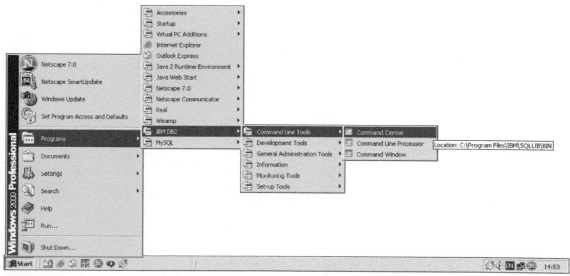

Figure B-45

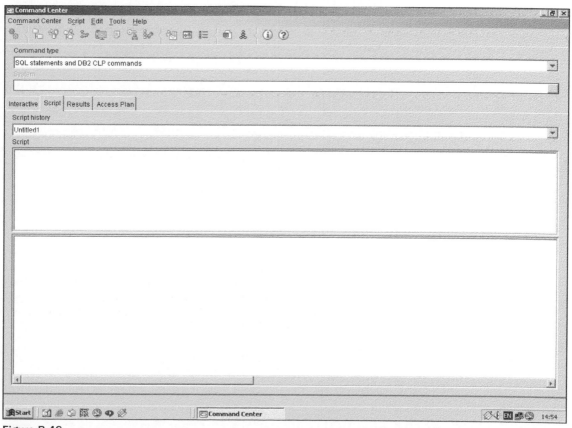

Figure B-46

You can also enter and execute SQL statements one at a time in the Interactive tab. Click the Interactive tab, and you'll see the screen change to that shown in Figure B-47:

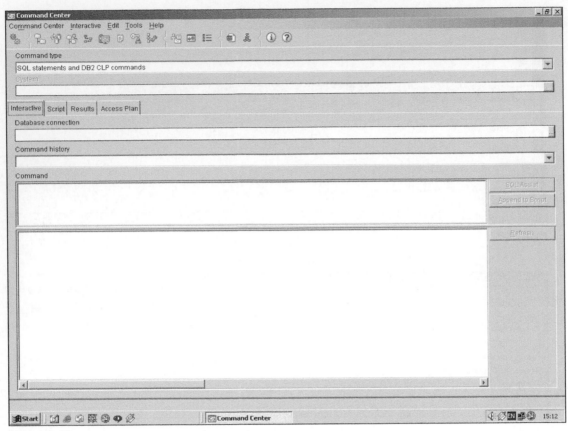

Figure B-47

To select a database connection (to choose which database the SQL queries are executed against), you can type the following SQL:

```
CONNECT TO database_name
```

Alternatively, you can click the button to the right of the database connection line, which allows you to browse the database system for databases to connect to. Currently there are no databases on the system, so you can start by creating the Film Club database. Type the following SQL into the Command box (as shown in Figure B-48) and click Execute or click the Execute icon from the Interactive menu.

```
CREATE DATABASE FILMCLUB USING CODESET UTF-8 TERRITORY US
```

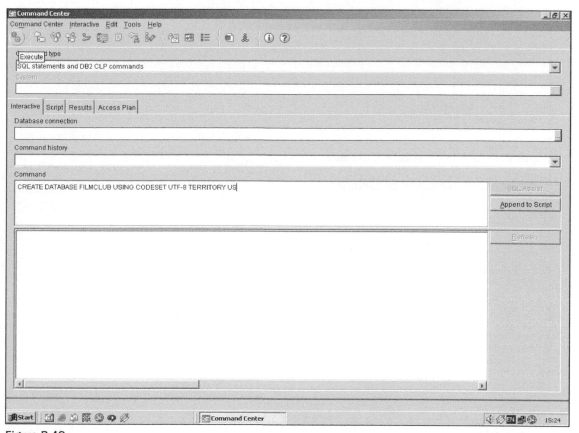

Figure B-48

Depending on the speed of your computer, it may take a while to complete the database creation, but eventually you should see what appears in Figure B-49:

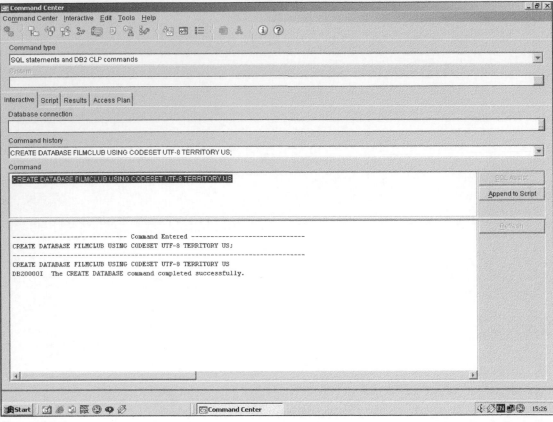

Figure B-49

The Film Club database is now created, but you haven't actually connected to it. If you try executing any SQL, you receive an error message (similar to the one shown in Figure B-50) telling you to connect to a database first:

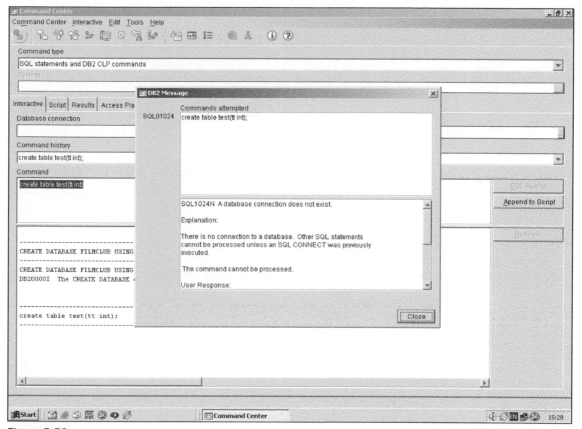

Figure B-50

You must reconnect to the database each time you open the Command Center. To connect to the Film Club database, you can either type the following SQL or browse to the database using the database connection button discussed previously:

```
CONNECT TO FILMCLUB
```

Chapter 1 already contains all the SQL for adding tables to the example database, and Chapter 2 covers how to insert data. So this appendix demonstrates creating one new table, adding two rows to it, and then deleting the table. Don't worry if the SQL itself doesn't make sense; it does once you've read Chapters 1 through 3.

Ensure that you're still in the Interactive tab and connected to the Film Club database, and then type the following statement into the Command textbox:

```
CREATE TABLE MyTable (MyColumn int)
```

Now click Execute, and the table is created.

Now you need to insert some data. You can either use the interactive screen to insert data one statement at a time, clicking Execute after each statement, or you can click the Script tab and enter all the statements at once, making sure that you put a semicolon after each. There are two records to be inserted:

```
INSERT INTO MyTable(MyColumn) VALUES(123);
INSERT INTO MyTable(MyColumn) VALUES(888);
```

Enter the code into the Command window and click Execute. Note that you must have previously executed a CONNECT TO statement, either in the Interactive screen or in the Script screen, before you can execute SQL against the database.

To see what data is in the MyTable, return to the Interactive screen and type the following SQL in the SQL entry box:

```
SELECT * FROM MyTable
```

Click Execute, and you should see a screen similar to what appears in Figure B-51:

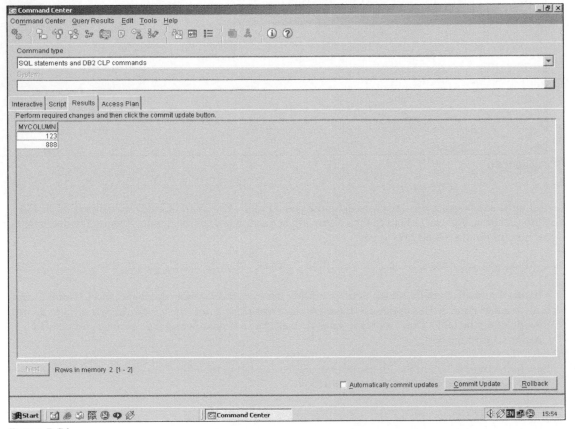

Figure B-51

You can see that DB2 automatically takes you to the Results screen whenever a query is executed.

The MyTable isn't needed again in this book, so delete it by switching back to the Interactive screen, entering the following code into the SQL entry box, and then clicking Execute:

```
DROP TABLE MyTable
```

The table is now removed from the Film Club database.

Installing and Using Microsoft Access XP

Unfortunately, there's no free trial software to download if you don't have Microsoft Access, but you can order a CD with a trial version of Microsoft Office, which includes Access, from the Microsoft Web site.

The installation of Access is fairly straightforward. All the default or typical options are acceptable for the purposes of this book, and when given a choice, you should simply select typical options. Otherwise, installation is mostly a matter of clicking Next.

Once installed, click Start ➪ Programs and select the Access icon. Once it's loaded and activated, you should see the default screen, which appears in Figure B-52:

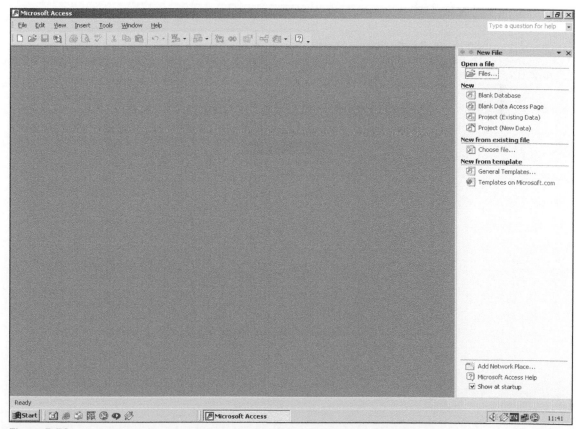

Figure B-52

In Access it's not possible to create a new database using SQL, so you need to click the Blank Database link under the New File tab on the right of the screen. Click the link and you're presented with the New Database dialog box, shown in Figure B-53:

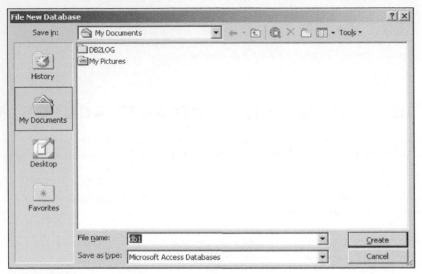

Figure B-53

The only option is to select the location and name of the new database's file. Enter `FilmDatabase` for the name of the file and then click the Create button. The database is created and opened and the default view displayed as depicted in Figure B-54:

Figure B-54

The box in the middle of the screen shows a list of possible database objects, such as tables, queries, forms, reports, and so on. Currently the Tables tab is selected and the list of tables in the database is shown, which at the moment contains no tables. You can create a new table by ensuring that the Tables tab is selected and then clicking the New icon in the Tables tab. Because this book is all about SQL, this appendix shows you how to use SQL to create a table. To enter SQL queries and code, you must click on the Queries tab and then double-click the Create Query in Design View option, which causes the screen shown in Figure B-55 to be displayed:

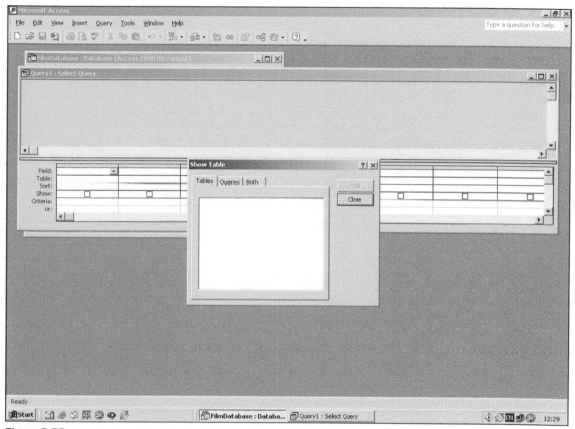

Figure B-55

Click Close to clear the dialog box. Now the view currently displayed is the MS Access Query Design view. To enter SQL code, you need to switch to the SQL Editor view. From the Design view, this can be achieved by either clicking the SQL icon on the far left of the toolbar or selecting the SQL View option from the View menu. Once you've switched to SQL view, a textbox is displayed (see Figure B-56) where you can enter SQL code:

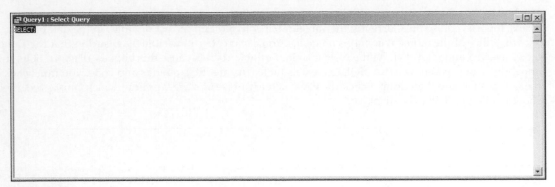

Figure B-56

You need to use the SQL view in order to try out the SQL code in this book. Access allows you to create more than one query, and you can save each query under a unique name. The SQL needed to create all the tables in the database is discussed in Chapter 1. So, this appendix takes you through a brief example of how to create a table, insert data, and then delete the table. However, because this is a book on SQL, you use SQL code to do all this, but you can use the user interface to perform these actions if you prefer.

Type the following SQL into the Query textbox:

```
CREATE TABLE MyTable (MyColumn int)
```

Now execute the query by clicking the Run icon (a dark red exclamation mark) in the middle of the toolbar. Alternatively, from the main menu bar, you can select Run from the Query menu. Executing the query results in the creation of MyTable. If you switch back to the Tables view, you can see that MyTable has been added to the table list, as shown in Figure B-57:

Figure B-57

If you select MyTable from the list, you can view its design by clicking on the Design icon, or you can open it for entering data by clicking on the Open icon. Figure B-58 shows you MyTable in Design view:

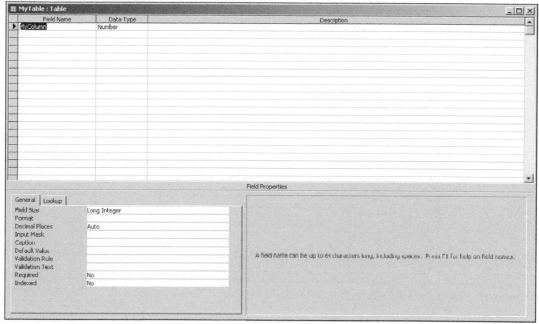

Figure B-58

Design view is MS Access's way of letting you see what each table looks like and change each table's design. Because this book is about using SQL to make design changes, return to the Query view and back to the query where you entered the table creation SQL.

After creating the table, you need to insert some data. Although there are two records to be inserted, each INSERT statement must be entered and executed separately, so first type the following code into the SQL entry box:

```
INSERT INTO MyTable(MyColumn) VALUES(123);
```

Then click the Run icon and you're warned that you're about to append one row to the table. Click Yes and the data is entered into MyTable. Now clear the SQL entry box, type the following statement, and click Run:

```
INSERT INTO MyTable(MyColumn) VALUES(888);
```

To see what data is in MyTable, clear the SQL entry box and type the following statement:

```
SELECT * FROM MyTable
```

Click Execute, and you should see the screen that appears in Figure B-59:

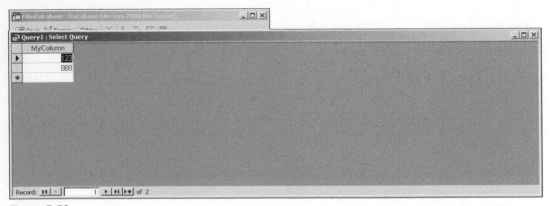

Figure B-59

To return to the Code view, you need to either select SQL View from the main menu's View menu or click on the Design icon on the far left of the toolbar and hold down the mouse button and select the SQL icon. MyTable isn't needed again in this book, so delete it by entering the following statement into the SQL entry box and clicking Execute:

```
DROP TABLE MyTable
```

Close the query, saying no to saving it. Return to Table view, and you can see that MyTable is no longer listed.

Installing and Using Microsoft SQL Server 2000

If you have access to a full, licensed copy of Microsoft SQL Server, that's great news. If you don't have one, a 120-day evaluation version can be downloaded from: www.microsoft.com/downloads/details.aspx?FamilyID=d20ba6e1-f44c-4781-a6bb-f60e02dc1335&DisplayLang=en

If the hefty price tag of the full MS SQL Server is off-putting, you may be pleased to know that SQL Server 2005 Express Edition is due out in 2005, and it's free! It has many of the features of the full SQL Server and is ideal for learning SQL with this book. The main difference between the Express Edition and the full SQL Server is scalability; SQL Server 2005 Express Edition is not designed for very heavy workloads, like sites such as Amazon.com *might get. As the time of this writing, SQL Server 2005 Express Edition is still in beta 2, which means it's not 100% stable, so it's not a good idea to install it on any essential machine. SQL Server 2005 Express Edition can be downloaded from the Microsoft.com Web site:* www.microsoft.com/downloads/details.aspx?FamilyID=62b348bb-0458-4203-bb03-8be49e16e6cd&DisplayLang=en.

You can learn more about SQL Server 2005 Express Edition at the following Web site: http://msdn.microsoft.com/library/default.asp?url=/library/en-us/dnsse/html/sseoverview.asp.

If you're installing the downloaded evaluation version, you have downloaded a single file, SQLEval.exe, that needs to be run so that it decompresses itself. Select Start ➪ Run, and then browse to the file and run it. Extract the file's contents to a convenient location on your hard drive. Once the files are unpacked, the installation is pretty much the same whether you downloaded the evaluation or the full version.

To start the SQL Server installation, select Start ➪ Run and browse to the setup.bat file. You should be presented with the screen shown in Figure B-60. Click Next to continue installation:

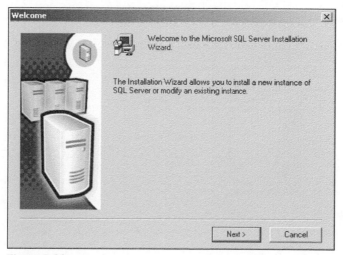

Figure B-60

The next screen (see Figure B-61) allows you to choose the computer on which you want to install SQL Server:

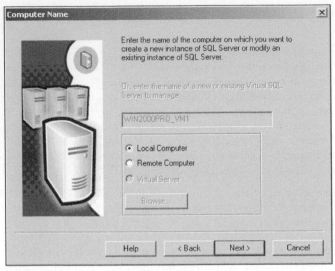

Figure B-61

Ensure that the Local Computer option is selected and click Next, and you're presented with the screen shown in Figure B-62:

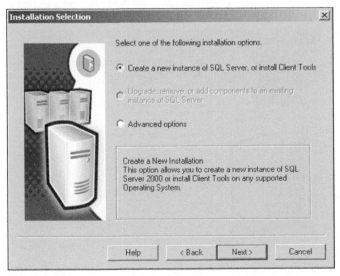

Figure B-62

Select "Create a new instance..." and click Next. You're asked to enter your username and company name, as shown in Figure B-63:

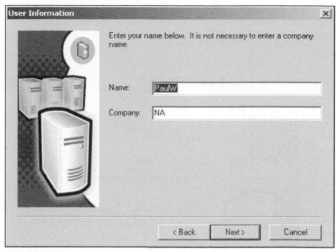

Figure B-63

What you enter here is not that important. You're not selecting a database system username; you're simply letting the system know your personal name. Enter your name and click Next, and you're taken to the usual license agreement screen.

Click Yes if you agree and want installation to continue. The next screen (see Figure B-64) allows you to choose what part of the database system you're installing. You want to install both the database system itself and the tools that allow you to manage it and run queries, so select the Server and Client Tools option and click Next:

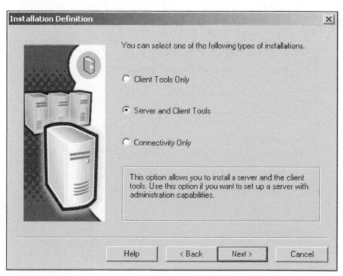

Figure B-64

On the next screen, shown in Figure B-65, you get to choose the name given to your particular installation of the database server. For the purposes of this book, leave the default box checked and let the installation choose a name for your database server. The name is based on the name of your computer. Click Next to continue:

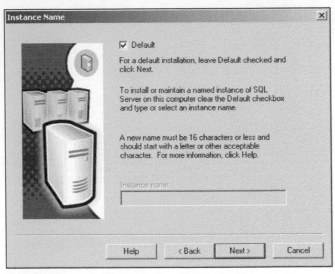

Figure B-65

The next screen (see Figure B-66) allows you to customize which parts of the database system are installed. For the purposes of this book, and for most general purposes, the default Typical option is fine. If you're short on hard drive space, the Minimum install should also be sufficient for this book:

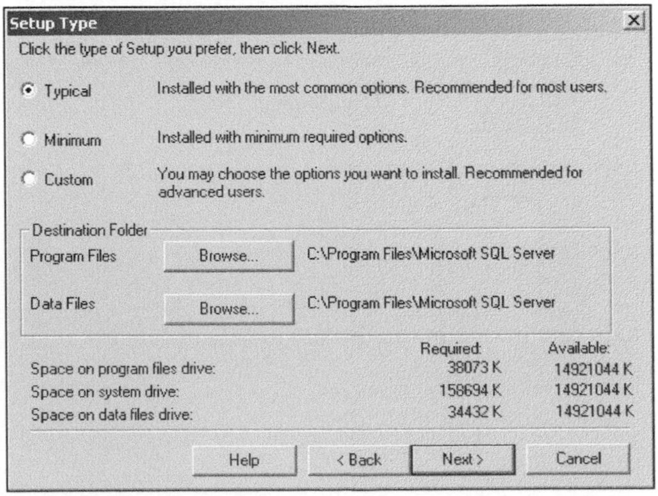

Figure B-66

Click Next to continue. Figure B-67 shows you the screen that asks you whether you want to install SQL Server to use a Local System account or whether you want to use a specific Domain User account. For the purposes of this book, Local System account is fine. However, the Local System account prevents access to SQL Server's more advanced features, which you might want to use later. It's advisable to use a Domain User account. The installation selects a suitable account, so you simply need to enter the password:

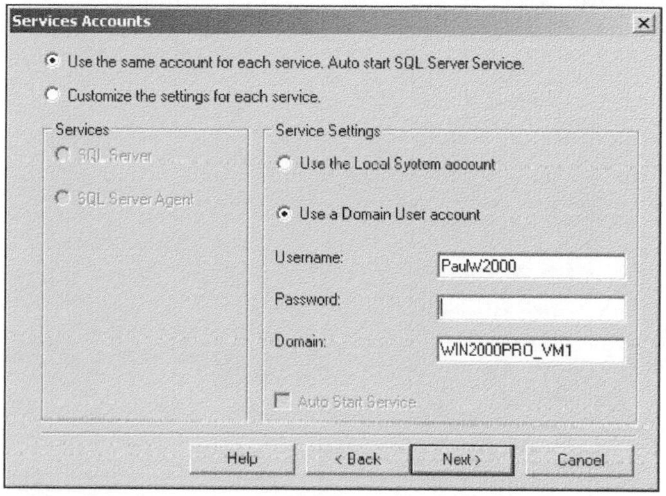

Figure B-67

Obviously your system has different accounts and users. For this book, choosing "Use the same account for each service" at the top of the dialog box is the easiest option. Click Next to continue. The more secure option on the screen displayed in Figure B-68 is to choose the default option, Windows Authentication Mode:

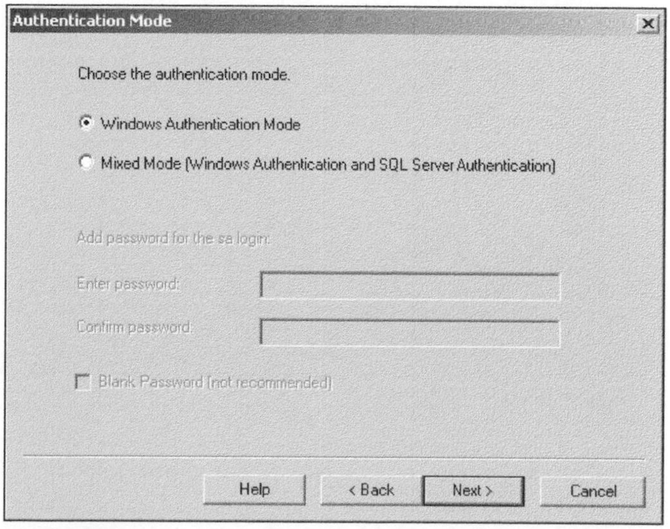

Figure B-68

Click Next to proceed to the final screen (see Figure B-69), and you're ready for installation to start:

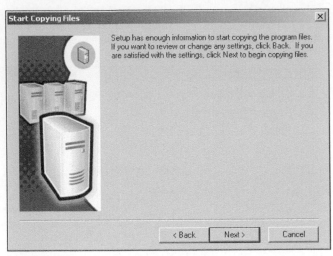

Figure B-69

If you're happy with all the settings made so far, click Next and wait for the installation to do its thing. Installation takes a while, so you can grab a cup of coffee.

Once installation is complete, you should see the screen depicted in Figure B-70:

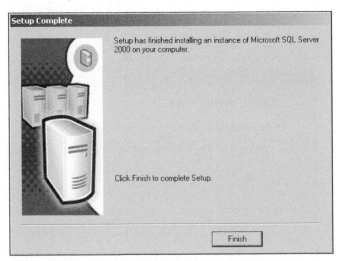

Figure B-70

Click Finish and everything is almost ready to go, but it's advisable to download and install SQL Server 2000 Service Pack 3a, which fixes a few bugs and increases security. You can download it from www.microsoft.com/sql/downloads/2000/sp3.asp.

Although it's not strictly essential, you may want to restart your PC after installation. Now that you've installed SQL Server, you can learn how to use some of the tools included with it.

Using SQL Server Tools

The two main tools for administering the database system and running SQL queries are Enterprise Manager and Query Analyzer. You can access both by clicking Start ➪ Programs ➪ Microsoft SQL Server. Enterprise Manager provides an easy-to-use user interface for managing the database system.

In order to run SQL queries, you need to use Query Analyzer, which is the tool you need to use for this book, so a brief discussion of how it works follows.

Load Query Analyzer by clicking Start ➪ Programs ➪ Microsoft SQL Server, and you're presented with the database system login screen, shown in Figure B-71:

Figure B-71

Select the Windows Authentication option. You need to log in to the PC as the same user as you entered when installing the database system and it asked for a Domain User name and password. If you log in with a different username, you receive a login error. Alternatively, you can select the SQL Server Authentication option and enter sa for the username and whatever password you set for the username; if you installed Service Pack 3, you probably already set a password for the sa user. If you've never set a password for the sa user, just leave it blank — no spaces, just blank. Having a blank password for the sa user is not considered particularly secure, but it's not so important if your PC is only a development machine. New users can be added and changes to existing users of the database system can be made using Enterprise Manager, which is a topic beyond the scope of this book.

Having successfully logged in, the screen shown in Figure B-72 appears:

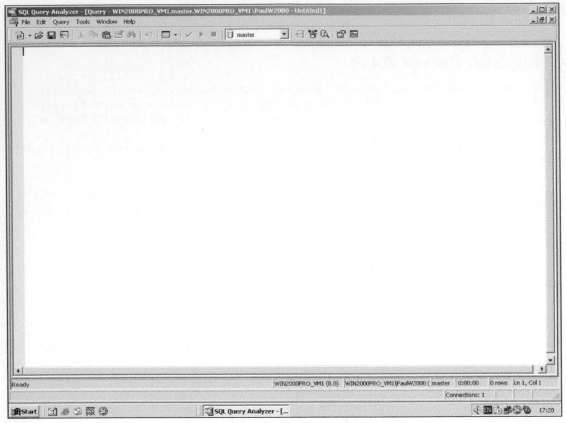

Figure B-72

The huge textbox is where you can enter your queries. The drop-down box in the middle of the toolbar (currently set to master) shows which database the queries are executed against. The master database records important database system information and is best left untouched unless you're sure of what you're doing. If you click the database selection drop-down box, you see a few more of the databases installed, as shown in Figure B-73:

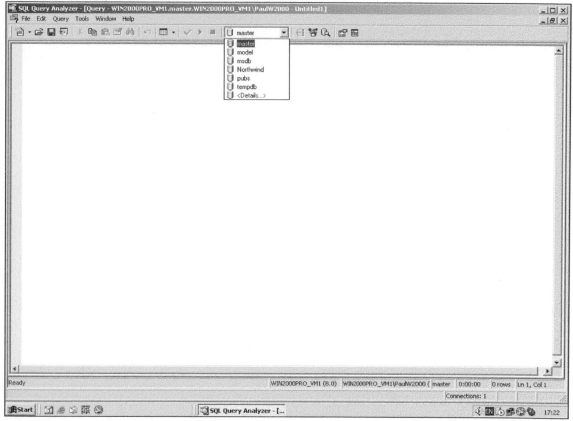

Figure B-73

Most of the databases are system-related, except Northwind, which is a handy example database. The tempdb is just that: a temporary database. Any tables you create there are lost when the database system is restarted — for example, if you restarted your computer.

An additional window that usefully shows details of databases and tables in the system is the Object Browser window (see Figure B-74). In order to view the Object Browser window, select Tools ⇨ Object Browser ⇨ Show/Hide or press the F8 key:

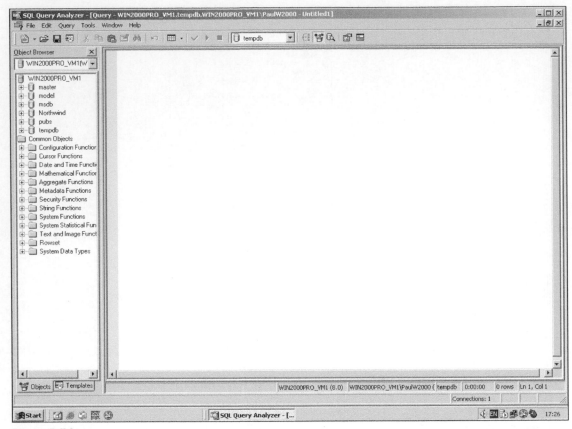

Figure B-74

Notice that six databases are already installed; four of them are related to the database system in some way and best left alone unless you're sure of what you're doing. However, the Pubs and Northwind databases are both example databases that you can play around with and modify. Click the plus sign next to the Northwind database to reveal more details. Click the plus sign next to User Tables to see the tables that the database contains. Click next to a particular table to see the columns in the table.

The second half of the Object Browser, called Common Objects, shows the various functions that the database system supports and acts as quite a handy reference guide.

Query Analyzer allows you to enter one or more queries and to save and load queries to or from a file. Each statement must end with a semicolon. Once a statement is entered and you're happy with it, click the Execute button; usually this is the second icon to the left of the database selector drop-down menu, and although you can't see it from the screenshot, it's actually an icon with a green triangle. You can also hit the F5 key to execute a query. The first task is to create the Film Club database. Enter the following SQL into the SQL box, as shown in Figure B-75:

```
CREATE DATABASE FILMCLUB;
```

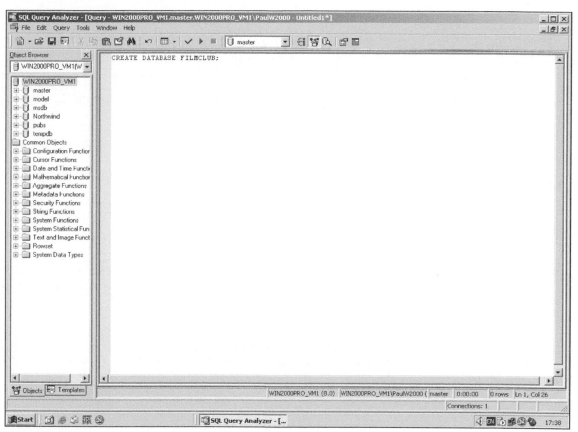

Figure B-75

This is not a query that returns information; rather, it is SQL that changes the database system, in this case adding a new database. After a few seconds, the database is created and the results screen (see Figure B-76) lets you know whether your attempt was successful:

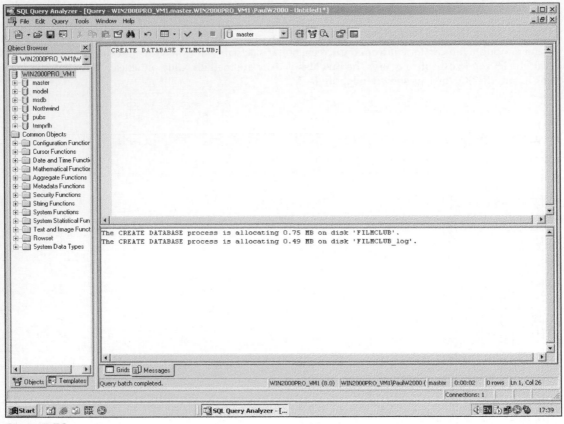

Figure B-76

The Object Browser view on the left doesn't show the changes unless you refresh it by right-clicking one of the items in the box and selecting Refresh, as demonstrated in Figure B-77:

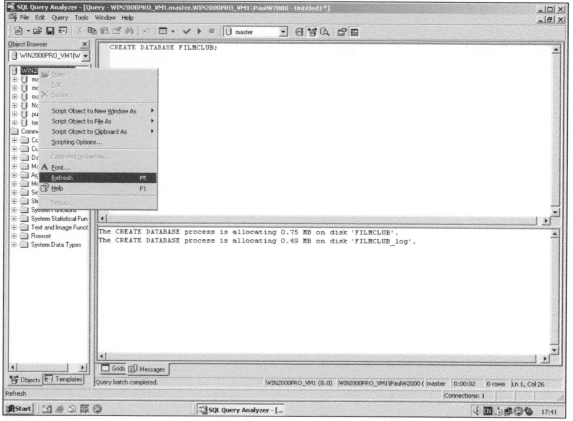

Figure B-77

Notice in Figure B-78 that the database called FILMCLUB appears in the Object Browser:

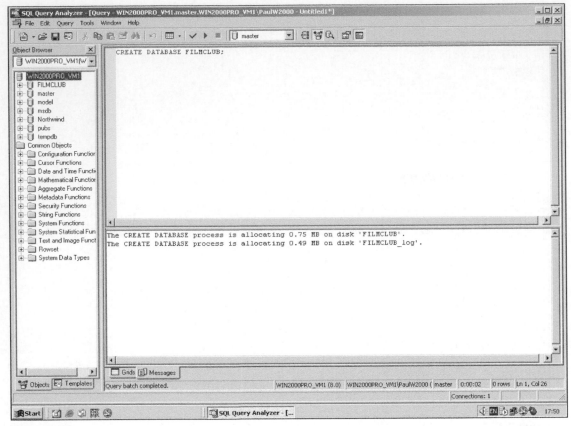

Figure B-78

Chapter 1 already contains all the SQL for adding tables to the example database, and Chapter 2 covers how to insert data. This appendix simply demonstrates how to create one new table, add two rows to it, and then delete the table. Don't worry if the SQL itself doesn't make sense; it does once you've read Chapters 1 through 3.

Some commands, such as CREATE DATABASE, affect the database system rather than a particular database. However, nearly all of the SQL in this book is aimed at the Film Club database. To ensure that queries are executed against the Film Club database, you can either select Film Club from the drop-down menu in the middle of the toolbar or type and execute the following command:

```
USE FILMCLUB;
```

Type the following statement into the large textbox at the top of the Query Browser:

```
CREATE TABLE MyTable (MyColumn int)
```

Click the Execute icon and the table is created. Now you need to insert some data. Type the following statements into the SQL entry box and click Execute:

```
INSERT INTO MyTable(MyColumn) VALUES(123);
INSERT INTO MyTable(MyColumn) VALUES(888);
```

In order to see what data is contained in MyTable, clear the SQL entry box and execute the following statement:

```
SELECT * FROM MyTable
```

You should see a screen similar to Figure B-79:

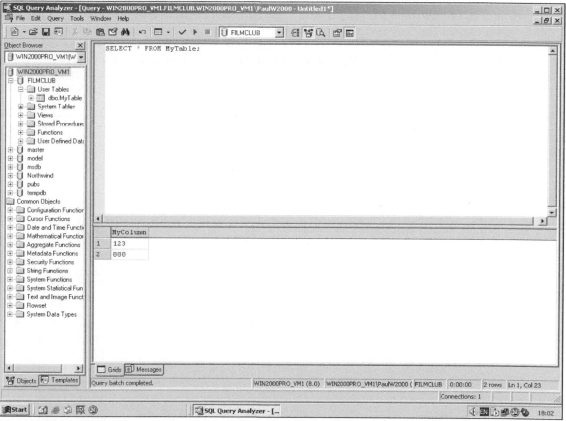

Figure B-79

You don't need MyTable again in this book, so delete it by entering the following statement into the SQL entry box and clicking Execute:

```
DROP TABLE MyTable
```

If you refresh the Object Browser view, MyTable is no longer listed under the Film Club database.

Installing and Using Oracle 10g

A fully working evaluation version of Oracle 10g can be downloaded from the Oracle Web site; it's a massive download (more than 500MB), so patience is definitely a virtue necessary for that download!

The current link to the download page is www.oracle.com/technology/software/products/database/oracle10g/index.html.

Once you've downloaded Oracle 10g, you need to run the single file download so that it's decompressed to a convenient location. After decompressing the file, select Start ⇨ Run and browse to the setup.exe file from where you decompressed the files. Figure B-80 depicts the first screen in the installation process:

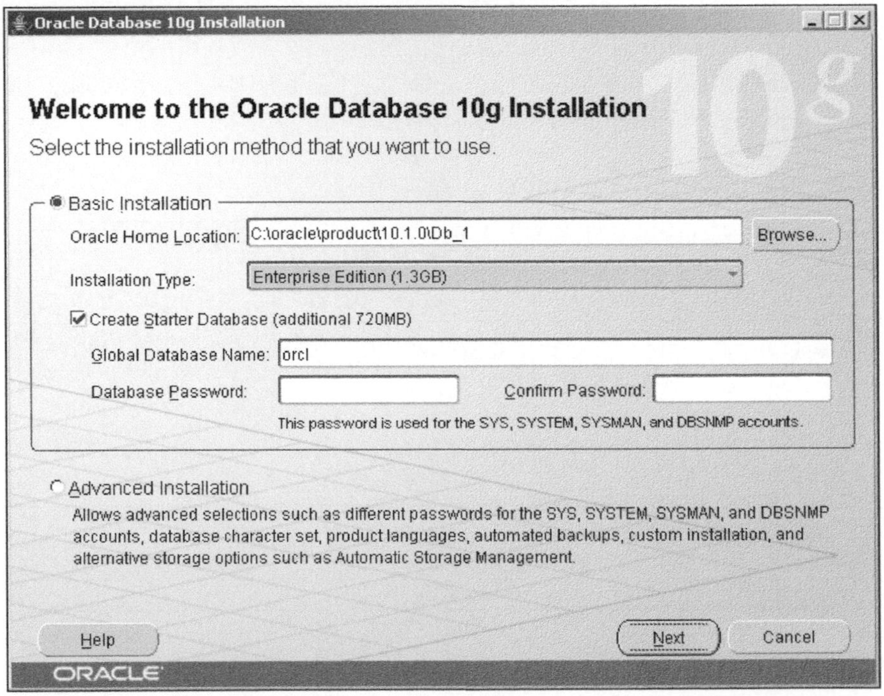

Figure B-80

From the Installation Type drop-down menu, select Standard and enter `filmclub` into the Global Database Name textbox. Choose and enter a password of your choice into the Database Password box, as shown in Figure B-81:

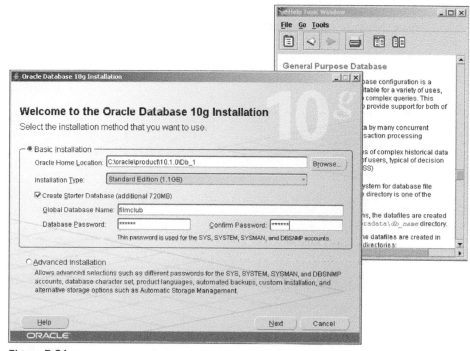

Figure B-81

When Oracle has finished installing, it creates the Film Club database, which you use throughout this book. Click Next, and shortly the Summary screen (see Figure B-82) is displayed:

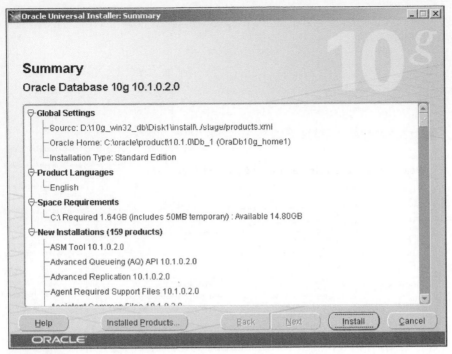

Figure B-82

To begin the installation, simply click Install. Once installation is complete, you see the screen shown in Figure B-83:

Click OK to close the Database Configuration screen, whereupon the Installation Complete screen is shown (see Figure B-84):

Click Exit. Oracle is now installed and you've created this book's example database. This appendix finishes off by demonstrating how to use the Oracle SQL*Plus Tool to enter SQL statements, create an example table, and fill that table with data.

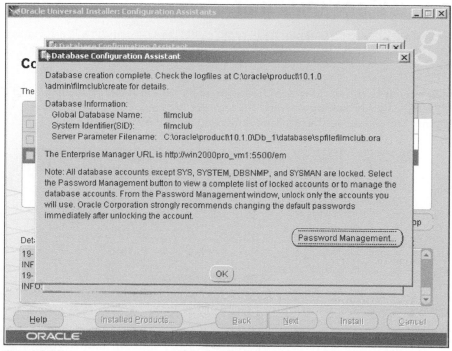

Figure B-83

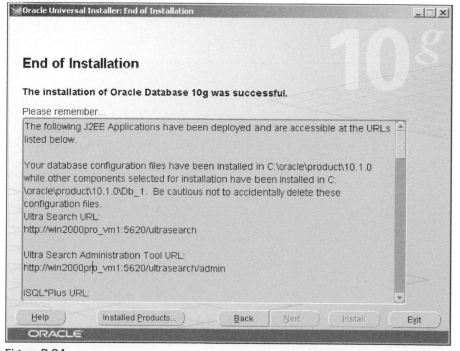

Figure B-84

Using Oracle's SQL*Plus Tool

Oracle 10g is a very powerful and extremely complex database system. Oracle's documentation alone runs longer than 50,000 pages! This section shows you enough to be able to run the examples in the book.

You can use a number of tools to write SQL queries in the Oracle system, namely the SQL*Plus tool. First, launch SQL*Plus by selecting Start ↪ Programs ↪ Oracle ↪ OraDB10g_home1 ↪ Application Development. You should see the window shown in Figure B-85:

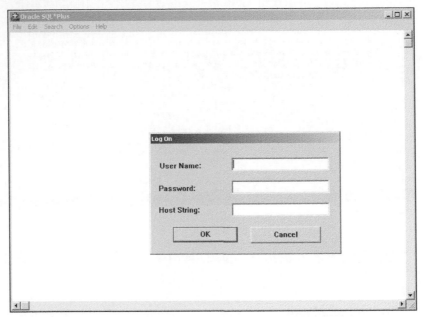

Figure B-85

Type system in the User Name field and the password you selected during installation in the Password field. Click OK and you should be logged in to the Film Club database, which is the only database on the system. When you log in to the SQL*Plus command line tool, you should see a screen similar to Figure B-86. It's all ready and waiting for you to enter some SQL code.

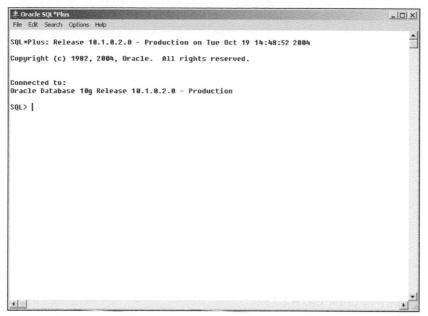

Figure B-86

You enter SQL queries in the command line. Type the following statement:

```
CREATE TABLE MyTable (MyColumn int);
```

Press Enter to execute the SQL and create MyTable. You should receive a confirmation message from the console. After creating MyTable, you need to insert some data. Type the following statement and press Enter:

```
INSERT INTO MyTable(MyColumn) VALUES(123);
```

Enter and execute the following line of SQL code:

```
INSERT INTO MyTable(MyColumn) VALUES(888);
```

In order to see what data is contained in MyTable, clear the SQL entry box and type the following statement:

```
SELECT * FROM MyTable;
```

Press Enter and you should see a screen similar to what appears in Figure B-87:

It's vital to note that none of the data is permanently stored in the database unless you tell Oracle to store the data by issuing a COMMIT command. If you don't issue a COMMIT command, the data you entered is deleted when you close the SQL*Plus tool. Type the COMMIT command as shown below in the command line:

```
COMMIT;
```

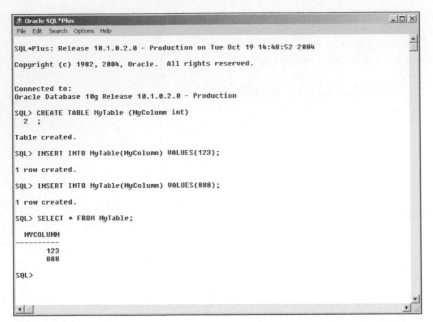

Figure B-87

Another option is to select Options ⇨ Environment and set the autocommit option to On.

You don't need MyTable again in this book, so delete it by executing the following statement:

```
DROP TABLE MyTable;
```

You add all the example tables and data to the Film Club database in Chapters 1 and 2. Note that if you download the book's code files, you need to load them into SQL*Plus using the START command. The files contain more than one SQL statement, each separated by a semicolon. If you load the files by selecting File ⇨ Open, then SQL*Plus treats all lines in the file as one big statement and you receive an illegal character error message where the first semicolon appears. Instead, to load a file, type the following statement:

```
START file_name
```

For example, if the file to insert film data is called FilmsTable_Data.txt and is located in your Z: drive under the BeginningSQL\Chapter2 directory, you would need to type the following command:

```
START Z:\BeginningSQL\Chapter2\FilmsTable_Data.txt
```

Doing so loads and executes the SQL statements in that file.

Initial Data Setup

In Appendix B and Chapter 1, you created the Film Club database, this book's example database. In this appendix, you insert some initial data into the Film Club example database. Before reading this appendix, you should have read and executed the code in Appendix B and Chapter 1 and the first part of Chapter 2, up to and including the section entitled "Inserting Data into the Case Study Database."

This appendix walks you through the data to be inserted table by table. Generally speaking, the SQL is the same for all five database systems supported by this book; instances when the SQL differs are noted in subsections containing the SQL for the database system that requires changed SQL code.

If you want to save yourself a whole lot of typing, don't forget that you can download this code from www.wrox.com. Under each table is a reference to the correct file. All files are contained in the directory AppendixC. Note that when you do a file open operation—either from a menu or a toolbar—the dialog box to select a file usually displays only files with .sql extensions. Because this book's downloadable files are saved as text files (.txt), you need to make sure to change the dialog box so that it shows all file types. The downloadable files are saved as text files because you might be working with a database system (such as Microsoft Access) that doesn't load .sql files, so you need to use a text editor instead.

Most of the database systems allow you to load in a whole file and execute it all at once. MS Access, however, doesn't allow you to load an entire file at once, so you need to cut and paste one SQL statement at a time into a new query—though you can just reuse and execute the same query and cut and paste over the text. If you're using Oracle, then don't load the file using the Open command under the File menu; instead, use the START command as in the following:

```
START C:\temp\CategoryTable_Data.txt
```

Note, however, that you need to modify the START command to reflect wherever you've stored the downloaded files on your hard drive.

Category Table

The following SQL inserts data into the Category table, and it runs on all 5 of the database systems:

```
INSERT INTO Category (CategoryId, Category) VALUES (1, 'Thriller');
INSERT INTO Category (CategoryId, Category) VALUES (2, 'Romance');
INSERT INTO Category (CategoryId, Category) VALUES (3, 'Horror');
INSERT INTO Category (CategoryId, Category) VALUES (4, 'War');
INSERT INTO Category (CategoryId, Category) VALUES (5, 'Sci-fi');
INSERT INTO Category (CategoryId, Category) VALUES (6, 'Historical');
```

You can find this text in the file CategoryTable_Data.txt.

MemberDetails Table

The default installation of Oracle usually requires dates in the following format:

```
day_of_the_month month_name year
```

For example, you would type January 23, 2004, as 23 Jan 2004.

The other four database systems are happy with the following format:

```
year-month-day_of_the_month
```

You would type January 23, 2004, as 2004-01-23.

Since there are two different date formats, this section is divided into two subsections: non-Oracle databases and Oracle databases.

Database Systems Other Than Oracle

If you've downloaded the code, the file named MemberDetailsTable_Data.txt contains the information that populates the MemberDetails table in SQL Server, MS Access, MySQL, and IBM DB2.

```
INSERT INTO MemberDetails
(
  MemberId,
  FirstName,
  LastName,
  DateOfBirth,
  Street,
  City,
  State,
  ZipCode,
  Email,
  DateOfJoining
)
VALUES
```

```
  (
  1,
  'Katie',
  'Smith',
  '1977-01-09',
  'Main Road',
  'Townsville',
  'Stateside',
  '123456',
  'katie@mail.com',
  '2004-02-23'
  );

INSERT INTO MemberDetails
(
  MemberId,
  FirstName,
  LastName,
  DateOfBirth,
  Street,
  City,
  State,
  ZipCode,
  Email,
  DateOfJoining
)
VALUES
  (
  2,
  'Bob',
  'Robson',
  '1987-01-09',
  'Little Street',
  'Big City',
  'Small State',
  '34565',
  'rob@mail.com',
  '2004-03-13'
  );

INSERT INTO MemberDetails
(
  MemberId,
  FirstName,
  LastName,
  DateOfBirth,
  Street,
  City,
  State,
  ZipCode,
  Email,
  DateOfJoining
)
VALUES
```

```
  (
  3,
  'Sandra',
  'Jakes',
  '1957-05-15',
  'The Avenue',
  'Windy Village',
  'Golden State',
  '65423',
  'sandra@her_mail.com',
  '2004-04-13'
  );

INSERT INTO MemberDetails
(
  MemberId,
  FirstName,
  LastName,
  DateOfBirth,
  Street,
  City,
  State,
  ZipCode,
  Email,
  DateOfJoining
)
VALUES
  (
  4,
  'Steve',
  'Gee',
  '1967-10-05',
  'The Road',
  'Windy Village',
  'Golden State',
  '65424',
  'steve@gee.com',
  '2004-02-22'
  );

INSERT INTO MemberDetails
(
  MemberId,
  FirstName,
  LastName,
  DateOfBirth,
  Street,
  City,
  State,
  ZipCode,
  Email,
  DateOfJoining
)
VALUES
```

```
  (
    5,
    'John',
    'Jones',
    '1952-10-05',
    'New Lane',
    'Big Apple City',
    'New State',
    '88776',
    'jj@jonesmail.org',
    '2005-01-02'
  );

INSERT INTO MemberDetails
(
  MemberId,
  FirstName,
  LastName,
  DateOfBirth,
  Street,
  City,
  State,
  ZipCode,
  Email,
  DateOfJoining
)
VALUES
  (
    6,
    'Jenny',
    'Jones',
    '1953-08-25',
    'New Lane',
    'Big Apple City',
    'New State',
    '88776',
    'jj@jonesmail.org',
    '2005-01-02'
  );
```

Oracle

This SQL, which is used to populate the MemberDetails table if you're running an Oracle database system, is contained in the book's download file called `Oracle_MemberDetailsTable_Data.txt`.

```
INSERT INTO MemberDetails
(
  MemberId,
  FirstName,
  LastName,
  DateOfBirth,
  Street,
  City,
  State,
```

```
  ZipCode,
  Email,
  DateOfJoining
)
VALUES
 (
 1,
 'Katie',
 'Smith',
 '9 Jan 1977',
 'Main Road',
 'Townsville',
 'Stateside',
 '123456',
 'katie@mail.com',
 '23 Feb 2004'
 );

INSERT INTO MemberDetails
(
  MemberId,
  FirstName,
  LastName,
  DateOfBirth,
  Street,
  City,
  State,
  ZipCode,
  Email,
  DateOfJoining
)
VALUES
 (
 2,
 'Bob',
 'Robson',
 '9 Jan 1987',
 'Little Street',
 'Big City',
 'Small State',
 '34565',
 'rob@mail.com',
 '13 Mar 2004'
 );

INSERT INTO MemberDetails
(
  MemberId,
  FirstName,
  LastName,
  DateOfBirth,
  Street,
  City,
  State,
  ZipCode,
```

```
    Email,
    DateOfJoining
  )
VALUES
  (
   3,
   'Sandra',
   'Jakes',
   '15 May 1957',
   'The Avenue',
   'Windy Village',
   'Golden State',
   '65423',
   'sandra@her_mail.com',
   '13 Apr 2004'
  );

INSERT INTO MemberDetails
  (
   MemberId,
   FirstName,
   LastName,
   DateOfBirth,
   Street,
   City,
   State,
   ZipCode,
   Email,
   DateOfJoining
  )
VALUES
  (
   4,
   'Steve',
   'Gee',
   '05 Oct 1967',
   'The Road',
   'Windy Village',
   'Golden State',
   '65424',
   'steve@gee.com',
   '22 Feb 2004'
  );

INSERT INTO MemberDetails
  (
   MemberId,
   FirstName,
   LastName,
   DateOfBirth,
   Street,
   City,
   State,
   ZipCode,
   Email,
```

```
    DateOfJoining
)
VALUES
  (
  5,
  'John',
  'Jones',
  '05 Oct 1952',
  'New Lane',
  'Big Apple City',
  'New State',
  '88776',
  'jj@jonesmail.org',
  '02 Jan 2005'
  );

INSERT INTO MemberDetails
(
  MemberId,
  FirstName,
  LastName,
  DateOfBirth,
  Street,
  City,
  State,
  ZipCode,
  Email,
  DateOfJoining
)
VALUES
  (
  6,
  'Jenny',
  'Jones',
  '25 Aug 1953',
  'New Lane',
  'Big Apple City',
  'New State',
  '88776',
  'jj@jonesmail.org',
  '02 Jan 2005'
  );
```

Location Table

The SQL that you use to insert information into the Location table works on all five database systems. Its filename is LocationTable_Data.txt.

```
INSERT INTO Location
(
  LocationId,
```

```
        Street,
        City,
        State
    )
    VALUES
    (
    1,
    'Main Street',
    'Big Apple City',
    'New State'
    );

    INSERT INTO Location
    (
      LocationId,
      Street,
      City,
      State
    )
    VALUES
    (
    2,
    'Winding Road',
    'Windy Village',
    'Golden State'
    );

    INSERT INTO Location
    (
      LocationId,
      Street,
      City,
      State
    )
    VALUES
    (
    3,
    'Tiny Terrace',
    'Big City',
    'Small State'
    );
```

FavCategory Table

The SQL that is used to populate the FavCategory table works on all five database systems. Its filename is FavCategoryTable_Data.txt.

```
    INSERT INTO FavCategory
    (
      CategoryId,
      MemberId
    )
```

```
VALUES
 (
  1,
  3
 );

INSERT INTO FavCategory
(
  CategoryId,
  MemberId
)
VALUES
 (
  1,
  5
 );

INSERT INTO FavCategory
(
  CategoryId,
  MemberId
)
VALUES
 (
  1,
  2
 );

INSERT INTO FavCategory
(
  CategoryId,
  MemberId
)
VALUES
 (
  1,
  3
 );

INSERT INTO FavCategory
(
  CategoryId,
  MemberId
)
VALUES
 (
  2,
  1
 );

INSERT INTO FavCategory
(
  CategoryId,
  MemberId
)
```

```
VALUES
 (
  2,
  3
 );

INSERT INTO FavCategory
(
  CategoryId,
  MemberId
)
VALUES
 (
  3,
  3
 );

INSERT INTO FavCategory
(
  CategoryId,
  MemberId
)
VALUES
 (
  4,
  6
 );

INSERT INTO FavCategory
(
  CategoryId,
  MemberId
)
VALUES
 (
  4,
  1
 );

INSERT INTO FavCategory
(
  CategoryId,
  MemberId
)
VALUES
 (
  5,
  2
 );

INSERT INTO FavCategory
(
  CategoryId,
  MemberId
)
```

```
VALUES
  (
   5,
   3
  ) ;

INSERT INTO FavCategory
(
  CategoryId,
  MemberId
)
VALUES
  (
   5,
   4
  ) ;
```

Films Table

The SQL that you use to insert data into the Films table works on all five database systems. One point to note is that the film description for the film *15th Late Afternoon* contains the word `Shakespeare''s`— the second apostrophe tells the database systems that the first apostrophe isn't the end of the text. The code to populate the Films table is contained in the download file called `FilmsTable_Data.txt`.

```
INSERT INTO Films
(
   FilmId,
   FilmName,
   YearReleased,
   PlotSummary,
   AvailableOnDVD,
   Rating,
   CategoryId
)
VALUES
  (
   1,
   'The Dirty Half Dozen',
   1987,
   'Six men go to war wearing unwashed uniforms. The horror!',
   'N',
   2,
   4
  ) ;

INSERT INTO Films
(
   FilmId,
   FilmName,
   YearReleased,
   PlotSummary,
   AvailableOnDVD,
```

```
    Rating,
    CategoryId
)
VALUES
  (
   2,
   'On Golden Puddle',
   1967,
   'A couple find love while wading through a puddle.',
   'Y',
   4,
   2
  );


INSERT INTO Films
(
  FilmId,
  FilmName,
  YearReleased,
  PlotSummary,
  AvailableOnDVD,
  Rating,
  CategoryId
)
VALUES
  (
   3,
   'The Lion, the Witch, and the Chest of Drawers',
   1977,
   'A fun film for all those interested in zoo/magic/furniture drama.',
   'N',
   1,
   3
  );


INSERT INTO Films
(
  FilmId,
  FilmName,
  YearReleased,
  PlotSummary,
  AvailableOnDVD,
  Rating,
  CategoryId
)
VALUES
  (
   4,
   'Nightmare on Oak Street, Part 23',
   1997,
   'The murderous Terry stalks Oak Street.',
   'Y',
   2,
```

```
  3
);


INSERT INTO Films
(
  FilmId,
  FilmName,
  YearReleased,
  PlotSummary,
  AvailableOnDVD,
  Rating,
  CategoryId
)
VALUES
(
  5,
  'The Wide-Brimmed Hat',
  2005,
  'Fascinating life story of a wide-brimmed hat',
  'N',
  1,
  5
);


INSERT INTO Films
(
  FilmId,
  FilmName,
  YearReleased,
  PlotSummary,
  AvailableOnDVD,
  Rating,
  CategoryId
)
VALUES
(
  6,
  'Sense and Insensitivity',
  2001,
  'She longs for a new life with Mr. Arcy; he longs for a small cottage in the
Hamptons.',
  'Y',
  3,
  6
);


INSERT INTO Films
(
  FilmId,
  FilmName,
  YearReleased,
  PlotSummary,
```

```
  AvailableOnDVD,
  Rating,
  CategoryId
)
VALUES
 (
  7,
  'Planet of the Japes',
  1967,
  'Earth has been destroyed, to be taken over by a species of comedians.',
  'Y',
  5,
  4
 );


INSERT INTO Films
(
  FilmId,
  FilmName,
  YearReleased,
  PlotSummary,
  AvailableOnDVD,
  Rating,
  CategoryId
)
VALUES
 (
  8,
  'The Maltese Poodle',
  1947,
  'A mysterious bite mark, a guilty-looking poodle. First class thriller.',
  'Y',
  1,
  1
 );


INSERT INTO Films
(
  FilmId,
  FilmName,
  YearReleased,
  PlotSummary,
  AvailableOnDVD,
  Rating,
  CategoryId
)
VALUES
 (
  2,
  '15th Late Afternoon',
  1989,
  'One of Shakespeare''s lesser-known plays',
  'N',
```

```
  5,
  6
);


INSERT INTO Films
(
  FilmId,
  FilmName,
  YearReleased,
  PlotSummary,
  AvailableOnDVD,
  Rating,
  CategoryId
)
VALUES
(
  2,
  'Soylent Yellow',
  1967,
  'Detective Billy Brambles discovers that Soylent Yellow is made of soya bean.
Ewwww!',
  'Y',
  5,
  5
);
```

Attendance Table

Again, because of the date issue, there are separate code listings for Oracle and non-Oracle systems.

Database Systems Other Than Oracle

The download file AttendanceTable_Data.txt contains the following code:

```
INSERT INTO Attendance
(
  LocationId,
  MeetingDate,
  MemberAttended,
  MemberId
)
VALUES
(
  2,
  '2004-01-01',
  'Y',
  1
);

INSERT INTO Attendance
(
```

```
  LocationId,
  MeetingDate,
  MemberAttended,
  MemberId
)
VALUES
  (
  2,
  '2004-01-01',
  'N',
  2
  );

INSERT INTO Attendance
(
  LocationId,
  MeetingDate,
  MemberAttended,
  MemberId
)
VALUES
  (
  2,
  '2004-01-01',
  'Y',
  3
  );

INSERT INTO Attendance
(
  LocationId,
  MeetingDate,
  MemberAttended,
  MemberId
)
VALUES
  (
  2,
  '2004-01-01',
  'N',
  4
  );

INSERT INTO Attendance
(
  LocationId,
  MeetingDate,
  MemberAttended,
  MemberId
)
VALUES
  (
  2,
  '2004-01-01',
  'Y',
```

```
   5
 );

INSERT INTO Attendance
(
  LocationId,
  MeetingDate,
  MemberAttended,
  MemberId
)
VALUES
 (
  2,
  '2004-01-01',
  'Y',
  6
 );

INSERT INTO Attendance
(
  LocationId,
  MeetingDate,
  MemberAttended,
  MemberId
)
VALUES
 (
  1,
  '2004-03-01',
  'Y',
  1
 );

INSERT INTO Attendance
(
  LocationId,
  MeetingDate,
  MemberAttended,
  MemberId
)
VALUES
 (
  1,
  '2004-03-01',
  'N',
  2
 );

INSERT INTO Attendance
(
  LocationId,
  MeetingDate,
  MemberAttended,
  MemberId
)
```

```
VALUES
 (
 1,
 '2004-03-01',
 'Y',
 3
 );

INSERT INTO Attendance
(
 LocationId,
 MeetingDate,
 MemberAttended,
 MemberId
)
VALUES
 (
 1,
 '2004-03-01',
 'Y',
 4
 );

INSERT INTO Attendance
(
 LocationId,
 MeetingDate,
 MemberAttended,
 MemberId
)
VALUES
 (
 1,
 '2004-03-01',
 'N',
 5
 );

INSERT INTO Attendance
(
 LocationId,
 MeetingDate,
 MemberAttended,
 MemberId
)
VALUES
 (
 1,
 '2004-03-01',
 'N',
 6
 );
```

Oracle

To save some typing, you can find the following code in the download file called
`Oracle_AttendanceTable_Data.txt`:

```
INSERT INTO Attendance
(
  LocationId,
  MeetingDate,
  MemberAttended,
  MemberId
)
VALUES
 (
  2,
  '1 Jan 2004',
  'Y',
  1
 );

INSERT INTO Attendance
(
  LocationId,
  MeetingDate,
  MemberAttended,
  MemberId
)
VALUES
 (
  2,
  '1 Jan 2004',
  'N',
  2
 );

INSERT INTO Attendance
(
  LocationId,
  MeetingDate,
  MemberAttended,
  MemberId
)
VALUES
 (
  2,
  '1 Jan 2004',
  'Y',
  3
 );

INSERT INTO Attendance
(
  LocationId,
  MeetingDate,
  MemberAttended,
  MemberId
```

```
)
VALUES
  (
  2,
  '1 Jan 2004',
  'N',
  4
  );

INSERT INTO Attendance
(
  LocationId,
  MeetingDate,
  MemberAttended,
  MemberId
)
VALUES
  (
  2,
  '1 Jan 2004',
  'Y',
  5
  );

INSERT INTO Attendance
(
  LocationId,
  MeetingDate,
  MemberAttended,
  MemberId
)
VALUES
  (
  2,
  '1 Jan 2004',
  'Y',
  6
  );

INSERT INTO Attendance
(
  LocationId,
  MeetingDate,
  MemberAttended,
  MemberId
)
VALUES
  (
  1,
  '1 Mar 2004',
  'Y',
  1
  );

INSERT INTO Attendance
(
```

```
  LocationId,
  MeetingDate,
  MemberAttended,
  MemberId
)
VALUES
 (
 1,
 '1 Mar 2004',
 'N',
 2
 );

INSERT INTO Attendance
(
  LocationId,
  MeetingDate,
  MemberAttended,
  MemberId
)
VALUES
 (
 1,
 '1 Mar 2004',
 'Y',
 3
 );

INSERT INTO Attendance
(
  LocationId,
  MeetingDate,
  MemberAttended,
  MemberId
)
VALUES
 (
 1,
 '1 Mar 2004',
 'Y',
 4
 );

INSERT INTO Attendance
(
  LocationId,
  MeetingDate,
  MemberAttended,
  MemberId
)
VALUES
 (
 1,
 '1 Mar 2004',
 'N',
```

```
    5
  );

INSERT INTO Attendance
(
  LocationId,
  MeetingDate,
  MemberAttended,
  MemberId
)
VALUES
  (
  1,
  '1 Mar 2004',
  'N',
  6
  );
```

Index

Symbols

A

Printed and bound by CPI Group (UK) Ltd, Croydon, CR0 4YY

14/02/2023

03191646-0001